Making War, Forging Revolution

Making War, Forging Revolution

RUSSIA'S CONTINUUM OF CRISIS, 1914–1921

PETER HOLQUIST

HARVARD UNIVERSITY PRESS

Cambridge, Massachusetts
London, England   2002

Library of Congress Cataloging-in-Publication Data

Holquist, Peter.
    Making war, forging revolution : Russia's continuum of crisis, 1914–1921 /
Peter Holquist.
        p. cm.
    Includes bibliography and index.
    ISBN 0-674-00907-X (alk. paper)
    1. Don River Region (Russia)—History—Revolution, 1917–1921.
    2. Don Cossacks—History—20th century.   3. Don River Region (Russia)—
Rural conditions.   I. Title.

DK265.8.D596 H65 2002
947'.49—dc21   2002075942

To Diana

Acknowledgments

This book would never have come into being without the generosity of a large number of individuals and institutions. Although I bear full responsibility for all errors and opinions in this book, its strengths build upon the support, criticism, and collegiality of others.

This work began as a dissertation at Columbia University. There Leopold Haimson taught me to see history as a system; Mark von Hagen was and remains a wonderful supporter, and now friend; and Richard Wortman helped me see the imperial period in all its depth, preventing me from thinking of it only as an antechamber to Soviet history. I benefited from a wonderful dissertation committee, consisting of these three scholars as well as Alfred Rieber and Boris Gasparov. Their criticisms of that dissertation have made this a better book. Stephen Kotkin's seminar on Russia through the prism of European history was a cathartic intellectual experience. He has remained a wonderful critic and source of ideas.

I had the good fortune to enter Columbia with a remarkable cohort of graduate students. My discussions with them suffuse this entire work. I cannot say where our collective approach ends and where my own thinking begins. Seminars and endless discussions with Nathaniel Knight, Fred Corney, Yanni Kotsonis, Laurie Manchester, Igal Halfin, Amir Weiner, Jochen Hellbeck, and Charles Steinwedel shaped my horizons. I am especially grateful to Igal Halfin and Jochen Hellbeck for expanding these horizons far beyond where they began—and making graduate school not only tolerable but enjoyable. Michael David-Fox spent one semester at Columbia, which was only the beginning of an ongoing friendship. David McDonald, Frank Wcislo, and David Hoffmann served as avuncular guides to Columbia University and to history. This group continues to sustain me. Igal Halfin and Jochen Hellbeck inspire me, in life and in scholarship; Amir Weiner has maintained a faithful friendship and ongoing dialogue with me, even when I exasperate him; Yanni Kotsonis and Charles Steinwedel have been generous with their friendship, time, and knowledge. My continuing dialogue with Michael David-Fox has shaped me and my work. I am grateful also for his good humor.

Russian colleagues and friends supported me in Russia and helped me see the joys and tragedies of Russian history: Aleksandr Kozlov and Andrei Venkov in Rostov; Boris Kolonitskii; Vladimir Shishkin; and Sveta Semenova and her family.

A new generation of scholars focusing on Russia during the First World War graciously shared their work and tutored me in their own specialties: I thank Eric Lohr, Joshua Sanborn, and Peter Gatrell. Laura Engelstein, Daniel Orlovsky, Donald Raleigh, and William Rosenberg shared their knowledge of late imperial and revolutionary Russia and demonstrated a remarkable generosity of spirit. I am especially grateful to Donald Raleigh, who is the "godfather" of this book. He shared his knowledge of provincial Russia and local archives; he read the grotesquely long dissertation with patience; and he then read the manuscript as well. Through it all, he showed unflagging support for my work.

The anonymous reviewers for Harvard University Press later unmasked themselves. Donald Raleigh and Daniel Orlovsky were remarkably helpful and constructively critical. Their criticisms have vastly improved the book. Michael David-Fox read and commented on the entire manuscript. Those who read large portions, often at very short notice, and who have contributed significantly to the book at various stages include Paul Bushkovich, Andrea Graziosi, David Hoffmann, Isabel Hull, Yanni Kotsonis, David McDonald, Benjamin Nathans, Dan Orlovsky, William Rosenberg, Charles Steinwedel, Frank Wcislo, and Amir Weiner. Participants at a variety of conferences have contributed invaluable comments and criticisms. I thank Teresa Howley for preparing the map of the Don Territory.

Since 1997 the Cornell History Department has been my home. It has provided an unparalleled intellectual environment. I am indebted to the European History Colloquium and to the Department's encouragement of team-teaching. I particularly wish to thank Itsie Hull for providing a warm example of what a colleague, teacher, and scholar should be; and Sherm Cochran, for his warmth, patience, and overall cosmopolitanism.

Much of the argument in *Making War* is built upon research and reading in Russian archives. Several institutions made it possible for me to read broadly and deeply. Initial research was supported by an IREX dissertation grant; further research was made possible by an SSRC Eurasia grant. The Kennan Institute for Advanced Russian Studies of the Woodrow Wilson Center in Washington, D.C., and the National Fellows' Program of the Hoover Institution on War, Revolution, and Peace each supported long stretches of time to write. Without the help of archivists at GARF, RGVA, RGASPI, RGVIA, RGIA, GARO, and TsDNIRO, I would have been lost. I particularly thank Nonna Tarkhova at RGVA and the archivists of GARF and GARO. They and their selfless efforts represent Russia at its very best.

My editor at Harvard University Press, Joyce Seltzer, saw promise in an unwieldy manuscript. Her suggestions have made this book immeasurably better. It has been a joy to work with her.

Most of all, I am indebted to my family. To my parents, for their unstinting support of me, through thick and thin. To Katerina Clark, for always believing in me. To my brothers, for helping me keep everything in perspective. To Albert and Deborah Kaplan, who have loved and supported me as their own. My children, Hana and Isaiah, have literally lived with this project for all their young lives. My only regret about this book is the time it has taken from them. I dedicate this book to my wife, Diana. Her love has sustained me through all and has shown me what is really important in life.

Contents

Note on Usage

Through February 1918 Russia adhered to the Julian calendar, which ran thirteen days behind the Gregorian, or Western, calendar. Dates are given in the Julian style (Old Style) until January 31, 1918, when Russia adopted the Gregorian calendar (New Style). Dates of anti-Soviet publications, which followed the Julian calendar, have been converted to New Style.

I have employed the Library of Congress system of transliteration, except for names widely employed in English (for example, "Trotsky" instead of "Trotskii").

A pood is approximately 36 pounds; a desiatin is 2.7 acres.

The following terms refer to specifically Cossack forms of administration:

ataman: a Cossack headman, a post of administrative responsibility;

stanitsa: a Cossack community, both the stanitsa proper (often numbering up to 20,000 inhabitants) and the administrative unit encompassing the stanitsa and smaller, outlying Cossack settlements;

khutor: a Cossack settlement within a stanitsa.

Making War, Forging Revolution

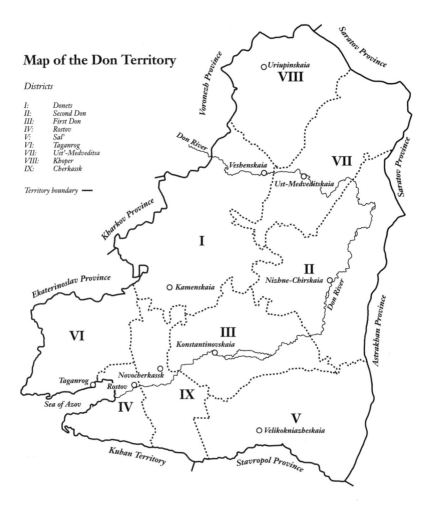

Map of the Don Territory

Districts

I:	Donets
II:	Second Don
III:	First Don
IV:	Rostov
V:	Sal'
VI:	Taganrog
VII:	Ust'-Medveditsa
VIII:	Khoper
IX:	Cherkassk

Territory boundary —

Saratov Province

○ *Uriupinskaia*

VIII

Voronezh Province

Don River

Veshenskaia

VII

○ *Ust-Medveditskaia*

Saratov Province

Kharkov Province

I

II

Ekaterinoslav Province

○ *Kamenskaia*

Nizhne-Chirskaia ○

Don River

Astrakhan Province

VI

III

Konstantinovskaia

Taganrog ○ *Novocherkassk*

○ *Rostov* ○

IX

Sea of Azov

IV

V

○ *Velikokniazheskaia*

Kuban Territory

Stavropol Province

Introduction

> In our own century there has arisen . . . an altogether different type of
> event in which it is as though even the fury of war was merely the
> prelude, a preparatory stage to the violence unleashed by revolution.
>
> ⁓ Hannah Arendt, *On Revolution*

*I*t has become customary to date the true beginning of the
twentieth century not from 1900 but rather from two events: the First
World War and the Russian Revolution. While scholars have long recognized the interrelationship between these two seminal episodes, few
studies have analyzed their interaction. This oversight resulted in part
from the revolution's own image of itself. For seventy years, the Communist Party and the Soviet state insisted that the October Revolution
marked a radical break in the history of humankind. October's opponents inverted the Communist signifiers from positive to negative but
ironically retained the underlying structuring chronology.[1] Communism's advocates and foes alike dated their narratives from 1917.

There were good reasons to do so. One of the essential features of
the revolutions in both February and October 1917 was the belief
among their participants that they were making—and experiencing—a
radical break with the past, that they were bringing about a new order.
In the course of 1917, people across the political spectrum shared a belief that revolutionary politics could transform society and each individual in it. This narrative of the revolution as a foundation event elevated the Bolsheviks and their revolution above the historical context
that had produced both the revolution and the Soviet state. In this way,
the Russian Revolution became uncoupled from the wartime crisis out
of which it had emerged. Only in Russia did a self-proclaimed revo-

1

lutionary, Marxist regime emerge at the other end of the crisis that marked the end of the Great War throughout central and eastern Europe. This gulf in outcomes had the effect of drawing a line between Russia and the rest of Europe.

Contemporaries and subsequent analysts telescoped Russia's path through the common European deluge (1914–1921) into its period of revolution. As a result, Russia has largely fallen out of the general story of the Great War and twentieth-century European history. Yet reinserting the Russian experience is crucial for understanding the First World War in general. Russia's 1917 revolutions exerted a reciprocal impact upon the European wartime ecosystem. The Russian Revolution served as a major precipitant for the wartime "remobilization" after 1917 that took place across Europe.[2] It had an equally great impact upon the politics of war aims and peace making.

Some contemporaries underscored this linkage between war and revolution. In November 1919, in the middle of the Russian civil wars, Peter Struve—one of Russia's preeminent political figures, who had traveled the path from legal Marxism to opposing the Bolsheviks—delivered a lecture in Rostov-on-Don, one capital of the anti-Bolshevik struggle. Struve proclaimed that "the world war formally ended with the conclusion of the armistice . . . In fact, however, everything from that point onward that we have experienced, and continue to experience, is a continuation and transformation of the world war."[3] Struve's observation suggests that rather than distinguishing between a period of war (1914–1917) and one of revolution and civil wars (1917–1921), one might instead speak of a broader 1914–1921 cataclysm, with 1917 serving as its fulcrum.[4]

Reinserting Russia's revolution within the war makes it a European, rather than a solely Russian, story. The Soviet state crystallized at a particular moment, amid the more generalized 1914–1921 European crisis. Historical studies have not overlooked the linkage between the First World War and the Russian Revolution. In its most common formulation, however, the relationship between the two is reduced to a question of whether the war served as a causal trigger, a catalyst, for revolution. This approach focuses more on the viability of imperial Russia before the war than on the ways in which Russia changed during the course of the war. Studies devoted to Russia's participation in the war demonstrate that profound changes were taking place during these years. These works convincingly show how the war caused the fall of the old regime, but they are less interested in examining how the war shaped the emergence of the new regime. Hence they rarely carry their analyses from the war years into 1917 and beyond.[5] Similarly, there are excellent studies of how the Soviet state consolidated its power, but these commonly date developments from October 1917 and do not seek the pre-October (and especially pre-1917) roots of many revolutionary practices.

The war and revolution, as Struve suggests, were not two discrete events but rather points along a common continuum. Analyzing the revolutionary period as a process rather than as an event radically recasts its points of reference. As with the French Revolution, the years immediately preceding the Russian Revolution shaped the conceptual terrain and institutional framework in which the revolution unfolded.[6] Yet unlike Old Regime France, Russia in the years immediately preceding the revolution experienced not only administrative reform but also wartime mobilization. With the revolution occurring amid wartime mobilization, there developed a reciprocal relationship between total war and revolution. In particular, Russia's political class harnessed tools of wartime mobilization for its political projects.[7] Whereas other European societies and governments incorporated wartime practices of total mobilization, they could dispense with them or subordinate them to an existing order. In revolutionary Russia, these institutions and practices instead became the building blocks of the new state and socioeconomic order.

In 1930 Ernst Jünger, whose worldview had been shaped by the war, asserted that "these two phenomena, world war and world revolution, are much more closely interrelated than a first glance would indicate. They are two sides of an event of cosmic significance, whose outbreak and origins are interdependent in numerous respects."[8] Throughout much of central and eastern Europe, the war wound down in an extended convulsion of revolutions and civil strife. In this light, the violence of the Russian civil wars appears not as something perversely Russian or uniquely Bolshevik, but rather as the most advanced case of a more extended European civil war, beginning with the Great War and stretching several years after its formal conclusion. Rather than viewing these civil wars, and the Russian civil wars in particular, as distinct episodes in their own right, we might instead think of them, as

Struve suggested, as a "continuation and transformation" of the world war. In the aftermath of this European "Time of Troubles," domestic politics "could no longer be described as peacetime politics." Not just in Russia but in other European states as well, "domestic politics after 1918 became an expression of a latent civil war."[9]

Yet the Soviet state and its opponents emerged not only from the shared experience of European war but also from a common Russian heritage of revolution. In tsarist Russia, educated society's political impotence and sense of social obligation had fused into a powerful commitment to reforming the political order and society. Because of their oppositionist stand toward the autocracy and sense of backwardness in regard to their own ideals, members of Russia's educated society were committed to a revolutionary transformation of society, although revolutionary not necessarily in the terms advocated by political radicals.[10]

In the years before 1914 educated society's ability to act on its aspirations had been blocked by the autocracy's opposition to public involvement in policy. Wartime mobilization led to the emergence of structures in which the public could finally play a role in policy making. Russia thus telescoped the stages of the establishment of many public organizations, which existed in most other combatants before the war, with their reorganization to the ends of war mobilization. Thus the resulting network of semipublic, semistate structures was less a public sphere autonomous of the state than a "parastatal complex" in which society and state were tightly intertwined.[11] The February Revolution in 1917 brought to power the class that was staffing this complex and provided it with the long-desired opportunity for realizing its aspirations. The structure from which members of educated society would operate, however, was now this parastatal complex that had developed during the war; the tools for achieving their prewar dreams became, increasingly, tools derived from wartime mobilization.

The Russian Revolution in 1917 marked a tectonic shift in the nature and scope of politics in the Russian Empire, a shift encompassing both the use of modern state practices and the crystallization of a revolutionary political ecosystem.[12] The course of 1917 witnessed both a quantitative increase in traditional politics and a qualitative transformation in its definition and scope. Whatever their party or ideological affiliation, all political movements in the post-February period engaged in a form of revolutionary politics, seeking to remake Russian society as much as its political order. In this sense, the Russian Revolution was a "social revolution" not only because various social groups made it, or because the social order was changed, but because all political actors sought to employ politics as a tool to transform society.[13] This heritage of revolutionary aspirations informed the programs not only of the Bolsheviks but also of their opponents. The anti-Soviet activists were not simply reactionaries or restorationists; while opposing the Bolshevik variant of revolution, they, too, aimed to reform—some even to transform—Russian society.

The Provisional Government established in February 1917 was a revolutionary government, defining itself explicitly in contrast to the "Old Regime" that preceded it. Total mobilization in Russia took place against this background of a longstanding and powerful critique of the existing order. As a result, revolutionary governments in Russia—in February and October—implemented measures for total mobilization common to other warring powers, but in a supercharged and concentrated form. The implementation of wartime policies overlapped with the revolutionary reordering of the political system and society. Elsewhere, governments relied upon a thick network of existing public institutions to mobilize society for war. The Provisional Government promulgated many revolutionary programs, but because of the attenuated development of public structures, it proved unable to realize them. Confronting this situation, proponents of the Provisional Government in particular came to view the state and the army as surrogates for the structures of civil society missing in Russia. The Soviet state, which in the absence of public structures relied on coercive means, implemented many of these programs initially proposed by the Provisional Government.

Seen from this perspective, the Russian Revolution did not exist in hermetic isolation from the civil wars that followed. (What is termed the "Russian Civil War" in fact was a series of overlapping civil wars and national conflicts. To highlight the multiple vectors of this struggle, throughout this book I employ the plural "civil wars" rather than the homogenizing "Russian Civil War.")[14] The traditional chronology dividing the Revolution of 1917 from the civil wars implicitly suggests that the latter were external to or separate from the revolutions they followed. Yet political movements, including the anti-Soviet ones, fought the civil wars precisely over the question of how to interpret and implement "the Revolution." State practices—many developed in the wake of the First World War—were the means for realizing this fundamentally political project.

In examining the unfolding of revolutionary aspirations, this book concentrates on political practices. It is less a social history of politics than a political history of social movements. To be sure, political programs needed to find purchase in lived experience and existing collective aspirations. Yet social and economic preconditions alone do not satisfactorily explain people's political behavior.[15] Rather than examining the mobilization of social groups, well studied for 1917, I instead focus on Russia's political class and how it shaped preexisting collective aspirations into self-consciously identified "social movements"; that is, I examine the mechanisms for instituting and reinforcing political projections, the methods for finding a political purchase in sociological experience.

Political practices are the measures that political movements employ to achieve their ideological goals, along with the behaviors and assumptions—conscious and unconscious—that underlie such practices. Practices and the ideologies that envelop them exist in a mutually constitutive and symbiotic relationship. Ideology shapes the means and ends to which political practices are applied. Such practices, for their part, determine the scope and form of political intervention. This study concentrates on the emergence and transformation of three particular state practices: state management of food supply; the employment of official violence for political ends; and state surveillance of the population for purposes of coercion and "enlightenment." These three vectors of state activity were among the most intrusive and unavoidable points of contact between citizens and various contenders for political power.

All movements in the Russian Revolution employed a shared heritage of political practices that were emerging out of Russia's total war experience. As Alexis de Tocqueville noted for the French Revolution, revolutionaries "took over from the old regime not only most of its customs, conventions, and modes of thought . . . in fact, though nothing was further from their intentions, they used the debris of the old order for building up the new."[16] Such political practices were not the product of any particular ideology. They predated the new revolutionary ecosystem, but after 1917 they could be deployed, massively and without constraint, to accomplish new ideological ends. Political movements, in 1917 and afterward, incorporated, intentionally and unintentionally, certain working assumptions and categories that were implicit in these wartime state practices. Thus ideology alone did not make the Bolshevik regime. The tools of state it inherited to pursue its ideological project were the tools of wartime coercion and mobilization. An aim of this study is to identify particularities in how the competing sides actually employed these practices for their very different ideological projects. The specificity of Bolshevik policies, however, can be appreciated only against the more generalized European background of total war.

A study of practices requires the kind of in-depth examination that only a local study can provide.[17] The Don Territory, a region in Russia's south, is the locus for this analysis. A regional focus permits an examination of the interplay between state policy and local implementation, of how national policies unfolded and were transformed in a specific local context. This level of analysis underscores the varying degrees of slippage between official aspirations and the forms of their realization.

The Don Territory had its own particularities and specificities, as does any region. It recommends itself for this analysis, however, for several reasons. It was one of Russia's premier grain-growing regions. Throughout the 1914–1921 period successive regimes assigned it an important role in their increasingly frantic food-supply operations. The region's repeated failure to meet these expectations provides an opportunity to analyze the divergence between official expectations and people's actual behavior.

The most significant distinguishing feature of the Don Territory, however, was the fact that it was a Cossack region. Cossacks, Russia's martial estate, occupied a special place in the Russian political imagination. Because actors across the political spectrum assumed that Cossacks would be a major force in the revolution, the Don Territory figured prominently in the political calculations of all national movements. For this reason, the Don Territory and its inhabitants came to play a disproportionately large role in the course of 1917 and the ensuing civil wars.[18]

During the civil wars of 1917–1921, the front line repeatedly passed over this region. As a consequence, the territory was variously controlled for extended periods by the Reds and the Whites. Moreover, the documents generated by both sides, while widely dispersed, are largely extant. Thus the region affords a unique opportunity to analyze the ways that both the Soviets and their opponents actually practiced politics. This comparative analysis demonstrates some striking and hitherto under-appreciated similarities in the political practices of the Soviets and their opponents. In doing so, it provides a perspective on the development of Soviet political culture that is much different from that found in the existing literature, both in Russia and in the West, which has tended to focus on either the Soviets or their opponents in isolation from each other.

The Don Territory was an administrative region, equivalent to a province, in Russia's southwest.[19] By 1914, it numbered nearly four million inhabitants. Cossacks gave the region its distinctive face, but they composed only 39 percent of the population. Peasants native to the Don made up 24 percent, and "outlanders"—non-natives who had settled in the Don Territory—29 percent.[20] Although by the early twentieth century Cossacks were no longer the majority of the population, the Don Territory continued to be defined by the corporate structure for the Cossack estate, the Don Host [*donskoe voisko*]. (For reasons of accessibility in English, I have employed "Cossack" rather than "Host" throughout this work.) This link to the corporate Cossack administrative structure accounted for several distinctive features. Rather than the "districts" [*uezdy*] found in most other provinces, the Don Territory was divided into "military districts" [*okruga*]. By 1917 there were nine such districts: three known as "northern" (Ust'-Medveditsa; Khoper; Second Don); one "middle" (Donets); three "southern" (Cherkassk; First Don; Sal'); and two overwhelmingly peasant districts, located to the west (Rostov and Taganrog). In late 1917 a tenth district—Upper-Don—was formed.

Below the district level, Cossacks and peasants inhabited segregated administrative structures. Peasant regions had "counties" [*volosti*], as existed in regular provinces, which were further subdivided into villages [*derevni*] and settlements [*slobody*]. Cossacks, by contrast, had "stanitsas" [*stanitsy*] in place of "counties." A stanitsa was both the large settlement proper as well as the administrative unit encompassing several dozen smaller Cossack settlements [*khutora*]. The stanitsa proper was usually quite large—in some cases numbering twenty thousand or more inhabitants—and often was more akin to a small town than to a village.

The Don Territory lacked the *zemstvo*, the local self-governing structure that was established by the Great Reforms and existed in most of the rest of European Russia. It had actually been introduced in the Don Territory in 1875, only to be withdrawn in 1882 under pressure from Cossacks, fearing that the zemstvo leveled their privileges to those of the peasantry. From that date Cossacks remained under their traditional atamans, paternalistic administrators appointed from above. In place of Cossack atamans, peasants had district peasant boards and county elders.

In addition, there were several large urban and industrial areas. Rostov-on-Don (hereafter, Rostov) was one of the empire's largest and most vibrant cities. An important city with a very heterogeneous population, it had been appended to the Don Territory only in 1888. Along with the largely Armenian settlement of Nakhichevan', it numbered nearly 230,000 inhabitants in 1915. It was the region's leading industrial and trade center and home of a vibrant regional press. The administrative capital, Novocherkassk, was home to the Cossack corporate administrative organs, and the Cossack nobility and service elite dominated it. There were several other urban centers, such as Taganrog, the port of Azov, and several district capitals. There also were industrial areas located outside cities, primarily in the Donbass mining region.[21] Given the focus of previous studies on the workers, and this book's intention to focus on the politicization of the rural population, I do not concentrate on these urban and industrial centers.

The Cossack estate was a martial estate. Its distinguishing features were universal male military service in specific Cossack formations and the attendant privileges for such service, most notably exemption from taxation. Between them, Cossack communities and the Cossack corporate administration held the majority of land in the Don Territory. The "Host estate" [*voiskovoe soslovie*]—the official title—was itself a microcosm of Russia's estate structure, encompassing nobles, priests, merchants, and "Cossacks," who were the vast majority. "Cossacks" were those members of the "Host estate" living in stanitsas, working the land, and serving in the territorially raised Cossack units. Such was the official definition by estate criteria. Rank-and-file Cossacks, however, increasingly defined themselves in terms of their lifestyle: living and farming in a stanitsa and serving in a territorially raised Cossack regiment. These experiences set them apart from the Cossack elite as much as from neighboring peasants. During and after the 1905 Revolution, many Cossacks in fact contrasted this lived form of Cossack identity to the purely ascriptive identity favored by the Cossack elite and the corporate Cossack administration.

In the countryside there were effectively two groups of non-Cossacks. "Native peasants" [*korennye krest'iane*] had lived on the Don prior to the emancipation of the serfs in 1861. With emancipation, they had received official land allotments, originally between three and four desiatins (one desiatin is equivalent to 2.7 acres). Population growth had reduced allotments to 1.4 desiatins per soul by 1906. Peasants supplemented these meager collective holdings through both private and collective purchase of land and through extensive rental. In 1905 peasants held 23 percent of all privately owned land, almost double the amount of communal allotment land they held.[22] The dynamics of agrarian unrest in 1917 would therefore be different in the Don Territory than in other parts of Russia: the prospect of seizing large amounts of land from private estates did not exist. Although they resented the vast amount of land held by Cossacks, peasants themselves were among the leading holders of private land, both as property and through rental.

The other group, the "outlanders" [*inogorodnie*], was more amorphous than native peasants. Officially, this term designated someone of any estate (noble, merchant, or peasant) living on the Don but not officially registered there. However, Cossacks sometimes used "outlander" to refer to all non-Cossacks, thus collapsing together both native peasants and true outlanders. Because they had no allotment land, outlanders primarily rented land either from the Cossack host or from private landowners.[23] Consequently, they often had the most strained relations with Cossacks and were more closely identified with market practices undermining the traditional estate system in landholding.

The land issue caused serious tensions between Cossacks and non-Cossacks. But the issue was not simply Cossack land wealth and non-Cossack "land envy." Indeed, the structure of landholding itself exacerbated tensions. Collectively, Cossacks possessed the lion's share of the land in the Don Territory, holding on average nearly seventeen desiatins per household, more than double that of native peasants and vastly more than that of outlanders. Peasants, both native and outlander, engaged in large-scale rental of land. Thus, the amount of land actually sown by Cossacks and non-Cossacks—and especially native peasants—was much more equivalent.[24] While holding less allotment land, peasants engaged in more intensive forms of agriculture than did Cossacks, employing more hired laborers and utilizing more advanced agricultural technology.[25] Tensions between Cossacks and non-Cossacks therefore stemmed as much from the *type* of agricultural relations—traditional estate relations or those of the market—as from the amount of land.[26]

Thus on the eve of war and revolution, there were several axes of identification and tension. How the population of the Don Territory negotiated claims to make sense of these collective experiences and aspirations in the maelstrom of war, revolution, and civil wars is the focus of this study.

~ 1

Russia at War

I simply understand nothing about these questions of
food supply and provisioning.
~ Nicholas II, letter to Empress Alexandra
(September 20, 1916)

$\mathcal{D}$uring the First World War, food supply became one of
the most important areas of expanded state intervention and public debate in Russia. Agriculture was central to the Russian economy (it was
by far the largest sector), to Russian society (more subjects were engaged in agriculture than in any other pursuit), and to Russian political
life (the peasant and land questions were burning issues of the day).
During the period of war and revolution, state measures pertaining to
the food supply became, along with military recruitment, one of the
most intrusive and prevalent points of contact between individuals and
the state, especially in the countryside. Food supply therefore provides
a particularly useful lens for examining the political economy of imperial Russia at war.

Imperial Russia entered the First World War amid an ongoing political crisis. The autocracy had barely survived the 1905 Revolution,
when nearly the whole nation had aligned against it. In October 1905
Nicholas II granted the October Manifesto, promising a semiconstitu-
tional order, including an elected legislature, the State Duma. Peter
Stolypin, since 1906 the chairman of the newly reformed Council of
Ministers, oversaw a dual program of repression and reform. The repression was violent but effective. As to reform, Stolypin in June 1907
restructured the State Duma's electoral laws in order to make it more
pliant but also a more effective partner in governing. His controversial

agricultural reforms sought to provide the autocracy with a new and firmer sociopolitical foundation.

Beginning in 1912, however, the Russian Empire entered a new "crisis of autocracy." This crisis would profoundly influence how the empire would negotiate the war. Nicholas II, who had never made peace with the 1905 reforms on his autocratic powers, turned against even Stolypin's system.[1] He despised the State Duma and its parties, even those loyalists who sought to reform the autocracy, such as the Octobrists. He had even less patience for the more oppositionist Constitutional Democrats, or Kadets (from the Russian initials of the party's name), who viewed themselves as supraparty, supraclass agents for bringing a progressive, mighty Russian state into being.[2]

Nicholas II was no more pleased with the form of his own government, the Council of Ministers. In Nicholas's eyes, the council's claim to administrative routine infringed upon his prerogatives, just as the State Duma claimed to place limits on his powers by invoking the national good. The Romanov dynasty's tercentenary celebrations in 1913 reinvigorated Nicholas's belief that there existed an unshakeable bond between tsar and people. After Stolypin's assassination in 1911, Nicholas made sure that chairmen of his government did not ever again exercise such authority. With Nicholas's having intentionally weakened his own government, court favorites and ministerial infighting became important features of political life in the years that followed.[3]

Yet the opponents of autocracy were no more united. After 1905, and especially after 1912, the Russian Empire experienced a crisis of "polarization."[4] The gulf between Nicholas and his own government was one axis of polarization. The rift between "society" and the political parties born of the 1905 Revolution, on the one hand, and the autocracy, on the other, was a second such axis. Because the autocracy so jealously protected its own prerogatives, Russia lacked any institutionalized network, such as France's national school system, that might have served to stitch together the "common people" and "educated society" into one sphere of "society." Public activists in Russia thus confronted challenges on two fronts: from the autocracy's arbitrary authority from above, and from the benightedness and backwardness of the masses below. Although a vibrant public sphere arose in the cities, Russia's autocratic system prevented the emergence of a true civil society, institutionalized in the law and concrete political structures.[5] This

context profoundly inflected the programs and ideals of Russian educated society. The absence of the institutions necessary to secure a true
civil society, compounded by the intelligentsia's own conceits and aspirations, fostered attitudes antithetical to civil society among precisely
those groups who would have been candidates for constituting it. Educated society's political impotence and sense of social obligation fused
into a powerful sense of mission. Invoking its own "consciousness," the
public set itself the task of taming and channeling the Russian people's
"spontaneity."[6]

Because Russian society telescoped phases of development that unfolded sequentially in western Europe, there emerged a form of "combined development," "an amalgam of archaic with more contemporary
forms."[7] Many activists and bureaucrats held that Russia might by-
pass the pitfalls experienced by those societies that had already passed
through industrialization, what Trotsky later termed the "privilege of
historic backwardness."[8] When Russia began to implement forms of
specialist intervention, especially after 1905, it did so as its preferred
models of progress were themselves developing critiques of the modern order. Harnessing these critical programs, Russian professionals
and reformers produced "an anticipatory critique of institutions not yet
endowed with the authority of an established order."[9] Thus, Russia's
political class combined a desire to change the existing state of affairs
with a repudiation of the defects of a modern industrial, capitalist order, which they found already existing in England or Germany, but
which had not yet become established in Russia. Public activists anticipated changing the established order and replacing it, not with modern
society as it already existed in western Europe, but with an idealized
projection of it. In the years immediately preceding the war, even Russian economic and legal thought, while critical of the autocracy proper,
championed a special role for the state rather than the commercial
structures prevalent elsewhere.[10] Thus public activists in Russia were
committed to a revolutionary transformation of society, although revolutionary not necessarily in the terms advocated by political radicals.

Opponents of autocracy came increasingly to view a powerful state
as both a political ideal and a concrete instrument, the antithesis of as
well as the remedy for Russia's backwardness. The polarization was less
a gulf between "state and society" than a struggle between autocracy
and educated society over how best to employ the state to transform

Russian reality.[11] This emphasis on state consciousness was a distinctive feature of Russian political culture, and its leading proponents were the Kadets. Although its members were drawn overwhelmingly from the urban free professions, this party had always viewed itself as a supraparty and supraclass organization. For Kadets, the state would be the instrument for creating both a civilized nation and enlightened citizens. This ethos predisposed Kadets to speak of collective sacrifice for the commonweal.[12]

After 1912, as a result of the failure of the Duma system to forge a common, reformist agenda between government and educated society, those parties that had committed themselves to working through the State Duma—the Octobrists, the Kadets, and the Progressists—were confronted with a crisis of identity. Whereas such parties had previously been the predominant institutional form of political expression, they seemed increasingly irrelevant. Over the course of 1914, all leading political parties in the State Duma were fracturing over whether it was better to pursue further reform with a hostile government or to court revolution again, as they had in 1904–1905.[13] In place of parties, some members of the educated elite proposed a new broad political alliance across party lines, capable of mobilizing the support of all sectors of Russian society, including representatives of the revolutionary left. Indeed, the State Duma's parliamentary activities over several years had fostered a new form of sociability across party lines.[14] To many in Russia's political and educated elite, the threat of war in July 1914 represented an opportunity to break out of this impasse. War held forth the prospect of building an "all-nation struggle," just as in 1905, in the course of which Russian society could overcome divisions both within and between parties, as well as finally seal the rift between society and the regime.[15]

A third axis of polarization ran between this educated society and the masses, in whose behalf educated society claimed to speak. The 1905 experience and its aftermath had increasingly estranged "the plebs" [*nizy*] from progressive educated society. The State Duma and all parties within it claimed to speak in the name of "the people." But Stolypin's restrictive suffrage laws had in fact created a State Duma with an artificial majority that was far more propertied, rightist, and ethnically Russian than the empire's population as a whole.[16] After a lull in the aftermath of the 1905 Revolution, social unrest intensified again after 1912. The war would see an almost immediate drop in industrial conflict, and this domestic peace would last for some time. Many convinced themselves that the gulf between "society" and "people" would disappear of its own accord once the autocracy was reformed or destroyed. The course of the war and 1917 itself, however, would demonstrate the tenaciousness of this third axis of polarization.

War and the Food Supply

In order to fund Russia's industrialization program, Ivan Vyshnegradskii, the finance minister under Alexander III, had declared, "Let us starve, but let us export grain." This the Russian Empire did. Eighty percent of the empire's total exports, measured by value, were agricultural. Owing both to its immense size and to this calculated government policy, Russia was one of the world's largest grain exporters: it accounted for 42 percent of the world export in wheat. More than half of Russia's marketed grain was exported, with Germany, Holland, and Great Britain the chief customers. Three-quarters of these agricultural exports passed through the ports of the Black Sea. With the war's outbreak, that outlet closed.[17]

Agricultural production in Russia took place primarily on peasant holdings, which had a lower productivity than either private farms or large estates. Peasants produced more than three-quarters of both the empire's grain harvest and its marketed grain.[18] Yet the majority of peasant farmers themselves had very low rates of consumption.[19] Russia was simultaneously one of the world's leading grain exporters and a country in which the consumption norms among those producing these huge surpluses were quite low.

Given Russia's grain surplus and the widespread belief that the war would not last for any extended period, the Russian government did not worry much about its food supplies as war threatened. The 1914 harvest was average, but the previous two harvests had been excellent. The vast amounts of grain that Russia traditionally exported abroad, which would be choked off with the closing of the Black Sea, could simply be shifted to meet the needs of the vastly expanded army.

Two weeks into the war, the Council of Ministers addressed the question of grain supplies for the first time. The government's concern, however, was not a shortage of grain but rather "speculation on grain and profit at the expense of the poor." A cessation of exports and the anticipated grain abundance had caused a precipitous fall in grain prices. Alexander Vasil'evich Krivoshein, the minister of agriculture and a protégé of Stolypin, offered the services of his ministry to address the problem.[20] He urged the Council of Ministers to empower his agency to coordinate the work of *zemstvos* [elective local government assemblies] in overseeing the acquisition of grain supplies for the army. Krivoshein cast his agency in the role of "the rear guard for the army quartermaster." The Council of Ministers accepted Krivoshein's offer and assigned his ministry responsibility for acquiring grain for the army, hoping that this measure would have a "moral impact" and that the country would see it as a "new step" by the government.[21]

This decision to assign the task of acquiring grain for the army to the Ministry of Agriculture had a profound influence on Russia's wartime food-supply network. The choice was not inevitable. Internal food supply before the war had traditionally fallen within the purview of the Ministry of Internal Affairs. In early 1915, Nicholas II briefly established an abortive food-supply organ under the Ministry of Trade and Industry.[22] But there were strong reasons for preferring the Ministry of Agriculture for this task. The army's head quartermaster noted that his agency had only a skeletal organization. The Ministry of Agriculture, in contrast, "had created over the course of the past several years a large number of trained specialists in all branches of agricultural life."[23] The government also knew that the educated public considered Krivoshein the most intelligent and reform-minded minister remaining in government. In July 1913 Krivoshein had given a speech portraying his ministry as eager to cooperate with "society." Zemstvo specialists, such as agronomists, especially respected him. He was one of the few ministers who could boast the confidence of both the emperor and government circles, on the one hand, and the educated public on the other.[24]

But the Ministry of Agriculture did not abruptly inherit the task of grain supply in August 1914. Since the turn of the century a new generation of agrarian experts had emerged within the government, a group with more direct knowledge of rural life than their predecessors and with greater aspirations to transform it.[25] After 1906, this generation would shape the agrarian reforms pressed by Prime Minister Stolypin—reforms that sought to undermine the peasant commune and to use property as an instrument for transforming the inert (and, after 1905, the potentially revolutionary) *muzhik* into a responsible, patriotic citizen. Krivoshein, who headed the Ministry of Agriculture from 1908, had been responsible for implementing Stolypin's reformist agenda in the countryside. These reforms went far beyond agronomic improvement and land consolidation. While property was to be a mechanism for turning peasants into citizens, the reformers simultaneously sought to combat the putatively corrosive forces of faceless "commerce." Productive labor was the ideal. As part of the government's reform program, credit and cooperative policies divided the rural population into categories of "laborers" and "nonproducers," with the latter defined as an alien and undesirable element. Government-sponsored cooperatives were meant to serve only "direct producers," marginalizing the grasping, capitalist middlemen.[26]

Krivoshein, to be sure, was neither a reactionary nor a doctrinaire opponent of capitalism. Even more than Stolypin, he favored the involvement of large capital in opening up Siberia and Central Asia. He also supported large private capital in industry, not least because he believed private investment in that sector would free up more state funds for agriculture. For agriculture, however, he favored the individual "strong peasant" and resourceful individual noble landowner, both of whom he believed were threatened by large, faceless capital.[27] During ministerial debates over a new law for joint-stock companies in 1913–1914, Krivoshein's ministry did not oppose their expansion in industry, but it fought to limit their role in land purchases. Joint-stock companies, the ministry argued, would permit "Jewish capital" to circumvent existing laws that limited Jewish landholding. While not opposing any "ethnic" limitations for joint-stock companies in industry, the Ministry of Agriculture demanded—and got—a ban on Jews' holding managerial positions in stock companies involved in land purchases.[28]

Although the Ministry of Agriculture fought the spread of commerce to the countryside, it was by no means "reactionary." Whereas other ministries (notably the Ministry of Internal Affairs) opposed any form of public involvement in government, Stolypin and Krivoshein had consistently advocated stronger links with local bodies. Both proved eager to involve the new generation of agronomists, statisticians, and economists that had emerged after the 1905 Revolution.[29] While they often opposed the form of Stolypin's reforms, these specialists shared the antipathy of the new breed of bureaucrats to private commerce. Cooperative activists wished "to protect grain, our country's main product, from any encroachments by any stock speculation." Cooperative spokesmen aspired to drive out private traders and to take commerce into their own hands.[30] Those who participated in the cooperative movement described their involvement as part of a campaign of enlightenment and liberation. Respondents to one questionnaire elucidated why they supported the cooperative movement: "to help the peasantry"; "to protect society from the kulaks [wealthy peasants usually identified with commercial pursuits]"; "a desire to free [the peasantry] from the clutches of the kulak usurer (or kulak-trader) and raise his well-being"; "to aid in the cause of freeing him from the clutches of Israel."[31] These specialists sought to implement their professional vision in league with, rather than in opposition to, the state, even as they decried the autocracy heading it.[32]

Nonetheless, after 1910 Stolypin's own political entanglements and the government's financial limitations came to stymie the prime minister's vision.[33] Moreover, after 1912 the growing disharmony in government policies complicated any attempts to fashion an overarching reform agenda. For Krivoshein, then, the war represented an opportunity to pursue the Stolypin agenda that had been obstructed in the years preceding the war. His son later recalled that "for Krivoshein, the war opened up perspectives for implementing the principles contained in his [July 1913] Kiev speech," the speech in which he called for society to aid in his reform efforts.[34] In war conditions, he could now cast his ministry's reformist agenda in terms of national defense, claiming that the ministry served as "the rearguard of the army quartermaster." Funding would no longer be a problem. In this program explicitly intended to support the cooperative and zemstvo institutions favored by the Ministry of Agriculture, the War Ministry would provide the credits for all expenses. The people heading this new wartime edifice would be the new generation of agricultural bureaucrats.

The activist and anticommercial ethos animating the Ministry of Agriculture's reform initiatives came to suffuse the entire wartime food-supply network. Reacting to the specter not of shortage but of "speculation," the Council of Ministers in early August 1914 approved guidelines for the agriculture minister, Krivoshein, to appoint "commissioners for army grain purchases." The goal of such state grain acquisitions was *"to get as close to the producer directly, bypassing the middle-man."* To do so, Krivoshein would rely on his ministry's officials in the localities, working in collaboration with zemstvo and cooperative orga-nizations.[35] With this goal in mind, the guidelines instructed commis-sioners to purchase grain directly, either from peasants and landowners or from cooperatives. Only as a last resort were they to turn to grain traders—"middlemen" and "speculators." These officials often anthro-pomorphized their distaste for commerce by identifying it specifically with "Jewish middlemen."[36]

This anticommercial disposition stands in stark contrast to that of other combatants. In Germany, Secretary of the Interior Clemens von Delbrück proclaimed several weeks before the outbreak of war that food supply was not the government's problem: "Commerce and in-dustry must take the matter in hand on their own." In Britain the presi-dent of the Board of Trade, Walter Runciman, insisted at the beginning of the war that food supplies could best be maintained through nor-mal commercial channels.[37] In Russia, however, the government's food-supply network extended its prewar tendency to work with cooperative and zemstvo activists, all the while seeking to marginalize private com-mercial networks.

Most of the commissioners appointed by Krivoshein were members of the public rather than administrators or businessmen.[38] The war provided both government officials and members of society with an opportunity to pursue their joint project to transform Russia's political and social order. In mid-August 1914 Viktor Anisimov, one of Russia's foremost cooperative activists and a leading member of the Popular Socialist Party, convened a meeting of the Committee of Cooperatives to determine how Russia's cooperatives could aid the war effort. This was not his only objective, however: Anisimov argued that the war effort could also further the cause of cooperatives in their struggle against private trade. He proposed that the government conduct all its purchasing operations for the army solely through cooperative organi-zations, thereby bypassing private trade structures.[39] Throughout the war, economists and cooperative officials trumpeted the conflict as pro-viding a welcome opportunity for the "revitalization" [*vozrozhdenie*] of both the Russian economy and Russian society.[40]

This fusion of government structures and public efforts mirrored developments in other countries. In the course of the First World War, all combatant societies saw the emergence of a "parastatal complex," a dense network of professional and civic organizations that became closely intertwined with the state.[41] But in Russia, society's side of these efforts had been stunted before the war owing to the autocracy's opposition to almost any public involvement in policy. In other countries public organizations had developed before the war and then were restructured for wartime mobilization. In Russia, by contrast, wartime mobilization telescoped the establishment stage of many such structures with their wartime reorganization under the state. Lacking a preexisting civil society, Russia "amalgamated" the emergence of technologies of public intervention with statist wartime mobilization. A parastatal complex developed under the aegis of the state, without the prior development of a civil society autonomous from it.[42]

At first, collaboration between state and society seemed to work. With prices still low, commissioners initially succeeded in their purchasing operations for the army. For all the Ministry of Agriculture's desire to engage the producer directly, however, neither it nor the cooperatives had the infrastructure necessary to replace the prewar trade apparatus, especially its network of storage facilities. Such storage points were all the more necessary as the war disrupted the regular transportation system. Once the cooperative and state trade apparatus managed to obtain grain "directly from the producer," its officials then often watched it rot at rail sidings.[43] As a consequence, commissioners in the 1914–1915 acquisition campaign were forced, against their own wishes, to turn to intermediaries—"middlemen and speculators"—for more than 60 percent of their grain. They managed to acquire only 28 percent directly from producers (15 percent from peasants and 13 percent from landowners) and 12 percent from cooperative organizations.[44]

The commissioners' greatest complication was an administrative one. In July 1914, with war looming, the military had hastily introduced a document entitled "Regulations on the Field Administration of the Armed Forces during Wartime." This document granted vast powers to the military authorities in the large swath of territory under their command, thereby bifurcating administration between areas of civilian and military control. In particular, military authorities profligately invoked their authority to ban exports from those regions under their command.[45] As a result, grain prices were rising sharply by the end of

1914 and commissioners increasingly failed to meet their targets.[46] The imperial government responded in February 1915 by permitting its purchasing commissioners to impose price limits on goods purchased for the army. Implemented by a "historic" imperial decree on February 17, these policies in fact exacerbated supply and distribution problems and were subject to much subsequent criticism.[47]

The decree reflected the convergence of views, over the course of 1915, between government administrators and public activists staffing the acquisition network regarding the need for state management and centralization of the economy.[48] The most progressive ministries, those of agriculture and war, had been the first to propose the measures. Krivoshein then convened a meeting of purchasing commissioners for the army, men drawn from among zemstvo and cooperative activists. The commissioners overwhelmingly agreed that they could not conduct their work any longer on a commercial basis, a view strongly endorsed by the War Ministry. This meeting proposed that the Ministry of Agriculture's civilian officials be granted the same powers as military authorities to prohibit "speculative" private purchasing and to ban the export of grain from areas suffering from "speculation." It requested the right to requisition grain at discounted prices whenever grain holders refused to sell it at fixed prices. The February 17 decree implemented all these proposals. The Kadet organ *Rech'* warmly endorsed these policies, citing them as a model of government cooperation with "the public."[49]

At first, these measures produced a dramatic increase in grain acquisitions, as commissioners overfulfilled their acquisition targets.[50] As critics later noted, however, the decree had several unintended effects. It introduced a two-tiered price system—fixed prices for army purchases but market prices for all other grain transactions. Civilian officials invoked their new authority to ban grain shipments even more broadly than the military had, leading to disruptions in the existing trade network. In particular, such bans prevented milling centers from receiving grain from traditional supply areas that happened to be located outside their administrative boundaries.[51]

The government could issue decrees from Petrograd, but official decrees gained purchase only in a local environment. To feed the army, the government looked to Russia's traditional grain regions. For any such food-supply operation, the Don Territory would be crucial. Located in "New Russia," Russia's rich agricultural southwest, the Don Territory accounted for 8 percent of the empire's total wheat harvest. Wheat, unlike rye or barley, was predominantly a market crop, and more than three-quarters of the region's wheat harvest was marketed.[52] In the immediate prewar period, the Don Territory ranked second in the empire in the amount of marketed wheat it produced, accounting for 11 percent of the empire's total. Owing to its location, the vast majority of all marketed grain from the Don Territory—more than 70 percent—was bound for foreign rather than domestic markets.[53] Thus the outbreak of war and the subsequent cessation of exports through the Black Sea would profoundly disrupt the Don Territory's agricultural system.[54]

Because of the vast amount of land held on behalf of the Cossack estate, however, this surplus was produced by peasant-type households rather than by large private estates. One 1916 study found that "peasant-type households" accounted for 94 percent of the overall wheat harvest in the Don Territory.[55] (Much of this peasant-type agriculture, however, was not on allotment land, but rather on land purchased or rented in addition to allotment land.) Agriculture in the Don Territory thus had a particular profile: it was more linked to the market than the empire-wide average, but with a disproportionately large involvement of small peasant producers.[56]

It was not only its agricultural profile that made the Don Territory distinct. Although Cossacks numbered less than half the population (39 percent), the territory's identity as a Cossack region determined both a special administrative status and special treatment. The area was subordinated to the War Ministry rather than to the Ministry of Internal Affairs. As a Cossack region, it also lacked the zemstvo, the local self-governing structure set up in most of European Russia as part of the Great Reforms of the 1860s and 1870s.

Official circles viewed the Cossack estate as a bulwark of order. Land impoverishment did not spare even the Cossacks, however, and by 1905 many Cossacks were finding it increasingly difficult to meet their equipping obligations for state service, a mount and saddle. After 1905, the autocracy had other reasons for concern. Despite their reputation as the autocracy's most faithful safeguard, Cossack units had proved no less susceptible than other troops to revolutionary sentiments during the crisis of 1905–1907.[57] Within the Don Territory itself, the call-up of middle-aged Cossack reserves to suppress revolution *after* the end of the Russo-Japanese War precipitated a "Cossack movement" directed equally against the autocracy and the territory's Cossack administration.[58]

In response, the autocracy attempted to shield the Cossacks from the corrosive forces supposedly sapping their reliability. In 1880 it banned Jews from settling in the Don Territory, and during the First World War it barred Jewish refugees from even temporarily settling in Cossack territories. Beginning in the 1890s the government attempted to shelter traditional Cossack landholding from the threat of non-Cossack rental and purchase through lavish distribution of loans and outright grants.[59]

The 1905 Revolution, however, had also introduced electoral politics, which served both to give shape to popular expectations and to magnify them. To the frustration and even consternation of the autocracy, the oppositionist Kadet Party became a major force in Cossack regions, beginning with elections to the First State Duma.[60] Among those Cossack Kadets elected to the First State Duma from the Don Territory was Vasilii A. Kharlamov, who would be elected to all four State Dumas. Throughout the entire Duma period, Kharlamov and other Cossack deputies criticized the War Ministry's paternalistic administration of Cossack life. By 1915, the Ministry of Internal Affairs predicted that if elections to the State Duma were held (the Fourth Duma's term was set to expire in 1917), the Don Territory would likely return "leftist" deputies. This predilection for Kadet deputies, the Ministry of Internal Affairs noted with some bewilderment, "seems so incompatible with the general spirit of the Cossacks."[61]

The autocracy, however, had made sure to appoint a staunch supporter, General V. I. Pokotilo, as *ataman* for the Don Cossack administration, in which post he acted as the territory's overall administrator. The Ministry of Internal Affairs placed great hopes on Pokotilo's activism in support of the old order.[62] Thus a vital Kadet branch operated in a region where the local administration was particularly committed to buttressing the status quo. In early 1915, Pokotilo had petitioned the government to curtail the activities of public organizations in the Don Territory, charging that the Kadet Duma deputies Kharlamov and Mitrofan Voronkov were using them for political ends. If not for their immunity as Duma members, Pokotilo would have liked to threaten them both with administrative exile to Siberia.[63]

Pokotilo and his Cossack administration, committed to sheltering Cossacks from the vicissitudes of modern life, were therefore opposed to many of the new parastatal structures decreed from Petrograd. In the Don Territory, Krivoshein's appointee as purchasing commissioner for the army—the "rear guard of the army quartermaster"—had to operate alongside this highly traditionalist Cossack administrative structure. Since the Don Territory lacked zemstvo institutions, Krivoshein appointed Aleksei Ivanovich Kirillov, the head of the credit branch of the Southeast railroads, as commissioner for army grain purchases.[64] (The railroad had a network of elevators and had much experience in grain acquisition and transport.) Kirillov would have a difficult task. Although the Don Territory was rich in grain, the specifically Cossack nature of its administration deprived him of an existing infrastructure of zemstvos or a network of Ministry of Agriculture agents, both of which existed in most other provinces. The lack of such institutions would significantly complicate his assignment.[65]

Cooperatives, here as elsewhere, were supposed to bridge the gap between production and government acquisition. The Ministry of Agriculture's chancellery in charge of army grain purchases telegraphed Kirillov in no uncertain terms that he was to give cooperatives preferential treatment. Kirillov bypassed offers from commercial grain dealers and instead concluded deals with cooperatives, although their prices were usually higher and they often were unable to meet their contracted deliveries.[66] To Kirillov's frustration, the cooperatives mustered the support of several Duma members—particularly Kadet delegates.[67] Despite his misgivings, Kirillov dutifully continued to observe the Ministry of Agriculture's guidelines. Following "instructions which I am receiving from Petrograd," he declared, his goal for the second grain campaign of 1915–1916 was "to avoid any intermediaries, except where it is necessary, and deal only with sowers and cooperatives."[68]

Cooperatives, for their part, were eager to participate in Krivoshein's new network. With the declaration of war, the massive Don-Kuban'-Terek agricultural society and thirty-six other cooperatives immediately petitioned the Ministry of Agriculture to direct the quartermaster to refrain from contracting with grain dealers "who might exploit the peasant population." Rather, they argued, the ministry should rely exclusively on "the public"—meaning the cooperatives.[69] Cooperatives participated so eagerly because they saw this moment as an opportunity to transform the existing economic structure. In early 1916 two cooperatives in the Don Territory, both of which had come into existence only during the war, separately petitioned the Ministry of Agriculture's army purchasing office to provide them each with huge, interest-free loans to purchase their own river flotillas. The stated purpose for their requests was "to liberate agriculturalists once and for all" from dependence on the large private grain-trading firms, whose control of the river trade guaranteed their dominance. Citing the need "to combat large firms," both Commissioner Kirillov and a local Kadet Duma deputy, Anrissarkh Savvateev, supported the petitions. The Ministry of Agriculture was sympathetic to the request but was barred from spending the War Ministry's credits on such expenses.[70] Many public organizations thus willingly collaborated in the state's war-mobilization plans because they believed they provided an unparalleled opportunity to transform society according to their own programs.

The Food-Supply Crisis

Summer 1915 brought significant changes in the state's involvement in food supply. Owing to the administrative chaos, some cities had already begun to experience food shortages. Yet the government's new measures resulted more from the overall political crisis than from any particular crisis in food supply. The "Great Retreat" in the spring and summer of 1915, when the Russian army was driven out of Galicia and Poland, led to charges that the government was mismanaging the war effort. Reformers in the military and even within the government joined the public in its criticisms of the government's conduct of the war.

An "economic-military-political alliance of 'respectable' Russia" emerged out of the web of public organizations that the government had reluctantly sanctioned to channel public involvement in the war effort: war-industry committees, the union of zemstvos, and the union of towns.[71] These institutions provided public activists with a forum, denied them before the war, to discuss and implement their programs of reform. This web of supraparty organizations came to supersede the fractured prewar party organizations. The political networks of the Duma parties atrophied as their members threw themselves into work in parastatal organizations.[72] Yet these parastatal organizations, like the Duma parties before them, did not so much represent the country as harbor pretensions to speak for it. Thus the war years reproduced the axis of polarization between "society" and "the masses," but now in organs fashioning themselves as supraparty and supraclass.

One of these new parastatal organizations consisted of "special councils," established in summer 1915. Based upon German and British models for bringing together government ministries and public organizations, each special council—defense, transport, fuel, and food supply—was chaired by the minister from the most relevant government ministry. Krivoshein, as the minister of agriculture, headed the "Special Council for Discussing and Coordinating Measures for Food Supply."[73] Hitherto, the minister of agriculture had overseen a network of commissioners whose task was to purchase grain only for the army, originally with the hope that such purchases would help grain producers. In 1915, the Special Council extended the state's responsibility from covering just the army to feeding the entire civilian population.

At precisely the same time, also in response to the military defeats, Nicholas II decided, against much advice to the contrary, to assume the post of commander in chief. His ministers expressed their concern that further defeats would tarnish the imperial reputation. Even more, they feared that Nicholas's presence at Headquarters would increase the influence of court favorites, grouped around the Empress Alexandra and Rasputin, on government policy. The Council of Ministers took the entirely unprecedented step of petitioning the emperor to reconsider. This collective ministerial protest occurred just as secret discussions between certain reformist ministers (among them, Krivoshein and War Minister Polivanov) and a broad spectrum of centrist Duma parties culminated in the program for a Progressive Bloc, formed to press a minimum agenda of longstanding demands against the autocracy. Learning almost simultaneously of his ministers' protest and the formation of the Progressive Bloc, Nicholas felt betrayed on all sides. He prorogued the State Duma and curtly rejected his ministers' advice. Nicholas came to rely even more on court favorites rather than on government officials.[74] As a result, there was little stability in the Council of Ministers. Because of his progressive views and role in the "ministers' rebellion," Krivoshein was dismissed less than three months later. His replacement, the old zemstvo hand Aleksandr Naumov, continued Krivoshein's policy of seeking to involve public organizations.[75] After Krivoshein, however, there would be little stability: three different people would occupy the post of minister of agriculture over the next fifteen months. August 1915 marked a watershed. After this point, the government and parastatal organizations did not so much work together as stand in opposition to one another.

Complaints of government inefficiency provided the backdrop for the formation of the Special Council on Food Supply. Like all other special councils, it was staffed by representatives of the government departments concerned and, in a major departure for the autocracy, included representatives from the legislature and public organizations. In the Special Council for Food Supply such members outnumbered government officials. Peter Struve, a leading public figure and critic of the autocracy, participated as the delegate from the Union of Zemstvos. Krivoshein, a friend and admirer of Struve, had earlier recommended him to head the committee charged with restricting the flow of enemy trade.[76]

On the ground in the Don Territory, Kirillov, the commissioner for army grain purchases, confronted the task of meeting a grain assignment for 1915–1916 that represented 10 percent of the empire's total assessment for wheat and flour.[77] The grain-rich Don Territory did not yet suffer from grain shortages, but there was concern over its rising cost, especially in urban centers. In confronting this problem, Kirillov and Ataman Pokotilo found common ground in their antipathy to "speculation." City councils in Rostov, Taganrog, and Novocherkassk protested rising prices on essential goods, excoriating "the purely speculative activities of local merchants and private banks." Pokotilo supported these charges, criticizing merchants for having "excessively inflated" food prices in the cities. The Special Council for Food Supply concurred with such findings. (Food supplies, except those intended for the army, were not yet under any price controls, so the merchants' actions were entirely legal.)[78]

Responding to an avalanche of such complaints from throughout the empire, the Special Council in October 1915 established a "commissioners of the chairman of the Special Council on Food Supply" for each province. The commissioner was to work alongside the already existing network of commissioners for army grain purchases. These two networks were unified at the top in the same individual, the agriculture minister, in his dual role as agriculture minister and chairman of the Special Council. The local commissioners were then to form their own provincial special councils for food supply. Whereas the army commissioners were to acquire grain for the army, the food-supply commissioners were to coordinate food supply for the civilian population. Ataman Pokotilo vetoed the original nominee for the post, Vasilii Chernitskii, a member of the State Council from the Don Territory. Pokotilo denounced him as holding a hostile attitude to "Cossack life." In his place, Pokotilo proposed Privy Councilor I. T. Semenov, who had served for many years in the Cossack administration. "Recently," Pokotilo added, "he was my junior aide." The Special Council promptly appointed Semenov.[79]

Rather than seeking to involve "society" in affairs of governing, Pokotilo attempted merely to extend traditional bureaucratic oversight into new spheres. Krivoshein's instructions for local commissioners allowed them to hand pick the individual participants for each particular meeting. But they also directed the commissioners to include the new public organizations in deliberations. Despite his distaste for members of the new public structures, Semenov felt obligated to invite them to participate in his gatherings. Kadets were very prominent in these organizations. Pokotilo's *bête noire*, Vasilii Kharlamov, the perennial Cossack Kadet Duma deputy, was the local representative of the Union of Zemstvos. (While the Don lacked zemstvos, Kharlamov represented the union's empire-wide activities there.) Among other participants were the heads of the Rostov and Novocherkassk war-industry committees, both of whom were also prominent local Kadets, as well as delegates from the Union of Towns, local cooperative societies (including the prominent G. P. Urusov from the Don-Kuban'-Terek society), city boards, and the Territory's War-Industry Committee.[80]

Even under Semenov, then, the local special council fostered the emergence of a professional apparatus, even if it lacked much power. His council secretary, Pavel Ageev, had participated in the antiregime unrest in 1906 and been arrested, along with Filipp Mironov, for composing a petition of protest for northern Cossack communities.[81] He and Mironov had delivered this petition to the leading Cossack Duma deputy in St. Petersburg—Vasilii Kharlamov. In the intervening years, Ageev had taken up his teaching duties and served without problem. Kharlamov and Ageev met again in late 1915 over the table of the local special council, headed by the traditionalist Semenov. There Ageev increasingly pressed a program of state management of the food supply and even the partial expropriation of privately held grain and flour stocks. Semenov's council rejected Ageev's suggestions in mid-1916, but only because there was insufficient data to carry them out effectively.[82]

Semenov and his political opponents, then, agreed on a common foe. For the next six months Semenov would repeatedly press the Special Council to place limits on grain merchants and millers in order to guarantee a "fair" price and "normal" profits. Regardless of how bad the food-supply situation became, Semenov refused right down to the collapse of the autocracy to turn to the long-established network of private grain traders in Rostov.[83]

Throughout 1915, the government's initial response to the food-supply problem had been a series of measures to prevent "speculation." For traditionalist bureaucrats, these were predictable responses to fears about the specter of faceless commerce. Agricultural specialists, seeing in these measures the potential for rational administration of the chaotic and unjust market, also endorsed them. Thus there emerged a widespread consensus favoring centralized, technocratic state intervention in the economy, symbolized by the Special Council's burgeoning staff and secretariat. Despite the fervent desires of reformist ministers like Krivoshein, however, the autocracy involved "society" only begrudgingly. In the Don Territory, Pokotilo and Semenov acquiesced to the requirement to include public organizations, but they did not welcome their participation. The government's intransigence and the Kadets' own role in parastatal organs allowed Kadets to imagine they spoke on behalf of society. As the food-supply situation continued to deteriorate, the government's reluctance to involve "the public" became the target of public criticism, much more than the government's actual measures in food supply.

By the autumn of 1916, Russian newspapers regularly carried banner headlines on "the food-supply crisis." Even in the grain-rich Don Territory, shortages led authorities to ban the making of sweets and cakes, for which the region was renowned. Why were there such shortages in the Russian Empire, previously one of the world's largest exporters of grain, and, even more remarkably, in the grain-rich Don Territory?

Clearly, there were objective factors related to the war. The vast numbers of men drafted into the army had produced a shortage of labor in the countryside.[84] The labor shortage led to a contraction in sown territory overall, but it particularly affected the large estates that had depended upon hired agricultural labor. Before the war, these estates had been the most efficient producers of grain. By 1915, the amount of territory sown throughout the empire on large private estates had dropped by half, and on the Don the decrease was even more precipitous, to 75 percent of the prewar figure.[85]

Even so, the harvests in 1915 and 1916 were generally considered good. The Don Territory, however, suffered a localized drought in 1916. According to the Ministry of Agriculture's standardized categories, the wheat harvest there was judged to be "poor" and the rye harvest as "below average."[86] By 1917 both the sown territory and harvests throughout the Russian Empire had contracted. On the Don, the drop was especially precipitous in 1916, with nearly a 25 percent falloff in sown territory (the empire-wide average was 12 percent). Owing to the contraction in sowings and the drought, the region's wheat harvest was only 40 percent that of the prewar average, compared with an empire-wide average of 80 percent.[87]

Despite all these problems, as late as 1917 the country had enough stocks to cover its needs.[88] Indeed, contemporaries and subsequent scholars can be so certain that these grain reserves existed because they can rely on a mass of empirical studies generated by the Special Council, such as the first empire-wide agricultural census in 1916. This census had the unintended consequence, "impossible to exaggerate," according to two former officials of the Special Council for Food Supply, of leading "the Government in the first place to convince itself of the inexhaustible productive resources of the nation."[89] Russia, then, produced the necessary amount of grain. What was wrong?

Contemporaries blamed much of the deteriorating situation on the transportation network. It was not just a question of Russian "backwardness." Prewar planners had been correct that, in aggregate terms, the amounts of grain exported in peacetime should have covered wartime demands. Such estimates, however, failed to take into account the geography of the market. Much of European Russia's surplus marketable grain was produced in the south for foreign export. In peacetime these surpluses were generally transported away from Russia's industrial centers, along an established river and rail network, toward ports from whence they were shipped abroad. Thus, while vast amounts of grain existed in Russia, they often were situated at points that had not developed market and transport links to the *internal* market. In addition, those rail lines best suited to distribute grain internally now happened to be precisely the ones required by the military to support its operations. Furthermore, demands of war led to a cumulative deterioration of the rolling stock.[90]

Although all these factors contributed to the food-supply crisis, the transportation system became the convenient scapegoat, both at the national level and within the Don Territory, for all problems related to the breakdown in distribution.[91] The government could and should have better coordinated its existing grain stocks. The transportation problems were not inevitable. Rather, they resulted from the government's failure to coordinate the activities of provincial-level bodies, such as provincial commissioners for food supply, who had been granted the power to ban exports and control local transportation.[92]

Equally important, however, was the emergence of Russia's first "scissors crisis." This was the term employed in the 1920s to describe the diverging price curves between the industrial and the agricultural sector, with rising prices on scarce manufactured goods and stagnant or falling prices on agricultural goods. In such conditions, farmers held their grain from the market and planted no more than was necessary for the household's own consumption. Wartime mobilization disproportionately affected the industrial sector, leading to a shortage of manufactured consumer goods. At precisely the juncture at which the government wished to coax grain from the countryside, it was unable to offer any goods in return.

Moreover, peasants no longer needed to sell their grain to obtain cash. The wartime prohibition on alcoholic beverages deprived the government of its greatest revenue source, the tax on alcohol. This patriotic gesture left this money—one-quarter of state revenues in prewar years—in the hands of peasants. This, plus massive state outlays to families of mobilized servicemen, provided peasant households with more disposable cash than ever before to purchase fewer and fewer goods. These conditions in an inflationary economy gave peasants little incentive to sell grain for money that could purchase little and that was declining in value.[93] Rather than sell grain at fixed prices in these conditions, peasants instead increased consumption for themselves and their cattle, or brewed their grain into moonshine. Economists at the time estimated that peasant households increased consumption by 25 percent over the course of the war (admittedly from a very low base). In Struve's formulation, "Here was not a case of anemia but rather a pathological blood congestion of agriculture."[94]

Given the available models of wartime mobilization, some imbalance between the industrial and the agricultural sectors—a scissors crisis— was probably unavoidable. The predominance of the agricultural sector in Russia made this problem more acute than in other countries, but all combatants faced it in one form or another. All states that relied upon domestic sources for food supply had difficulties in extracting grain. In this sense, the British government's dependence on foreign imports gave it a paradoxical advantage. While the British Food Controller had to worry about ensuring imports from abroad, this same reliance on imports saved him from having to extract foodstuffs from Britain's own producers, which was the primary axis of dissatisfaction in the food-supply policies in both Russia and Germany.[95] From March 1917 the German government employed military units for conducting house-to-house searches of peasant households for hoarded grain, a practice repeated in spring 1918.[96] Beginning in January 1918 the Austro-Hungarian Empire likewise employed field units from the army to assist with requisitions in Hungary. In March 1918 the Austro-Hungarian government even withdrew an additional 50,000 men from the front to assist with food-supply requisitioning.[97] By 1918, Russia would be employing similar measures to extract grain from the countryside.

Russia, however, was distinct among major powers in seeking to eliminate its existing commercial and trade networks. As a matter of policy, Russia used wartime measures to establish a new, "direct" relationship with its millions of agricultural producers. In the process, the war revealed a vast gulf between the educated elite's aspirations for the peasants and the peasants' actual goals and behavior. During the war years, however, most politically minded Russians neglected this rift, preferring instead to indict the regime rather than the peasant producers. In excoriating government incompetence, contemporary observers overlooked the extent to which the distribution crisis in fact resulted from the fulfillment of the Ministry of Agriculture's original goal: the elimination of the middleman and the establishment of direct relations between the government and the producer. Russia's educated elites across a broad spectrum had shared this goal, seeking to shield peasant producers from the corruption of commercial relations. Toward the end of 1916, these government officials and public professionals had driven out the middlemen and forced the grain back into the hands of producers. They now faced a cruel irony. War conditions, which had made it possible to implement anticommercial measures so energetically, also meant that the state, when confronting peasant producers directly, now had nothing to offer them but exhortations. The Russian government had removed the market's "invisible hand" with the intention of replacing it with the state. But this role then made the state the focus for all dissatisfaction.[98]

In Russia, the hostility of both state officials and the public toward private trade mechanisms from the earliest stage of food-supply organization exacerbated structural problems common to other combatant societies. By 1916, most other combatants had moved toward state intervention in the economy. These measures usually took the form of some kind of corporatism, retaining private trade structures but subsuming them under a broader collectivist agenda. In constructing their state food-supply apparatuses, for instance, the German and British governments both drew upon the expertise and infrastructure of existing commercial networks. In January 1915 the German government established an "Imperial Grain Corporation" (note even the commercial title), which was "composed of the sector's leading capitalists, the grain farmers and wholesalers." Wherever possible, the German food-supply apparatus integrated existing corporations and cartels.[99] Despite its goal of protecting the consumer, "merchants continued throughout the war to work at the heart of Germany's food organization . . . The government continued to rely on mercantile relationships throughout the years of controlled food distribution."[100]

Confronting an admittedly different set of problems, Britain shifted toward the central organization of food supply only in 1916. When it did, however, the British Ministry of Food retained the existing channels of trade even during "the heroic age of food control."[101] Some in England thought private trade "too circuitous," as did many in Russia. But the British Food Controller, Lord Rhondda, "insisted that it was more important to preserve continuity of supply and distribution and to let each trader work through the men whose ways he knew."[102] The two heads of the British Ministry of Food from 1916 to mid-1918, first Lord Devonport and then Lord Rhondda, were both liberal businessmen and traders. In Britain, then, the "machinery of state food control was superimposed upon existing commercial patterns of production and distribution, and Rhondda went to great lengths to accommodate both large and small traders and to disrupt as little as possible the normal methods of supply."[103] France and Austria-Hungary pursued similar corporatist policies.[104]

Russia was thus not alone in facing a scissors crisis or difficulties in cajoling millions of small producers to surrender their grain. But unlike nearly all other major combatants, the Russian government, with significant support from civic activists, attempted to employ wartime measures to supplant, rather than incorporate, existing market structures. Whereas in most other combatant countries the administrators in charge of food supply were businessmen, in Russia they were not. Nor did Russian trade organizations have any great influence over food-supply measures.[105] Perhaps the only analogue to Krivoshein's attempts to squeeze out the "middleman" and "to engage the producer directly" was the effort of Kemal Bey in Turkey to use wartime food-supply measures to "Turkify" economic life. By forming Turkish consumer cooperatives, Bey sought to squeeze out the non-Turkish, and especially Greek, merchants who dominated the grain trade.[106]

By mid-1916, government officials recognized that they were facing a serious distribution crisis. In the 1915–1916 grain-acquisitioning campaign, commissioners for army grain purchases obtained 15 percent of their grain directly from peasants, the same percentage as in 1914–1915. Cooperatives provided 17 percent (up from 12 percent in 1914–1915) and landowners—18 percent (up from 13 percent the year before). Although middlemen dropped from providing 60 percent in 1914–1915 to 50 percent the following year, they still remained by far the largest supplier of grain. Confronted by these results, the Special Council enjoined its agents to increase their reliance on the private trade apparatus.[107]

The public activists within the special council apparatus, however, insisted upon a continuation of measures that the government now wished to moderate. From late autumn 1915 into the winter of 1916, the representative of the Union of Towns, the renowned economist Vladimir Groman (a Menshevik), and that of the Union of Zemstvos, Peter Struve, formed a common front in agitating for more systematic state intervention. It was government officials who opposed their suggestions. Indeed, it fell to government officials to defend the necessity of involving the private trade apparatus in food-supply operations at all.[108] The cooperative activists whom the state itself had drawn into the wartime food-supply network, however, violently opposed this shift, despite the continuing deterioration in the food-supply situation. Throughout 1917 local food-supply officials, especially cooperative activists, continued to oppose government proposals to grant the private trade apparatus any role at all in the failing food-supply effort.

The imperial state's failure to deal with food-supply demands ultimately led to the regime's collapse in February 1917. Educated society naturally criticized the autocracy's poor performance in food supply. The focus of the intelligentsia's criticism, however, was not the government's antimarket measures themselves, but the execution of those measures. Nikolai Kondrat'ev, who was involved in food supply throughout the period of war and revolution and published a seminal study of the question in 1922, testified that over the course of 1916, "public opinion proceeded from the view that the growing supply crisis demanded consistent state regulation of supply. Moreover, civic circles—representatives of towns, cooperatives, and even some zemstvos—advanced in this regard an even more radical program, extending the principle of regulation to all significant branches of the economy."[109] By February 1917, reformist bureaucrats and their allies in public organizations had achieved their long-cherished goal. They had driven middlemen and private traders almost entirely from the scene, and grain was now concentrated largely in the hands of its producers. When they came to power after the February Revolution, these specialists and reformers would confront the consequences of their policy.

The Political Economy of Crisis

After long debate, in autumn 1916 the government implemented fixed prices for all grain transactions. In doing so, it inadvertently opened a major public discussion of the political economy of food supply. In February 1915 the government had established a dual price policy for purchasing grain: fixed prices for army purchases and market prices for all other transactions. In early 1916 the Special Council had discussed fixed prices for all grain purchases, but only Struve had supported the measure. Only when Naumov, Krivoshein's replacement as the minister of agriculture, proclaimed his support for fixed prices in May 1916 did the Special Council reverse itself and direct provincial special councils to draw up "fair" fixed prices for their regions.[110] Just as the Special Council was preparing to introduce them, however, the old zemstvo hand Naumov was removed as the minister of agriculture. He was replaced by Count Aleksei Aleksandrovich Bobrinskii, a leader of the arch-reactionary United Nobility and a noted advocate for the "agrarians," the large landed interests.[111]

One month after Bobrinskii's appointment, both the Special Council's civilian commissioners for food supply and the Ministry of Agriculture's commissioners for army grain purchases gathered in Petrograd to determine the rates for fixed prices. This conference provided a forum for the public activists who had been drawn into the government's food-supply apparatus during the war to criticize the autocracy's programs. These criticisms were covered extensively by the national press. It was during these debates that Mitrofan Voronkov, the Kadet Duma deputy from the Don Territory, came to national prominence. Originally elected to the oppositionist Second State Duma (1906–1907), he had devoted himself in the prewar years mainly to educational issues. During the war, however, Voronkov became involved in food-supply issues through a variety of government and Duma committees. From the first days of the war he had strongly advocated government reliance on cooperative structures, arguing that they should receive orders even if their prices for grain were higher than those offered by private firms.[112] At the congress of commissioners in August 1916, Voronkov formed a common front with Vladimir Groman, the Menshevik planning specialist based in the Union of Towns. Together they championed low fixed prices and attacked Bobrinskii as a spokesman for the parochial interests of the wealthy "agrarians." When the Special Council voted on the fixed prices proposed by the conference, the Menshevik Groman and the Kadet Voronkov drafted the opposition resolution. The Special Council, led by Bobrinskii, narrowly voted it down and passed higher fixed rates.[113]

Reformers in other ministries refused to accept Bobrinskii's victory. The Special Council for Defense—chaired by War Minister Shuvaev, who had previously served as army quartermaster—had the power to overturn Bobrinskii's decision. When Shuvaev summoned a special joint meeting of his council, he invited Groman and Voronkov to present their case. They were joined by Andrei Shingarev, the Kadet Party's point man on food supply. After February 1917, all three would play key roles in the Provisional Government's food-supply apparatus. As a result of their lobbying, the government lowered the fixed prices originally set by Bobrinskii.[114]

This debate catapulted Voronkov onto the national scene, turning him overnight into a nationally recognized "specialist" in food supply. Leading newspapers interviewed him, national journals reprinted his observations, and he began receiving telegrams from throughout the country.[115] Voronkov and Groman, a Kadet and a Menshevik brought together in the war's supraparty parastatal structures, continued their advocacy of state intervention and their public criticism of Bobrinskii's policies.[116] In early December 1916, Voronkov gave a major speech to the State Duma on the food-supply issue, echoing Groman's criticism of the government for failing to develop a systematic economic plan.[117] In both the State Duma and the Special Council for Food Supply, Voronkov continued to harry Bobrinskii's replacement as minister of agriculture, Aleksandr Rittikh, as part of the Kadet Party's overall campaign against the government.[118] It was at this time that Nicholas II frankly confided to his wife in late September 1916, "I simply understand nothing about these questions of food supply and provisioning."[119]

By late 1916 a wide-ranging consensus had emerged across much of the political spectrum, from the radical Duma parties to many reformist members of the tsarist bureaucracy and military, that the autocracy was conducting the war in an incompetent manner. Although parastatal organizations provided an institutional forum for opposition, they did not of their own accord generate any concrete program. Ironically, it was Germany's war economy that provided a successful and tested roadmap for economic mobilization and social reorganization. In looking to Germany, Russian policy-makers, officials, and revolutionaries drew upon that national economic model they had known best for decades.[120] And there were indeed good reasons for Russians to study Germany's model of wartime mobilization. Blockaded Germany seemed to be coping successfully with the most difficult situation of any combatant. Additionally, the German *intensive* economic mobilization more closely approximated Russia's situation than did the *extensive* economic mobilization of France or Britain, which was predicated on their dependence upon overseas colonial holdings and, ultimately, the United States.[121]

Russian specialists came to view German wartime measures as a model of what the state could do if it harnessed the forces of "society." Struve covered German measures in articles for the monthly journal *Russkaia mysl'* and, in his capacity as the chairman of the Russian Committee for Restricting Enemy Trade, compiled regular reports on the German war economy.[122] From neutral Stockholm, "M. Lur'e" reported in copious detail on German wartime economic policies for both the liberal newspaper *Russkie vedomosti* and the popular monthly *Vestnik evropy*. "Lur'e" was in fact a pseudonym for the Menshevik Iurii Larin.[123] Vladimir Groman, who from his post in the Union of Towns was the leading Russian proponent of economic planning, also closely followed German developments. Knowing no foreign languages, Groman relied upon Larin's reportage for his understanding of German measures.[124] Groman would become a prominent planning expert for the Petrograd Soviet in 1917, and throughout the 1920s he would continue this work for the Soviet state. Larin joined the Bolsheviks in August 1917 and during the civil wars became the architect for the Bolshevik policy of War Communism.

Yet however much Russians believed they should be emulating German policy, Russian wartime measures were not simply carbon copies of German measures. Until the collapse of the old regime, the German form of war mobilization did not so much provide the model for actual Russian measures as serve as the basis for a critique of existing policy, a critique implemented only after the autocracy's collapse. The proposal to introduce a "grain monopoly" in August 1916 was a case in point. While Bobrinskii was pursuing his campaign against low fixed prices, officials within his very own ministry floated a draft proposal "for the monopolization of the grain trade." The proposal represented a consensus that had emerged between the professional staff of the Special Council's burgeoning secretariat, on the one hand, and the activists in public organizations and legislative bodies, on the other. On the last day of the congress debating fixed prices, the "draft" appeared in newspapers. It invoked German measures as the blueprint for future economic planning, both for the course of the war and afterward:[125]

The war has advanced the social life of the state [*sotsial'nuiu zhizn' gosudarstva*] as the dominant principle, in relation to which all other manifestations of civic life must be subordinated . . . Germany's military-economic practice, which is the most intensive in the world conflict, shows how far this process of *étatisation* [*ogosudarstvlenie*] can proceed . . . All these state measures related to the war . . . represent a hitherto under-appreciated foundation for the systematic construction of future domestic and foreign trade . . . The state cannot allow grain to remain a circumstance of free trade.

Members of the Special Council's secretariat pursued a veritable press campaign on behalf of this measure. Iakov Bukshpan, a former student of Struve's serving as editor of the Special Council's official journal, published an article strongly advocating a state grain monopoly. Echoing the draft proposal, Bukshpan argued for the establishment of a state organ to oversee grain distribution, to be modeled explicitly on the German *Reichsgetreidestelle*.[126] Andrei Shingarev, the Kadet spokesman on food-supply issues, also pressed the idea of a state grain monopoly in meetings of the Special Council in early September 1916.[127] As the Provisional Government's first minister of agriculture, Shingarev would implement the grain monopoly as one of his very first measures.

These proposals demonstrated the emergence of a wide-ranging consensus among officials in the new parastatal organs and the general public for interventionist state measures. But under Bobrinskii such measures had no chance of realization. Bukshpan's article was published in the journal's "unofficial" section. The court and ministers appointed by the tsar refused to implement these policies favored by the professional staff of the ministries and public activists. As a result, the political contours of the food-supply debate in Russia differed from those of its German ideal. In Germany, the political struggle over food supply increasingly reflected the divide between rural producers and urban consumers.[128] In Russia politicians and the public concentrated their criticism not on this aspect of the problem but rather on government incompetence and the iniquity of private trade. This myopic focus on the autocracy's bumbling allowed food-supply technocrats—within and outside of government ministries—to overlook the looming gulf that had opened between themselves and the mass of agricultural producers.

Criticism of the existing regime's policies on food supply became even more urgent as autumn passed into winter, and the food-supply situation only worsened. With nearly all factions in the State Duma, including the right, arrayed against Nicholas's obstinate government, the tsar jettisoned several of his ministers, including the arch-reactionary Bobrinskii. He was replaced by Aleksandr Rittikh, who was a member of the new generation of bureaucrats. Rittikh had served under Krivoshein as head of the land-consolidation department during Stolypin's reforms.[129] Immediately upon taking up his post, Rittikh received a telegram from General Brusilov indicating that the army had absolutely no reserves at hand and threatening to employ his units to acquire grain for the army. Rittikh responded by sending all available grain to the army, leaving him with no reserves. To address this situation Rittikh instituted a grain levy [*razverstka*].[130] He intended the levy less as an effective extraction mechanism than as a means to transform the nature of the food-supply nexus. A protégé of Stolypin and Krivoshein, Rittikh hoped to eliminate the commercial aspect of food supply altogether. In describing his policy, both to the State Duma and to the Special Council for State Defense, he proclaimed that "the idea of the levy was to transform the delivery of peasant grain from the sphere of a simple commercial transaction [*torgovaia sdelka*] to the sphere of fulfilling a civic duty [*grazhdanskii dolg*], obligatory for all who hold grain."[131]

Although Rittikh's measures initially speeded up grain deliveries, they disrupted the previous system, however inefficient it had been, leading to even greater shortages by early 1917. The abrupt introduction of the new distribution plan also meant that the assessments allocated to provinces often did not correspond to existing grain reserves.[132] Few doubted that Rittikh, as minister, represented an improvement on Bobrinskii. Yet he was a minister in a government now detested by nearly the entire political spectrum.[133]

Under Krivoshein, a government food-supply system had been tried, and it had failed. Rittikh attempted exhortation, and it too had failed. Confronting a catastrophic shortage of grain amid evident plenty, several food-supply officials by late 1916 broached the need for "compulsion." Under pressure from the war minister, Bobrinskii in early October 1916 had asked his commissioners to present their views "on the possibility of registering the population's grain reserves and acquiring them in a compulsory manner." Soon afterward two Duma deputies— a Kadet and an Octobrist, characteristically now acting in new roles within the wartime food-supply apparatus—proposed compulsory alienation of peasant grain to supply the army.[134] These suggestions were in fact enacted less than three months later, by the Provisional Government's grain monopoly.

Rittikh's levy had assigned the Don Territory the second-largest grain assessment of all European provinces. But by autumn 1916 Kirillov was finding it impossible to meet the assigned shipments of grain for the army.[135] Most provinces with large assessments failed to meet them. Even so, the shortfall in the Don Territory, where grain was dispersed to an even greater extent among small peasant producers rather than concentrated among large landowners, was dramatically worse. Choosing to blame Kirillov rather than structural problems, the chancellery for army grain purchases removed him and appointed M. P. Krinitskii, who prior to the war had been involved in the Ministry of Agriculture's land-consolidation program.[136] Krinitskii would be no more successful than Kirillov. In January 1917 the Don Territory failed to dispatch even *one* of its assigned 4,040 railcars of grain, and the situation did not improve over the next two months.[137] In his 1915–1916 operations, Kirillov procured 53 percent of his assessment from landowners, a figure that included peasants farming on private and rented land (the empire-wide average was 18 percent); 22 percent from cooperatives (17 percent empire-wide); 21 percent from middlemen (50 percent); but only 4 percent directly from "peasants" (15 percent). While the cooperatives' success in procuring one-fifth of the total led some to consider the Don a model of cooperative activity, the figures overall demonstrated a total collapse of the government program.[138] In a region dominated precisely by the small producers whom the government viewed as the pillar of its food-supply and civic programs, efforts by the central authorities had failed spectacularly.

But the failure to ship grain out of the Don Territory did not mean that the surplus found its way to the region's cities. The mills of Rostov were some of the largest and most modern in Russia. Before the war they had depended on grain shipments from the Black Sea, but now they had to depend on irregular rail shipments. In October 1916 an assembly of state officials and food-supply organizations of the region's six largest cities introduced flour rationing.[139] Owing to a shortage of wheat and wheat flour—in a province that before the war had provided 11 percent of the Russian Empire's marketed wheat—Pokotilo's replacement as the Cossack ataman, Count Grabbe, banned the sale of wheat bread in January 1917. The following month, on account of shortages of sugar and flour, he banned the production of cakes and sweets.[140]

Local officials did not limit themselves to rationing. Newspapers reported both official and popular actions against "speculators." Merchants convicted of "speculation" (meaning either hoarding goods or selling them at inflated prices) regularly received sentences of several months in jail.[141] Concerned that "speculators" were descending upon the Don from neighboring provinces to purchase foodstuffs and then carting them out of the territory, Ataman Grabbe ordered district authorities in September "to detain all small-scale purchasers of goods."[142] Conservative administrators as well as Kadet-dominated municipal "inhabitant committees" conducted intermittent store-to-store searches.[143]

The tsarist government's resistance to the further development of parastatal organs provided a convenient explanation for all shortcomings. While Rittikh called for unity, the Ministry of Internal Affairs "was closing down food-supply congresses left and right. Aleksandr Chaianov remarked a few months later, 'the government feared hunger, but it feared public organizations even more.'"[144] In the Don Territory organizers of a meeting of cooperatives, scheduled for mid-January 1917, had to cancel when they failed to receive the government's permission to convene. One week later, the ataman's aide for civic affairs declared that he would not permit food-supply committees to hold any public meetings to discuss price policy.[145] When Semenov finally permitted a food-supply conference under his personal supervision, meeting from February 19 to February 21, he dutifully telegraphed the Special Council secretariat with the resolutions the conference had passed. He failed to report, however, that his aide had banned participants from discussing an increased role for civic organizations, an act that led the vast majority of participants demonstratively to walk out of the gathering.[146]

Two weeks later these very same delegates met again. Summoned by a new national government, they constituted themselves as the Don Territorial Food-Supply Committee. In place of an appointed chairman, they elected one. He was Mitrofan Voronkov—Cossack, Duma deputy, Kadet, food-supply specialist. As chairman, he would be primarily responsible for implementing the Provisional Government's grain monopoly. The monopoly epitomizes the tight nexus forged in the wartime parastatal structures. It was formulated in a committee chaired by Voronkov's comrade in arms for fixed prices, the Menshevik Groman; it was drafted by Struve's student, Bukshpan; and it was proclaimed by Voronkov's Duma and Kadet colleague Andrei Shingarev, in his duty as the new government's minister of agriculture.

Food Supply as a Prism of Russia at War

Revolution brought down Russia's old regime in February 1917. The immediate cause was worker demonstrations over food-supply shortages in the capital, Petrograd. The crisis shifted from rebellion to revolution when soldiers sided with the strikers and members of the moderate opposition abandoned the autocracy to form new organs of power. A grain-rich country—the world's leading exporter of grain—had found itself facing grain shortages by the third winter of the war. This situation resulted not from any shortage of grain but from a sharp decline in marketed grain. Particular policies of the imperial regime exacerbated structural constraints facing all combatants. Krivoshein's Ministry of Agriculture had entered the war with a sense of mission inherited from its frustrated efforts to carry out the Stolypin reform. Paradoxically, many of the Russian state's food-supply problems in 1916–1917 were the result of the success of the Ministry of Agriculture's wartime program—to marginalize the middleman and deal directly with the producer. When the government reluctantly decided in 1915 that it was necessary to harness the private trade apparatus, its own commissioners and broad sectors of the public opposed this concession. Wartime food-supply operations thus fostered among those who staffed them a shared antimarket, pro-planning, *étatist* consensus across the political spectrum.

This antimarket outlook conditioned the behavior of political actors throughout 1917 and into the civil wars. The events of 1917 would demonstrate that this overarching antimarket consensus, further fostered by war measures, was mapped onto a fractured political field. Yet however great the differences over the extent of state intervention during 1917, the planning ethos was not a product of 1917 or Bolshevik ideology alone.[147] Its roots were in a broader ecosystem in which both the Bolsheviks and their political competitors were situated.

The food-supply shortage alone did not cause the collapse of the old regime. Other countries, such as Germany, faced more dire food-supply problems. Indeed, one historian has convincingly argued that Russia's *economic* crisis in these years "was not of decline and relapse into subsistence, but rather growth."[148] Russia did not collapse as an economy. Rather, the autocracy failed in political terms, with the war serving to radicalize and extend existing political fissures. Peter Struve, in a later analysis of events in which he had participated, wrote: "the student of economic factors will not ascribe the political catastrophe that overwhelmed Russia in 1917 to the economic condition of the country in general and its food situation in particular. For an explanation of the Revolution, first and foremost, the political forces should be considered." He further observed that it was precisely the heavy accumulation of food supplies in the fertile south that prefigured both the alignment—a grain-deficient, industrialized north versus a grain-rich south and west—and the nature of "the civil war of 1917 and succeeding years."[149]

Struve's comments suggest that food supply was important beyond its role in the collapse of the autocracy. Certainly, the intransigence of the autocracy during the war alienated many people who formerly sought its reform and thereby hastened its collapse. However, wartime food supply was significant not only as one of the key precipitants for revolution but also as a productive phenomenon. The parastatal organizations fostered the personal networks, institutional structures, and a supraparty political sociability that served as the foundation for the Provisional Government and the initial cooperation between it and the Petrograd Soviet.

A defining feature of the First World War was precisely this self-mobilization of society for the ends of total war.[150] In Russia, as in other European powers, the educated public and professional organizations contributed to mobilizing society under the aegis of the total war state. Only by such means did the wartime state in Europe manage to extend its reach so radically and to produce a revolutionary reordering of society. In Russia, this program coalesced with a widespread repudiation of the existing sociopolitical order, making the critique especially radical. The particular parastatal complex that emerged in Russia was arrayed against the autocracy ostensibly heading that state. Rejecting the old order, the organizations composing the public side of the complex simultaneously embraced many critiques of liberal society that had yet to be established in Russia. Wartime mobilization came to be viewed not as a necessary concession to circumstance but as an instrument for achieving far-reaching and long-desired change.[151]

In the aftermath of the 1905 Revolution, many members of the public had come to see the state as both a tool and an ideal for "consciousness" to channel the masses' "spontaneity" toward progress and enlightenment. Before the war, the autocracy's opposition to any public involvement in policy had stunted the public side of these efforts. Wartime mobilization in Russia thus telescoped both the developmental stages of many public organizations, which already existed in most other combatant countries before the war, and their reorganization to the ends of war mobilization. As a result, Russia developed not a public sphere existing autonomous of the state but rather a specific wartime parastatal complex, one "amalgamating" public participation and state-led mobilization. To a greater degree than in other combatant societies, the state played a dominant role in this parastatal complex, which, together with its mobilizational techniques and the ethos fostered by it, provided a common heritage for all political movements after 1917.

~ 2

"Radiant Days of Freedom"

Inspired by the event that has occurred for the renovation of our
Fatherland's state order, the Novocherkassk stanitsa at the election of
its representatives on March 4–5 enthusiastically and unanimously . . .
passed a resolution to subordinate ourselves to the central government
and by all means necessary defend it, for the good of the great Russian
people, from the dark forces of the fallen regime.

~ signed by the stanitsa ataman, the chairman of the Novocherkassk
mining commission, and the chairman of the stanitsa economic council

$\mathcal{T}$wo and a half years into the Great War, Russian society
welcomed the February Revolution as a definitive break with the old
order, a bright new beginning for Russia and its citizens. The men of
February—those specialists and public activists who had been staffing
wartime parastatal organizations—established the political matrix for
Russia's new order. Through the institutions established by these activists an ever-broadening circle of participants sought to transform their
own lives and the society around them. The true measure of the revolutionary transformation in 1917 was to be found in the massive participation of citizens in this new political universe.

Political parties and radical movements mobilized various social
groups over the course of 1917.[1] These social groups did not exist,
however, outside of politics: politics and the social world functioned in
a symbiotic relationship. For centuries, the state had imposed legal
identities on social groups. By the turn of the twentieth century, educated society, seeking to mobilize these groups against the autocracy,
had formulated alternative models for social identity. Educated society—what one may term Russia's "political class"—had "assumed the
collective representation of an 'intelligentsia' in their efforts to divine

as well as direct the shaping of the new society that they saw in the making on Russian soil."[2] In the aftermath of the February Revolution, this political class attempted to establish a new political order.

The public activists who established the February order imposed the new form of politics—typified by elections, the concept of popular sovereignty, and the representation of "society"—on a deeply divided country. The wartime experience had focused the public's widespread dissatisfaction on the old regime and forged a consensus on immediate measures. But while the war had helped forge a dense network among professional and civic organizations, the wartime parastatal complex, the autocracy had not created an analogous network linking this complex to the vast majority of the population.

Given the attenuated development of public institutions prior to the war, the government appointed and coopted people who claimed to speak for society. Before 1917, members of educated society had largely thought of "the regime" and "society" in purely binary terms. This claim by public actors to represent society, however, remained meaningful only insofar as "society" represented an antipode to the autocracy's own claims. Even in the aftermath of the February Revolution, members of Russia's political class conceived "society" as those bearing "consciousness" in opposition to the masses' "spontaneity." Looking back after the civil wars, one member of Russia's political class ruefully observed that the late imperial period had fostered a sense of mission among Russian liberals, predisposing them to rely on force rather than to build a consensual social basis.[3]

The educated public had seen state intervention for war as the precursor to an increased state role in restructuring the economy and society more generally. This aspiration became the Provisional Government's *raison d'être*. "In the revolution's initial period," testified Sergei Chakhotin, a leading public intellectual and Kadet, "the overwhelming majority of the intelligentsia were on the side of the Provisional Government."[4] For members of educated society, the state was necessary because the autocracy had bequeathed so few institutions binding "society" and the common people together. Such institutions were essential for cultivating benighted subjects into rational, responsible citizens. In their absence, public activists turned to the state.

Educated society at first held out much hope that democratic practice and popular enlightenment would overcome the gulf between it-

self and the common people. Writing in the Kadet newspaper *Rech'*
in May 1917, Vladimir Vernadskii—one of Russia's most prominent
scientists and a leading member of the Kadet Central Committee—
observed that "at present we have democracy without the political organization of society."[5] As 1917 progressed, however, the institutions
established by the technocratic elite to create that organization instead
magnified preexisting social and political rifts. The makers of the February system saw the revolution as the crowning achievement of their
prewar and wartime campaign for an enlightened and technocratic order. By contrast, new citizens who were not members of educated society saw February as the opening of a revolutionary project to obtain
their rights in full by overthrowing superordinate authority—that of
Russia's educated society as well as that of the autocracy.

In November 1917, Vernadskii confided to his diary: "It is a tragic
situation. Forces and layers of the people are now playing a role in determining our structure of life [*zhizennyi stroi*], but they are in no condition to understand [this structure's] interests. It is clear that unre-
strained democracy, the pursuit of which I set as the goal of my life,
requires corrections."[6] The predisposition among public activists, fostered during their apprenticeship to power during the war years, was to
reaffirm—with force, if necessary—their own tutelary role through reliance on the state. When political organization did not, as expected,
develop organically among the people, they increasingly saw their task
as imposing this political organization on the masses. This tendency to
view the state as the organizing principle of political life, as both an
ideal and an instrument, extended across the political spectrum. To the
dismay of the proponents of this ideal, their desires to exert such authority waxed just as their ability to do so waned.

The Provisional Government embodied this ethos of "state consciousness" and would do so until its demise. Members of the Duma's
provisional committee forged this new, revolutionary fulcrum of legitimacy as Nicholas II was forced to abdicate. Kadets were particularly
prominent in its formation.[7] Although empowered only until the convocation of the Constituent Assembly, the Provisional Government set
itself a very clear task: to secure a great and democratic Russia, while
avoiding the "anarchy" born of revolution. This program, however, left
unresolved the relationship between the stated principles of "democracy" and "statehood." Over the course of 1917, supporters of the Pro-

visional Government—Kadets first and foremost, but also moderate socialists—increasingly favored "statehood," upheld, if need be, by force.[8]

From the very first, of course, the Provisional Government had to share power with the Petrograd Soviet and, later, with the national Soviet structure, the All-Russian Central Executive Committee of Soviets. This system of "dual power" was in fact the institutional expression of the polarization between "(educated) society" and "democracy." At first, each side collaborated with the other out of a sense of common cause, to secure the revolution's achievements.[9] Leaders of "society" feared anarchy, which they hoped the Soviet would control. Soviet leaders feared counterrevolution, and to counterbalance it they relied on the support of "progressive" bourgeois elements, meaning first and foremost the Kadet Party. Thus the post-February political class extended beyond any one party, encompassing both the constitutionalist advocates who established the Provisional Government as well as those moderate socialists for whom dual power would become a program rather than simply a compromise. One branch among the moderate socialists remained committed to this program of dual power throughout 1917.

Yet the principle of "dual power" challenged the pretensions of the Provisional Government from its founding, for it suggested that the government operated not out of all-state or supraparty principles but out of class interests. The February Revolution would finally allow the wartime specialists to implement measures that the autocracy had previously blocked, such as the grain monopoly. When implemented by the Provisional Government, however, these policies could be cast as "bourgeois" measures, not measures of state. The Kadets conceived of themselves as advancing a supraclass, supraparty program of "state consciousness." (During the electoral campaign for the Constituent Assembly in autumn 1917, the Kadets refused on principle to form electoral alliances with parties that defined themselves as representing specifically bourgeois interests.) Yet outside their own ranks they were perceived as the archetypal representatives of census society, the party of professors and professionals.[10]

The Don Territory became a particularly prominent arena for defining the new revolutionary order because nearly all national political movements scripted its dominant social group, the Cossacks, to play a significant role in the unfolding of the revolution. Advocates of the Provisional Government identified the Cossacks with the cause of statehood. Forces of the left, by contrast, saw them as the paladins of counterrevolution. In the Don Territory, the institutions and practices of 1917 would compel all movements, Cossack and non-Cossack, to re-cast what had previously been estate identities and corporate attributes into a modern political form. Political movements at the local level would show a marked tendency to express themselves preeminently as "social movements."[11]

Revolution Comes to the Don Territory

The telegraph brought the Russian Revolution to the Don Territory. On March 1, the State Duma's Provisional Committee in Petrograd sent telegrams throughout the country informing local officials of the disturbances in the capital and of the formation of a new national gov-ernment. But in an act that would later seal his dismissal, Count Grabbe, in charge of the Don Territory as ataman, withheld news of the events in Petrograd from the press and public for more than a day. The following day, March 2, Grabbe convened a special meeting of the Cossack administration, which decided to submit to the Provisional Government's demands and to inform district atamans and public insti-tutions of the new government in Petrograd. Grabbe then summoned leading civic and public figures to his residence and notified them of the fall of the old order and the formation of the new government in Petrograd.[12]

The Don Territory, with its long history of Cossack rule and Cossack institutions, underscored the problems of transforming an administra-tive and social structure previously predicated on a system of estates into a new civic order. The Don Territory's special identity as a Cos-sack region in the late imperial period would profoundly shape the course of politics there in 1917. It was subordinate directly to the War Ministry rather than to the Ministry of Internal Affairs. Instead of a governor, the Don Territory had an appointed Cossack ataman who united civil authority over both the entire territory and the Cossack corporate administration specifically.[13] The Cossack administration in Novocherkassk then appointed the atamans who were in charge of each district. Non-Cossack inhabitants in the Don Territory were officially subordinate to this Cossack-dominated territorial administration.

Non-Cossacks in the Don Territory did not have zemstvos, the local self-governing structure that prevailed in most of European Russia. Beginning in 1900, and especially after 1905, local officials—including Cossacks—clamored to bring these administrative bodies to their territory. Three successive atamans in the early twentieth century, the territory's assembly of the nobility, and most Cossack stanitsas polled in a 1908 inquiry all expressed support for reintroducing the zemstvo. The War Ministry in St. Petersburg, however, resolutely opposed this reform and managed to block its implementation.[14] The tsarist government's intransigence prevented the emergence of any administrative institutions that would encompass both Cossacks and non-Cossacks. In 1917, then, the dilemma would be not only to establish an edifice for negotiating existing political claims, but first to create the civic institutions necessary for expressing those claims. For the vast majority of people who did not belong to educated society, the Don Territory in 1917 thus fully conformed to Vernadskii's description of "democracy without political organization."

For educated society, however, the wartime parastatal organs served as the framework for post-February institutions. Once informed of the February Revolution in Petrograd, the Novocherkassk War-Industry Committee immediately summoned a meeting of public organizations in its offices late in the evening on March 2. This gathering established a provisional Don Executive Committee, initially composed of representatives from Novocherkassk's civic, educational, and industrial organizations. "Owing to the worsening food-supply situation," the delegates proclaimed the need for closer ties with the countryside. They therefore immediately sought to coopt representatives from those organs that the delegates believed spoke on behalf of the rural population: the Don-Kuban'-Terek cooperative society and the agricultural society.[15]

The city of Rostov had changed greatly during the war, which had contributed to the development and concentration of industry. Although the number of industrial enterprises in the Don Territory had not increased substantially during the war, the number of workers had nearly doubled, to 35,000.[16] In addition, the garrison in Rostov alone numbered 30,000 soldiers. On the afternoon of March 2 Major General Petr Meier, the city's appointed administrator, summoned four men to his offices and suggested that they take power. The four were the head of the city's war-industry committee, N. E. Paramonov; the representative of the Don-Kuban' committee of the zemstvo union, Vladimir Feofilovich Zeeler; as well as the editors of two newspapers, the Kadet-leaning *Priazovskii krai* and the Kadet organ *Rostovskaia rech'*. Both Paramonov and Zeeler were prominent Kadets, with Zeeler serving as chairman of the city's Kadet organization. The four agreed to form a civic committee. That evening a small group of public activists held a meeting in the offices of the Kadet-dominated war-industry committee and drew up a program for the public organ that would run the city. They then presented this program to a larger gathering of public and cooperative activists, the local press, and the Menshevik-dominated workers' organizations.[17]

Kadets dominated the emerging revolutionary organs for both the Don Territory and Rostov, its largest urban center. Kadets did not dominate because they were the largest party, although they did have significant support in the urban centers. (When City Duma elections were held in July 1917, moderate socialists—Mensheviks and Socialist Revolutionaries—outpolled Kadets and Bolsheviks in all major urban centers.)[18] The dominance of the Kadets in the February Revolution resulted instead from the role they occupied in the political ecosystem of the old regime. While at odds with each other, both Kadets and tsarist bureaucrats thought of "state" and "society" in binary terms, with the autocracy representing the state and Kadets speaking for society. Kadets were held to represent society both by virtue of their prominence in the wartime parastatal organs and by the nature of their critique of the autocracy.

The war years, however, had changed the texture of party political life. First, the networks and local committees of almost all political parties had withered during the war. For the Kadets and moderate socialists such as the Popular Socialists, the supraparty wartime parastatal organs became the new focus of their energies.[19] The war had further fostered the ethos of "state consciousness"—the ambition to incorporate under the aegis of the state all citizens through overcoming particular interests. This ethos extended far beyond particular party lines. Nor was it limited to Russia. Like their counterparts throughout Europe during the First World War, many Russian public and civic leaders did not merely accept the state's growing role in economic and so-cial life; they celebrated it. State intervention during wartime was seen as the precursor of an increased role for the state in restructuring not only the economy but social relations more generally along rational, productivist lines.[20] In Russia this program coalesced with a widespread repudiation of the existing sociopolitical order, making the critique particularly radical.

The Provisional Government represented the age of "specialists in power."[21] During the war, these activists proposed measures for mobi-lizing society, but the autocracy often stymied their efforts. The revo-lution would permit their introduction. Moreover, the February Revo-lution crystallized existing institutions and personal networks into new structures. The Don Executive Committee, the new executive organ for the region, emerged directly out of the Novocherkassk War-Indus-try Committee and a local network of Kadets. The first chairman of the committee, A. I. Petrovskii, was both chairman of the Novocherkassk War-Industry Committee and head of the Novocherkassk branch of the Kadet Party. He had been a Kadet deputy in the oppositionist Second Duma (1906–1907). To secure recognition from the Provi-sional Government, the Don Executive Committee promptly dis-patched a deputation to Petrograd. The delegation was headed by K. P. Kakliugin, also a former Kadet deputy to the Second Duma and an-other member of the Novocherkassk War-Industry Committee. (In the Second Duma, he served alongside Petrovskii, Mitrofan Voronkov, and Vasilii Kharlamov, all also Kadets and Cossacks.) His instructions from the Don Executive Committee excoriated Ataman Grabbe as a reac-tionary and asked that the Don Executive Committee be sanctioned to act as the new authority for the entire Don Territory.[22]

The Provisional Government, through its new minister of agricul-ture, the Kadet Andrei Shingarev, dispatched an encouraging telegram to Petrovskii in Novocherkassk on March 12. There was no institu-tional reason for the minister of agriculture to respond, as the Don Territory certainly was not subordinated to it. Shingarev's involvement resulted, rather, from preexisting personal and party networks. It was fairly predictable, then, that the Provisional Government on March 14 extended its temporary recognition to the Don Executive Committee as its accredited authority throughout the Don Territory.[23] This condi-tional recognition was followed a month later, on April 15, by a decree from War Minister Guchkov, declaring the Don Executive Committee to be the sole legitimate organ for the entire region until special laws could be drafted.[24] On the day preceding formal recognition from the Provisional Government, the Don Executive Committee—still a self-appointed organ drawn almost exclusively from Novocherkassk's public and professional circles—announced that it was summoning a territorial congress for October, to which it would transfer its authority. Until that time, the committee declared, its task was "defending the people's interests and the achievements of the Revolution."[25] The Don Executive Committee had invoked a new form of legitimacy: popular sovereignty and safeguarding the revolution.

But until then, how was the new authority to be constituted? On March 5 the Provisional Government had issued a circular removing all governors and appointing instead the chairmen of the provincial zemstvo boards, now titled "provincial commissars of the Provisional Government."[26] As the Don Territory had neither zemstvos nor a governor, this instruction did nothing to resolve the situation. When the provisional Don Executive Committee dismissed Count Grabbe as a holdover of the old order two days later, on March 7, it therefore repeated its request for a commissar from the Provisional Government to serve as the region's civil administrator. Grabbe, however, had simultaneously served both as the region's administrator and as head of the territory's Cossack administration. To fill the now-vacant post at the head of the Cossack administration, the Don Executive Committee appointed Lieutenant Colonel E. A. Voloshinov as "acting ataman." The provisional Don Executive Committee intended the new ataman to administer purely Cossack affairs. Voloshinov was a Cossack by estate but, more to the point, he had headed the military department of the Novocherkassk War-Industry Committee. He also was a Kadet, as were Petrovskii, Kakliugin, and Voronkov.[27]

But the Don Territory still required a "provincial commissar" from the Provisional Government to head the civil administration. (Voloshinov as ataman oversaw only Cossack affairs.) The Don Executive Committee had repeatedly petitioned for one. The Provisional Government, while hoping local democratic structures would foster unity and harness the vital forces of the nation, intended its commissars to integrate the free-standing local structures that were emerging into the central government's national and statist program.[28] The Provisional Government appointed Mitrofan Voronkov, who had come to prominence during debates over food-supply policy in 1916, to serve this function for the Don Territory. The new government initially dispatched him to serve as its "emissary" to the Don Territory for coordinating local food-supply efforts with the new state food-supply organs. The Don Food-Supply Committee promptly elected him *in abstentia* to serve as its chairman. Only the following day did the Provisional Government also empower Voronkov to serve as its provincial commissar.[29] Voronkov was thus not simply a spokesman for the Cossack elite or the Kadet Party; indeed, he was equally a statist technocrat and food-supply specialist.[30] Throughout 1917 Voronkov believed he was acting, as both a Cossack and a Kadet, from a statist point of view.

Popular Sovereignty

The Russian Revolution was a social revolution. This was so not simply because social actors were the driving force behind events, but rather because political actors self-consciously defined the object of their concerns and activity to be society itself.[31] The new representative organs in 1917 had a symbiotic relationship with the social groups in whose name they spoke and in whose interest they acted. Social interests and collective actors were "defined in the course of political practice, rather than existing prior to it."[32] This does not mean, of course, that a conceptual realm of ideas and discourse triumphed over people's lived experience. Rather, political programs and institutions asserted a claim to give meaning to people's experience. Thus the "strength and staying power" of competing political claims and institutions would "ultimately hinge on their degree of correspondence with these groups' own collective experience."[33] Political claims in 1917 collapsed when they failed to resonate with these existing collective social aspirations.

Although entirely self-appointed, the provisional Don Executive Committee claimed to act in the name of the revolution, protecting the people's interests and expressing the people's will. This rhetoric had concrete institutional consequences. Claiming popular sovereignty as the fulcrum of legitimacy, the provisional committee on March 8—the day following its dismissal of Count Grabbe—directed local communities throughout the Don Territory to form organs termed variously "public committees" or "civic committees." The purpose of these organs was "to establish calm and civil security among the population and to provide the army and population with food supplies."[34] Throughout 1917 such structures led to a qualitative expansion in the population's political participation.

Through the autumn of 1917, civic committees were far more prevalent and embraced far more participants than did soviets or any political party.[35] By summer 1917, the Kadet Party numbered no more than 1,000 members. The socialist parties were larger, but they still numbered only in the tens of thousands in a region with a population of nearly four million. The Socialist Revolutionary Party was the largest, numbering perhaps 45,000 members, 8,000 of them in Rostov. Mensheviks followed, numbering 10,000, half of whom were concentrated in the Mensheviks' stronghold of Rostov. The Bolshevik Party in the summer of 1917 numbered a paltry 3,500.[36] The channel for political activity was thus not so much political parties as the political institutions of 1917. To the extent that people came to participate in the politics of revolution, they did so originally and, for much of 1917, predominantly through new political organs, such as civic committees, rather than through political parties.

Yet while they became the gateways to the new political culture, these civic organs did not spring forth spontaneously.[37] A few larger communities formed such committees almost immediately on their own. Most committees, however, were summoned into being first by the new Don Executive Committee and later by the Provisional Government. Through the network of district atamans, holdovers from the tsarist system, the Don Executive Committee proclaimed its intent to uphold order and to "unfailingly implement the intentions of the People's Government." Soon afterward, on March 8, it issued a call for local assemblies to organize—but not yet elect—civic committees.[38] In direct response to the directive from Novocherkassk, a groundswell of communities and the districts above them constituted "civic committees."[39] While these telegrams praised the new order's democratic nature, they equally expressed hope that the government would conduct the war effort more effectively and foster national productivity.

Officials constituting the Don Executive Committee viewed the public good as a transcendent entity beyond particular interests.[40] The committee's agenda was much like that of the Provisional Government, which "aimed to deny the reality not only of class conflict but of any conflict between the multi-layered propertied and laboring groups in the provinces."[41] Tellingly, the Don Executive Committee's first directive did not specify that committees be elected, only that local gatherings "organize" them.

On March 14, one week after the Don Executive Committee's initial directive, the Provisional Government issued its own instructions regarding "civic committees." It directed that the activities of such organs be unified and standardized into a hierarchy of provincial, district, and county committees. But the Provisional Government also explicitly decreed that these committees should represent "the interests of all groups of the population of a given locality." Provincial commissars, appointed directly by the Provisional Government, were to oversee and coordinate this entire structure.[42] In the wake of these instructions, this time from Petrograd rather than from Novocherkassk, communities that had not yet done so now established civic committees.[43]

These organs invoked a new fulcrum of legitimacy: society. All movements operating in the new revolutionary ecosystem of 1917 embraced the social theory of representation, resting "on the basic assumption that the entity to be represented is society." Proponents of this theory therefore "sought to summon society into active existence and to endow it with representative institutions that would offer a means of articulating its needs and interests."[44] Yet, while it was now clear that "society" was to be represented, neither the instructions from the Don Executive Committee nor those from the Provisional Government resolved the problem of how it was to be represented. In the two weeks following its vague March 8 directive, the Don Executive Committee was deluged by telegrams from communities either complaining about self-styled but improperly constituted civic committees or just requesting clarification. Several days after the Don Executive Committee directive decreeing the "formation" of civic committees, but before the Provisional Government's March 14 directive, the ataman of Bogaevskaia stanitsa informed his superior, the Cherkassk District ataman, that the stanitsa had dutifully elected a civic committee. Reflecting the ambiguity of the post-February period, the telegram fastidiously noted that the civic committee was formed "in accordance with directive no. 1275," yet at the same time asserted that the committee's election took place "at the people's demand" and "for the good of Russia."[45]

The Don Executive Committee had already learned of the civic committee in Bogaevskaia, but not from its ataman. Three separate telegrams from the stanitsa's merchants, employees, and local students had complained that the ataman's "civic committee" included only delegates from the Cossack population. The telegrams, all written after the Provisional Government's March 14 instruction calling for representation of "all groups of the population in a given locality," complained that other groups—students, the local cooperative, non-native inhabitants, merchants, employees, craftsmen, and even war refugees —had been barred from delegating representatives. Such a state of affairs, one of the telegrams warned, "is leading to the cessation of trade and the disruption of normal life, which at the present moment helps only internal and external enemies." Order, it was stressed, would return only if the "executive committee is constituted from all layers of the stanitsa's inhabitants." These telegrams, like those from the stanitsa ataman they were protesting, pleaded for "precise directives" on civic committees.[46]

Directives from the Provisional Government and the Don Executive Committee in the third week of March unambiguously established that civic committees should represent "society" in its entirety. On March 20 the Provisional Government ordered its provincial commissars to organize county committees that were to be entrusted temporarily with the functions of county administration.[47] The following day, March 21, the Don Executive Committee issued its own "temporary instruction to all district, stanitsa, county, village and other executive committees in the Don Territory," clarifying how "society" was to be represented: "representatives from various groups in the population enter the committee with a deciding vote in a number proportionate to each of these group's number and significance for local life."[48] Such committees were to oversee the local administration and maintain contact with the Don Executive Committee, carry out the directives of the national Provisional Government, maintain order, and address food-supply needs. A copy of the temporary instruction was sent to Bogaevskaia, where the local ataman had constituted an entirely Cossack executive committee, with instructions to include "representatives from all layers of the population."[49] This reproof, it should be noted, came from an organ—the Don Executive Committee—heavily dominated by Cossack Kadets. Other executive committees, in submitting complaints and appeals, referred explicitly to the Don Executive Committee's instructions on how executive committees were to represent "the population."[50] In place of the old regime's ordering of the political structure by estates, the new authorities identified individual citizens as the fundamental political actors. The new order was to be a democratic and egalitarian one, in which the rights of non-Cossacks and Cossacks would be leveled in the political sphere.

Although the Provisional Government and the Don Executive Committee could issue orders, it was local activists, often lawyers and teachers, who summoned local civic committees into being. The driving force behind the establishment of the district-level civic committee in Nizhne-Chirskaia, the capital of the Second Don District, was Nikolai M. Mel'nikov, a local inhabitant and justice of the peace. A Cossack, he had graduated from the law faculty of Moscow University and then completed his military service in a Cossack regiment, where he had organized reading circles for the rank-and-file. Mel'nikov then returned to the Don in 1908 to work as a justice of the peace in Donets District. He came home to his native Second Don District in 1912 when his predecessor there, A. P. Savvateev, was elected as a Kadet deputy to the Fourth Duma.[51] With the outbreak of the February Revolution, Mel'nikov attended the founding assembly of the "Second Don District Executive Committee of Public Organizations" as a delegate from several institutions, ranging from the local library to the committee for aiding poor students. Mel'nikov described himself as a "nonparty leftist." Although opposed by more radical Cossack delegates representing the local cooperative, he was elected chairman of the District Executive Committee of Public Organizations.[52] In late April, Territorial Commissar Voronkov appointed Mel'nikov the Provisional Government commissar for the Second Don District.[53] Civic proselytizers brought the good news of revolution to those communities that had either not heard of it yet or had failed to act on it. One week after the Provisional Government and the Don Executive Committee directives on civic committees, the principal of the local elementary school in Starocherkasskaia stanitsa took it upon himself to organize meetings in several outlying communities, helping to establish civic committees in at least five settlements in one day.[54] Duma members elected from the Don Territory also toured local communities, informing citizens of the new order and pressing them to form civic committees.[55]

Both the Provisional Government and the Don Executive Committee had now clearly indicated their expectations for the new civic order. It was to be founded on two principles: popular sovereignty and a social, rather than corporate or honorific, theory of representation.[56] Communities now scrambled to form executive committees constituted along these lines. Kazanskaia stanitsa sent the following telegram, ringing with enthusiasm for the revolution, to the Don Executive Committee:

> The free citizens of Kazanskaia stanitsa, having welcomed with a feeling of deep emotion and joy the happy news of the fall of the old despotic order which had brought ruin to Russia and having now gathered for the organization of our civic committee, unanimously send the Don Committee our warm and heartfelt wishes that it work for the flourishing of our dear region in these new radiant days of freedom.
> Citizens and Ataman Dronov[57]

For all its revolutionary rhetoric, this telegram was not composed in the immediate flush of revolution; it was sent three weeks later, in direct response to the Don Executive Committee's guidelines instructing each community to form a civic committee. Despite its citizens' "deep emotion and joy," Kazanskaia stanitsa had not established a civic committee before sending the telegram.

As a result of its guidelines, then, the civic ideals of the Don Executive Committee took on institutional form. Executive committees mushroomed in local communities throughout late March and April. By the beginning of May, a network of more than three hundred executive committees existed, with one in nearly every major community.[58] Following the directives of the Provisional Government, by late March the Don Executive Committee had organized them into a formal structure under its direction.[59] At that time the number of soviets totaled several dozen, at best. One Soviet-era study identifies only twenty-five soviets throughout the entire Don Territory by late April, and most district-level soviet organs did not form until June–July.[60] New forms of political behavior fostered by such institutions—elections, public gatherings, and the collective dispatch of telegrams on events of national significance—were as important as the institutions themselves.[61]

These civic organs represented the emergence of a new political space, with inhabitants now participating directly in national politics within their own communities.

The new committees existed in an ambiguous relationship with the Provisional Government's commissars.[62] The Provisional Government repeatedly insisted that ultimate authority lay with its commissars. War Minister Guchkov, under whose ministry the Don Territory remained, reiterated this principle on April 6 when he issued his own guidelines for civil administration in the Don Territory. Guchkov explained that "the Provisional Government's organs in the localities are to be only its provincial and district commissars," whereas civic committees "are considered to be exponents of public opinion." The Provisional Government's agents, however, were to cooperate with the committees, which were encouraged to propose candidates for the post of district commissar.[63] Three weeks later Voronkov appointed as district commissars people who had been proposed by local public groups, including three officers, two judges (including Mel'nikov for the Second Don District), and an agronomist.[64] Through the summer both executive committees and commissars proclaimed their goal to be the transcendent public good, "the Great Russian Revolution."

Uses of the Social Theory of Representation

In this environment, however, a particularistic Cossack organ, the reconstituted Don Cossack corporate administration, emerged to challenge and then triumph over the more universal civic organs. Soviet accounts long portrayed the Don Cossack administration in 1917 as merely a stalking horse for the Kadets and the bourgeoisie. Western accounts have presented it as the unmediated political expression of Cossack social interests.[65] Both presentations capture aspects of the Don Cossack administration's appeal in 1917, but only in part. At the local and national level it was indeed strongly linked, both in its agenda and in its personnel, with the Kadet Party. The administration became a formidable factor on the political scene because it, unlike the Kadet Party itself, could mobilize a degree of popular support among many Cossacks. Because of this support, it had at its disposal a rare commodity in 1917: a relatively reliable military force, in the form of Cossack detachments.

Despite longstanding myths of a uniformly loyal Cossackry, however, Cossacks never were one monolithic bloc. Owing to electoral politics and less restrictive censorship, there emerged after 1905 competing narratives of Cossack identity. Cossacks had long justified the "liberties" they enjoyed by reference to "the blood of our ancestors and our continued [military] service." But Cossack identity was reshaped in the last decades of the nineteenth century and the first decade of the twentieth.[66] An abortive attempt in the 1880s to introduce the zemstvo to the Don had led to an orchestrated campaign against it. Opponents of the zemstvo mobilized rank-and-file Cossacks through a petitioning and press campaign, one that delineated Cossacks from non-Cossacks in the postreform civic order. Debates over the land issue during the 1905 Revolution led to more vociferous political expression of the peasant-Cossack division, with members of the Peasant Union advocating the expulsion of all Cossacks. The "union for the peaceful resolution of the land question" countered that Cossacks had the right to "expel all peasants and other landholders who do not belong to the Cossack estate."[67]

Cossack "liberties" had also meant special obligations, which Cossacks were finding increasingly hard to meet. Rank-and-file Cossacks came to distinguish the Cossack aristocracy from authentic Cossacks. The latter, in this view, served in the territorially recruited Don Cossack regiments and lived in Cossack communities, rather than in the administrative centers. The 1905 Revolution gave political expression to these incipient rifts, as a "Cossack movement" demonstrated against both the autocracy and the Cossack territorial administration.[68] This period increasingly saw Cossack demands expressed in new ways. Ordinary Cossacks now participated in mass politics, such as Duma election gatherings, and Cossacks now invoked the principle of popular sovereignty alongside traditional estate privilege.

The traditionalist narrative favored by the Cossack administration posited the Cossackry as a corporate group. This program was not simply the spontaneous "expression" of a preexisting sociological group, but rather the political projection of that group in the ideal. It scripted corporate actors—most notably, Cossacks and peasants—as the fundamental performers in the revolutionary drama. This Cossack narrative and its institutionalization in Cossack organs of governance helped project a specific Cossack identity. Although this program of Cossack ideals was not an unmediated representation of the views of rank-and-file Cossacks, it overlapped to some degree with their inchoate demands. Indeed, it played a cardinal role in drawing the boundaries around the Cossackry as a political actor in the revolution, in distinction to its previous role as a juridical estate.

The narrative favored by the Cossack administration emerged among local officials and Cossack intellectuals with much national experience, not least in the Kadet Party and State Duma. In 1917 the leadership of the Cossack administration—and later of the "Cossack government" that grew out of it—came primarily from among prewar career military officers, members of the established Cossack intelligentsia, and local political figures. Most had not served at the front during the war. Many had not lived on the Don for many years. These men propounded a vision of a patriotic Cossackry serving as a bulwark of Russian order and statehood, the most faithful of Russia's sons. Wartime propaganda highlighted this image, lionizing Cossacks as the archetypal embodiment of Russian patriotism.[69] The Cossack administration welcomed the February Revolution for returning to the Cossack estate "liberties" [vol'nosti] that had been usurped by the tsarist regime. In the new order, however, the corporatist Cossack narrative insisted on continued administrative separation and asserted that the Cossack administration remained the corporate embodiment of all Cossacks.

Against this idealized corporate image emerged a competing Cossack republican narrative, lionizing Cossacks as a tribe of "free" [svobodnyi] men, Russia's earliest citizens. Advocates of this outlook tended to come from Cossack communities primarily in the northern districts, rather than from Novocherkassk or places outside the Don Territory. Whereas many of the proponents of the corporatist narrative had been career officers before the war, Cossack republicans were nearly all front-line soldiers. By the time of the February Revolution, these men were officers of some rank, most having been swiftly promoted in the course of the war.[70] They frequently bore conspicuous military decorations for their bravery at the front. Indeed, many leading Cossack republicans were holders of the order of St. George, Russia's highest military decoration. Cossack republicans' conceptions of the Cossackry were grounded in particular communities and their own regiments, rather than in the Cossack administration as a corporate structure. Their outlook took on political form first in Cossack executive and regimental committees and later in Cossack soviets and military revolutionary committees. While retaining a strong sense of their identity as Cossacks, these republicans argued for the civic inclusion of Cossacks in a more universalistic political order.

The Provisional Government had abolished all restrictions predicated on estate and religion, thereby putting an end to the estate structure upheld by the tsarist system.[71] Cossack traditionalists, especially Cossack administrators and career military officers, now had to find a new foundation for a continued corporatist definition of the Cossackry. In the aftermath of February, they scrambled to construct specifically "Cossack" representative organs, the new form of legitimization required to sanction continued Cossack separateness. Cossack traditionalists now presented their corporatist organs not as estate institutions but as expressions of popular political will. If the Don Executive Committee emphasized the unity of popular sovereignty and the representation of all society, Cossack organs claimed to represent a specific social group, albeit one that allegedly transcended its own interests and embodied Russian statism. Opponents of the new civic order—imperial officials and career officers—sought to transpose a formerly unambiguous estate identity into the forms of modern mass politics.

But Cossack organs drew on support from beyond the defenders of particularist Cossack corporatism. As the revolution unfolded through the late spring of 1917, many advocates of the statist principle [*gosudarstvennost'*] who originally had embraced republican organs became disillusioned with the revolution's growing "anarchy." Because of the Cossacks' mythic relationship to the Russian state, these people came to view Cossack organs as an embodiment of the statist principle itself. This statist principle led many Cossacks and non-Cossacks alike, in the Don Territory and throughout Russia, to support the Don Cossack government, as the Don Cossack administration came to term itself after mid-1917. Cossack Kadets (Voronkov, Kharlamov, Kakliugin, and Petrovskii), as well as some Cossack socialists (Ageev and Mel'nikov), found a common platform in this ideal of organic, progressive statism. The conviction that the Don Cossack government was a bulwark for Russia's transcendent state interest attracted support at the national level as well, extending from the far right through to moderate socialist ministers in the Provisional Government.

The Provisional Government in all its changing manifestations, whether with Kadet ministers or socialist ministers, not only tolerated the Don Cossack government but seemed to welcome it, to the immense frustration of the region's non-Cossack population. In stark contrast to the hostile reaction of the Provisional Government to "nationalist" demands in Finland or Ukraine, its ministries never treated the Don Cossack government in 1917 as a "nationalist" or "separatist" movement.[72] The Provisional Government embraced Cossack organs not because they were any more representative or democratic than "separatist" ones, but because its officials conceived of Cossacks as distinctively devoted to Russia's "state interest." Among its advocates were not only those opposed to revolution but also those who originally had welcomed it but who came to oppose what they viewed as its "anarchic" and "antistatist" course. And it was "Cossack" only with the understanding that true Cossacks were paladins of Russian statehood, a principle upheld irrespective of how many actual Cossacks endorsed this ideal themselves.

To be sure, Cossack community assemblies passed resolutions recognizing the Don Executive Committee but pointedly demanding the retention of "Cossack administration" and "the rights of our forefathers." Similarly, Cossacks at the front insisted that their new oath as citizen-soldiers did not signify any renunciation of their "Cossack title."[73] But these assertions did not coalesce into an overarching political agenda. Exclusive Cossack organs at first shaped rather than reflected a sense of Cossacks as a political collectivity. In Novocherkassk, the administrative capital of the Don Territory, several officers in the Don Cossack military headquarters, a branch of the Don Cossack administration responsible for Cossack military affairs within the territory, formed an initiative group. This group discussed the need to counteract the Don Executive Committee's pretension to speak for the whole territory and especially for all Cossacks. To counteract this claim it formed a "Cossack Union" around the nucleus of the existing "Officers' Union" in Novocherkassk, the first meeting of which was held on March 14.[74]

The very first day that the Cossack Union met, it received support from an entirely unexpected quarter. Responding to an appeal from the Ural Cossacks—and completely unaware of the Cossack Union's plans for the Don Territory—War Minister Guchkov in Petrograd issued an order on March 14 for the reorganization of the civil administration of all Cossack territories. His order called for congresses in each Cossack territory to discuss current events and to debate the future form of Cossack self-government.[75] Guchkov's telegram played an inadvertent but important role in legitimizing Cossack organs. Here as elsewhere, the Provisional Government initially seemed unaware of what type of new organs might result from its sanction. Members of the Cossack Union and Cossack administrators in the localities seized upon the war minister's telegram to justify their own call for elections to a specifically Cossack organ.[76] They summoned a Don Cossack congress in April, in opposition to the Don Executive Committee's call for a universal, territorial congress in October. One month later Guchkov, in a telegram confirming the Don Executive Committee as the organ responsible for the new order in the Don region, attempted to correct any misimpressions about the breadth of the Cossack congress's mandate. While noting that the ataman was a duly constituted agent of the Provisional Government, Guchkov indicated that he was to coordinate his activities with the Don Executive Committee. He took pains to stress that the Cossack congress, summoned "in accordance with my last instruction," was to consider "purely Cossack issues," and that all its actions would require the approval of the War Ministry.[77] Despite this attempted clarification, Guchkov's earlier telegram of March 14 had unwittingly sanctioned the establishment of separate Cossack political structures.

Cossack officials in Novocherkassk were not alone in their attempts to create a specifically Cossack form of representation. One Cossack recalled that in Cossack formations at the front demands for self-determination "originated, of all places, among the regular officers," who "thought up the 'self-determination' principle—proclaimed by the Russian Provisional Government—as an excuse for the creation of purely Cossack soviets of front-line troops. The idea was to prevent the disintegration of Cossack units and help preserve order in the Russian state as a whole."[78] Officers in Cossack units, who were often not Cossacks themselves, drew up "Cossack programs" for their men in which they advocated the creation of separate Cossack bodies. They then dispatched agitators back home with these programs.[79] Once there, these delegates toured native stanitsas, touting the advantages of all-Cossack organs and often benefiting from introductions by the stanitsa atamans. In May one such Cossack noncommissioned officer toured Cossack

communities in Ust'-Medveditsa District, proselytizing for separate
Cossack organs. At a gathering in Eterevskaia stanitsa, he called upon
the Cossacks to expel the non-native peasants as well as all non-Cossack intellectuals and professionals, even priests. His speech directly
contributed to a worsening in relations between Cossacks and non-
Cossacks in the community.[80] In the following days, the local executive
committee sought to serve the stanitsa ataman with a resolution compelling him to cooperate in local administration, but the ataman an-
grily refused, prompting the Eterevskaia committee to appeal to the
Don Executive Committee.[81] Tensions between Cossacks and non-
Cossacks, in Eterevskaia and throughout the Don Territory, had certainly existed before. But after February a new form of Cossack separateness, one based on the social theory of representation rather than
on legal ascription by estate, had emerged.

At the national level, Prime Minister Lvov sanctioned a request from
Cossack delegates from the Fourth Duma to hold a national Cossack
congress. These Cossack Duma deputies then dispatched telegrams to
communities in their regions, calling on them to elect delegates. The
congress met in late March, with delegates elected from each stanitsa
of all eleven corporate Cossack communities throughout the empire.[82]
The Cossack assembly in Kamenskaia stanitsa, prompted to act by a
telegram from one Cossack Duma deputy, elected as delegate the head
of the local high school, Metrofan Petrovich Bogaevskii. Bogaevskii
was a Cossack nobleman whose estate was surrounded by Ukrainian
peasant settlements, meaning he had little contact with stanitsa life.
His brother recalled that "as children we knew almost nothing about
Cossack life." After attending Petersburg University, he returned to
the Don, where he had served as principal of the local gymnasium.
Thus he had experienced neither life in a Cossack community nor wartime service at the front. Yet in 1917, as the chairman of the First Cossack Circle and deputy ataman, this prototypical intellectual became
the leading spokesman for the Cossack narrative on the Don.[83]

Non-Cossacks living in Cossack communities noted that the election of delegates and the ensuing press coverage drew rank-and-file
Cossacks into the new Cossack organs. Matvei Mokhov, a peasant living in a Cossack community, wrote a letter to his nephew serving in the
army on the Caucasus front. "In Petrograd at the end of March," he
wrote, "there was a Cossack Union [*sic*], a congress of all eleven corpo-

rate Cossack communities, and at that congress they decided to defend all their rights and privileges . . . Aleksandr Petrovich Bokov, the former ataman, went from our stanitsa. Then on Easter there was a stanitsa gathering and at that gathering he preached on all topics . . . He told them that 'we conquered this land and it belongs to us Cossacks,' and they drew up resolutions and signed them."[84]

As a result of the politics of 1917, electoral gatherings were taking place almost continually. Soon after elections to the Cossack congress in Petrograd, Cossack communities participated in elections to the Cossack congress for the Don Territory, which was to meet in April. Invoking the ideals of the new order, non-Cossacks immediately protested their exclusion from this new representative organ. The Mikhailovka Executive Committee remonstrated Territorial Commissar Voronkov—who as representative of the Provisional Government was to safeguard the new order—that "the freedoms which have been proclaimed grant equality to all. Thus the convocation of only one portion of the population is one-sided and violates the rights of the other part of the population."[85] Voronkov, a Cossack, did not reply. Other communities wrote to the Provisional Government itself, protesting its apparent acquiescence to the establishment of Cossack mastery in the Don Territory. One peasant community complained that its sons in the army were shedding blood for the new democratic Russia, only to be rewarded with the introduction of a second serfdom in their native region.[86]

When the Don Cossack congress met in mid-April, it defended particularist Cossack structures. Yet it declared that these organs were to exist alongside the new universal and egalitarian political order, in which Cossacks would also participate.[87] Regarding Cossack governance, the congress declared that Cossack structures would be retained but democratized, with the establishment of elected local councils. Non-Cossacks were to be permitted to participate in Cossack assemblies on non-Cossack issues that concerned them directly. The congress described local executive committees as "temporary public organizations," elected but with proportional representation for Cossacks and non-Cossacks. The congress even declared itself in favor of a democratically elected and unified zemstvo for Cossacks and non-Cossacks alike, the proposal that had been met with such opposition in the 1880s. The Cossack congress then appointed delegates to the Don Executive Committee and recognized that body as the supreme administrative organ for all affairs not directly touching on Cossack life.[88] The congress's measures suggested that Cossacks remained distinct, but nevertheless partook of one common civic order alongside the Don Territory's other inhabitants.

On the symbolically weighty land issue, the congress passed a resolution insisting that "all land located within the boundaries of the Don Territory constitutes the historic property of the Don Cossackry, acquired by the blood of its ancestors [and] paid for many times over by the Cossacks' burden of service to the state." (Predictably, the congress described Cossack sacrifice to be in the service of the state rather than the nation.) These words would be repeated often throughout 1917. Yet the congress also voted to seize all private land above a certain labor norm in order to form a special land fund. This fund was intended to meet the needs of land-hungry rural inhabitants, first and foremost native peasants. Only after their needs had been addressed would any remaining land pass to the Don Cossack administration's own land fund, to Cossacks.[89]

But the most significant decision of the April congress was its call for the convocation of a Cossack Circle [voiskovoi krug], the traditional elective assembly of the entire Cossack community from the times before Peter the Great.[90] The Cossack congress directed that elections to the circle be conducted on the basis of free, secret, equal, and direct suffrage by Don Cossacks over the age of twenty, women as well as men. The congress explicitly indicated that the circle was to be composed solely of Cossacks, elected from each Cossack community and settlement.[91] By employing the term "circle," its advocates underlined the idea that the February Revolution had returned to Cossacks their age-old "liberties." An elective and representative circle, however, also had a more recent provenance. In 1909 the imperial administration had summoned a consultative Cossack assembly to discuss the Cossack land shortage in the Don Territory.[92] The War Ministry had prevented any repeat of the 1909 consultative assembly, prompting Cossack Duma deputies to excoriate the War Ministry's paternalistic administration of Cossacks.

Elections to what would become known as the "First Cossack Circle" were held in the third week of May, 1917. By this point the February consensus was breaking down, on the Don and throughout Russia.

The original Provisional Government was no more. War Minister Guchkov's note to the Allies, indicating support for the previous regime's annexationist war aims, precipitated the April Crisis. Street demonstrations and opposition in the Petrograd Soviet forced Guchkov out and brought down the government. The Provisional Government reconstituted itself as the first coalition government. Representatives of the moderate socialist parties, who continued to participate in soviets, now also served in the Provisional Government alongside Kadet ministers.[93]

Despite the Cossack Circle's pretension to speak for all Cossacks, rank-and-file participation in the initial May elections was less than overwhelming. The elections demonstrated that the seemingly self-evident identification of Cossacks with organs claiming to speak for them had yet to be fully established by May 1917. In Ust'-Medveditskaia stanitsa and its outlying settlements, for which the most detailed results are available, only 3,006 ballots were cast in a community of more than 12,000 Cossacks. In the stanitsa itself, only 393 of the more than 4,000 Cossacks eligible to vote did so.[94] Judging from election protocols from other Cossack communities, it appears that only one-third to one-half of eligible Cossack voters participated in elections to the First Circle.[95]

Those who did vote demonstrated a high degree of solidarity with the leading candidates, who often received significantly more than 90 percent of the vote. (In these elections, voters cast both negative and positive ballots for each candidate.) Yet this solidarity testified less to unanimity among all Cossacks than to the like-mindedness of those who chose to participate. Young Cossack males, often identified as more leftist than their elders, were concentrated in military units, and thus voted separately from their home communities. While claiming to speak for all Cossacks, the delegates from the stanitsas were drawn disproportionately from among the Cossack intelligentsia, with a leavening of officers.[96] The delegates were therefore often the same people responsible for disseminating the Cossack narrative in the first place.[97]

The "First Large Circle" met from May 26 to June 18, 1917, with 444 delegates from Cossack settlements and a further 224 delegates from Cossack military units. The circle was divided along a major sociopolitical rift between Cossacks from the upper districts (Khoper, Ust'-Medveditsa, and Second Don) and those from the lower districts (Cherkassk, First Don, and Sal'). This division would continue to be significant throughout the civil war.[98] The Cossack administration was concentrated in the lower districts (one-third of all hereditary nobles in the Don Territory lived in Cherkassk District alone) and benefited from better and more diverse natural resources. Consequently, Cossacks from the northern districts tended to resent their brethren from the lower districts and especially the Cossack administration, located in Novocherkassk.[99] It is no accident that both Pavel Ageev, the secretary of the wartime Special Council for Food Supply who became the leading spokesman for the leftist faction in the Don Cossack government throughout the civil war, and Filipp Mironov, the most prominent leader among pro-Soviet Cossacks, were both "northerners" from Ust'-Medveditsa District. Together they had been leaders of a 1906 demonstration against the autocracy and the Don Cossack administration.

Representation at the circle was by district rather than by head, which further magnified the collective differences between Cossacks from the "upper" and "lower" districts. This system of representation replicated the practice of Cossack electors in Duma election assemblies and at the 1909 "circle."[100] In order to prevent the formation of interest-group constituencies, delegates from each district met in preliminary caucuses and nominated one representative to speak in the district's name at the circle. Individual delegates could not address the circle.[101] By mid-June 1917, newspapers in the upper Don had taken to characterizing their own delegates as "radical" and those from the lower districts as "counterrevolutionary."[102]

The circle passed resolutions on all burning issues of the day.[103] Its decisions indicated a watershed in attitudes among those Cossacks who had hoped to unite a commitment to statist principles with support for the post-February civic order. Men like Voronkov, Petrovskii, Kharlamov, and Mel'nikov had opposed particularist and traditionalist structures throughout much of 1916 and early 1917. Fearing the revolution's further course, Cossack Kadets and moderate socialists now joined Cossack traditionalists in abandoning the post-February order and sided instead with particularist Cossack organs.

This shift took place somewhat earlier on the Don than at the national level. In the Don Territory there was more common ground between the statist and the traditionalist opponents of the revolution. The Duma period had fostered longstanding ties between Cossacks and local Kadets, with the result that Kadets in 1917 could entertain Cossacks as perhaps the only truly popular base that might support them. Additionally, the Cossack government provided Kadets with an instrument of power unavailable elsewhere. As their power waned at the national level, the Kadets could look on the Don to an organ of real power. For Kadets and other advocates of state consciousness, the Cossack government represented an ideal type: a democratic institution that acted responsibly in revolution.

Three of the First Circle's decisions deserve special attention. First, the circle formed a "Cossack government" [*voiskovoe pravitel'stvo*] and elected Aleksei Maksimovich Kaledin to head it as "Cossack Ataman." The circle proclaimed that Kaledin held his post "by right of ancient custom of election, violated by the will of Peter I in 1709 and currently restored."[104] Kaledin was a general well known throughout Russia for his successes as commander of the Eighth Army during the 1916 Brusilov offensive in Galicia against the Austrians. In his effort to democratize the army, Alexander Kerensky appointed Brusilov, Kaledin's superior in 1916, as commander in chief. Brusilov then dismissed Kaledin because he refused to embrace democratization of the army.[105] Heading to the resort of Kislovodsk upon his dismissal, Kaledin literally passed through Novocherkassk on his way. Members of the circle convinced him to stand for the post of Don ataman.

By estate Kaledin was a Don Cossack, but his worldview was that of a career officer of the imperial army. Having graduated from the General Staff Academy, he had served as deputy chief of staff for the Don Cossack administration from 1906 to 1910, the period of reaction immediately following the 1905 Revolution. His wife was a Frenchwoman, and during the circle's deliberations he stayed in the house of General Zerebkov, the last Cossack adjutant general to Nicholas II.[106] Given his national prominence, almost all other contenders withdrew when he declared his candidacy. Delegates from the upper districts and from units at the front were displeased over the candidacy of a former imperial general and a member of the Cossack elite. Under great pressure from other delegates, however, they dropped their electoral opposition. Kaledin was thus elected by a deceptively lopsided vote of 562 to 24, with 23 abstentions.[107] On its last day, the circle renamed the previously existing Cossack council [*voiskovoi sovet*] a Cossack "government," although at this point the duties and functions of this new "government" were unclear even to the twenty-four people who composed it. The Provisional Government endorsed all the circle's administrative changes, but predictably insisted that its own commissar serve at the head of the Cossack hierarchy. The Cossack government refused, reiterating that there could be no outside interference in Cossack affairs.[108] In practice the point was moot, as the Provisional Government's commissar, Voronkov, was both a Cossack and a Kadet and proved quite solicitous of the Cossack cause.

The circle's second significant decision concerned civic administration. The April Cossack congress had sought to establish a system by which separate Cossack organs would exist alongside the newly emerging universalist political order. The host circle in June instead sought to disentangle Cossack organs from the now ubiquitous executive committees, which had been founded upon the principle of universal and equal representation. The June circle ordered that all Cossacks must withdraw from non-Cossack institutions. Hitherto many Cossack delegates had participated in both Cossack organs and supra-estate, republican civic committees. Cossacks now had to choose between Cossack organs and more universal civic ones. Insisting on the need for firm authority, Kadets—many of whom were also Cossacks—threw their support behind the Cossack government and withdrew from the Don Executive Committee.[109] The commitment to statehood thus led many "Constitutional Democrats" (the name from which the acronym "Kadet" in fact derived) to side with the particularist, estate-based Cossack government.

As a direct result of this decree, Cossacks serving on executive committees, including the central Don Executive Committee itself, resigned en masse. Their action left such committees solely in the hands of non-Cossacks. The circle's action directly repudiated the decisions of the April Cossack congress, which had constituted the Don Executive Committee in its current form. Petrovskii, who had served as the chairman of the Don Executive Committee since its formation in March, was both a Cossack and a Kadet. After the circle's resolution, he resigned his post as chairman. Other Cossacks on the committee joined him.[110] Symbolically, the circle expelled the Don Executive Committee from the ataman's palace in Novocherkassk and transferred control of the region's official newspaper from the Don Executive Committee to the Cossack government, renaming it from *Donskie oblastnye vedomosti*

[*The Don Territorial Gazette*] to *Vol'nyi Don* [*The Free Don*]. In addition to the change in title, the newspaper's previous editor, a moderate Socialist Revolutionary, was replaced by a Kadet.[111]

The circle's move to the right expressed the will of the delegates. Despite its pretensions, however, it did not express the will of the majority of Cossacks. It was the circle's final decision of significance that linked it more closely with those in whose name it spoke, rank-and-file Cossacks in their communities. This was the debate over who was to benefit from the alienation of private lands. The topic was largely symbolic, since private land represented a paltry 17 percent of the total.[112] At issue was not whether this private land should be alienated, which was a foregone conclusion. Rather, the question was who should benefit from this windfall: the relatively land poor native peasants, or Don Cossacks. On the second ballot and by a slim margin, the circle passed a resolution granting the land to needy native peasants, thus ratifying the earlier decision of the April Cossack congress. But the issue was so divisive that the vote was not considered definitive, and stanitsa assemblies were encouraged to express their own views on the issue.[113]

The land issue was a sensitive point for both peasants and rank-and-file Cossacks. Although peasants did have less land in aggregate than Cossacks, the shorthand measure of landholding (land ownership, including allotment land) corresponded poorly to actual land use. Statistics on landholding overlooked extensive peasant land rentals. The most detailed analysis of agriculture in the Don Territory, an overview compiled on the basis of the 1917 agricultural census, found that the territory of actual peasant sowings was six times greater than peasant landholding. Peasant agriculture was also much more intensive than Cossack agriculture. Harvest yields on peasant fields were significantly higher than those on Cossack ones. Peasant households were even much more likely than Cossack households to employ hired labor. Cossacks, by contrast, were much more likely to lease their holdings, in whole or in part.[114] Owing to the extensive purchase of private land, peasants in fact held more land as private property than as communal allotment land. Rather than being universally impoverished, peasants on the Don occupied both ends of the economic spectrum. By far most land seizures and violations in 1917 concerned not Cossack community holdings but private landholding, which was much more likely to be held by wealthy peasants than by Cossacks.[115]

To be sure, peasants in 1917 did stake a claim to "Cossack" lands. But they rarely demanded the farmland in use by Cossack communities. There were three main categories of "Cossack land": plots allotted to individual Cossacks by their communities; the land belonging to the Cossack communities themselves, from which the community apportioned land to its members and met communal needs, while frequently renting out the remainder; and the Cossack corporate administration's own land reserve, primarily leased in large plots to middlemen who then subleased the land to peasants at much higher rates. The Cossack government conveniently collapsed all categories of Cossack corporate landholding under the rubric of "Cossack land," thereby rhetorically linking the Cossack administration's vast system of land rental with an individual Cossack's own farming plot.

But peasants almost never laid claim to individual Cossack holdings. Indeed, peasant demands usually concerned lowering rental fees or tranferring outright land they were renting from the host administration or from Cossack communities. That is, peasants usually demanded possession of land they were already farming. For example, peasants in Sulinskii settlement seized hayfields belonging to the Sulinovsko-Kundriuchevskii Cossack settlement. But their act was not directed against the Cossacks. The Cossack community had leased its hayfields to wealthy renters. Under the influence of soldiers returning from the front, the peasants began mowing the hay for themselves. In order to uphold its claim, the Cossack community then requested that the Cossack Circle either take immediate action or permit it to deploy a Cossack company quartered nearby against the peasants. What had begun as a peasant action against wealthy, non-Cossack renters had become instead a struggle between Cossacks and non-Cossacks.[116]

In this environment, delegates to the circle returned to their stanitsas to report on the land resolution. Land stood at the center of rank-and-file Cossacks' sense of their identity. Many stanitsa Cossacks invoked their ties to the land to demonstrate their true Cossack nature, as opposed to those Cossack spokesmen who were only nominally Cossack, by virtue of juridical estate. By the early twentieth century, Cossacks were particularly concerned about a perceived land shortage in their communities and the encroachment of capitalist relations on their traditional lifestyle.[117] Thus Cossack communities responded with a veritable wave of resolutions condemning the circle's decision to apportion land first to peasants and only then to Cossacks. Delegates to the circle also returned to Cossack military formations at the front and in distant garrisons, which scripted similar proclamations to the circle on this issue. The resolution of Kazanskaia stanitsa is typical of many others in asserting that Cossacks had a moral claim to noble and all other land in the Don Territory. This claim was based on the assertion that "all land located in the boundaries of the Don Territory composes the historical possession of the Don Cossackry, acquired as it was through the blood of our ancestors and paid for many times over by the burden Cossacks have borne for the state."[118] This and other resolutions thus directly incorporated language from the circle's own formulaic proclamation on the land question. Such petitions, as well as the community assemblies that drafted them, drew Cossacks into the framework of the particularist Cossack institutions in ways they had not been previously involved. To be sure, before 1917 Cossacks had desired more land. Significantly, however, these aspirations were now being formulated not as an appeal to a tsar but as a demand to a "representative" political organ.

The land issue had long been a sensitive point for both peasants and rank-and-file Cossacks. More important than any resolution, the circle's very existence and activity served as a blueprint for the new Cossack political narrative and the new political practices required to sanction it. Participation in the May elections to the circle had been dismal in Ust'-Medveditskaia stanitsa. Yet once the circle had begun to meet, the local newspaper noted the groundswell of interest in its activities.[119] Elections to future circles would encompass ever more voters. Only 3,006 votes out of a possible 12,000 were cast for elections to the First Circle in May; in elections to the Constituent Assembly in October, more than 9,000 Cossacks voted for the slate of the Cossack government. Although the figures are not entirely comparable, they give a sense of proportion. Cossack participation in later circles during the height of the civil wars averaged 50 percent of all eligible voters, a relatively high proportion for such times.[120] The circle thus elaborated a new *political* form of Cossack separateness. Participation in the institutions and practices of the revolution's new-style politics had transformed the Cossackry from an estate into a modern-style social movement.

Both Cossacks and non-Cossacks increasingly employed new forms of political mobilization, thereby expanding the circle of political participation. As the emerging Cossack structures encompassed an ever-broadening number of Cossacks, they in turn prompted non-Cossacks to respond through their own political structures. In the face of claims for Cossack "liberties" in the form of particularistic local and territorial organs, non-Cossacks responded with calls for an egalitarian, civic order.[121] In principle the civic organs established in March and April remained universal and egalitarian. But with the mass resignations by Cossacks from executive committees, they became more and more non-Cossack in composition and anti-Cossack in outlook. What were originally intended as all-inclusive organs began to resemble estate structures, as peasant-dominated executive committees now confronted rejuvenated Cossack organs.

In the spring of 1917 the Don Executive Committee, along with Cossack Kadets and nonparty socialists heading the new organs, had championed a system in which Cossack organs dealing exclusively with Cossack issues operated alongside more universalistic civic organs of administration, encompassing Cossack and non-Cossack alike. The repudiation of that policy in June 1917 by Cossacks and their Kadet and moderate socialist supporters produced two entirely independent structures for civic administration and political representation, one for Cossacks and one for non-Cossacks.

The Cossack Circle's resolution to recall Cossacks from non-Cossack organs thus helped shape the Cossack and non-Cossack population into distinct and separate social movements, each requiring separate political representation. And this disaggregation of the population into distinct political structures extended from territorial organs, such as the Don Executive Committee and the Cossack government, down to individual communities throughout the Don Territory. By mid-May civic committees had spread throughout the Don Territory. While there was certainly friction between the two groups, almost everywhere these organs encompassed Cossacks and non-Cossacks alike. The circle's resolution, however, provided a powerful new principle for framing political institutions. In Siniavskii settlement, the circle's resolution splintered the local executive committee, which after its establishment in February had encompassed both Cossacks and non-Cossacks. The community also had a local cooperative society, which had existed from 1916 and included both Cossack and peasant members. It was only with the circle's political resolution in June that this cooperative also split along estate lines.[122] In some communities Cossacks went beyond recalling their delegates and instead advocated "destroying" universalistic executive committees outright, proposing in their place purely corporate organs: Cossack committees for Cossacks, peasant committees for peasants.[123]

A parallel process occurred in the army. Initially, Cossack sections claimed to look after the special interests of Cossack units, but they encouraged Cossacks to participate in their general front organizations as well. By June and July, at the time of the First Circle, Cossacks both at the front and in garrisons began to withdraw from elected organs and formed their own, specifically Cossack, institutions.[124]

Cossacks who had at one time been the driving force behind certain committees now abandoned them for specifically Cossack organs. Nikolai Mel'nikov had played a major role in establishing the Second Don District Executive Committee in Nizhne-Chirskaia stanitsa and served as a district commissar for the Provisional Government. But like Territorial Commissar Voronkov, Mel'nikov was also a Cossack by estate. In addition to his civic posts, he was elected to Cossack congresses and circles. After the First Cossack Circle Mel'nikov returned to Nizhne-Chirskaia and demanded the dispersal of the executive committee—which he had helped form—and the local soviet. While non-Cossacks protested, most Cossack members joined Mel'nikov in abandoning the executive committee. The remaining non-Cossack members submitted a complaint to the Provisional Government against Kaledin and the Cossack government.[125] The Provisional Government, however, did not act on their protest.

Mel'nikov, whose gateway to political activity had been a civic committee in March 1917, now participated only in Cossack organs. He was elected to all circles held in 1917, rising to ever more prominent posts. He served as deputy chairman of the April Cossack congress and the first "large" circle in May, and was elected chairman of both the August "small" circle and the second "large" circle in September. In December 1917 he would be elected to the All-Russian Constituent Assembly as a member of the Cossack slate.[126]

Russians across the political spectrum had welcomed the February Revolution as a decisive break with the old regime. But while nearly all Russians welcomed the collapse of the autocracy, they entertained dif-

ferent visions for Russia's revolution. Wartime institutions had forged
something of a consensus on the immediate steps that needed to be
taken. The makers of February envisioned a responsible, democratic
order, one in which local elected institutions would mature organically
to support "state consciousness" and would unite all the vital forces of
the nation. It is easy in hindsight to see how misplaced these hopes
were. But the institutions constructed on these assumptions, such as
the ubiquitous executive committees and food-supply boards, had real
effects. It was largely through such institutions established by the Provisional Government that citizens came to participate in a national
form of politics at the local level throughout much of 1917.

Russia's political class had imposed a democratic and elective political structure on a highly fractured political field. The institutions it had
summoned into being thus became the vehicles for expressing and mobilizing existing social divisions and new political ones, rather than
overcoming them. People became politically active and participated in
elective institutions, but Russia's new citizens failed to mature in the
ways the spokesmen of society had hoped or anticipated. The gulf between such anticipations and people's actual behavior had existed earlier, but during the war the political class had been able to hold the autocracy, rather than the people, responsible for this shortcoming. The
events of 1917 forced these people to confront their illusions head on.
Whereas the makers of February hoped new institutions would foster
the maturity posited by the "Great Russian Revolution," workers and
peasants sought to employ these same institutions as instruments to
pursue what they understood as their "rights" in the new order. By
summer, both on the Don and throughout Russia, it had become clear
that the post-February institutions were not fostering state consciousness among the population. Defenders of the state principle, from the
right through to the moderate left, gave up on persuasion. What would
replace it?

~ 3

Persuasion and Force

> We must cease our attempts at persuasion . . . a shift to compulsion is
> now absolutely necessary. It is necessary, and without this shift
> we will not be able to save either the cause of our homeland
> or the cause of our revolution.
> ~ Minister of Food Supply Sergei Prokopovich,
> October 16, 1917

$\mathcal{S}$ummer 1917 represented a watershed in the development
of wartime societies throughout Europe. The Russian Revolution, together with America's entry into the war, had transformed the global
conflict. In Russia, the framers of the February order had hoped that
the revolution would radically improve the war effort. They found,
however, that continuing to mobilize for war only deepened existing
rifts, thereby hobbling the war effort even more.[1] By the summer of
1917, hopes that "the Great Russian Revolution" would unite Russia's
citizens had given way to divisions over the future course of the revolution. Under attack from both left and right, the Provisional Government in these months confronted the collapse of its framers' illusions
about the people's capacity for democracy. As the masses failed to sub-
scribe to the type of citizenship its supporters had hoped for, the Provisional Government increasingly turned to state force as the only alternative to persuasion.

The Collapse of the Post-February Order

As the Cossack government staked its claim to the Don Territory, the
Don Executive Committee did not sit idly by; indeed, it aspired to a
universal and egalitarian order, one in which it spoke for the entire
population. But after the Cossack Circle's resolution in June recalling

Cossacks from civic organs, most Cossacks had abandoned the committee. When the Don Executive Committee reconstituted itself in late July, it relied heavily on soviets, organs that explicitly cast themselves as class institutions. The committee's new board drew two-thirds of its members from the Soviet of Workers' Deputies, the Soviet of Soldiers' Deputies, and the Soviet of Peasants' Deputies. G. L. Kariakin from the Soviet of Peasants' Deputies assumed the position of chairman of the committee after Petrovskii, a Cossack Kadet, resigned the post.[2] In both public proclamations and complaints directed to the Provisional Government, the Don Executive Committee asserted that only it could unite the population, as it alone was committed to a republican and democratic order. "Any attempt to subordinate the general interests of the territory to the special interests of the Cossackry," it asserted, "is a crude violation of the rights of the remaining portion of the population and contradicts the basic demands of the laboring revolutionary people."[3]

The Don Executive Committee, however, was supposed to coordinate its actions with the Provisional Government's commissar in the region, Mitrofan Voronkov. The Provisional Government made the Don Executive Committee even more dependent on Voronkov by declining to fund it directly and insisting that it receive credits only through him.[4] As a Cossack and a Kadet, however, Voronkov had come to oppose what he imagined was the committee's antistatist program. For its part, the committee repeatedly expressed its lack of confidence in Voronkov to the Provisional Government.[5] District executive committees and soviets, as well as individual citizens, also criticized Voronkov's pro-Cossack line and support for Kadet statist principles. One letter excoriated the commissar as a "lackey of the Kadets" and described how he catered to the needs of landowners.[6] As a general principle, the Provisional Government had decreed that commissars ought to rely on local committees, which "unite all organized local democratic forces and which enjoy their trust." In cases of conflict, the government permitted executive committees to petition for another appointee who would enjoy authority among the local population.[7]

The Provisional Government's own emissaries were highly critical of Voronkov. One commissar dispatched by the Ministry of Internal Affairs reported that Voronkov had failed to win the support of the "organized democratic forces," meaning the soviets. Moreover, so vague was the delineation of authority between Voronkov and Ataman Kaledin, the head of the Cossack government, that the two had taken to deciding jointly all administrative questions for the entire territory. In conclusion, the Provisional Government's emissary decried "the absence of a territorial organ that would unite the entire population." Although the Ministry of Internal Affairs did query Voronkov directly about the division of authority between his administration and that of the Cossacks, the Provisional Government did not remove him.[8]

Along with the withdrawal of all Kadets and Cossack delegates in June, the Provisional Government's acquiescence to the Cossack government's activities sealed the fate of the Don Executive Committee. The Provisional Government's tolerance for the Cossack government did not result from neglect or ignorance. Rather, it was conditioned by the national government's own growing isolation. During the July Days in Petrograd (July 3–5) demonstrators had called for the reluctant Bolsheviks to overthrow both the Provisional Government, with its coalition of moderate socialists and Kadets, and the moderate socialist leaders heading the Soviet. At that time the sole armed force upon which the government could call were two Don Cossack regiments quartered in Petrograd. A third was soon rushed to their aid.[9] The July Days led to the resignation of the Kadet ministers in the Provisional Government's first coalition and brought Alexander Kerensky to the post of prime minister.

With the collapse of the army after its failed June offensive and the government's demonstrated lack of any reliable military force in the July Days, proponents of "state consciousness" cast about for forces upon whom they could rely. Cossacks, almost alone, had demonstrated loyalty to the government. Provisional Government agencies tracking attitudes to the government purportedly showed the Don Territory as one of the few regions that consistently supported it.[10] On July 8, the day after he became prime minister, Kerensky sent a telegram to Ataman Kaledin directing him "to act decisively, without awaiting further instructions" to suppress any disobedience or armed resistance to the government's authority.[11] Soon afterward, Kerensky confirmed Kaledin as the ataman of the Don Cossacks and also appointed him commander in chief of all forces in the Don Territory, encompassing both Cossack units and army troops in rear garrisons. Kaledin was directed to secure the mining regions and protect the rail lines.[12] Voronkov continued to occupy the post of commissar in part because Kaledin informed the Provisional Government in no uncertain terms that the Cossack administration would not accept any other appointee.[13]

The Provisional Government was tolerant of the Cossack government because it, unlike the Don Executive Committee, could exert a modicum of military force. Despite protests of the Don Executive Committee, the Cossack government claimed the right to resolve not only Cossack issues but also more general issues such as agrarian unrest and food-supply problems.[14] Whereas the executive committee could do no more than issue protests and proclamations, the Cossack government could dispatch Cossack military units to deal with unrest.[15] Kaledin could thus exert some authority amid the growing anarchy of 1917. This attracted support from advocates of statehood and order, Cossacks and non-Cossacks alike.[16] The Don Food-Supply Committee, chaired by Voronkov, relied exclusively on the Cossack government rather than on the Don Executive Committee, even in non-Cossack regions.[17] This program of state-consciousness and order led the non-Cossack Rostov Union of Landowners as well as leading non-Cossack Kadets, such as Zeeler in the Don Territory and Shingarev at the national level, to support the Cossack government.[18]

The summer of 1917 witnessed the rise of class-based soviets as organs of representation in the territory as throughout the rest of Russia.[19] For non-Cossacks, there were few other options, since the Cossack government in August blocked the Provisional Government's planned introduction of the zemstvo.[20] Soviets on the Don therefore did not compete against "bourgeois" organs (executive committees, zemstvos, dumas) but rather formed a common front with them against Cossack structures.

In the early months of 1917, soviets existed only in a handful of large urban and mining centers (Rostov, Taganrog, Aleksandrovsk-Grushevskii, and Makeevka). By the summer, soviets had coalesced into a semi-unified structure. Soviet representatives met at a territorial level for the first time in July, and a territorial congress of soviets elected an executive committee in early August.[21] By that time, soviets had become the preeminent base of support for the Don Executive Committee. Through the autumn, moderate socialists—Mensheviks and Socialist Revolutionaries—dominated soviets as well as city dumas.[22]

Soldiers at the front transmitted the soviet paradigm to their relatives back home in rural areas. In an explanatory cover letter to "the executive committee of the Novocherkassk soviet of soldiers' and workers' deputies," the soldier Aleksandr Tarakanov wrote in May 1917:

> In forwarding my uncle Matvei Nikolaevich Mokhov's letter, I ask you to take measures (if you find it necessary) to stop Aleksandr Petrovich Bokov from propagating monarchist ideas, which are harmful to freedom. Mr. Bokov is an old Cossack officer who was wounded in the present war and was released from service for this reason . . . He is the enemy of any form of public interest and of all society's undertakings for the common good; he was a loyal servant of the tsar and so he advocates ideas of monarchism.
>
> As is evident from the letter, the stanitsa executive committee is composed of bourgeois, which is entirely intolerable—it must be reelected. Hear the call of the dark village! Tear the freedom-loving citizens from the iron grip of the bourgeoisie!
>
> Soldier Aleksandr Trofimovich Tarakanov[23]

The young soldier appealed to the Novocherkassk city soviet, in the southern Cherkassk District, to intervene in the affairs of Veshenskaia stanitsa, located far away in the Upper Don District. He presumed that the Novocherkassk soviet had both an interest in defending non-Cossacks in a distant Cossack community and the power to do so.

Tarakanov was not alone in advising his non-Cossack relatives to seek support from soviets against local Cossacks. In early August, Ivan Perfil'ev, an outlander serving as a postman in Ust-Khoperskaia stanitsa, received a letter from his son, who was serving in a Guard regiment at the front: "Dear father, yesterday I received your letter. You write that Cossacks don't give you any peace and curse you. What you should do is get all the outlanders together and write to Petrograd, to the Soviet of soldiers' and workers' deputies." For reading this letter aloud, Perfil'ev, a father of six, was expelled from the stanitsa by the Cossack community assembly and forced to return to his place of official registration.[24] Elsewhere, non-Cossack soldiers returning from the front pressed their communities to form soviets.[25]

The ultimate triumph of the soviets imparts a sense of inevitability to the rise of these new organs. Yet as late as autumn 1917 soviets had not yet emerged as the definitive form of representation for the non-Cossack population outside the large cities and mining regions. Even in autumn 1917, the boundary between executive committees and soviets remained indefinite and fluid. Because the Don Territory had lacked zemstvos and the Cossack government had prevented their introduction throughout 1917, in this region they represented not so much the old regime as the repudiation of the Cossack-dominated administrative order. As late as October 1917, even district soviets demanded the introduction of the zemstvo to serve as "the cornerstone of economic and legal life in the territory."[26]

The transformation of the Ust'-Medveditsa District Soviet of Peasant Deputies into a civic executive committee, and then back again, demonstrates the fluidity between these organs.[27] Voronkov's appointee as the Provisional Government's commissar for Ust'-Medveditsa District, I. I. Popov, was a Cossack. In mid-September the Ust'-Medveditsa District Soviet informed the Don Executive Committee that Cossacks had their own organs and no longer participated in universal civic bodies. Thus it petitioned to replace Popov, the "Cossack" district commissar, with "citizen" F. I. Klimenko. The Don Executive Committee replied that only Territorial Commissar Voronkov could confirm district commissars and then proceeded to lecture its distant pupils on how to constitute a proper civil organ. Such an organ should represent all of society rather than particular segments, and thus must be a universal executive committee rather than a particularistic soviet. As a result, in November 1917 the district soviet dutifully went about reconstituting itself as a "congress of soviets and executive committees from all of Ust'-Medveditsa District." Now authorized to speak for all of local society, the congress promptly elected as chairman of the new district executive committee the same man who had earlier served as chairman of the district soviet.

Despite such actions, all efforts to secure approval from the Don Executive Committee brought meager results. On December 10, a month and a half after the Soviet seizure of power in Petrograd, the exasperated executive committee remonstrated the Don Executive Committee for its repeated failure to respond to the committee's inquiries. "We . . . don't know how to explain this silence and find ourselves in an uncertain position," the district committee wrote. "What should we do? Please respond, since the inactivity of executive committees completely discredits them in the eyes of the population." The Provisional Government's acquiescence to the Cossack government and the Don Executive Committee's impotence led many non-Cossacks to see Soviet power as the sole effective authority to challenge Cossack claims.

The Don Executive Committee, to be sure, continued to insist on its authority throughout the autumn of 1917, proclaiming itself "the Provisional Government's organ for administering the Don Territory."[28] But the Provisional Government had little power and perhaps even less interest in supporting the Don Executive Committee. In the last week of October, just before the Provisional Government was itself overthrown, the Don Executive Committee petitioned it to intervene against Kaledin, whom the committee charged had destroyed the universal civic order and was now fomenting civil war.[29] Voronkov, meanwhile, told the Cossack government's newspaper that "the Don Executive Committee is an unburied corpse. The Cossackry has turned away from it and the peasantry doesn't know it. There is not one social group in the city or the [Don] Territory which would support it."[30] Responding to the Provisional Government's query regarding the demarcation of authority between himself and Cossack organs, Voronkov replied that "the only stable organization which shares a statist perspective is the Cossack government, with which I am in full contact."[31] Voronkov, with his Kadet background, was not alone in speaking of a "statist perspective." Many socialist officials in the Provisional Government by this point had come to share his concern for the statist principle. In fact, in his response Voronkov employed the very same phrase found in a Ministry of Internal Affairs circular from three days before, which had directed commissars to utilize "all local forces with a statist point of view, regardless of party affiliation" to form a militia to combat anarchy and secure food supplies.[32]

Dual power on the Don did not so much counterpose "census society" and "the people," or organs of the Provisional Government and soviets, as "democratic" models of representation—executive committees as well as soviets—and exclusive Cossack organs. The triumph of soviets was not preordained. Soviets became the preeminent counterweight to the Cossack government because they were the only organs not implicated in the Provisional Government's acquiescence to the Cossack government. After October, the new revolutionary government would provide support to local soviets in a way that the Provisional Government had failed to do.

How Cossacks Became Counterrevolutionaries

"When the revolution began," noted Anton Denikin, "all political groupings focused much attention on the Cossackry—some placing inflated hopes on it, others regarding it with undisguised suspicion. Rightist circles expected a restoration from the Cossacks; the liberal bourgeoisie—an active buttress of order; and the left feared their counterrevolutionary nature."[33] During August and September 1917, political activists across the ideological spectrum came to accept civil war as inevitable. Nearly all assessments of the situation predicted that Cossacks would play a prominent role in the forthcoming struggle. Although Kaledin's Cossack government did not represent the views of most Cossacks, its activity on the national political stage tended to confirm existing stereotypes of Cossacks as either paladins of order or tools of counterrevolution, depending on one's point of view.

During the July Days, Don Cossack regiments quartered in Petrograd had saved the Provisional Government and its coalition with the moderate socialists. Leading political figures hastened to read generic Cossack attitudes into the actions of these three units. The military commander in Petrograd telegraphed Ataman Kaledin, thanking the Don Cossacks for the sacrifices of their sons during the demonstrations. Leaders of the Kadet Party waxed lyrical about the Cossacks' devotion to Russian statehood at the funeral of seven Cossacks killed during the Petrograd disorders. Pallbearers for the fallen Cossacks represented the leadership of parties from the right—the Octobrist Mikhail Rodzianko and the Kadet Miliukov—to the moderate left, in the person of Kerensky himself.[34]

Over the course of 1917, the Kadet Party in particular looked to the Cossacks as an island of commitment to the statist principle in a sea of anarchy. Even before 1917, the Kadets had enjoyed a special relationship with the Don Cossacks. In late May 1917 Shingarev traveled to the Don Territory, as did many Kadet leaders in 1917. While there he made speeches to several large public gatherings and conducted a meeting of the local Kadet Party.[35] Although the Kadet Party was generally loath to sanction any particularistic demands, Shingarev insisted that the Kadets exempt Cossack lands from the party's land program, which called for alienating all land above a certain norm.[36]

When a national Kadet Party congress met in July to discuss electoral alliances for the Constituent Assembly elections, it voted for an electoral bloc with the Cossack government. In some sense, the Cossacks represented the one potential arena for popular electoral support for the Kadets. Yet the Kadets were not simply chasing votes. Because of their self-identification as a supraclass party, they declined to form alliances with those parties that defined themselves explicitly as parties of the bourgeoisie.[37] For the Kadets, Kaledin's Cossack government represented not a particular interest but rather a pillar of state consciousness.

Immediately after this congress, a delegation of nationally prominent Kadets traveled to the Don to attend the regional Kadet congress in Rostov.[38] At the same time, the Cossack government summoned a "Small Cossack Circle" to discuss the proposed electoral alliance and other issues. (The circle was termed "small" because it did not include delegates from Cossack units at the front—precisely the most revolutionary constituency.) Kharlamov, the four-time Duma deputy from the Don Territory and the senior Kadet in the region, addressed the circle on the questions of the Constituent Assembly and the proposed Cossack-Kadet bloc. The speaker summarizing the day's presentations pointed to three dominant themes: the country is in mortal danger; Cossacks will play a great role in saving the motherland; and the savior of Russia will be the Kadet Party.[39] As debate continued, some speakers protested that it was inappropriate for the "free Cossackry" to ally itself with "the party of the bourgeoisie." Delegates from the northern districts, more democratically inclined than others in the territory, were further displeased to learn that Kadets were to be granted places on the electoral slate that had been previously reserved for their delegates.[40] In the end the leadership managed to force through the electoral bloc. A closed meeting of the circle nominated the candidates for the joint slate. Among them were six former Duma deputies, five of whom were Kadets (including Kharlamov, Voronkov, and Kakliugin), as well as the nonparty Cossack socialists Mel'nikov and Ageev.[41] The Cossack leadership would later judge this alliance one of its greatest errors.

The Cossack government's alliance with the Kadet Party testified to the Cossack leadership's growing national prominence as one of the putative bulwarks for order. Ataman Kaledin's appearance at the Moscow State Conference, meeting less than one week after the Cossack-Kadet alliance had been concluded, further identified the Don Cossacks with the forces of law and order. Prime Minister Kerensky had summoned the Moscow conference in an attempt to forge unity out of the growing divisions in Russian society. He called upon all significant forces in society, from officers to members of socialist parties, to unite behind the revolutionary state. Before the conference opened Kaledin met with General Kornilov, the commander of the Russian Army and the darling of those, such as the Kadets, who opposed the "anarchic" turn in the revolution. Kornilov was of Cossack background himself. The two men decided to orchestrate their presentations, with Kaledin giving an intentionally inflammatory speech in order to make Kornilov's speech appear more moderate.[42]

Kaledin addressed the conference as speaker for all eleven corporate Cossack communities [*voiska*] throughout the empire.[43] Rejecting charges that Cossacks were counterrevolutionaries, he presented them instead as a force for order and freedom, the revolution's truest defenders, representing "an all-national and statist point of view" [*obshchenatsional'naia i gosudarstvennaia tochka zreniia*]. Having established the Cossacks' impartial credentials to speak on Russia's current condition, Kaledin proceeded with his proposals for restoring order to the revolution. He unabashedly opposed the revolution's post-February course. He proposed to eliminate politics in the military by abolishing army soviets, and called for strengthening discipline in both the front and the rear "since the rear and front are an indivisible whole." (Despite society's focus on revolution, Russia was still at war.) Miliukov, the head of the Kadet Party, attested that this speech "caused more disturbance in the hall than even Kornilov's speech . . . When Kaledin stepped down from the tribune, the hall's agitation reached a crescendo. The right and portions of the center clapped wildly and at great length . . . The left protested and expressed its outrage."[44]

Kaledin's portrayal of a Cossackry united in defense of the Russian state resonated widely among those on both the right and the left. However, Cossack republicans, even at the State Conference, advanced a countervailing historical narrative. They looked not to old-style Cossack corporate institutions but to their own revolutionary organs, most particularly Cossack regimental and military revolutionary committees.[45] By and large, Cossacks at the front and in Cossack communities on the Don rejected the alliance with the Kadets, charging that Kaledin had choreographed the agreement by summoning a small circle with restricted representation.[46] Cossack regimental and army committees passed resolutions challenging Kaledin's claim to speak for all Cossacks when he demanded an end to these "democratic organs."[47]

Kaledin clearly shared Kornilov's negative assessment of the "anarchic" course of the revolution. Kornilov, with backing from Kadet and rightist circles, was planning to become dictator. In that capacity he intended to suppress the Soviet and thereby, he believed, save the war effort, the nation, and the revolution. Kornilov hoped for the support of Prime Minister Kerensky, but he was willing to take action against him if necessary. In the last days of August he began his attempt to seize power. Owing to a misunderstanding between Kerensky and Kornilov as to who would take charge after order was restored, Kerensky ended up opposing Kornilov when the general finally dispatched troops to Petrograd.[48] On August 27 Kornilov issued an appeal to the people of Russia, referring both to his humble origins and to his Cossack background. He simultaneously issued an appeal specifically to Cossacks, calling on them to come to his aid in saving Russia.[49] During the course of the uprising, Kornilov sent telegrams and couriers to Kaledin, urging him, "with your Cossacks," to support the attempted seizure of power.[50]

Given preconceptions about Cossacks in general, and Kaledin's performance at the Moscow Conference in particular, nearly everyone expected him to support Kornilov.[51] Kaledin was on a tour through districts of the northern Don when news reached him of Kornilov's move, and therefore he was in no position to take concrete measures to support the general. Voronkov, as the territorial commissar, prevaricated.[52] Nonetheless, reports swirled throughout Russia that the Don Cossacks supported the rebellion. Aleksandr Verkhovskii, the commander of the Moscow military district, sent a telegram to Kaledin warning that any move to aid the rebellion would be crushed. The following day, Kerensky declared Kaledin to be a rebel and telegraphed orders that he be arrested.[53] On the final leg of his trip back to Novocherkassk, Kaledin had to avoid worker detachments, executive committees, and even republican Cossack troops seeking to arrest him. By the time Kaledin had returned to Novocherkassk, the attempted coup had collapsed and Kornilov himself was under arrest.

Although the extent of Kaledin's foreknowledge of Kornilov's plans remains a matter of dispute, no one doubted that Kaledin sympathized with Kornilov's goals. Miliukov, for instance, described the Don Territory and the army general staff as the two pillars of the Kornilov rebellion.[54] Meanwhile, both the Provisional Government and revolutionary organizations in areas surrounding the Don, similarly convinced of a unified and reactionary Cossackry, took measures to crush the supposed counterrevolution there, often speaking in blanket terms of Cossacks as counterrevolutionaries.[55] The Provisional Government, erroneously believing that Kaledin had issued telegrams in support of Kornilov, ordered his arrest. Thus, while a majority of Don Cossacks opposed the Kornilov affair, Kaledin's actions and his claims to speak for them nevertheless served to confirm widespread notions of Cossacks as counterrevolutionaries.

The Kornilov affair crystallized rank-and-file Cossack opposition to the Cossack leadership. Cossack garrisons throughout the Don passed resolutions condemning Kornilov's actions.[56] At the front, one officer in the Don Cossack Life Guard regiment recalled that the Kornilov affair caused the first conflicts between officers and enlisted men, as officers refused to promote an "agitator" who had opposed Kornilov while enlisted men passed motions of no-confidence in their officers.[57] In the northern part of the territory, *Ust'-Medveditskaia gazeta* condemned the Cossack government and its newspaper, *Vol'nyi Don*, for their equivocating response to the attempted coup.[58] These events also worsened relations between Cossacks and non-Cossacks "by a factor of several times," in the words of a Provisional Government emissary to the region.[59]

In the immediate aftermath of the Kornilov fiasco, the Cossack leadership hoped to utilize the "Second Large Circle," meeting in the second week of September, to rehabilitate itself before Cossacks and the Provisional Government.[60] The circle roundly condemned the Provisional Government for its allegations that Kaledin was involved in the Kornilov affair. It further insisted that the Provisional Government had no authority to remove an official, in this case Kaledin, whom the government had not appointed. (Kaledin, although nominally an official of the Provisional Government, had been elected by the First Circle in June.) It steadfastly refused repeated demands from the Provisional Government that Kaledin present himself before an investigative commission, proudly invoking the slogan from the times when serfs had sought freedom on the Don: "From the Don there is no extradition" [*s Dona vydachi net*]. Taking upon itself the responsibility for investigating Kaledin, the circle predictably exonerated his actions.[61] The Provisional Government, itself shaken by the whole adventure, could only acquiesce. It was rumored that the Provisional Government might remove Territorial Commissar Voronkov, who had refused to condemn Kornilov's actions against the government he supposedly represented. But Kaledin indicated his strong support for Voronkov, insisting that he could be replaced only with the consent of the Cossack government, and the Ministry of Internal Affairs hastily concurred.[62]

But the Cossack government also had to account for its actions before the Cossack delegates. Clearly responding to widespread disapproval over the proposed alliance with the Kadet Party, the circle voted that the Cossack government should review its decision and, in doing so, should "take into consideration the interests of the districts and the front." In fact, most delegates were opposed to the bloc, and the Cossack government belatedly annulled the agreement in October.[63] The circle also took up the issue of Lieutenant Colonel Golubov. Golubov, a Cossack, had participated in the formation of the Don Executive Committee in March and had opposed Kaledin's election at the First Circle in June. At the Moscow conference he had spoken against Kaledin's speech; during the Kornilov rebellion, he had addressed crowds in Rostov and even dispatched military detachments to arrest Kaledin. The entire circle, with the exception of seventy delegates from the front and from Ust'-Medveditsa District, voted to exclude him from the Cossack estate for his "treason." The dissenting delegates demonstratively walked out. In an attempt to prevent a schism, the circle voted only to reprimand Golubov, rather than to expel him outright from the Cossack estate. But in case the message was lost on anyone, the circle also voted itself the authority to expel individuals from the Cossack estate in the future.[64] The circle thus declared itself to be the arbiter for determining who was and who was not a Cossack, a consideration based on one's political behavior as much as on one's background.

Following Kornilov's attempted coup, all sides began bracing for the anticipated civil war. Within the Don's borders, the Cossack government had long ceased dealing with the Don Executive Committee and took simply to issuing its own orders for the entire population. On October 12, the Cossack government informed both the Provisional Government and the local population that henceforth, "considering the current political and economic situation of Russia overall," it would enter "onto a course of taking decisive, independent, and responsible measures."[65] Less than two weeks later, on October 25, the October Revolution overthrew the Provisional Government and established a Soviet government. The Cossack government would then attempt to extend its "decisive, independent, and responsible measures" beyond the boundaries of the Don Territory.

From Persuasion to Compulsion

The general shift of the post-February political class from a politics of exhortation to one of compulsion was most clear in food supply. The wartime policies of food supply had demonstrated, to those who wished to see it, that there existed a gulf between the expectations of Russia's political class and much of the rural population. From the very first days of the war, the imperial government's food-supply network, organized under the aegis of the reformist Ministry of Agriculture, sought to involve cooperative and zemstvo activists while excluding commercial channels. This wartime policy represented an extension of the Ministry of Agriculture's prewar pro-producer reform program, for which many public and professional activists had much sympathy. Government measures in food supply, and especially these measures' anticommercial bias, reflected not just the views of an isolated administration but the program of a broad spectrum of public professionals as well. Until 1917, these public men and officials chose to believe that their wartime food-supply efforts had failed because of the autocracy's incompetence.[66]

The February Revolution allowed the near-immediate implementation of mobilization programs that had been gestating since mid-1916, but which until that point had been blocked by the autocracy. Wartime food-supply specialists, such as Vladimir Groman, Andrei Shingarev, and Iakov Bukshpan, immediately formed a Joint Food-Supply Commission, constituted from members of both the embryonic Provisional Government and the Petrograd Soviet.[67] On March 2 this joint committee issued a telegram calling for the establishment of provincial food-supply committees, to be formed "on democratic principles." The following day the Kadet Shingarev was appointed the Provisional

Government's first minister of agriculture. As minister, he issued a circular confirming the committee's earlier directive on provincial food-supply committees.[68]

Food-supply officials in the Don Territory did not act on the original March 2 telegram from the Joint Food-Supply Commission, but upon receiving Shingarev's confirmation of that directive they immediately convened a "territorial food-supply committee" on March 7. This assembly's composition resembled the gathering only three weeks earlier, when Semenov's aide had caused most of the assembly to walk out when he had banned them from discussing a greater role for public organizations. Semenov, the conservative bureaucrat appointed in 1915 to oversee food-supply in the Don Territory, read Shingarev's telegram to the gathering, and then ceded his chairman's seat. Once again, the Provisional Government's guidelines directed zemstvos to take over for the organs of the old regime. In their absence on the Don, delegates decided to form a food-supply committee on the model of a zemstvo, with an elected board. Elections were held immediately, with Mitrofan Voronkov elected *in absentia* as chairman.[69] This choice was logical, for Voronkov had served in several national food-supply organizations and had come to national prominence in debates over food-supply policy in late 1916.

Shingarev had appointed Voronkov, his Kadet and Duma colleague, to the Don Territory as a government "emissary" for coordinating local food-supply efforts with the new state food-supply organs.[70] The following day the Provisional Government also named Voronkov as its commissar for the Don Territory.[71] Throughout 1917 Voronkov would combine the posts of Provisional Government commissar and chairman of the Don food-supply board. There was a good deal of continuity in the food-supply organization itself. Voronkov's deputies had earlier played roles in the wartime food-supply apparatus, and two of his three deputies held posts in the Don-Kuban'-Terek cooperative society. All the agents responsible for army grain purchases in the Don Territory had held similar posts before February in the tsarist Ministry of Agriculture's food-supply organization.[72]

The situation these specialists faced was dire. Three years into the world war, both the army and the civilian population were confronting shortages of food, caused less by actual shortfalls in production than by problems with distribution. The immediate solution seemed to be to implement those measures that the technocrats had earlier proposed but which had been blocked by the autocracy. Without any discussion, the All-State Commission on Food Supply, which superseded the short-lived Joint Food-Supply Committee, proposed the introduction of a grain monopoly, a measure that had caused much debate in late 1916. The commission members, from Mensheviks to the moderate right, agreed across party lines on the necessity of this measure.[73] Iakov Bukshpan, who as editor of the special council's official journal had advocated its introduction throughout the autumn of 1916, drafted the law, employing existing German measures as his model. Indeed, one reason the measure caused so little opposition was that people believed that Germany's wartime economy had already tested it and proven its worth.[74] The Provisional Government introduced this measure on March 25.

This decree—"The Directive on Placing Grain at the Disposal of the State"—encapsulated the wartime and post-February consensus among specialists on food supply.[75] All grain, but for a quota to be left to grain producers for their own consumption and sowing, was to be turned over to the state at prices the state itself dictated. The decree simultaneously established the fixed prices for grain and guidelines for instituting local organs to carry out this monopoly. One contemporary treatment described the decree's "grandiose task" to be "the destruction of the trade in grain and the transfer of its exchange to state authority."[76] The state had now staked its claim to *all* grain in the country, marketed and unmarketed. In fact, the March 25 decree only indicated the intended contours of government policy. During its eight months in power, the Provisional Government never completed the detailed inventory required to determine how much grain should be taken from producers. Moreover, it proved unable to extract the grain from them.[77] The grain monopoly would remain in force, however, longer than the government that had instituted it. For the first several months of their rule, the Bolsheviks retained the grain monopoly and followed the same basic principles in food supply as had their predecessors. Although the Bolsheviks attempted to implement the monopoly much more aggressively, they had no great success, causing them to adopt new policies over the course of 1918.[78]

Although the measures introduced immediately after the February Revolution had already been gestating for several months before February, the revolution created an entirely new context for their implementation. When it introduced the grain monopoly, the government decided not to implement a parallel monopoly and fixed prices on manufactured goods, a program proposed by Groman since 1916. This decision led many peasants to charge that they were being asked to sacrifice disproportionately. Socialists across the spectrum, Groman among them, focused precisely on this disparity. Industrialists criticized and increasingly attacked the Provisional Government from the opposite direction. A series of conferences on food supply held throughout May proved that the overall polarization in politics also affected the food-supply issue. The Provisional Government defended its policies but was attacked as too timid by socialists and as too interventionist by trade and industrial circles.[79]

The Provisional Government had appointed Voronkov as its commissar in part because of the Don Territory's importance to national food-supply efforts. The reports at the first Don food-supply congress, held on April 20–21, indicated that the new order was proving no more successful than the old at exhorting small producers to surrender grain. At that congress Voronkov read aloud telegrams from the army reporting the total lack of grain and fodder for military units at the front. Still, the majority of delegates at the congress continued to favor privileging cooperatives over the existing private trade and storage network, effectively continuing the ban on the latter's involvement in food-supply operations.[80] Delegates from private trade organizations participated in the congress, but they were swamped by the delegates from cooperative and public organizations. Even Shingarev as minister of agriculture ordered a continuation of the wartime policy of preferential treatment for cooperatives, although he did sanction the use of private traders wherever necessary. Many local food-supply officials criticized even this concession to private trade organizations, opposing any role for them at all.[81]

As Kadets, both Shingarev and Voronkov attempted to foster unity out of this division. Shingarev favored a continued reliance on cooperatives, but he defended the need to take advantage of the trading class's knowledge and expertise.[82] In mid-May he traveled to the Don to meet with local Kadets and to campaign on behalf of the food-supply effort. In several public speeches he summoned all groups to self-sacrifice, extending his hand even to grain merchants, who, he claimed, could contribute to the cause with their knowledge and organization. At several gatherings he concluded his speech with the same slogan: "Secure grain for the country, and you secure it its freedom."[83] While in Rostov he participated in the second territorial congress on food supply. Hearing of the poor levels of fulfillment, he declared the situation "tragic." "If we previously were able to condemn the tsarist regime," he lectured, "now the food-supply issue is entirely in your hands, and if it does not meet its required level, then the fault lies entirely on the local organizations." In the face of faltering food-supply deliveries, Shingarev tried to convince the local food-supply congress, dominated by cooperative activists brought into food-supply efforts by the tsarist Ministry of Agriculture, that private grain traders ought to be harnessed to food-supply operations. His pleas had little effect.[84]

At the state food-supply congress in early May, Shingarev explicitly tied food-supply efforts to both self-sacrifice and "state consciousness." "The State [sic]," he declared, "cannot allow economic decline due to personal self-preservation."[85] In several public speeches in Rostov and Novocherkassk, Shingarev argued that the population was seeking "to live as well as possible" [vo vsiu shir'] at a time of national crisis, conducting "a feast in time of famine." The desire for personal profit and speculation, in his view, had poisoned the Russian state organism.[86] Throughout 1916 Shingarev had held the autocracy responsible for the food-supply failures. By mid-1917 he was blaming the peasants— behaving no differently than in 1916—for "feasting" themselves amid the state's "famine."

In late April the All-State Food-Supply Committee, including both moderate socialists and representatives of the Provisional Government, established an "agitational commission," which sought to familiarize the population with the new laws and to explain the necessity of their fulfillment. Aleksandr Chaianov, Russia's leading agronomist, lectured and wrote pamphlets to familiarize student "cultural-enlightenment activists" with the food-supply situation, so the students in turn could edify peasant-producers. Shingarev testified, "We sent everyone that we possibly could to the localities in order to instill among the population a sense of the terrible danger confronting the state's food-supply effort."[87] The Ministry of Food Supply, established in May, included its own subdepartment for information and agitation.[88] Provincial organs imitated this model. The Don Food-Supply Committee employed university students for its "propaganda in the localities" and depended upon these *Kulturträger* for much of its information.[89]

The Provisional Government, however, confronted the same problem that had undercut tsarist food-supply efforts: it had few industrial goods to offer in exchange for peasant grain. By mid-summer spiraling inflation meant that rural producers were being asked to surrender their goods at state-dictated prices for near-worthless currency. By autumn 1917, the state price for grain often was less than half what it could fetch on the market.[90] Large landholders generally adhered to the grain monopoly, but grain was concentrated overwhelmingly in the hands of small producers, especially in the Don Territory.[91] Cajoling them to hand over grain to meet state targets fell to district and county food-supply boards established by the March 25 decree. Torn between meeting their state obligations and carrying out the will of their constituents, such boards fell far behind their assignments. By August, the flow of grain had nearly ceased. Farmers were also refusing to turn over their cattle.[92] Some farmers complained that, after three years of war, they simply had nothing left to give. Others declared, "We aren't against handing over cattle or produce for the army—but not for the bourgeoisie." (This statement from a Cossack community.) Such farmers expressed skepticism that their sacrifices were reaching the front. Others demanded payment at market prices.[93] As 1917 progressed, the Provisional Government increasingly blamed peasant producers themselves for failing to meet the national government's expectations. An analysis of food-supply offenses compiled by the militia's Department of Information in October 1917 blamed the worsening situation on "the position taken by the peasantry in regard to providing grain to the cities and the army."[94]

Despite the conceptions of the Kadet Party and the Cossack leadership, rank-and-file Cossacks were no more likely to adhere to statist principles than were non-Cossacks. Throughout the spring and summer of 1917, some Cossack communities boarded passing barges to seize the grain for themselves, while others declined to turn over grain and cattle at fixed prices. To the consternation of stanitsa food-supply committees, their own community assemblies passed resolutions that defined state requisitions as merely "voluntary" and called for payment at market prices. Outlying Cossack settlements then employed these stanitsa resolutions as precedents for their own, similar resolutions.[95]

The chairman of the Ust'-Medveditsa District Food-Supply Committee reported that he had to work alone, without any help. (Ust'-Medveditsa was a northern, predominately Cossack district.) "No one," he lamented, "wants to recognize the laws. The chairman often hears, 'I'll give as much as I want to give.' One also frequently hears threats, such as 'we'll slit your throat,' or 'we'll sit you on a pitchfork.'"[96]

Throughout the country, the Provisional Government's militia department noted, the population tended to view the food-supply committees themselves as the cause of all their problems, leading to demands for their abolition and even to assaults on committee members.[97] By summer, the Don Food-Supply Committee noted a growing hostility both to its measures as well as toward the intelligentsia upon whom it relied for its agitational efforts. Unable to believe that Cossacks themselves would oppose state measures, the committee charged that Cossack atamans opposed to the new order must be inciting average Cossacks against it.[98]

Cossack communities increasingly took to registering and distributing grain among themselves, while opposing all efforts by their food-supply committees to remove grain from the community. In Krasnyi khutor, a large number of Cossack soldiers home on leave in mid-June appeared at the community's assembly. Here they learned that some individuals were hoarding grain and selling it on the free market to speculators and moonshiners. Such measures, the soldiers charged, were harmful to the state and were unfair to families of Cossacks serving at the front. The returning Cossacks insisted upon reelecting the food-supply committee, and seated their own candidates. At the prompting of the assembly, the new food-supply committee then drew up a precise inventory of all grain holdings in the khutor. In the ensuing house-to-house search, some Cossacks attempted to block the committee's entry by force, but they were overcome. The Provisional Government was hoping for precisely such determination and autonomous action. Yet the grain obtained by the local committee was intended solely for internal redistribution, not for shipment to the state.[99]

By mid-summer, state acquisition operations were faltering badly. Army officials frantically bombarded the Provisional Government with reports that they were receiving nowhere near the required amount of supplies.[100] Moderate socialists now held many of the key posts in the

Provisional Government. Among them was Aleksei Peshekhonov, a leader of the Popular Socialist Party, who was serving as the minister of food supply. In May Peshekhonov had declared, "By means of state intervention we will not only eliminate necessities and shortages, but also demonstrate that our Motherland does not lag behind other states."[101] But with government food-supply efforts flagging disastrously, socialist ministers in the Provisional Government began to speak of using force against the rural population. In mid-July 1917 both Kerensky and Peshekhonov advised local committees to turn to force; in particular, Peshekhonov directed the committees to employ "the most energetic and firm measures" to secure the harvest, which he noted now "constitutes state property."[102]

Kerensky and Peshekhonov modeled their directives on an order issued one week earlier, on July 8, by Lavr Kornilov, at the time the commander of the Southwest Front. Noting that grain had been declared state property, Kornilov threatened punishment for any actions preventing the orderly gathering of the harvest in areas of the Southwest Front. While the legal basis for the order derived from authority granted to Kornilov by article 19 of the regulations for regions under martial law, it was issued in consultation with the Provisional Government's commissar for the front. When Kornilov was made commander in chief, he reissued the order on July 31 to cover the entire front.[103]

The Provisional Government, however, did not have to press local officials to use force; indeed, they had come to accept the necessity of force on their own. In early August Peshekhonov reported that the decrease in sowings on private estates meant that the state would have "to place its hopes on peasant grain." Given the peasantry's reluctance to surrender its grain, the state was having little success. He noted in the ministry's official news summary, however, that in "several provinces local organs have taken their own initiative to employ force to obtain grain, and sometimes this has given favorable results."[104]

The Don Territory was one such region where a local food-supply committee had come to embrace the use of force. As the summer progressed, the Don Executive Committee sought to mediate between landowners and peasants. Often it was reduced to pleading with violators to desist. Much like the Provisional Government itself, the Don Executive Committee alienated landowners by failing to protect them, and it exasperated peasants by lecturing them that "private property remains inviolable until the Constituent Assembly."[105] In contrast, Kaledin's Cossack government was both willing and able to dispatch military force. At the request of landowners in Rostov District, Kaledin sent Cossack units in late July to uphold order in two peasant communities, prompting vain protests from local peasants, the district peasant soviet, and the Don Executive Committee.[106]

Kaledin's actions, however, represented more than simply Cossack oppression of peasants. The food-supply board of Rostov District, an overwhelmingly peasant area, worked in conjunction with the Cossack government "to induce inhabitants to fulfill their State [sic] obligations." To this end the committee in early August expressed its willingness to employ "all measures of exhortation and influence, up to and including armed force."[107] The Cherkassk District food-supply board similarly petitioned the Cossack government to provide it with armed force to compel compliance from the population.[108]

A Don territorial food-supply congress meeting in the third week of August formalized this emerging consensus on the desirability of force.[109] Although the congress was chaired by Voronkov, cooperative activists and moderate socialists predominated among the delegates. With no reserves and a drought looming in the northern districts, the food-supply board decided to temporarily cease shipments of grain. The board, headed by Voronkov, again raised the issue of employing private trade organizations. The vast majority of delegates, opposed only by Voronkov and the board, for the third time that year voted to employ the private trade organizations for grain storage "only when cooperatives proved incapable of handling it themselves." In light of the dire state of affairs, it was clear that this was simply a formula for excluding the private trade organizations under any conditions.

While foreclosing reliance on private trade organizations, the congress that very same evening passed a resolution declaring that "the existence and integrity of the army and all the achievements of freedom now depend on providing food supply." Therefore, it advocated employing "all measures," meaning "persuasion first and foremost," but "the employment of armed force" in "cases of necessity." (Employing "all measures" clearly did not extend to resorting to the private trade organizations.) "We appeal to the Ministry of Food Supply," the resolution continued, "to provide committees with the right to demand, in cases of necessity, military units for fulfilling the law on the grain monopoly." A member of the territorial Soviet of Peasants' Deputies protested this decision to use force. He was shouted down by virtually the whole congress. S. M. Gurvich, a Menshevik and a member of the territorial Soviet of Workers' Deputies, denounced the speaker as an "irresponsible demagogue." Grigorii Urusov, head of the Don-Kuban'-Terek cooperative society and the deputy chairman of the food-supply board, declared, "You are opposed to employing armed forced against ill-willed elements. Then tell us what means we should employ to deal with them." Vasilii Mazarenko, an organizer for the Peasant Union in 1905 and a food-supply official in 1917, corrected the cowed speaker. The territorial Soviet of Peasants' Deputies had indeed condemned the Cossack government's dispatch of Cossack units to peasant regions. But the soviet had not voted to oppose the use of force, he lectured; it had simply demanded that the soviet be informed of all cases where force was employed.

The congress's appeal to the Ministry of Food Supply for the right to employ force could not have been more timely. On August 20 Peshekhonov issued a circular directing local committees to employ "coercive measures, up to and including armed force," should the population decline to turn over its grain. "Needs of state," he proclaimed, "dictate these extreme measures." In particular, he proposed that local committees, now obviously viewed as state executive organs rather than as democratic structures, resort to military detachments to secure grain.[110]

Divisions within the Provisional Government soon cast doubt on the firmness of this policy. In the third week of August the head of the Special Council for Defense informed Kerensky that "the entire cause of defense now depends on getting grain from the population." In his opinion, the shortfalls resulted primarily from the low fixed prices on grain. Kerensky therefore sanctioned a doubling of the fixed prices established by the March 25 decree.[111] Given their longstanding anti-commercial ethos, most food-supply specialists, including the Don Food-Supply Committee, predictably opposed this measure. They charged that it encouraged producers to hoard their grain in anticipation of further price increases.[112] The increase in prices also undercut confidence in the government, which only three weeks before had declared that prices would not be raised under any circumstances. Peshekhonov, who had just threatened to use force to uphold requisitioning at these prices, resigned in protest.[113] Kerensky's gamble on higher prices did not mean, however, that he eschewed the use of force. In the telegram to local officials laying out the price increase, Kerensky and V. N. Zel'geim, the lifelong cooperative activist now heading the All-State Food-Supply Committee, directed local committees that if producers still declined to turn over grain, the committees were to "employ the most determined means of compulsion."[114]

These decisions were taking place as the Kornilov affair was unfolding. In its immediate aftermath Kerensky, who took over the post of commander in chief from Kornilov, issued an order on September 8 that substantially repeated Kornilov's July 31 order directing the use of force to overcome any obstruction to state food-supply efforts.[115] Although Kerensky issued the order, its origin lay elsewhere. Indeed, it was prompted by the fervent appeals of Nikolai Aleksandrovich Gavrilov, an official in the Ministry of Agriculture since 1899 who during the war had served under Krivoshein as the head of the grain department in the Special Council for Food Supply. After the February Revolution Gavrilov became the Ministry of Food Supply's special agent attached to the army's commander in chief. Concerned that Kornilov's arrest would lead the population to doubt the validity of his July 31 order, Gavrilov sent a telegram on September 4 to Kerensky, pleading with the prime minister to reissue the order under his own name. Gavrilov further proposed that the Provisional Government extend the authority for enforcing the decree from provincial commissars to local food-supply committees. To give them the "real force" required to carry out this task, Gavrilov—a civilian with a long history in the tsarist regime's reformist Ministry of Agriculture—proposed that food-supply committees be *required* to appeal to the army's quartermaster for armed detachments. Kerensky's order, issued four days later, incorporated all of Gavrilov's suggestions.[116]

While taking Kornilov's earlier orders as its foundation, Kerensky's order went much further in conflating the military and civilian spheres.[117] Kornilov's orders had been issued on the basis of powers granted to him in regions under martial law, and they had covered only areas of the front. Kerensky's order, issued by him in his capacity as supreme commander in chief but while he also occupied the post of prime minister, did not invoke any legal foundation. In effect, it extended to the entire political space of Russia an order originally intended exclusively for the front and derived from martial law powers. Whereas in his order Kornilov had invoked only "the interests of the army," Kerensky expanded the justification to include preserving the nation's economy and overcoming food shortages facing the country's entire civilian population. Thus in 1917 the use of armed force was conceptually extended from "requisitioning" for the armed forces to the "state task" of feeding the entire population. Moreover, only governmental commissars had been hitherto empowered to summon military force.[118] Kerensky's decree extended this authority to a new civilian organ, local food-supply committees, for addressing essentially civil concerns. Indeed, the order obligated the committees to use such force. The right of such committees to summon military force would become a key feature of Soviet food-supply policy. The shift, however, came before October and at the prodding of Gavrilov, a civilian and longtime food-supply technocrat.

The public had lost faith that the common people were gradually educating themselves in the ways of responsible citizenship. It had come to place its hope on force instead. Sergei Chakhotin, a Kadet heading the Provisional Government's "Central Committee for Sociopolitical Enlightenment," recalled that the intelligentsia in early 1917 harbored a near-mystical faith that "the people" would instinctually find their way to state consciousness. Over the course of 1917, however, "these unfounded expectations were replaced by disappointment, mixed often with animosity toward that very same people in whom they had up until then believed."[119] This was precisely the trajectory of Viktor Anisimov. A leading zemstvo statistician, agronomist, and cooperative activist, as well as a prominent Popular Socialist, in 1914 he had advocated increased participation by cooperatives in the war effort in order to foster new cooperative structures. (He sat on the board of five cooperative organizations.) After the February Revolution he served the Provisional Government's Ministry of Food Supply, headed by his party colleague Peshekhonov. Addressing a gathering of food-supply inspectors in late September, he described his disillusionment with democracy. "The initiators of the law on the grain monopoly," he declared, "demonstrated too great a fascination with a democratic system for organizing the cause of food supply." They had, he argued, placed too much hope on the ability of the local population to understand the tasks of state: "We ought to acknowledge that the wager on the autonomous activity and statist outlook by broad sectors of democracy has failed." Anisimov argued that food supply would have to rely instead on "organs that are capable of taking a statist point of view." These conclusions prepared the ground for his future service as a cooperative specialist for the Soviet state.[120]

It had become clear that the doubling of prices in August had not dramatically improved food-supply deliveries. Peshekhonov's replacement as the minister of food supply, the nonparty socialist Sergei Nikolaevich Prokopovich, came to share the views of Peshekhonov, Gavrilov, and Anisimov on employing force. Soon after his appointment, Prokopovich toured several agricultural regions in late September, including the Don Territory. He consulted with Voronkov, who informed him that the Don Territory had a surplus of eleven million poods of grain. Voronkov explained that acquiring it, however, was proving "complex."[121] The revolutions of 1917 had changed nothing about the nature of grain holding in the Don Territory. Food-supply boards in both peasant and Cossack communities continued to resist the removal of grain reserves from their villages.[122] As a result, Voronkov managed to send off only thirty of the fifteen hundred railcars he was supposed to dispatch in the first half of September.[123]

Things were not much better elsewhere, and from early October the Provisional Government, with the backing of many cooperative and public activists, was preparing to use force to obtain grain from the countryside. Prokopovich's speech to the Council of the Russian Republic on October 16 signaled this shift to the use of military force for internal political ends. (The Council of the Republic was yet another all-national gathering intended to shore up support for the government.) Prokopovich declared that the government had not been able to bring itself to use force in August, and so had doubled fixed prices instead. Declaring that exhortation had failed owing to the Russian people's own excesses and ignorance, Prokopovich concluded: "We must cease our attempts at persuasion . . . a shift to compulsion is now absolutely necessary. It is necessary, and without this shift we will not be able to save either the cause of our homeland or the cause of our revolution."[124]

The following week the ministries of war, internal affairs, and food supply worked out measures for providing government food-supply officials with armed detachments to compel Russia's citizens to meet their "State obligation."[125] The socialist Prokopovich; the Menshevik minister of internal affairs, Aleksei Maksimovich Nikitin; and the leftist minister of war, Alexander Ivanovich Verkhovskii, were all eager to dispatch cavalry units to large cities and the countryside to extract food supplies. General Nikolai Dukhonin, the chief of staff for the acting supreme commander in chief, was understandably less eager at the prospect of having to remove these units from the front against the Germans. He contended that military requirements and disorders at the front made it impossible to dispatch cavalry units to "internal provinces."[126]

The idea of employing armed force to secure grain from reluctant peasant producers did not derive solely from the circumstances of Russia's revolution. Indeed, by 1917 Germany, too, had resorted to employing armed force to secure its requisitions, and Austria-Hungary would soon follow suit. In countries other than Russia, however, the use of force operated within an established political and institutional order and was directed toward the clear goal of the war effort. In revolutionary Russia, by contrast, the Provisional Government's endorsement of violence occurred in a society deeply divided over the goals and even legitimacy of that government.

The Provisional Government sought to pursue an aggressive and forceful policy in the sphere of food supply—in fact, a quasi-military policy. That the Provisional Government lacked the means does not imply that it lacked the will; that it lacked sufficient means does not imply that it did not find some support for its measures.[127] In response to the requests of local commissars and food committees, the civilian chancellery attached to the supreme commander's headquarters issued a flood of telegrams to the quartermaster departments of the various fronts, ordering them to provide military units for securing grain for the state. Kerensky's September 8 order, issued at Gavrilov's prodding, provided the legal foundation.[128] Such units, particularly cavalry detachments outfitted with machine guns, were indeed dispatched to "impose order." These measures to deal with the post-summer crises did not save the government. But they became the institutional legacy directly inherited by the Bolsheviks. A neat line between governments and policies thus can be drawn no more for October 1917 than it can be for February. Contemporaries themselves understood the Soviet state's revolutionary food-supply measures as an extension of preexisting policies.[129]

To pursue these coercive policies in the Don Territory, Voronkov came to rely exclusively upon Cossack structures, issuing directives jointly in his name as Provisional Government commissar and in the name of the Cossack government. In early October, Kaledin established military cordons around the territory's borders to prevent the illegal private trade in grain.[130] Voronkov informed the Ministry of Internal Affairs that he was relying upon the Cossack government because it was the sole viable organ operating from a statist point of view.[131]

Yet while Voronkov relied on Cossack structures to carry out these measures, the measures themselves corresponded to the Provisional Government's own policies. Prokopovich, in his speech to the Council of the Republic, singled out Voronkov's measures for special praise.[132] Following directly upon Prokopovich's call to shift from persuasion to compulsion in mid-October, Voronkov issued an order directing all inhabitants to turn over their grain in accordance with the grain monopoly. The Cossack government cosigned the order. Those declining to turn over grain voluntarily, it warned, "will face requisition conducted with the aid of armed force." An accompanying appeal urged Cossacks to cease their selfish behavior and sacrifice on behalf of the government and their starving fellow citizens in the northern districts.[133] Instructors from the Ministry of Food Supply, agents dispatched to the Don Territory over the summer to ensure proper fulfillment of central policy, heartily endorsed Voronkov's measures. Neither Cossacks nor counterrevolutionaries, they sourly declared that "there are now no hopes for voluntary delivery." While noting that Voronkov was relying on the Cossack government to carry out this measure, Inspector P. A. Sebriakov defended this decision because only the Cossack government could deploy any "real force."[134] These reports arrived in Petrograd amid the Bolshevik seizure of power.

The day after the Bolsheviks took control in Petrograd, the new Council of People's Commissars officially formed a "People's Commissariat of Food Supply" on the foundation of the previous government's ministry. Nikolai Kondrat'ev, the preeminent economic specialist and student of food supply and price regulation, pointed out that "under Soviet power, the basic principle of food-supply policy—the monopoly—remained the same as it had been under the Provisional Government." "But," he noted, "qualitatively, and in its relative significance, it had changed radically. As much as the moment of freedom and persuasion had been hypothesized under the Provisional Government, under Soviet power the moment of compulsion increased by an unprecedented degree."[135]

Kondrat'ev suggested that what distinguished the two was not so much their policies as the ability of Soviet power to mobilize support for coercive measures to carry out those policies. Even so, the linkage between the Soviets' use of violence in acquiring food and their predecessors' plans was genealogical, rather than coincidental. Before the Soviet seizure of power, government commissars, emissaries from the Ministry of Food Supply, and provincial food-supply committees—invoking Kerensky's September 8 order—had been petitioning the army for military units to secure grain. After October, many of these same officials, remaining at their posts, continued to request armed force to impose compliance with food-supply policies. Almost irrespective of the change in regime, through November and December the army quartermaster continued to dispatch military detachments from the front to be placed at the disposition of these committees.[136]

In January 1918 the Soviet government dissolved the old army in order to establish its own Red Army. When it did so, it transferred the functions of the military agency responsible since before October for dispatching armed force for civilian requisitioning, "the interfront commission for supplying military organizations," to the "Ministry [*sic*] of Food Supply."[137] Under the Soviets, the People's Commissariat of Food Supply (its proper term) would rely not only on armed units placed at its disposal by the military but also on its own "food-supply army."[138] In addition to the extensive loan of military force to civilian ministries practiced under the Provisional Government, the Soviet state would provide certain civilian ministries with their own military formations.

The Don Territory, however, did not recognize the new government, and Voronkov's Don Food-Supply Committee continued to meet through December. In this period the committee's activities were no more successful than they had been earlier. In addition to Voronkov, Urusov—the food-supply committee's leading cooperative activist—continued to participate in its meetings. Because local committees, Cossack and non-Cossack alike, continued to cater to their constituents rather than carry out their state tasks, the food-supply committee abolished elected food-supply boards and reassigned their responsibilities to the local administrative bodies. While the Cossack government prepared to crusade against Bolshevism in Russia, on the Don, Voronkov removed elected Cossack food-supply officials for insubordination and attempted to lecture Cossack communities that they couldn't simply seize grain in storage elevators, since "the grain in the Morozovskaia elevator belongs to the state."[139] Ominously for the cause of "state consciousness" and the Cossack government, his appeals had no more success among Cossacks than among non-Cossacks.

The Provisional Government and the Political Culture of 1917

The Russian Revolution had entered a new phase, that of civil war. The roots of civil war, however, are to be found within the revolution itself. "Educated society" had sought first to cultivate state consciousness through exhortation and agitation, only to see its hopes disappointed. The people who had established the post-February order did not sit by passively as it eroded. Advocates of "state consciousness," extending from the right through to moderate socialists, attempted to impose order on the system they had created, thereby further polarizing the political landscape.

Lacking a true civil society before 1914, Russia's educated society had coalesced over the course of 1914–1917 into a wartime parastatal complex under the aegis of the state. This was the first of two telescoped phases of development for Russian educated society during the period of war and revolution. This parastatal complex and its mobilizational techniques provided a common heritage for all political movements after 1917. The February Revolution finally provided Russia's political class with an opportunity to pursue its long-deferred dreams. Members of educated society initially held out much hope for the organic and spontaneous development of consciousness among the masses. But when the masses' behavior increasingly deviated from their own expectations, members of the political class turned to the state as the instrument necessary, in Vernadskii's words, to impose a "political organization of society" upon a chaotic "democracy." Here was the second telescoped stage of development: the growing willingness over the course of 1917 among members of Russia's educated society to employ wartime policies, not for warfare, but for reordering the political system and society. By autumn 1917 the Provisional Government had embraced a militarized and mobilizational form of politics. Although the government's aspirations were far greater than its actual results, these measures constituted the legacy directly inherited by the Soviet regime.

In this respect the Don Cossack government takes on particular significance. Earlier treatments of the Don Cossack movement have portrayed it as the expression either of the Cossacks' particularistic will or of some generic counterrevolutionary program.[140] Of course, both are partly true. The Cossack government indeed originated among traditionalist officers and bureaucrats hoping to provide a new foundation for a corporatist Cossack identity. Yet they now had to cast these claims in terms of the new political universe, as representing a social movement, and in so doing they radically widened the circle of participants. But the Cossack government also drew support from another current. As local and national advocates of state-consciousness became disillusioned with the course of the revolution, they came increasingly to see the Cossack government as a counterweight to irresponsible revolutionary institutions.

In a sense, the dilemmas of the Don Cossack government were simply the local analogue to the dilemmas of the Provisional Government at the national level. Rather than the expression of Cossack particularism, the measures of the Cossack government, especially from late summer, largely corresponded to those of the Provisional Government. Indeed, in some ways the Don Cossack government was more viable than its national counterpart. Cossacks provided a potential popular constituency that the Provisional Government could not claim after mid-1917. Moreover, the ethos of Cossack patriotism managed to unite moderates and antirevolutionary forces in a way the Provisional Government never could. Voronkov's path, from calling for a democratic constitutionalist order in early 1917 to relying on Cossack detachments and the particularistic Don Cossack government to instill state consciousness among the population, demonstrates the difficult path trod by many advocates of this ethos.

But the Cossack government was a self-proclaimed Cossack institution, one aspiring to represent the Cossacks as a distinct social movement. As such, it all but drove non-Cossacks into opposition to it and to its statist agenda. Its pro-statist, antirevolutionary program similarly alienated those who saw the revolution as an ongoing project for social justice. To the extent that Soviet power triumphed on the Don in early 1918, it did so in large part as the antipode to this Cossack agenda. Yet the gulf between "society" and "democracy" on the Don did not run neatly along the divide between Cossacks and non-Cossacks. Proponents of a corporatist vision of the Cossackry projected their own image of what it meant to be Cossack onto their putative constituency. That many Cossacks did not share the Cossack movement's program did not shake its proponents' belief in the Cossackry's corporate mission. The months to follow demonstrated how both the Cossack movement and Soviet power at the national level sought to impart orthodox meaning to their respective political movements—to provide some form of "political organization" to 1917's chaotic "democracy."

∼ 4

Toward Civil War

> Citizens, it seems that we all understand who the Bolsheviks are and
> who the Left Socialist Revolutionaries are. I believe that
> they are the very same people.
> ∼ Comrade Tuchniaev, April 1918

$\mathcal{I}$n May 1917 the Kadet Vladimir Vernadskii exhorted his
fellow citizens to embrace politics as a way of liberating themselves and
saving the nation. He sought to tutor them in the ways of modern politics:

> There are ominous epochs in the life of a country, when not a sin-
> gle citizen should morally dare to remain outside of political par-
> ties, since only by this means can he become a free citizen, can he
> in a normal way express his will and his thought in political life.[1]

Vernadskii, unlike the Bolsheviks, insisted on adherence to a party system rather than loyalty to one party. But Vernadskii was not alone in
believing that parties constituted the sole legitimate form of modern
political representation. All party activists, regardless of their particular
affiliation, shared the belief that they alone were the legitimate channels for political expression. Throughout 1917 they set themselves the
task of "partifying" Russia's political life. This would be a major challenge.

The experience of 1917 had unquestionably politicized people. But
party organizations—at least through early 1918—were not people's
primary form of political expression.[2] Political movements therefore
employed a variety of practices to secure some correlation between
their own political projection of social support and people's actual be-

havior. The Cossack government, for instance, had to exert much effort to align Cossacks behind "their" movement, as did the Bolsheviks with workers. Whether these projects succeeded or failed depended on the relative efficacy of the tools they used to communicate their visions, as well as the degree to which their political projections mapped onto people's lived experience.

The Collapse of the Cossack Government

Upon receiving telegraph reports of the Soviet seizure of power in Petrograd, the Cossack government convened a joint meeting with various Novocherkassk civic organizations, including delegates from both the city duma and the city soviet. To the acclaim of these civic organizations, the Cossack government declared itself the supreme authority for the Don Territory and imposed martial law in the western mining regions. Participants at the joint gathering, Cossack and non-Cossack alike, enthusiastically endorsed the government's decisive action. Even the moderate socialist speaker of the Novocherkassk City Soviet declared that his soviet had never shared the Bolsheviks' views and welcomed the Cossack government's promise to maintain order.[3]

But the Cossack government viewed itself not simply as the local government for the Don Territory, but as a pillar of Russian state interest. On October 27 the Cossack government offered the Provisional Government refuge on the Don, "where it is possible to organize a struggle against the Bolsheviks," as well as the support of the Don Cossacks for that forthcoming struggle.[4] In deliberations of the Cossack government, Voronkov, Arakantsev, and Petrovskii—Kadets all—counseled that it was essential to constitute state authority temporarily on the Don until the Constituent Assembly could meet.[5] Voronkov, in his capacity as commissar of the Provisional Government, and Pavel Ageev, speaking as a delegate to the Council of the Republic, urged the Cossack government to take immediate measures to establish a firm national authority.[6] Tellingly, Ageev and Voronkov spoke not as Cossacks but as representatives of the Provisional Government.

Meanwhile, Lieutenant General N. N. Dukhonin, the new commander in chief of the Russian Army, asked Ataman Kaledin to dispatch Cossack units to Moscow to put down the Bolshevik uprising there. Presuming they would accomplish that task, he asked Kaledin to send these Cossack units north to support the drive of another general of Don Cossack background, Peter Krasnov, against Petrograd itself. This request was soon made moot by the victory of Soviet forces in Moscow and Krasnov's defeat at Pulkovo Heights, the "Valmy of the Russian Revolution."[7] (Subsequently, Krasnov would become ataman of the reconstituted Don Cossack government in April 1918.) The Cossack government responded immediately to Dukhonin's request, proclaiming, "The Cossack government has decided, in order to save the dying Motherland, to move to an active struggle with the Bolsheviks outside the borders of the Don Territory, setting as our first task the seizure of Voronezh."[8]

As Dukhonin's requests make clear, Cossack politicians were not alone in viewing themselves as the preeminent force for Russian statehood. As during the Kornilov affair, many national leaders and ordinary Russians shared the Cossack leadership's image of the Don as a natural bulwark of Russia's statist principle. Among those who flooded to the Don were Paul Miliukov (national head of the Kadet Party), Mikhail Alekseev (supreme commander in chief from March to May 1917 and subsequently Kerensky's chief of staff), and nearly all the generals jailed for involvement in the Kornilov affair.

Yet, as was also evident during the Kornilov affair, rank-and-file Cossacks did not share the enthusiasm of their self-appointed leaders for a national crusade against Bolshevism. In response to Kaledin's sweeping orders to take Voronezh, the Cossack headquarters received a stream of troubling reports from Cossack units. Although they were prepared to defend their home region, these men balked at carrying the struggle beyond the borders of the Don Territory.[9]

The Cossack government's assumption of power in the Don Territory placed non-Cossack civic institutions in a dilemma. They had to respond simultaneously to the Bolshevik seizure of power in Petrograd and to the Cossack government's own seizure of power in the Don Territory. District peasant congresses, congresses of soviets and executive committees, as well as the Don-Kuban'-Terek cooperative organization, excoriated both actions, calling on all sides to observe the will of the soon-to-be-elected Constituent Assembly.[10] (The Cossack government's seizure of power, however, did not prevent Grigorii Urusov, head of the Don-Kuban'-Terek cooperative, from continuing to serve in the Don Food-Supply Committee alongside Voronkov.) Two weeks

after the overthrow of the Provisional Government, a territorial congress uniting the presidiums of executive committees, city dumas, and
other "democratic" civic organizations met. It condemned the Cossack
government's actions as "a simple seizure of power" and protested that
the Cossacks' initiatives threatened "the Revolution and the rest of the
Republic."[11]

But the Cossack government had not only proclaimed power; it had
also ordered "decisive measures" within the Don Territory. On November 1, the government declared martial law in those districts where
"Bolshevism" was on the rise: Rostov, Taganrog, Cherkassk, as well as
most cities in the territory.[12] Tellingly, the geography of regions placed
under martial law roughly corresponded to the distribution of the non-
Cossack, and especially the worker, population. "Bolshevism" for the
Cossack government meant first and foremost any opposition to its
own agenda. It dispatched punitive detachments to mining settlements
along the western border of the Don Territory, where they dissolved
local soviets without regard to their party affiliation.[13] This indiscriminate assault on all soviets eliminated any middle ground. Local soviets
that otherwise had reservations about the Bolshevik-led Soviet government in Petrograd found in it the sole counterweight to the Cossack
units sent to punish those who opposed Cossack rule.

In this tense environment, elections to the Constituent Assembly
were held from November 12 to November 14. On the Don as
throughout Russia, the election was far from ideal, but neither was it a
farce.[14] Throughout the territory, the Cossack slate, headed by
Kaledin, received 45 percent of the vote; the Socialist Revolutionaries,
34 percent; and the Bolsheviks, 15 percent. The returns varied with the
social geography of the Don Territory. The Cossack slate won by a
landslide in Cossack districts (66 percent of the total vote in both
Khoper and Ust'-Medveditsa, 71 percent in the Second Don District,
and 76 percent in the First Don District). Socialist Revolutionaries ran
first in peasant districts and second in Cossack districts. They also per-
formed well in certain Cossack regiments. The Bolsheviks received 40
percent of the vote in the cities of Rostov and Taganrog and did even
better in industrial and mining settlements (77 percent in Aleksandrovsk-Grushevskii, and 75 percent in Makeevka). They also ran a
strong second to the Socialist Revolutionaries in peasant districts. The
Kadets received a paltry 3 percent of the vote, but many leading Cos-

sack Kadet politicians ran on the Cossack slate.[15] Of the nine delegates to the Constituent Assembly apportioned to the Don Territory, the Cossack slate took seven, though it is important to note that this slate provided an umbrella for a broad range of political beliefs. Indeed, the seven delegates from the Cossack slate ranged from rightist members of the Cossack government (Kaledin and Bogaevsky), to individuals with long experience in the Kadet Party (Voronkov, Kharlamov, and Arakantsev, all three of whom were also former Duma deputies), to "nonparty socialists" (Mel'nikov and Ageev).

Events would prove, however, that voters ascribed different meaning to their votes than did the parties for whom they voted. Most rural dwellers had become politically active during the revolution, not through the mobilization of any particular party, but rather through the new political practices, such as regular electoral assemblies and voting. For many, especially in the countryside, voting in the Constituent Assembly elections was their first experience with specific party programs.[16] The Provisional Government's own overview of reportage on the election campaign, noting a general apathy, observed that the "greatest activity in terms of party preparation" was displayed not by any political party but rather by the "soviets of workers' and soldiers' deputies."[17] Yet, as there was no slate for these soviets *per se*, the elections reduced political attitudes to a limited menu of party programs. Only by the end of 1918 would affiliation with a particular party overlap with allegiance to specific forms of political representation. Movements like the Don Cossack government viewed the outcome of the elections to the Constituent Assembly as an endorsement from an entire social group only at their own risk.

The Cossack government asserted its claim to sovereignty in the territory by ignoring non-Cossack executive committees and by dispatching punitive detachments to those regions where local soviets opposed it. The true test, however, was Rostov, the largest industrial and urban center in the Don Territory. There moderate socialists, whose base was the municipal organizations, and local Bolsheviks, who dominated the city soviet after reelections in mid-October, formed a joint "military revolutionary committee of united democracy."[18] This new organ responded to the Cossack government's declaration of power by proclaiming itself to be the supreme organ for the Don Territory instead. After the Soviet government appointed Vladimir Antonov-Ovseenko as its special commissar to combat counterrevolution in early December, Bolsheviks in Rostov requested aid from the revolutionary Black Sea Fleet. But the arrival of several ships from the fleet as a revolutionary shock force divided the once unified military revolutionary committee. When the moderate socialists balked at employing the new arrivals, the Rostov Soviet formed a new, hard-line military revolutionary committee without them. But before it could take any action, local officer cadets attacked both the Rostov Soviet and the Bolshevik Party headquarters.[19] This preemptive strike, however, only united workers of all political stripes in defense of "their" soviet. It had the additional effect of casting the Bolsheviks as the leading defenders of local soviets, and not just "Soviet power" at the national level. In a fatal error, the local Socialist Revolutionary and Menshevik committees called for "civil reconciliation," a call that fell on deaf ears among their own followers as well as among the officers.[20] Red Guards, aided by the Black Sea Fleet's transport ship *Kolkhida*, drove the officer cadets back to the train station. After two days of fighting, the Red Guards took control of the city.

When Ataman Kaledin ordered Cossack units to take back Rostov, he discovered that Cossacks in the ranks, and even many Cossack officers, did not share his crusading, anti-Bolshevik program. When one Cossack lieutenant colonel received orders to move on Rostov, he asked his troops, "Well boys, do we go?" They answered, "Let's not." The officer then responded, "I don't think it's worth it, either."[21] Unable to rely on its own Cossack regiments to take Rostov, the Cossack government was forced to depend on elite shock detachments, such as Cossack Captain Vasilii Chernetsov's "partisan brigade." Such units consisted almost exclusively of students, officer cadets, and volunteers who had come to the Don expressly to fight Bolshevism.[22]

Throughout Russia, however, people still believed in a monolithic, counterrevolutionary Cossackry. "Fantastic rumors circulated about Kaledin's forces approaching Moscow," Miliukov recalled, "and defenders of order and the legitimate Provisional Government, who had been routed in Moscow, began to flood to the Don."[23] Diarists in Moscow and Saratov awaited the arrival of Don Cossacks to put down Soviet power in their cities.[24] The Don's image as a Russian Vendée attracted to it all those who opposed the new Soviet government. Indeed, it was these arrivals, rather than the Cossacks themselves, who transformed the mirage of a "Russian Vendée" into a reality. Among the most prominent was General Mikhail Alekseev, the former commander in chief, who began establishing the core of what was to become the anti-Soviet Volunteer Army. Alekseev chose the Don, in his own words, because it "was a territory that was well-supplied in terms of grain" and because he "assumed that, with the Cossackry's help, we could calmly form the new, firm units necessary for restoring order in Russia and for strengthening the front. I viewed the Don as a base of operations against the Bolsheviks."[25] Generals Anton Denikin (who had served under Kaledin in 1916), A. S. Lukomskii, Sergei Markov, and later Lavr Kornilov joined Alekseev, all with similar plans for the Don.

Paul Miliukov and Boris Savinkov headed a long list of political activists who also flooded to the territory.[26] During the period after October and before the convocation of the Constituent Assembly in early January, most members of the Kadet Central Committee spent time in the Don Territory. Andrei Shingarev, the Provisional Government's first minister of agriculture, also traveled to the Don. It was from there that he returned to Petrograd as a delegate to the Constituent Assembly in January, to meet his death at the hands of revolutionary sailors. There was even talk of transferring the Kadet Central Committee to the Don.[27]

Not only the generals but also the foot soldiers of the future anti-Bolshevik movement streamed south. Officer cadets who had fought the Bolsheviks in Moscow in October 1917, rather than surrender after their defeat, went "south, to the Cossacks," in order to gather "forces for the further struggle."[28] As one non-Cossack officer recalled, they went because "Russia hoped to gather itself on the Cossack Don, under Kaledin's leadership." There they sought "a milieu particularly favorable to the growth of nationalist sentiments ... The Russian Cossackry, and particularly the Don Cossack government ... became the focus and source of national energy."[29] As a result of these visions, by the beginning of 1918 ten thousand officers and officer cadets had flocked to Rostov and another sixteen thousand to Novocherkassk.[30] Among these officers were men who, though officially Don Cossacks by estate criteria, had left the Don long ago. Some had never lived there. The anti-Bolshevik struggle brought them back to their "native Don."[31] Kaledin, who until this point had been ambivalent about working with these arrivals, found that he required their military support. Units of these anti-Bolshevik crusaders, rather than Don Cossacks, retook Rostov in December.

Such measures, added to Kaledin's previous actions, only confirmed preexisting views among Soviet supporters that Cossacks were counterrevolutionary paladins. In early December the Soviet government dispatched an expeditionary force to "wipe off the face of the earth the counterrevolutionary rebellion of the Cossack generals and the Kadet bourgeoisie."[32] On December 8 the new government appointed Vladimir Antonov-Ovseenko, who during the Bolshevik seizure of power had organized the storming of the Winter Palace, as "main commander in chief for the struggle against counterrevolution in the South of Russia," with specific instructions to act against Kaledin.[33] Red Guardsmen in these detachments, some literally brought up on lurid tales of Cossack violence against workers, thought of Cossacks as inveterate counterrevolutionaries.[34]

The Don Territory came to play an exaggerated role in the civil wars more because of long-standing stereotypes about Cossacks than because of actual Cossack behavior. By and large, rank-and-file Cossacks were willing to defend the Don Territory against Soviet expeditionary forces, but Kaledin's aggressive anti-Bolshevik actions found little support among them.[35] The Cossack government summoned a Third Large Circle to rally support for its actions, just as it had done earlier with the Second Large Circle following the Kornilov affair. The elections, however, demonstrate the splintering of Cossack opinion, despite the pretensions of traditionalist and republican Cossack leaders alike to speak for a united Cossackry. Election protocols for several communities show that by December Cossack voters, especially in Cossack military units, no longer united behind their primary candidates. Some delegates received less than half the possible positive votes—meaning that more people opposed than supported them. But they attended the circle because they had more support than any other candidates. Other delegates brought with them petitions from their constituents condemning the Cossack government's declaration of martial law and its plans for a military crusade against Bolshevism. These electors expressed fear that such actions would involve the Don in a struggle against the rest of Russia.[36]

The Cossack government managed to rally the delegates behind its suppression of the Rostov uprising, aided no doubt by the fact that the uprising had already been successfully put down. Yet so widespread was the desire for an end to confrontation that the circle, pressed by delegates from Cossack military units, voted to send a delegation to Moscow for negotiations with the Soviet government. The delegation met with Stalin in his capacity as commissar for nationalities in mid-December. (The shift from defining Cossacks as an estate to seeing them as an ethnic or national group was already occurring.)[37] The Cossack delegates asked why the Soviets were sending forces against the Don and argued in vain that Kaledin represented the true will of the Cossackry. Stalin countered that the Soviet government was for the laboring Cossackry but against counterrevolution, headed by Kaledin. If laboring Cossacks were indeed so blind as to support Kaledin, Stalin warned, the Soviet government would soon set this error right—even if in the process laboring Cossacks might suffer from the "ricochet" of Soviet actions. Delegates of the Eighth Cossack Division, which thus far had refused to carry out Kaledin's orders, hastened to assure Stalin that Cossacks themselves would set their own house in order. Invoking the Soviet government's own declarations on the right of self-determination, they declared that they did not need the help of Soviet punitive expeditions. Stalin concluded, "We prefer to work by peaceful means, by means of propaganda and agitation, but we will act with force when necessary." This exchange of views concluded without resolution.[38]

The circle also made a belated attempt at reconciliation with its opponents within the Don Territory. After having blocked the establishment of the zemstvo institutions in the Don since August, the Cossack government in late November finally approved their introduction in peasant districts.[39] It also permitted peasant representatives to attend the Third Circle, albeit with only a consultative vote. Yet even those few non-Cossack communities that considered sending delegates found the circle less than eager to have them. Just before the circle was to meet, the Donets District Soviet inquired whether the Third Circle would be held and, if so, whether it should send delegates. The soviet sent a second telegram after the assembly had already met, scolding the circle for failing to respond to its original request.[40] At the circle, however, Kaledin argued that the Cossack government could no longer rely on the Cossack population alone. He then proposed to include all segments of the population through a system of "parity," under which the government would be composed of seven Cossack delegates and seven delegates from all other segments of the population, to be elected by a special "congress of the non-Cossack population." Until then, three non-Cossacks (a Menshevik and two Socialist Revolutionaries) would enter the Cossack government as observers. To participate in the government, however, non-Cossack representatives would have to recognize the Volunteer Army, the only force upon which the Cossack government could rely, and support continued military operations against Soviet power.

Non-Cossack institutions did not respond with one voice. Most were unenthusiastic about a bald choice between either the national Soviet government or the territory's Cossack government. Mensheviks and Socialist Revolutionaries faced a particularly difficult choice. By October 1917, the Rostov Socialist Revolutionary organization was in shambles. Although it numbered 8,000 members at the height of its popularity, one Rostov activist reported to the party's national newspaper that by early November it could barely muster 150 members for meetings. During the October reelections to the city soviet, most Socialist Revolutionaries had voted for Bolshevik candidates.[41] The Menshevik speaker of the Novocherkassk Soviet had from the beginning supported the Cossack government's claim to power in the region.[42] During the Rostov uprising, Menshevik and Right Socialist Revolutionaries summoned a meeting of democratic organizations. This gathering of moderate socialists demanded the temporary transfer of all power in the territory to the Cossack government. Delegates from the two parties attended the Third Circle and detailed their attempts to mediate between the two sides during the fighting.[43] With the Bolsheviks facing repression after the December events in Rostov, Mensheviks and Socialist Revolutionaries dominated most city dumas and soviets. Their ascendancy in this period further linked moderate socialists with the Cossack government. Thus any backlash against the Cossack government would also strike at them.

Local soviets faced similar dilemmas. The Cherkassk District Congress of Peasant Deputies endorsed the formation of a joint government founded on the principle of parity in representation. It did so "despite the fact that Cossacks walked out of [the executive committees] over eight months ago . . . and although the [Cossack government's appeal for parity] does not recognize the equality of all citizens in government and self-government." Over much opposition, the congress dispatched four electors to the non-Cossack congress summoned by the Cossack government. But it also composed a petition to the Constituent Assembly demanding the redistribution of all land, including Cossack land.[44] For most people, however, the Cossack government's concessions were too little, too late. The Territorial Congress of Peasants (a different assembly from the Cossack government's proposed "congress of non-Cossacks") met in Rostov on December 27 and promptly voted to recognize the Soviet government.[45] Even the delegates elected to attend the "congress of non-Cossacks," sponsored by the Cossack leadership, were reluctant to endorse the Cossack government's parity proposal. After heated debates, the congress voted 62 to 44 to endorse a united government of Cossacks and non-Cossacks. Even then, the congress made participation conditional on the Cossack government's lifting martial law and exerting strict control over the volunteer detachments, acceptance of which the Cossack government had made a precondition of participation in the united government.[46]

The united government proved a dismal failure. Kaledin continued his active anti-Soviet measures behind its back. He entered into a "triumvirate" with Generals Alekseev and Kornilov and conducted negotiations with Miliukov, Struve, Rodzianko, and Savinkov to coordinate the national struggle against the Bolsheviks.[47] To achieve these goals, however, Kaledin found himself relying more and more on anti-Bolshevik "volunteer" detachments. All six detachments defending the approaches to Rostov in January 1918 were either officer or student formations. Of the forces directly subordinate to the Cossack government, the most reliable were again those made up of officers and students, such as Cossack Captain Chernetsov's partisan detachment. To stiffen the resolve of Cossack units, the Cossack government dispatched units of officers and students. Other officer units exacerbated the already poor relations between Cossacks and officers by breaking cease-fires established between individual Cossack units and Soviet forces.[48] By this point, a war mentality had enveloped the political struggle. The new Soviet government dispatched expeditionary detachments to crush "Counterrevolution," while the Cossack government relied more and more on its small, elite officer formations.

The evident disinclination of many Cossacks to fight Bolshevism did not cause anti-Bolshevik leaders to reconsider their faith in the

Cossackry. One officer, assigned after his arrival on the Don to the Cossack government's Department of Military Intelligence, noted the inability of the Cossack leadership to part with its quixotic vision of sixty full Cossack regiments ready to crusade against Bolshevism.[49] In part, Cossacks played to these images. When their officers rejected an appeal for a transfer from the overwhelmingly peasant Taganrog District, Cossacks in the Life Guard Regiment sent delegates directly to Kaledin himself. There they requested a transfer to their native Donets District, in order, they claimed, to protect their hearths from marauding Bolshevik hordes. Once they arrived in the district, they promptly dispersed to their homes.[50]

Cossack republicanism, which had been growing throughout 1917, and hostility to the Cossack government, which peaked in late 1917, coalesced and took political form in early January 1918.[51] Cossack units deployed in the Donets region to fend off Soviet expeditionary forces convened a "congress of front-line Cossacks," which met in the Donets District capital of Kamenskaia on January 10.[52] Twenty-one Cossack regiments, five artillery batteries, and two reserve regiments sent delegates. Kaledin sent a telegram to the congress while it was in session threatening its organizers with arrest. The congress indignantly responded by forming a Cossack military revolutionary committee, with a fifteen-member presidium headed by Fedor Grigorevich Podtelkov.

Opposing the Cossack government, however, was not the same as an endorsement of Soviet power on the part of the Kamenskaia military revolutionary committee. Although there were Soviet sympathizers at the congress, the Cossack delegates believed they had their own political program, one that they explicitly distinguished from the Soviet one. In addressing the population of Kamenskaia, Podtelkov declared that the military revolutionary committee "was composed not of some unknown Bolsheviks, but of those Cossacks who decided to make peace with the Bolsheviks and with Soviet power, in order to end the bloodshed and finish off the counterrevolution with as few victims as possible."[53] The fifteen-member Cossack military revolutionary committee numbered only two Bolsheviks: Ippolit Doroshov, a party member since June 1917; and S. I. Kudinov, a Social Democrat–Internationalist.

As Podtelkov's declaration makes clear, the Cossack delegates were willing to negotiate with Soviet forces but did not accept the Soviet program for themselves. The Cossack military revolutionary committee sought a cease-fire with Soviet forces and offered to end the Don's struggle against the rest of Russia by expelling all those officers who were attempting to turn the Don into a staging area against Soviet Russia. The commissar for the revolutionary forces from Moscow, who was in the territory attending the congress, telegraphed the Soviet government with his evaluation of the Cossacks. "Characteristic of the whole movement," he wrote, "is the desire, on the one hand, to finish off Kaledin and drive off the officers, officer cadets, and White Guards, but, on the other hand, a reluctance to allow Bolshevik forces to do this."[54] The congress pointedly did not embrace Soviet power for the Don Territory. It called instead for a "congress of the laboring Cossackry, workers, and peasants," in order to organize the true "power of the laborers" [*trudovaia vlast'*] on the Don. The phrasing was not an oversight. Indeed, A. V. Mandel'shtam, observing on behalf of Soviet military forces, noted that the congress "could not bring itself to declare itself a congress of soviets . . . It seemed to me that Podtelkov had serious doubts about the establishment of soviet power."[55] For Mandel'shtam, the term "soviet" signified much more than a mechanism of representation. The endorsement of "soviets" was meant to seal adherence to the new revolutionary republic. In refraining from using the word "soviet," Cossack delegates both indicated a specific form of power for their region and abstained from endorsing central Soviet control.

The Kamenskaia military revolutionary committee sent delegates simultaneously to both the Cossack government and the commander of the Soviet expeditionary force, Antonov-Ovseenko. In a meeting with members of the Kamenskaia committee, Antonov-Ovseenko made Soviet support for the military revolutionary organ dependent upon three conditions: the Cossacks would have to accept the Soviet government; convene not just another circle but a congress of soviets representing *all* segments of the population; and coordinate their military campaign against Kaledin with the Soviet command. The delegation from the military revolutionary committee equivocated, claiming it was authorized to discuss only military issues, and so the meeting ended without resolution.[56]

Meanwhile, a larger delegation from the military revolutionary committee, including its leaders, traveled to Novocherkassk to meet with the Cossack government. When the two sides met on January 15,

Podtelkov set out the military revolutionary committee's demands. The Cossack government must transfer command of all units to the military revolutionary committee; recall and disarm all volunteer detachments operating against revolutionary forces; and disperse the circle and transfer power to the military revolutionary committee until the "permanent power of the laborers can be established in the territory." In these discussions, the Cossack republicans' equivocal attitude to Soviet power was again evident. Mikhail Krivoshlykov, who had been elected secretary of the Kamenskaia Military-Revolutionary Committee, declared that "the Cossacks will not accept any organ that includes members of the Kadet Party. We are Cossacks and we ought to have our own rule, Cossack rule." When pressed by members of the Cossack government to state what they had in common with "Bronstein" (Trotsky's true name, and clearly invoked to emphasize his Jewishness), Podtelkov answered: "We have nothing in common with them. We are Cossacks and not Bolsheviks. We want to introduce Cossack rule, and not party rule."[57] In this response, Krivoshlykov and Podtelkov rejected not the Kadets or Bolsheviks *per se*, but the entire concept of party rule.

Kaledin's extensive interest in the views of the Cossack delegation had another purpose. In contrast to Antonov-Ovseenko, who had called off a planned offensive so as not to antagonize the rebellious Cossacks, Kaledin had surreptitiously dispatched the Chernetsov detachment to deal with the Cossack military revolutionary committee in Kamenskaia. That evening, upon learning that Chernetsov had surprised the unsuspecting Cossack units and driven them back, the Cossack government presented its response to the military revolutionary committee delegation in the form of a counterultimatum. Negotiations broke down.

Chernetsov's surprise attack enjoyed temporary tactical success, but this victory served only to drive the Cossack military revolutionary committee into the arms of the Soviet command. Feeling betrayed, the returning delegates rejected any further negotiations with the Cossack government. The next day, Chernetsov seized Kamenskaia itself, forcing the military revolutionary committee to relocate to Millerovo. Under pressure from Chernetsov, the committee telegraphed Antonov-Ovseenko: "the political question in principle is resolved. Absolutely yes, yes, yes [to each of Antonov-Ovseenko's three conditions]. An official yes. A declaration will follow shortly." To address fears that central Soviet legislation on the land issue would be foisted upon the Don, the subsequent official acceptance included an addendum indicating that the territorial congress demanded by Antonov-Ovseenko should also be the organ to determine the land question for the Don Territory.[58] Antonov-Ovseenko then issued orders for his forces to come to the aid of the Cossack military revolutionary committee. Within several days, revolutionary Cossack units had routed Chernetsov's detachment and killed Chernetsov himself. According to some accounts, Podtelkov personally cut him down.[59] The military threat had passed. But it had pushed Cossack republicans unambiguously into the camp of Soviet power.

Although they had agreed to joint operations with Soviet forces, the rebellious Cossack regiments retained their own commanders. At the recommendation of the Twenty-fourth Don Cossack Regiment, Antonov-Ovseenko appointed Mikhail Smirnov "commander of the revolutionary Cossack headquarters." Smirnov was a member of the Kamenskaia military revolutionary committee, but he was not a Bolshevik. He was a paragon of Cossack republicanism. During the First World War he had advanced from third lieutenant to full lieutenant, earning all four orders of the St. George's Cross along the way.[60] Golubov, who had barely escaped being expelled from the Cossack estate by the Cossack Circle in August 1917, also coveted the post of commander of revolutionary Cossack forces.[61] Neither Smirnov nor Golubov had any distinct party affiliation. Most Cossacks, however, had no problem identifying their political program.

With the death of Chernetsov, the Cossack government lost the one force upon which it could fully rely. The various non-Cossack volunteer detachments that had suppressed the Rostov uprising in November 1917 were now being formed into the Volunteer Army. The leaders of this new army informed Kaledin that they were planning to abandon the Don Territory, on account of both the deteriorating military situation and tensions with the Cossack government. By the end of January 1918, only a few Cossack communities around Novocherkassk itself remained true to Kaledin's government. The Cossack government resorted to what had worked before, summoning a Fourth Circle for February 1918. Only Cossack communities in the southern districts even bothered to hold elections this time, and in those that did the results did not bode well for the Cossack government. The unanimity so evident in elections to the First Circle in May 1917 had collapsed. Some delegates garnered more negative votes than positive ones, yet still attended as delegates because other candidates had even less support. In May 1917 Tsymlianskaia stanitsa, for instance, had sent three delegates, receiving 96 percent, 67 percent, and 60 percent, respectively, of the total vote, to the First Circle; in the January 1918 elections, the three delegates for the Fourth Circle could collect only 59 percent, 40 percent, and 39 percent, respectively, of the total vote.[62]

Reeling from the defection of Cossack units, Chernetsov's rout, and the imminent departure of the Volunteer Army, Kaledin's government relinquished power on January 29. Kaledin then retired to his office and shot himself. The Novocherkassk stanitsa assembly elected General A. M. Nazarov as his replacement until the Fourth Circle could meet on February 4. In the circumstances, only some of those few delegates elected actually arrived to attend the circle. The futility of attempting to continue the "parity" government was demonstrated when no delegates showed up for a "congress of non-native inhabitants." The Fourth Circle ordered a full mobilization of Cossacks to defend the Don "to the last drop of blood." But mobilization proved a dismal failure. In any case, most draft-age Cossacks had been in regiments that had already turned their backs on the Cossack government. Acting Ataman Nazarov had to inform the Volunteer Army that the Cossacks could offer it no help in its struggle, and the Volunteer Army then decamped to the Kuban' Territory.

The circle next dispatched a delegation to negotiate with the Soviet command, asking in particular why Soviet Russia was waging war now that Kaledin had killed himself. Speaking for the Soviet forces, Iurii Vladimirovich Sablin, a Left Socialist Revolutionary leading one of the two Soviet columns, responded that the Cossack government must recognize Soviet power and that all counterrevolutionaries and officers must be expelled from the Don.[63] While promising to allow Cossacks to retain as much land as they needed, Sablin also added that all estates, including the Cossacks, must be abolished, along with all their privileges.[64] The two sides were clearly irreconcilable, and the Soviet command continued its offensive. Soviet forces occupied Rostov on February 23, and revolutionary Cossack regiments marched into Novocherkassk on February 25. General Popov led the few remaining anti-Soviet volunteers and Cossack diehards out of the city, embarking on the so-called Steppe March, the Don Army's analogue to the Volunteer Army's "Ice March." Nazarov, Kaledin's successor as ataman, remained in the city. Golubov, leading the revolutionary units entering the city, arrested him in the nearly deserted meeting hall of the Cossack Circle. Upon arresting him, Golubov declared himself "revolutionary ataman." Nazarov was executed six days later. The Cossack government was no more.

Centralized "Soviet Power" versus Local "Power of the Soviets"

The Soviet expeditionary forces, operating alongside Cossack republican units taking orders from the Cossack military revolutionary committee, had achieved their joint objective: driving out the Don Cossack government. Despite their cooperation, Soviet forces and local Cossack formations continued to negotiate the nature of their relationship. Responding to questions from Cossack inhabitants of Mitiakinskaia stanitsa, members of the Cossack military revolutionary committee insisted that their group remained a specifically Cossack organ. They portrayed the Soviet expeditionary force as comrades-in-arms against the officers and generals in the Volunteer Army, but added that Soviet forces should leave the Don now that this task had been accomplished. In order "to avoid agitating the Cossack population," the Cossack military revolutionary committee insisted that it officially retain supreme command over operations against the Cossack government, even if Antonov-Ovseenko was in fact in charge of the overall campaign.[65] Finally, in the third week of February 1918, the Cossack military revolutionary committee merged with the rump Don military revolutionary committee, which had fled Rostov three months earlier.[66] This new body in principle claimed to represent the entire population, thereby fulfilling in part the Cossack military revolutionary committee's earlier promise to Antonov-Ovseenko to convene a congress of soviets to represent the entire population, and not just Cossacks.

For their part, central Soviet officials remained suspicious of the Cossacks.[67] Yet however much they might have distrusted Cossack sentiments, members of the new central Soviet government were in no position to disregard them. To the extent that Soviet power was advancing into the Don Territory, it was doing so alongside Cossack republican regiments. But Soviet officials had another concern. The Soviet advance into the Don was taking place at the very same time that Soviet delegates were negotiating the Brest-Litovsk Treaty with the Central Powers.[68] In the course of those negotiations, from December 22 (new style), 1917, to February 10, 1918, both sides loudly affirmed the principle of national self-determination. In response to German claims that the Ukrainian Rada in Kiev spoke for Ukraine, Soviet delegates insisted that the Khar'kov-based Soviet Ukrainian government held that privilege. Lenin was acutely aware of these disputes. In a telegram that only in passing congratulated Antonov-Ovseenko on his victory over Kaledin, Lenin lectured him on the need to retain the goodwill of the Khar'kov Soviet: "For God's sake, make every effort *to overcome any and all* disputes with the [Ukrainian] Central Executive Committee (the Khar'kov one). This is *of arch-importance* for *reasons of state*. For God's sake, make up with them, and grant them *any sort* of autonomy."[69]

Negotiations at Brest-Litovsk had broken down in mid-February, and the Central Powers advanced into Ukraine and toward the Don Territory. At this point questions of autonomy became even more urgent. At the Bad Homburg Crown Council, which met on February 13, 1918, Wilhelm II had decided to portray the advance as an attempt to provide assistance to national movements in combating "bandits." The council discussed orchestrating "appeals for help" from the areas slated for German occupation, so that the military operation could be cast as national liberation.[70] Five days later (February 18), German forces resumed their advance, occupying vast tracts of Ukraine and pushing to the borders of the Don Territory. At Lenin's frantic urging, Antonov-Ovseenko finally seized Rostov on February 23, and Cossack republican forces entered Novocherkassk the next day, thereby putting an end both to the Don Cossack government and, presumably, to any possibility that the Germans could claim to be acting in support of its "self-determination."[71]

As German forces continued to advance in Ukraine, Antonov-Ovseenko telegraphed Lenin on February 26 for guidance in his negotiations with Cossack spokesmen on the issue of autonomy. Lenin responded within two days: "I have nothing against autonomy for the Don Territory."[72] Several days later, on March 3, the Soviet government signed the Brest-Litovsk Treaty, recognizing Ukrainian independence. The treaty, however, did not demarcate the boundary between the German-supported Ukraine and Soviet Russia south of Brest-Litovsk. Thus, as German forces advanced into Ukraine as permitted by the treaty, there was no established territorial limit to their advance, so long as they claimed that they were advancing through "Ukrainian" territory. In fact, the German military command had decided at the very least to secure control of the Donbass coal fields (portions of which were in the Don Territory) and several Black Sea ports, including Taganrog, Rostov, and even Novorossiisk, in the Kuban' Territory.[73]

With the Soviet Republic lacking any real armed force, ethnoterritorial republics became the sole barrier to the advancing German Army in early and mid-1918. When the Germans threatened to advance beyond the newly established Ukraine, the Soviets on March 23 hurriedly proclaimed a "Don Soviet Republic." Sergei Syrtsov, the leading figure among the Bolsheviks in Rostov and a member of the new joint Don military revolutionary committee, justified this act to the Rostov Soviet. He explained that "the Don Republic is necessary to deny the Germans and Austrians . . . grounds for using their armed forces to come to the aid of self-determination. We should say to them: we have already practiced self-determination, and therefore you have nothing to do here."[74] The Don military revolutionary committee acted so swiftly that it did not even wait for a congress of soviets to be convened—one would meet two weeks afterward—before declaring a "soviet" republic.

The central Soviet government struggled to present a unified front in dealing with the Germans. But centralized "Soviet power" did not speak for all local soviets. There remained a gulf between the "power of [local] soviets" [*vlast' sovetov*] and the center's orthodox form of "Soviet power" [*sovetskaia vlast'*]. In Rostov, the city soviet repeatedly clashed with Antonov-Ovseenko's appointee as military commissar for the Don region, Voitsekhovskii. Repression under Kaledin had diminished the Bolshevik presence in Rostov and led to a renascence of the historically powerful Menshevik organization in that city. The Rostov Soviet and city military revolutionary committee condemned Voitsekhovskii's censorship of the local press (including the soviet's own organ) and the numerous arrests made on his orders.[75] In response, Antonov-

Ovseenko announced his intention to disperse the soviet. While recognizing that power belonged to the soviet in principle, Antonov-Ovseenko declared that it belonged "only to a revolutionary soviet, and your soviet is no good." Voitsekhovskii archly proclaimed that in order to strengthen the power of soviets, he was willing to suppress soviets standing in the way. A conciliatory speech by Evgenii Trifonov, a native of the Don and a leading Bolshevik with Antonov-Ovseenko's forces, called for revolutionary unity above parties. He brokered an agreement according to which Voitsekhovskii would henceforth "coordinate" his actions with the Rostov military revolutionary committee.[76] The Rostov Soviet's difficulties with Voitsekhovskii ended when he absconded with a large sum of money. City elections then returned a soviet narrowly dominated by Mensheviks. Soviet military authorities simply expelled the Menshevik and moderate Socialist Revolutionary members. Power then passed from the Rostov military revolutionary committee to this rump soviet, now "revolutionary" enough for Antonov-Ovseenko.[77]

Both the Bolshevik and the Menshevik accounts of this struggle reduce it to a conflict between the two parties. But this party lens, be it Bolshevik or Menshevik, fails to capture the political fluidity of the period. While the supposedly "Bolshevik" rump of the Rostov City Soviet indeed closed down the Menshevik newspapers, Left Socialist Revolutionary and even Anarchist newspapers continued to be published alongside the Bolshevik paper. During the "Bolshevik occupation" of Rostov, Left Socialist Revolutionaries occupied many key posts, including chairman of the Rostov Soviet and head of the Nakhichevan Red Guard.[78] Rather than a divide between clearly delineated parties, then, there was a ragged split between all those favoring a more radical course for the revolution, who tended to gravitate toward the Bolsheviks and the Left Socialist Revolutionaries, and advocates of a more moderate course, for whom the Mensheviks served as a compass. To be sure, Antonov-Ovseenko's high-handed actions weakened support for the Bolsheviks, but this did not necessarily benefit the parties opposed to the Bolsheviks. Delegates to a congress of Menshevik organizations reported that the decline of Bolshevik support in the industrial settlement of Aleksandrovsk-Grushevskii benefited the even more radical Anarchists. In the mining community of Makeevka, disillusionment with the Bolsheviks yielded a generalized distrust of *all* political parties.[79]

In the countryside, the fluidity of party identification was even greater than in urban and mining areas. Most rural inhabitants had become politically active over the course of 1917 through political institutions rather than through any specific party.[80] Just as in early 1917 the Don Executive Committee had mandated the formation of civic executive committees, in early 1918 the new Don military revolutionary committee issued guidelines describing how local soviets were to be established.[81] But for most rural inhabitants, the establishment of a local soviet did not signify adoption of "Soviet power" as understood by people such as Antonov-Ovseenko. Although the spread of rural soviets certainly represented the "power of the soviets," it was not necessarily "Soviet power."[82]

Soldiers returning to their home communities were the most common proselytizers of the concept of the "power of the soviets." This phenomenon was true throughout Russia. But returning soldiers established local soviets somewhat differently in the Don Territory than elsewhere. Cossack regiments were territorially based, and hence they often returned to their communities as entire units rather than as individual soldiers. Many soviets in Cossack communities arose precisely with the return of regiments from the front in early 1918.[83]

Soldiers were not the only proselytizers of the new order. By late 1917, many non-Cossack communities viewed "Soviet power" first and foremost as the only force willing and able to challenge local Cossack hegemony. In late 1917 and early 1918 local communities therefore dispatched delegates to investigate the new order. These delegates returned with reports that the new government recognized only soviets as legitimate organs of representation. In December 1918 delegates from peasant counties in the Rostov and Sal' districts traveled to the Third Congress of Soviets, meeting in Petrograd. Upon their return, the delegates pressed their communities to transform their local civic executive committees into soviets. These delegates had attended the congress of soviets not as representatives of any actual soviet, which came into existence only after their return, but out of interest in the policies supported by the congress.[84]

Even in places where citizens did not welcome the establishment of a soviet, they recognized that it was now the only accepted form of representation. Throughout December 1917 the Cossack settlement of Usov petitioned the food-supply board and Cossack authorities in Kepinskaia stanitsa, the Cossack community to which it belonged, to supply it with much-needed provisions. The Usov Cossack assembly met under the chairmanship of its Cossack ataman, who had been elected in April 1917 and reelected in August. In desperation, by late 1917 the Usov community assembly appealed to the Frolov settlement food-supply board to take it under its protection. Because it was located on the railway line, Frolov was better supplied than Kepinskaia. It had also recently established a soviet encompassing Cossacks, peasants, soldiers, and workers. The Frolov Soviet agreed to absorb Usov and look after its food-supply needs—but only if Usov elected a soviet. The community, supported by its ataman, unanimously voted to do so.[85]

Many communities simply re-christened existing local boards and executive committees as their "soviet." In Konovalov khutor (Migulinskaia stanitsa), news of the entry of Soviet forces into Novocherkassk prompted discussion about establishing a soviet. Many were opposed to the move, but Cossacks returning from the front were in favor of it. Aleksei Tret'iakov, a Cossack officer-trainee just back from Novocherkassk and a member of an influential family in the community, advised changing the name from a Cossack administration to a soviet. Although several Cossacks who had returned from the front were elected to the new "soviet," the community's former ataman became the soviet's chairman and Tret'iakov served as its secretary.[86] In this uncertain environment, other communities hedged their bets by both maintaining the old community boards and electing a new soviet, with the two cooperating to prevent outside intervention in the life of the community.[87]

The soviet as an organ offered a new, universal form of representation and implied new principles of legitimacy. Soviets were meant to represent all segments of the laboring population, especially when those segments had earlier been administratively segregated. One of the key demands of the Soviet expeditionary force to the Cossack military revolutionary committee at Kamenskaia was that it convene a congress of soviets representing the entire population. The Soviet command enforced this demand in late February, merging the previously separate Cossack military revolutionary committee and the rump Don military revolutionary committee, which had fled Rostov in December 1917, into a new, united "Don military revolutionary committee."[88] Rural inhabitants, too, were aware that the soviet as an institution dictated a universalistic syntax of representation. In January 1918 the Cossack settlement of Oblivskii elected a joint Cossack-peasant committee that could double, if need be, as the community's soviet.[89] The community was aware that even a semifictitious soviet must include both peasants and Cossacks.

Throughout the Don Territory, Cossack military revolutionary committees and regimental committees provided a means for Cossacks to embrace "Soviet power" without entering into joint soviets. Although a joint Cossack and non-Cossack "united Don revolutionary committee" was formed at the territorial level, beneath it Cossack military revolutionary committees, growing out of regimental organs of returning units, continued to stand in for district soviets. In northern Khoper District, the district peasant congress voted to recognize the (Cossack) military revolutionary committee only on the condition that it convene a joint peasant-Cossack congress, with proportional representation.[90] A district congress of soviets did not meet until March 10. Until that time the district military revolutionary committee implemented only those measures of the Soviet government that "did not contradict the conditions particular to the Don Territory." As late as May, however, one Bolshevik correspondent noted that revolutionary Cossacks still "consider a separate existence for Cossacks, and distinct Cossack political structures, to be essential."[91]

As the date for the First Don Territorial Congress of Soviets approached in early April—elections were now taking place in what had already been proclaimed an independent "Don Soviet Republic"—district-level soviets finally met. These organs claimed to represent the entire laboring population, but Cossacks were conspicuously underrepresented in them. This discrepancy reflected the disinclination even among Cossacks who ostensibly endorsed the Soviet program to participate in joint organs. The "First Donets District Joint Congress of Soviets of Cossacks', Peasants', and Workers' Deputies" met from March 5 to March 8, just after the Soviet government had signed the Brest-Litovsk Treaty. As the number of Cossack delegates did not correspond to their percentage of the general population, the congress actually debated whether it was competent to pass binding resolutions. However, Smirnov, the commander of Cossack revolutionary forces, intervened to defend the legitimacy of the district soviet. He proclaimed:

When we formed the [Kamenskaia] Cossack military revolutionary committee, we distributed circulars to Cossacks and non-Cossacks, we distributed them to [peasant] villages and to mines, and everybody obeyed us and responded to our appeals. *(Applause.)* Therefore I propose, brothers and comrades, that we consider ourselves competent, and constitute a competent authority for the district, one which operates with the faith of the entire laboring people.

The Donets District Congress of Soviets approved Smirnov's proposal and proceeded to form a district soviet.[92]

The central Soviet government viewed Cossack officers as the class foe. Many Cossacks, however, were uneasy with the wave of arrests and executions of Cossack officers. Even those who considered themselves pro-Soviet identified with Cossacks who had risen through the ranks in the course of the First World War. They were markedly less concerned for career officers of Cossack background and those officers who came to the Don solely to fight Bolshevism.[93] As a consequence, Cossacks serving in revolutionary organs often shielded fellow Cossacks from possible persecution. The revolutionary Cossack units that had occupied Novocherkassk protected former comrades-in-arms and complete strangers. They did so with the approval of their commanders, Smirnov and Golubov, who became renowned for their generous intervention on behalf of fellow Cossacks.[94] By April, when the Don military revolutionary committee had moved from Cossack Novocherkassk to proletarian Rostov, some revolutionary Cossack commanders were coming to the conclusion that their vision of the revolution diverged significantly from that of orthodox "Soviet power."

The "Two Soviet Parties" and the First Don Congress of Soviets

The First Don Territorial Congress of Soviets met in late April and triumphantly proclaimed itself the voice of the entire laboring population. As at the earlier Donets District congresses of soviets, however, Cossacks were seriously under-represented. The two peasant districts (Rostov and Taganrog) accounted for as many delegates as the five predominantly Cossack districts put together.[95] Even when communities dispatched a delegate to the congress, that delegate often did not speak for the whole community. The delegate from the Cossack community of Berezovskaia (Ust'-Medveditsa District) was V. N. Salishchev, an experienced Soviet activist. He had earlier been a delegate to the Fourth All-Russian Congress of Soviets and then had been elected to the Second Ust'-Medveditsa District Congress of Soviets. He was, however, an outlander peasant rather than a Cossack. His advocacy of the Soviet government's land legislation led the community that he claimed to represent to expel him.[96] Obviously, Salishchev represented at best the outlanders and a few Cossacks in Berezovskaia. Nevertheless, the syntax of representation required him to claim that he spoke for all laboring people in the community.

Because the Don military revolutionary committee had proclaimed a "Don Soviet Republic" on March 23, the First Don Congress of Soviets in late April was more than merely a provincial gathering. Under German pressure, the central Soviet government had granted broader autonomy for the Don than anything that the Cossack government had ever considered in 1917. The Don Soviet Republic dutifully declared that it was "bound by blood" to the Russian Soviet Republic. For its part, the Soviet Republic placed Sergo Ordzhonikidze, a leading Bolshevik who had been dispatched with Antonov-Ovseenko's forces to direct food supplies north, in charge of an extraordinary commissariat for the southern region. His task was to coordinate the struggle against the Germans and oversee the actions of the new southern republics.

The continued German advance and the terms of the Brest Peace were predictably the most important issues at the First Don Congress of Soviets (April 22–27, 1918).[97] The Soviet government's acceptance of the peace terms had already led the Left Socialist Revolutionary Party to withdraw from the national government. Anticipating a vote on the Brest Peace at the Don Congress of Soviets, the Left Socialist Revolutionary Party dispatched several members of its central committee and other nationally prominent representatives.[98] Ordzhonikidze spoke on behalf of the Bolsheviks. The congress counted 713 full delegates, 170 of whom identified themselves as Bolsheviks and 126 as Left Socialist Revolutionaries. Despite extensive agitation by both parties before and during the congress, the remaining 542 delegates did not identify themselves as belonging to any political party.

The congress's first act was to elect a presidium. The congress voted to elect only individuals belonging to specific parties, thereby magnifying the prominence of political parties beyond their actual weight among the delegates. Before the vote for the presidium, both the Bolsheviks and the Left Socialist Revolutionaries sought to define themselves for the delegates. One Left Socialist Revolutionary formulated the difference between his party and Bolsheviks in these terms:

> Two parties brought Soviet power to us: the Bolsheviks and the Left Socialist Revolutionaries. If anyone doesn't know the program of these two parties, I'll explain them simply to you. The party of Bolsheviks is that which promises many benefits to the factory, plant, and mine workers—in a word, to the urban proletariat. The Left Socialist Revolutionaries promise more good to the laboring peasantry and Cossacks.[99]

Students of the two parties might focus on Izvarin's portrayal of their differences. Equally striking, however, is Izvarin's description of the common terrain they shared: both Bolsheviks and Left Socialist Revolutionaries had "brought Soviet power to us." Somewhat earlier, in an appeal written in late January 1918, Filipp Mironov had felt the need to explain to the inhabitants of his district the differences between the various parties endorsing socialism. "Like those who believe in Christ," he instructed, "socialists are divided into many persuasions and parties." He then listed the Popular Socialists, the Right and Left Socialist Revolutionaries, and the Bolsheviks and Mensheviks. "While it is entirely true that they worship one god, they believe in different ways. But remember: *the final goal of all these parties is to reorder society on the type of foundations that socialism demands.*"[100] Even in early 1918 the gulf ran not so much between parties as between these broader political groupings.

The first test of each party's support among the delegates came in elections to the congress's presidium. The Bolsheviks garnered 308 votes to 285 votes for the Left Socialist Revolutionaries. As a result, the twenty-person presidium numbered eleven Bolsheviks, led by Syrtsov, and nine Left Socialist Revolutionaries, including the nationally prominent Boris Kamkov and Isaak Shteinberg and the two most prominent local Cossack advocates of Soviet power, Podtelkov and Krivoshlykov. From the composition of the presidium, however, one would not know that the majority of delegates belonged to neither party.

But even when delegates proclaimed a party affiliation, it was often far from definitive. Non-aligned candidates for the presidium simply picked one of the two parties prior to their nomination. For instance, Podtelkov, in his negotiations with the Cossack government on January 15, had proclaimed: "We are Cossacks, not Bolsheviks. We wish to introduce Cossack rule, not rule of the parties."[101] Two months later, when addressing a meeting of the Rostov Soviet, he had stated: "Comrades, I have never had anything to do with politics. But now I am a Bolshevik, because Bolsheviks are those who defend the laboring people and who stand for fraternity and equality."[102] The following month, Podtelkov and his colleague Krivoshlykov were elected to the presidium of the First Don Congress of Soviets as Left Socialist Revolutionaries. Filipp Mironov, in Ust'-Medveditsa District, declared his opposition to Bolshevism in September 1917. In October, he condemned the Bolshevik seizure of power but began to study the program of social-democracy. In November he balloted for the Constituent Assembly as a Popular Socialist. By January 1918 he had come to endorse the Bolsheviks as the party most committed to fighting for "popular rule" against the old regime and for an immediate social revolution.[103] The Menshevik observer Lokerman attributed the shifting party identity of Podtelkov and Mironov to political immaturity or uncertainty. Such shifts actually reflected the protean nature of party identity itself in this period. In this sense, Lokerman's firm sense of his Menshevik identity was much more anomalous than Podtelkov's or Mironov's firm commitment to "popular power" or "Soviet power" but equally fluid attitudes toward the particular parties advocating it.

After electing its presidium, the congress moved to debates over the Brest peace. The question was far from academic, as German forces were continuing their advance to the borders of the Don Territory. Kamkov, speaking for the Left Socialist Revolutionaries, spearheaded the opposition to the Brest treaty. Replicating rifts in the Bolshevik Party at the national level, many local Bolsheviks were also strongly set against the peace. The Bolshevik Turlo, clearly a proponent of "permanent revolution," argued that "there are no breathing spaces in revolutions, otherwise they die." Syrtsov, the leading Bolshevik in the Don Territory, also opposed the treaty. It was left to Ordzhonikidze, attending as the Soviet commissar to the southern regions, to defend it. All the Left Socialist Revolutionary leaders and many Bolsheviks thus opposed the treaty. Non-aligned delegates argued that, however unjust the peace and however firm Left Socialist Revolutionary opposition to it, the population in the line of the German advance simply did not want to continue fighting. Others argued that the revolution was currently occupied with fighting internal enemies and could not simultaneously combat an external foe. On a more prosaic level, several delegates anxiously pointed out that the fields had not yet been sown.[104]

When it came time to vote, there were four draft resolutions before the delegates: the orthodox Bolshevik proposal endorsing the treaty; a Left Socialist Revolutionary proposal calling for a decisive repulse of the imperialists and the unending war against both internal and foreign capital; a Left Communist "declaration"; and a Menshevik proposal. Only the first two received any significant support. The Left Communist "declaration" garnered only six votes, although several prominent local Bolsheviks later added their signatures, while the Menshevik proposal received all of two votes. The congress voted 348 to 106 in favor of the Bolshevik proposal; the Left Socialist Revolutionary proposal was defeated by a vote of 336 to 126.[105] Nonparty delegates thus overwhelmingly sided with the Bolshevik proposal against that of the Left Socialist Revolutionaries.

The congress next discussed how "Soviet power" should be constituted. Debate focused particularly on whether delegates to the Don Soviet Republic's Central Executive Committee should be elected by party or by district. The proposal to elect the executive committee by district, entirely ignoring party affiliation, replicated the Cossack Circle's system of representation, expressly intended to be supraparty. While acceding to "Soviet power," many Cossack delegates clearly continued to think in terms of the Cossack Circle's structuring of the body politic.[106] Comrade Tuchniaev, perhaps not incorrectly, charged that it was only distrust in the population's ability to act without party tutelage, whether Communist or Left Socialist Revolutionary, that motivated party delegates' opposition to elections by district. In opposing election by party, this same delegate also questioned the depth of party affinity even among self-proclaimed Bolsheviks and Left Socialist Revolutionaries:

Citizens, it seems that we all understand who the Bolsheviks are, and who the Left Socialist Revolutionaries are . . . The only thing is, they are unable to work out for themselves, or in fact do not even know, to which party they belong. [B]ut they are the same leftists: Bolsheviks and Socialist Revolutionaries.[107]

Tuchniaev was arguing that in most people's eyes, what bound Bolsheviks and Left Socialist Revolutionaries together as "leftists" was much more meaningful, at this stage, than the still vague differences that divided them. In the end, a compromise was reached: election would be by district, but according to party slates within districts. Thus, as late as April 1918, those who favored aligning political support by party were unable to carry the day at a congress of soviets, which claimed to speak for an entire region that had declared itself an independent soviet republic.

In the final election to the Central Executive Committee, to be the new republic's governing body, the Bolshevik slate received a total of 284 votes while the Left Socialist Revolutionary slate won 271. The two parties divided the positions nearly down the middle: the committee was composed of 26 Bolsheviks and 24 Left Socialist Revolutionaries. For the short duration of its existence, the Don Soviet Republic would be a joint Bolshevik and Left Socialist Revolutionary project.

The "Power of Soviets" as a Political Culture

Parties were not the primary forces animating political life in the Don countryside even after October 1917. Insofar as rural dwellers identified with the new revolutionary order, it was with the "power of the soviets" in general, rather than with any particular party vision of it. Both the Bolsheviks and the Left Socialist Revolutionaries colluded in presenting themselves as "the two Soviet parties." The "power of soviets" [*vlast' sovetov*] did not derive its legitimacy from these parties' endorsement. Rather, these parties gained much of their legitimacy from identification with the larger program of "power to the soviets." Party activists—Bolsheviks, Mensheviks, and Left Socialist Revolutionaries alike—sought to inculcate a sense of party identification in the population. But for much of the first half of 1918, popular allegiance to the revolutionary order manifested itself in loyalty to soviets as institutions rather than to any particular party.

To be sure, the population had demonstrated some degree of identification with political parties at the national level in the elections to the

Constituent Assembly. As drawn up by party activists on district and provincial electoral boards, however, the electoral lists presented voters with no other option than to express their political views through a party prism.[108] Failure to support the Constituent Assembly derived not from attenuated electoral identification, exhaustion, or political apathy.[109] (Indeed, many people actively supported soviets, to which they had also elected delegates, in a way they were unwilling to support the Constituent Assembly.) Rather, party leaders and activists ascribed more significance to these votes for particular parties than did the voters themselves. At this point many people did not share party activists' sense that political expression must necessarily be channeled through political parties.[110]

Inconsistent support for political parties, however, did not mean that rural inhabitants were unaware of the larger political universe. Support for the "power of the soviets" encompassed a very definite sense of how the political order should be structured. It meant a repudiation of the Old Regime and an inversion of the preexisting social hierarchy, at both the local and the national levels. The Provisional Government had promised civic equality and participation, but it failed to deliver on these promises, most concretely by its collusion with the Cossack government. For many, Soviet power must have seemed, if only briefly, to be the consummation of the new dawn promised nearly a year before. In marked contrast to the Cossack government, which had ordered political life by estate criteria, Soviet power promised a universalistic and egalitarian political order for the "laboring folk." Or, as Filipp Mironov expressed it, while socialists of various persuasions worshiped one god in different ways, their final goal was the same: "to reorder society on the type of foundations that socialism demands." As one aspect of a socialist society, supporters of Soviet power called for power to finally pass to *all* laboring people. Local soviets made such abstract ideals very concrete. Soviets, as rural inhabitants clearly knew, had to include members of all laboring groups—otherwise, that political entity was not a soviet. At the most basic level, soviets promised to obliterate the previous estate distinctions, upheld by the Cossack government and at least tolerated by the Provisional Government. This all was the "power of soviets." Inhabitants of the Don Territory would soon learn from both Reds and Whites, however, that the only acceptable variant of "power of [local] soviets" would be that of (centralized) "Soviet power."

~ 5

Forging a Social Movement

A punitive detachment is being dispatched in order . . . to put an end to
the harmful propaganda and to force the deluded [Cossacks] to come
to the defense of their native region at this critical moment.
~ Commander of the Don Army, General Poliakov,
April 26, 1918

$\mathcal{W}$hat is termed the "Russian Civil War" in fact was a series
of overlapping civil wars and national conflicts. In these struggles, all
competing political movements turned practices that had been deployed against external enemies during the First World War—punitive
detachments, occupation regimes, courts-martial—inward, for use in
domestic strife. There was nothing distinctively Russian about the
practices themselves; they were used by all combatants in the First
World War. What was unique to Russia was the extent to which these
practices became incorporated into the country's domestic political
scene during the course of the civil wars.[1]

After 1917 political movements began to deploy these wartime techniques in the service not of foreign war but of the new revolutionary
politics. One of the defining features of revolutionary politics was the
social theory of representation. By 1917, Russian educated and political
elites had come to describe politics through the analytical grid of social
groups. Russians across the political spectrum, from Bolsheviks to
monarchist officers, imagined politics as a play of social actors. This
way of thinking did not result just from observing actual political behavior. Indeed, political movements cast themselves as the embodiment of particular social groups and imposed their own projects onto
people's often very messy political behavior. They did so by a variety of

143

mechanisms intended to summon these "social" constituencies into being and then to bring them into proper political alignment. Although the success of such movements depended on their ability to gain traction on existing social demands, the "political" also shaped the "social" demands; the latter were totally imbricated within political imagineries. Our own analytical language for the Russian Revolution often reproduces these expectations about politics.[2]

The coercive measures utilized to fashion political behavior into social movements drew freely upon military practices designed to combat foreign foes, thereby importing violence into the very roots of the new political order. To be sure, other European powers during the First World War had incorporated institutions and practices of total mobilization into their societies and governments. But in most societies these wartime practices were appended to an existing political or social order, which could dispense with them once the war was over.[3] In revolutionary Russia, by contrast, the institutions and practices of total mobilization became the building blocks of both a new state *and* a new socioeconomic order.

Thus civil war practices derived not simply from the ruthlessness of both sides but from the new revolutionary ecosystem in which they operated. No one particular ideology alone accounted for them. Although such practices predated the new revolutionary ecosystem, they could now be deployed, massively and without constraint, to achieve new revolutionary ends. Consciously and unconsciously, all political movements in the revolutionary period incorporated categories and working assumptions implicit in these wartime state practices into their everyday conduct of politics.

A "Cossack" Insurgency?

In spring 1918 an insurgency made in the name of Cossacks overthrew Soviet power in the Don Territory. Historical treatments have presented the insurgency as a "Cossack" uprising, made in defense of Cossack privileges and in response to Bolshevik excesses. This narrative essentially recapitulates the account of the uprising set forth by the All-Great Don Host (AGDH), the reconstituted anti-Soviet Cossack government that claimed legitimacy as the capstone of this selfsame anti-Soviet movement. To cement its authority, the AGDH arrogated for itself the primary role in this narrative. In place of a diffuse insurgent movement, arising in many areas without any knowledge of the Cossack leadership's existence, the AGDH's literature portrayed the insurgency as radiating out from Novocherkassk, the Cossack government's capital. In this account, the Cossack leadership organized and extended the insurrection.[4]

The AGDH account not only provided a description of events but also unavoidably encoded its own conception of who constituted the narrative's social actors and simultaneously operated as the justification for the AGDH's claim to power in the region. Pavel Kudinov, who headed an important local insurgency against Soviet power one year later, in 1919, bitterly charged that the official AGDH histories written in emigration passed over local insurgencies in silence, precisely because they were headed by people independent of the AGDH and with more egalitarian views.[5] Western historical literature largely followed the AGDH's own account of the movement: Cossacks, seeking to protect their lifestyle, arrayed themselves behind the Cossack leadership and against covetous peasants.[6]

Rather than a single movement led by the Cossack leadership, however, the 1918 anti-Soviet insurgency on the Don was in fact several spontaneous uprisings. Most erupted without any central coordination and lacked any knowledge of the Cossack leadership's own struggle around Novocherkassk. When Soviet forces had occupied the Don, groups of officers had gone into hiding. By April 1918 these officers were conducting a low-intensity guerrilla war against the new order. At first Cossacks treated these officers with hostility, and even fired upon them when they tried to attack local soviets.[7] This small-scale raiding burst into full-scale rebellion in late April and early May 1918, when officers managed to find a base of support in many Cossack communities. Still, it was almost exclusively officers and students rather than ordinary Cossacks who initiated the uprising. One participant later recalled that the uprisings were originally led by "youthful officers who had once been teachers and agronomists . . . we soldiers who had served at the front extemporized for a long time . . . In a word, officers began the thing, and the community elders fostered it. And then we began to pull our share."[8]

The sea change in attitudes among ordinary Cossacks is usually attributed to the arrival in Cossack communities of marauding Red

Guard detachments retreating in the face of the German advance. Yet many of the insurgents' own accounts belie this description. While there was undoubtedly some pillaging in the southern districts, one observer commented that the Cherkassk stanitsas generally "did not experience the Red Guards; there were no seizures of property or requisitions." In Sal' District, another participant in the insurgency noted that "the Bolsheviks who occupied [the district capital Velikokniazheskaia] conducted themselves tolerably—they robbed and arrested a few people, but they did not engage in any executions or terror."[9] Similarly, in the northern districts "there were no violent occurrences . . . There were almost no cases of 'confiscations.' This all changed, of course, after the uprising." True, most insurgents had heard rumors of "Bolshevik" atrocities, but they often had no first- or even second-hand knowledge of them.[10] Cossack rebels, pressed by officers and hardliners in their midst, ambushed passing Red Guard detachments that were, by the insurgents' own account, behaving "properly" and seeking to accommodate Cossack communities.[11]

Why did these rebellions all break out so suddenly in late April 1918? German intervention played a critical role in the success of the 1918 "Cossack" insurgency. No one less than Ataman Krasnov, who was brought to power by the insurgency, attested that "without the Germans, the Don would not have been freed from the Bolsheviks."[12] Involvement in the Don Territory was an extension of more general German war aims for dismembering the former Russian Empire by establishing proxy states on the putative principle of national self-determination.[13]

German forces helped the Cossack insurgents both indirectly, by driving back routed Red Guard detachments, and directly, by aiding Cossack insurgents in overthrowing Soviet power. Toward the end of April, two weeks after the Don Congress of Soviets had voted to endorse the Brest-Litovsk peace, German forces occupied the strategic railway station at Chertkovo, cutting Soviet forces off from Voronezh. On May 1 German units took Taganrog; on May 6, Rostov. At the same time, anti-Soviet Cossack rebels seized Novocherkassk and immediately dispatched a delegation to the German forces in Rostov. By mid-May, German General Groener reported that "at the front Don Cossacks and Germans have joined forces against the Bolsheviks," and that the two had established an "extremely friendly relationship." The

German advance originally aimed at occupying the Black Sea ports and coal fields of the Donets basin, but Krasnov's welcoming attitude soon moved them to think of controlling the area politically as well as economically. Although there were disagreements among German military and diplomatic circles over the precise nature of German intervention, Germany would play a role in the AGDH's politics until the German defeat in November 1918.[14]

Cooperation with the Germans was widespread, and it did not derive solely from Ataman Krasnov's personal "pro-Greman" policy.[15] Local insurgents, with no knowledge of Krasnov's activities in Novocherkassk, began cooperating with German forces of their own accord. This cooperation was indicative of the shift from traditional wars between external enemies to the twentieth century's internationalized civil wars.[16] The anti-Soviet movement sided with the German army, which had been Russia's external enemy for more than three years, in order to combat domestic leftists. As German units moved into Donets District, they drove out Soviet detachments and engaged in joint operations with insurgent Cossack units. They provided the Cossacks with logistical and intelligence support (including aerial reconnaissance), all at the request of local Cossack commanders. While arming and aiding insurgent Cossack units, German forces simultaneously disarmed peasant communities.[17] Before they came into contact with the new authorities in Novocherkassk, district and stanitsa atamans first received their sanction from local German military authorities.[18] On the very day the Krasnov's Circle for the Salvation of the Don came into existence in Novocherkassk, the ataman of Donets District—oblivious to the existence of a self-proclaimed Cossack leadership in Novocherkassk—issued his own appeal to the neighboring First Don and Upper Don Districts. In it, he asked them to send delegates to form a Cossack government in *his* district capital, Kamenskaia. The district ataman explained his reasons for constituting such a regional authority: "The commander of the German division in Kamenskaia has indicated that he can take upon himself the liberation of the entire Don region from the Bolsheviks [*sic*], if a delegation from the districts, furnished with definite instructions, requests this."[19] Clearly, the Germans could offer significant military support to the insurgents. The insurgents, for their part, offered a fig leaf of popular sanction for the expansive German war aims, conducted under the guise of "national liberation."

The German advance created the conditions under which the insurgency was possible. But what motivated the insurgents to raise their rebellion in April 1918, providing a convenient pretext for German intervention? The disparate insurgencies were not primarily the product of Bolshevik marauding; indeed, they more closely resembled the "Great Fear" of the French Revolution.[20] In both cases the rural population was animated by fears of politically motivated brigandage, fears testifying as much to how rural inhabitants perceived a novel and volatile political environment as to what was actually occurring. In the disconcerting revolutionary situation of early 1918, new legislative organs— the Fourth All-Russian Congresses of Soviets (March 14–16, 1918) and the First Don Congress of Soviets (April 13–14)—propagated disturbing visions of the revolutionary order. Discussion at these high-level gatherings became terrifyingly concrete at the local level, for both congresses debated implementing two earlier decrees on the important land question: the December 13, 1917, guidelines on land committees and the February 19, 1918, decree on socialization of the land.[21] The new government directives on land issues fanned apprehensions among the Cossacks that their distinctive lifestyle would be eliminated. One insurgent leader testified that until April "it was a difficult task to involve the Cossacks of Ust'-Medveditsa District in overthrowing Soviet power, but the 'General Guidelines' [on land committees] made the task much easier." The guidelines directed that elections to the land committees be by "universal" suffrage (art. 5) and that they should redistribute the land fund so as to equalize holdings (art. 23, point g). Cossacks were particularly unsettled by the paragraphs granting land committees the authority to seize land on their own initiative.[22] The land socialization decree similarly disturbed Cossacks. Berezovskaia stanitsa expelled from the community its delegate to the First Don Congress of Soviets, an outlander, when he advocated implementing the decree.[23]

Many Cossacks believed that they were in a mortal struggle not only with peasants covetous of Cossack land, but also with the workers and miners of the Donbass region. Indeed, the Don Territory's western mining and industrial region was among the most pro-Bolshevik in the entire Don Territory. Such sentiments, however, derived at least in part from workers' and miners' previous experience with Cossack rule over the course of 1917 and early 1918, when Cossack authorities responded to worker demonstrations and strikes with military force. After the Bolshevik seizure of power, some Cossack detachments implemented a spontaneous form of White Terror in worker regions.[24] To be sure, fears also ran in the other direction. Soviet supporters and Bolsheviks viewed all setbacks as the result of the nefarious plotting of kulaks, bourgeois, and officers.[25] Both sides increasingly embraced a crude form of social typology. Many workers assumed that Cossacks were inveterate counterrevolutionaries who took pleasure in tormenting workers; Cossacks came to believe that all workers were Bolsheviks out to exterminate them.

The widespread rebellion against Soviet power was therefore not the result of a homogeneous Cossackry reacting to Bolshevik outrages. Instead it derived from the coalescence of a number of political currents, producing a "Great Fear," one that testified as much to popular suspicions and concerns about the new political order as to actual outrages. In an environment of menacingly vague legislative acts and misunderstood intentions of passing armed detachments, mutual suspicion and fear fed off each other.

French rural dwellers had seen the ubiquitous and malevolent aristocrat lurking behind every shadow in the French countryside. Cossack insurgents projected all their fears about the new order onto real and imagined "Bolsheviks." Although many pro-Soviet activists on the Don were Left Socialist Revolutionaries, Cossack insurgents routinely depicted all their opponents as "Bolsheviks." By equating "Soviet power" with "Bolshevik bands," they both delegitimized Soviet power and narrowed it to mean the rule of one political party.

Although the Cossack insurgents declared their crusade against "Bolshevism," the Don Soviet Republic through April 1918 remained a joint Left Socialist Revolutionary and Bolshevik project. The fate of an expedition of leading Cossack republicans, all of whom were Left Socialist Revolutionaries, demonstrates the narrowing of the political spectrum. Confronted by the German advance and the outbreak of rebellions all around them, members of the Don Soviet government decided to dispatch a conscription commission to the northern districts, home to many of the government's Cossack members. Fedor Podtelkov (chairman of the Don Soviet government and commissar for military affairs), Mikhail Krivoshlykov (commissar for local adminstration), and Petr Alaev, another member of the expedition, were all leading Left Socialist Revolutionaries and Cossacks native to the northern districts. A Communist detachment accompanied them, demonstrating the continued alliance between the "two soviet parties."

To the consternation of the expedition's leaders, Cossacks and peasants failed to respond to their summons. In the first week of May the detachment marched unawares into the middle of a rebellious region and was surrounded by insurgent forces. Assured by fellow-Cossacks that they would be spared if they turned over their weapons, the expedition members surrendered. Nonetheless, a court-martial, composed of officers, sentenced the entire expedition to death by firing squad, with the exception of Podtelkov and Krivoshlykov, who were hanged.[26] The divergent fates of the two delegates to the First Don Congress of Soviets in mid-April, both elected from the Upper Don District as Left Socialist Revolutionaries, demonstrates the fluidity of party identity in this period. Three weeks after the congress, one of the delegates, Mrykhin, perished with the expedition; the other, Rodin, participated in his trial and execution.[27]

In describing this expedition, the insurgents portrayed Podtelkov, who had balloted for the Constituent Assembly as a Left Socialist Revolutionary, as "conducting *Bolshevik* agitation."[28] Anti-Soviet insurgents similarly depicted the Soviet land decrees that so disturbed Cossacks as "Bolshevik," even though the decrees reflected Left Socialist Revolutionary views at least as much as Bolshevik ones.[29] The Manichean identification of all foes as "Bolsheviks" reduced all support for either local soviets or Soviet power to one party, the Bolsheviks. Such a narrowing of categories was a significant development, for many pro-Soviet Cossacks on the Don had earlier identified themselves with the revolution generally or somewhat loosely with the Left Socialist Revolutionaries. The insurgents' equation of all support for local soviets with "Bolshevism" unwittingly reinforced the Bolshevik Party's own attempts to claim for itself the mantle of sole party for the Soviet state.

Making Bolshevik Peasants and Anti-Soviet Cossacks

If Cossack insurgents imagined their foes in political terms as "Bolsheviks," they imagined them even more so in sociological terms as "peasants." (In mining districts, of course, they saw all workers as potential "Bolsheviks.") Cossacks obsessed about the threat they imagined neighboring peasant communities presented to their lifestyle. One Cossack insurgent recalled:

> The Cossacks feared the surrounding peasants, whose settlements were located throughout the Upper Don District . . . The Cossacks were extremely wary, fearing massive arms caches and machine-guns in the peasant settlements. However, upon searching them, it transpired that nothing other than a few rifles was found.[30]

Animated by rumors of shadowy "Kadet" and "Cossack" bands, peasants took to arming themselves as well. This move served only to justify the inchoate fears in the minds of many Cossacks. Who armed first is of less significance than the prevalent rumors of universal mobilization by all sides. In one instance, a peasant community formed a self-defense detachment and dispatched it to confront a rumored "counterrevolutionary band." When the peasant detachment came into contact with this "band," the peasants found that it was only a Cossack detachment from the neighboring community, itself mobilized to face a rumored Red Guard detachment. Upon this welcome discovery, both sides dispersed.[31]

Violence was not always avoided, however. Under the pretext of forestalling an assault by "Kadets," local peasants pillaged both Gundorovskaia and Mechetinskaia stanitsas and arrested several community leaders. Predictably, these two stanitsas eagerly joined the Cossack insurgency and received aid from German forces, thereby gaining the upper hand. Equating all peasants with "Bolsheviks" and "Red Guards," the Cossacks of Gundorovskaia expelled all peasants from the neighboring community.[32] One peasant recalled that "in April 1918 a civil war of local proportions flared up, the so-called war of Cossacks against peasants and peasants against Cossacks."[33]

Peter Krasnov, who as ataman of the AGDH had access to intelligence reports with much evidence to the contrary, nevertheless defined the conflict in purely estate terms:

> At that time the Don divided into two camps, Cossacks and peasants. The peasants, with few exceptions, were Bolsheviks. Where there were peasant settlements, uprisings against Cossacks did not

cease . . . War with the Bolsheviks on the Don had already taken on the character not of political or class struggle, not of a civil war, but rather of a people's war, a national war. Cossacks defended their Cossack rights from the Russians.[34]

(Cossacks often used the term "Russians" for native peasants, most of whom were indeed ethnically Russian, and the derogatory term "Ukes" [*khokhly*] for non-native peasants.) Krasnov's portrayal of the conflict as one between peasants and Cossacks is essentially the prevailing historiographical view of the rebellion.

The economic profile of the Don Territory—with native peasants engaged in market agriculture largely on rented and purchased land—should have suggested that many peasants would not welcome Bolshevism, even if they favored local soviets and civic equality with Cossacks. Elsewhere in Russia, the seizure of private estates cemented peasant support for Soviet power, or at least acquiescence to it. Given the small amount of private landholding in the Don Territory, this was not a salient factor. (Indeed, peasants themselves held a significant portion of what private land there was, especially in peasant districts.) Nevertheless, Cossack insurgents aligned political attitudes neatly, if erroneously, with sociological contours. Krasnov suggested that the rebellion succeeded in the southern districts, the cradle of the AGDH itself, owing to the large "Cossack" presence there. In point of fact, a greater percentage of the population was Cossack in the northern districts than in the southern ones. More relevant was the fact that the southern districts, where the insurgency indeed enjoyed its early success, had by far the highest concentration of Cossack officers and bureaucrats.[35]

Of interest here is not so much the veracity of the Cossack leadership's narrative as how the leadership came to interpret the conflict as one between monolithically anti-Soviet Cossacks and uniformly pro-Bolshevik peasants. From the very first, leaders of the insurgency reported, even if they failed to register, the variegated response of the peasantry. The Don government's own intelligence reports documented how peasants frequently shunned Bolshevik attempts to mobilize them, a far cry from Krasnov's portrayal of virtually all peasants as "Bolsheviks."[36] Some native peasant communities in fact embraced the anti-Soviet Cossack insurgency, often in an attempt to protect their property from other neighboring peasants.[37] Outlanders, who included large-scale farmers as well as impoverished renters, also did not respond monolithically. AGDH intelligence summaries reported that even outlanders, reputed to be the most uniformly Bolshevik, fought "side-by-side" with the Cossacks against "the common foe," and that "almost all outlanders are in the ranks of the Cossacks."[38] Public reports also testified to non-Cossack participation in the "Cossack" insurgency.[39] Indeed, when a full Cossack Circle convened in August 1918, Cossack authorities delegated several seats to those outlanders serving alongside Cossacks in certain insurgent regiments.[40] Categorizing political support by estate criteria ("the Don divided into two camps, Cossacks and peasants") did not so much synthesize "facts" as impose its ordering upon them. Despite the demonstrably nonmonolithic response of "the peasants" and "the outlanders," one government intelligence report noted that most people had come to believe that "'outlander' and 'Bolshevik' are synonyms."[41]

Without question, the vast majority of those participating in the insurgency belonged to the Cossack estate. The movement's social profile was attributable, however, as much to the political ideology of the uprising as to the sociology of its political support. Mass participation by Cossacks demonstrated not so much freely given consent by a like-minded collective social group, but rather the Cossack leadership's drive to recruit Cossacks, forcibly if need be, to serve "the Cossack cause." The movement's ideology prefigured as much as it described its base of support, by forcibly enlisting Cossacks to participate in their own "liberation."

The Cossack leadership affirmed that Cossacks unanimously rose up during the rebellion. At the time of the rebellion this version reflected how the Cossack leadership conceptualized the uprising; later it would serve as a legitimizing myth for the new Cossack government.[42] The link between rebellion and the Cossackry became entirely tautological. To support the rebellion was "Cossack," and failure to do so marked one as "non-Cossack." Officers who led the movement gained a foothold in Cossack stanitsas when a segment of the community supported their calls for mobilization against the terrifying prospect of "Bolshevik bands." In Migulinskaia stanitsa, a hard-core faction attacked a Bolshevik detachment despite the fact that "the Cossacks were equivocating and several had begun to curse the officers." The officers in fact began the assault despite an order from the ataman to parley with the Red detachment, thereby undermining negotiations.[43] Among Cossacks, the preference for "neutrality" was at least as widespread as total adherence to the insurgency. Within Cossack communities, a hard-line faction pressed all Cossacks to embrace the "Cossack cause," branding those who refused to share their vision as "traitors." Under the prodding of the hardliners, Cossack communities then passed resolutions ordering all members of the community to enter the ranks of insurgent detachments or face courts-martial for "treason." Deserters from the "Cossack cause" were to be executed.[44]

The spread of the rebellion in Ust'-Medveditsa District demonstrates how political opponents of Soviet power fashioned a "Cossack movement." Throughout early spring 1918, Cossacks in this northern district had offered little support to several officer detachments seeking to overthrow Soviet power.[45] In April, however, inflammatory rumors began to circulate that "the Russians" planned to confiscate Cossack land and deport all Cossacks to Siberia, leading some Cossack communities to turn to the officers they had previously spurned.[46] Ust'-Khoperskaia stanitsa emerged as the center of the insurgency. The community convened a stanitsa-wide "congress of soviets" for May 8. With Cossacks already uneasy about land legislation, the rebellion's spark was news that armed peasants from the town of Chistiakovo had attempted to free some captured Red Guard prisoners who had been detained by a neighboring settlement. The stanitsa "congress of soviets" passed a resolution declaring that it no longer recognized "existing Soviet power" and calling for resistance to the "Red Guards." Next it decreed a "compulsory mobilization" of the community's entire male Cossack population, from ages seventeen to fifty. Only officers were permitted to hold positions of command, and overall control of the insurgency's forces was entrusted to Lieutenant Colonel A. V. Golubintsev. Anyone avoiding mobilization would be subject to military law, up to and including execution.[47] The stanitsa's outlying Cossack settlements then passed analogous resolutions, some signed by the settlement ataman, others—by the settlement's "soviet."[48] Some Cossack settlements, however, were reluctant. Bobrovskii khutor had to intercede on behalf of four of its members—including a father and son, both noncommissioned officers—who had been arrested at the stanitsa assembly for their opposition to mobilization, offering a pledge of collective assurance for their future behavior.[49]

The rebellion's leadership then convened a "Soviet of Free Cossack Settlements and Communities," encompassing neighboring stanitsas. (The adjective "free" in the title derived from the term for Cossack liberties [*volia*], rather than from the word for egalitarian, civic freedom [*svoboda*].) The insurgent command, headed by Lieutenant Colonel Golubintsev, intentionally selected a "soviet" to head the movement in order to keep its appeal as broad as possible. Many Cossacks at this stage proclaimed outright that while they opposed Red Guards, they had no quarrel with local soviets. These views were common not only among Cossacks who had served at the front but also among officers who had advanced through the ranks during the war. The composition of the five-person committee elected by the "soviet" reflected the republican sympathies to which Golubintsev hoped to appeal. (Golubintsev made sure to retain *de facto* control as military commander of insurgent forces.) The soviet's chairman, Lieutenant Vedenin, had been a teacher in the local secondary school before advancing to officer rank during the First World War. He openly expressed doubts about Golubintsev's program. Another member, Sergeant Alferov, confided to Golubintsev that he considered himself "a Bolshevik, but one with principles."[50] The insurgents borrowed more than revolutionary rhetoric; they also employed organs born of the revolution. They established a "political department" for the purposes of "informing distant Cossack settlements about the movement and about the character of the popular uprising."[51]

To advance its cause, the insurgent leadership extended "compulsory mobilization" to the other participating stanitsas.[52] Far from all communities voluntarily embraced this measure. One week after the decree, Bukanovskaia stanitsa informed the insurgent leadership that it had convened an assembly "to discuss" the mobilization order. Three days later the stanitsa authorities reported that the stanitsa proper had mobilized its menfolk, but that its outlying settlements still had not. When most settlements still had not mobilized two weeks later, leaders of the uprising tartly instructed the Bukanovskaia authorities that they should confiscate the land allotments of any Cossack who failed to adhere to the insurgency immediately. (In July, six mounted militiamen seeking draft-dodgers in one of Bukanovskaia's settlements were fired on by relatives of one fugitive Cossack.)[53] As its control spread, the Soviet of Free Settlements continued to issue menacing mobilization orders, soon extending its claims to the entire Ust'-Medveditsa District.[54]

By this time, Cossack settlements in areas not yet controlled by the anti-Soviet insurgents had convened their own, pro-Soviet congress of soviets, which in turn issued its own mobilization orders for the entire district.[55] Both sides—Red and White—increasingly demanded exclusive and unambiguous allegiance. Soviet authorities employed many of the same measures as the insurgents to force communities to adhere to their cause and abandon their "neutrality." In Khoper District, the Cossacks of Akishevskaia stanitsa repelled the attacks of Dudakov's officer detachment. Despite being "well-disposed" to Soviet power, as the Soviets themselves testified, the community proclaimed its neutrality when Soviet district authorities sought to mobilize it. Such neutrality, however, was no longer an option. Soviet detachments sought to change the mood of the Cossacks in Lugovskaia stanitsa by training machine guns on them, and they shelled both Pravotvorskaia and Tishanskaia stanitsas in order to get the Cossacks to assemble.[56]

Skurshinskaia stanitsa, inundated by mobilization orders from both sides, informed its outlying settlements that it had joined with the insurgents, but simultaneously sought to assure them that the insurgents would not seek to wage war against the whole of Russia. This assurance did not sway several settlements, which begged their stanitsa leadership to seek a negotiated settlement.[57] Outlying settlements in Arzhenovskaia stanitsa expressed similar sentiments. The stanitsa leadership showed little patience for such views, though: "Those guilty of nonfulfillment of the above-cited order, and of failure to appear at the musterpoint, will be subject to harsh punishment, up to and including trial by court-martial. Arzhenovskaia stanitsa is under martial law."[58]

The Cossack leadership raised its revolt in the name of the entire Cossack estate, and it was fully prepared to compel Cossacks to participate in their own liberation. It expended a great deal of violence, in the form of both overt force and judicial coercion, to bring Cossacks into proper alignment with an imagined collective identity. During his interrogation by the Red Army, the captured commander of the Twenty-fourth Cossack Horse Regiment declared that Cossacks in his region had originally armed to defend their homes with little thought to the

Cossack government. They soon found, however, that the Don government "began to demonstrate a desire to subordinate the Cossacks to it."[59]

Imposing a Counterrevolution Orthodoxy

The view of the Cossack leadership became a veritable orthodoxy by subsuming the widespread but disparate opposition to "Bolsheviks" under the exclusive rubric of the "All-Great Don Host." The leadership's base was the area in Cherkassk District around the Don Territory's administrative capital of Novocherkassk, which was home to many nobles as well as bureaucrats who had served in the Cossack administrative structures. An insurgent detachment numbering around 350 men (mostly officers) briefly seized Novocherkassk in mid-April, just as the First Don Congress of Soviets was meeting in Rostov. Upon occupying the capital, the insurgents appointed I. A. Poliakov commander and S. V. Denisov as chief of staff of a not-yet-existent "Don Army." Although the "army" was forced to retreat soon afterward, the brief occupation of Novocherkassk allowed many officers trapped there to escape with the insurgents to nearby Zaplavskaia stanitsa, where they set up a defensive position. There they held out for nearly two weeks, growing to a force of nearly 6,500 men. This force formed the core of the Don Army.[60]

Most accounts describe Cossacks streaming to the insurgency's banner of their own accord.[61] Yet the increasing number of Cossacks in the insurgent ranks did not testify to some spontaneous social support for a Cossack agenda. The struggle to fit Cossacks within the insurgents' template required much effort even in the more conservative and loyal southern districts. In his memoir Poliakov, the commander of the Don Army, observed that "Cossack communities rose of their own accord against the Bolsheviks."[62] Poliakov's claim must be contrasted with his order from the time of the insurgency, in which he dispatched a punitive detachment to Starocherkasskaia to coerce its Cossack inhabitants "to defend the Don," threatening merciless punishment for any neutrality.

Almost from the beginning the leadership of the embryonic AGDH employed punitive detachments as a tactical tool, and before long it extended their use to other regions. Punitive detachments, military units authorized to act broadly against civilian populations, were an established part of European military practice. European militaries employed them most commonly in colonial situations, but the Russian imperial government used them against its own population at the height of the 1905 Revolution. Dispatching such units to Siberia, the Baltic, and the Caucasus, the imperial government granted them *carte blanche* to operate against civilian populations, in order to intimidate entire regions.[63] In 1918 the Cossack leadership relied on these same measures to bring ordinary Cossacks into the ranks of its counterrevolutionary insurgency. The Don Army's chief of staff at that time recalled that "the command's firmness caused outbreaks of unrest, and the campaign ataman was forced to dispatch detachments for pacification and even to equip repeated punitive expeditions."[64]

In mid-April the Cossack leadership faced its own rebellion among Cossacks pressed into service in its ranks. The insurgent command took stern measures. In late April Poliakov, the commander of the Don Army, issued the following public proclamation:

Today a punitive detachment is being dispatched by steamboat from Razdory to Starocherkasskaia, in order, by force of arms, to put an end to the harmful propaganda and to force the deluded [Cossacks] to come to the defense of their native region at this critical moment. Announcing this, the campaign ataman has ordered me to warn that any deviation or demonstration of neutrality will be mercilessly punished by military force.[65]

In this manner the Cossack leadership explained away those Cossacks who did not share its ideas by reference to their "delusion," a condition for which punitive detachments evidently were the best cure. Nor was Starocherkasskaia stanitsa an isolated case. The following day the command ordered a garrison to occupy the "politically unreliable" Melikhovskaia stanitsa and soon afterward dispatched it up the Don River to press recalcitrant Cossack communities to join the cause.[66]

As German units moved into Rostov, Taganrog, and Donets Districts and with local insurgencies elsewhere undermining Soviet power, the Don Army in Zaplavskaia succeeded in seizing Novocherkassk a second time from the disorganized Soviet forces. With the Don Territory's capital city in their hands, they could now present themselves as the authority representing the whole region. Two days after they seized the city, the insurgents convened a "Circle for the Salvation of the Don," which met from May 11 through May 18 and elected Peter Krasnov the new ataman. Krasnov extolled the circle as the true voice of Cossack sentiments, free of the "cowardly," meddling intelligentsia who claimed to speak on the Cossackry's behalf.[67]

The portrayal of the assembly as an authentic representative of the humble Cossackry relies entirely on the insurgency's own tautological definition of "Cossack." Representation was weighted toward those serving in insurgent detachments, which sent two delegates, whereas stanitsas under the insurgency's control sent only one. Consequently, of the circle's 130 delegates, only 33 were elected from the stanitsas, a further 48 came from insurgent Cossack units, and the remainder were officers and officials from Novocherkassk.[68] In constituting itself, the Circle for the Salvation of the Don proclaimed that it represented not all Cossacks but "those military units and stanitsas that have taken part in driving out Soviet forces."[69] Those Cossacks who did not share this goal were simply not represented, precisely because such behavior was *a priori* not Cossack. Conversely, simply by fighting "the Bolsheviks," others became impeccably "Cossack." When V. V. Shapkin, who had served in the Headquarters of the Russian Army and had then been appointed to represent Kaledin's Cossack government in Kiev, returned to the Don in this period, Georgii Ianov, as chairman, immediately registered him as a member of the Circle for the Salvation of the Don.[70] By virtue of his support for the insurgency alone, Shapkin—a career officer—had come to represent the "gray" Cossackry.

Humble Cossacks, however, did not necessarily share Krasnov's sense of what they supported. One AGDH intelligence report noted that

> among the officers, as well as among the Cossackry's rank-and-file, a hostile attitude is evident toward the ataman and the Circle for the Salvation of the Don, as well as toward those who elected it. Among simple Cossacks the ataman has the reputation, earned while he was commander [during the First World War], for being too strict, and they see in his current measures a manifestation of this excessive harshness.[71]

Several months later, a commander in the Don Army noted that "a feeling of duty before the entire Cossack community is poorly developed among Cossacks," who suffer at times from "selfish interests." By "selfish interests" he meant that Cossacks stubbornly failed to recognize the AGDH agenda as their own.[72] Such evaluations would not necessarily trouble members of the circle or Krasnov. In their view, they represented the Cossackry as a corporate entity and, as such, were responsible not to the plurality of individual Cossacks but to the good of the estate as a whole.

The circle translated its estate-based conceptualization of political affiliation into concrete legislation by passing a law granting Cossack status to all those who sided with it and who fought against "the Bolsheviks." Conversely, the circle passed a law expelling from the Cossack estate all Cossacks "participating in the Soviet forces and Bolshevik organizations."[73] The AGDH later officially confirmed this practice with a law expelling all individuals who had opposed "the Cossackry" (meaning the AGDH) and stripping them of their property. At the same time, all those who fought for their "native Don," regardless of origins, were admitted to the Cossack estate.[74]

The numerous resolutions granting Cossack status to non-Cossack participants of the insurgency, and those expelling Cossacks for their failure to embrace it, demonstrate that political allegiance could determine "social" identity. On the strength of the circle's resolution, authorities in Cossack communities purged those who did not share their view of the Cossackry and its interests. Kumshatskaia stanitsa excluded 282 of its own members from the Cossack estate for serving in Soviet forces, while Nagavskaia stanitsa expelled more than 200, one-quarter of all Cossacks in the community. Newspapers regularly published other stanitsa resolutions expelling hereditary Cossacks from the Cossack estate for their political views.[75] In their petitions, communities employed the insurgency's own categorization for Cossacks. The assembly of Krylov khutor (Esaulovskaia stanitsa) twice requested that the Novocherkassk authorities expel their co-villager Vasilii Samsonov from the Don "as an individual harmful to the Don Cossackry."[76]

At the same time that these communities were depriving hereditary members of the Cossack estate of their Cossack status, they were granting it to dozens and sometimes hundreds of non-Cossacks who had actively participated in the insurgency. Over a five-month period, the AGDH officially registered as Cossacks 1,400 "outlanders," only 150 of them officers, for their "active participation in the Don's defense."[77]

The Cossack leadership's estate-based conceptualization of political support transformed the category of "Cossack" from one of legal estate into a political one describing acceptance of the Cossack leadership and its cause.

Punitive detachments could secure Cossacks for the insurgency's ranks. But to be effective, such violence required clearly enunciated goals. The "Court for the Defense of the Don" and local courts-martial delineated for the population the insurgency's expectations and, more broadly, its worldview.[78] Cossacks who deviated from the leadership's standard of "proper" Cossack behavior were likely to find themselves facing either the court or its local analogue, a court-martial. The court punished Cossack parliamentarians who, contrary to the leadership's firm line, sought to negotiate with Soviet forces. It imprisoned other Cossacks for neutrality or for holding meetings in the ranks.[79] The Cossack leadership employed its courts to redefine desertion or neutrality into acts of treason "to the entire Cossackry and to the native Don."

Judicial coercion was effective not simply as an instrument of repression. Indeed, the courts not only punished the recalcitrant but also described for them the nature of their violation. In this sense the courts-martial were effective in communicating the insurgency's identification of "Cossack" with support for the anti-Soviet insurgency. The courts punished some individuals for such straightforward crimes as pillaging, robbery, and murder while in the service of "Bolshevik bands." Others it condemned for "agitation on behalf of Soviet power." However, the courts-martial also handed down sentences against individuals charged with participation, not in the Red Army or even in the "Bolshevik bands," but in "organizations that pursue as their goal the destruction of the Cossackry."[80] The courts even prosecuted individuals under the broad charge of holding "a hostile attitude toward the Don Cossackry."[81]

In addition to meting out punishments for those directly accused in its courts, the leadership of the insurgency forced the populace to employ its rhetoric in formulating petitions for amnesty. Entire communities sought to assure the Novocherkassk authorities that any complicity with "Bolshevism" on their part had been coerced, and they hastened to swear their allegiance to the insurgency.[82] A formulaic component of requests for clemency or amnesty was a petition from the accused's community, which required a community gathering to compose a resolution requesting pardon. Pavel Kadykov, along with his community, affirmed that the Bolsheviks had forcibly mobilized his son: "our whole khutor, as represented by its best citizens, mourns for my son, a true Cossack and defender of his native region."[83] The power both to sentence and to amnesty thus forced the populace to become conversant in the Cossack leadership's language and to orient themselves in its worldview.

With the western border secured by the German Army and with Soviet forces in disarray, the Don Army pushed northward, linking up with insurgent movements in other districts as it did so. As the AGDH expanded, it absorbed all local authorities that had been established by their own uprisings. The Donets District ataman placed all locally raised insurgent units under the command of his appointee Popov, instructing him to execute "all officers and Cossacks who resist existing authority and conduct agitation against the command."[84] One week later, he ordered that all locally raised units enter into General Fitskhelaurov's expeditionary force, which was extending the Cossack government's authority into the northern districts. As it moved north, Fitskhelaurov's force also incorporated the units of Golubintsev's Soviet of Free Cossack Communities and Settlements into the Don Army.[85]

But the disparate and diffuse unrest against "socialist measures" and "Bolshevik bands" that had motivated many local insurgencies was not synonymous with the program of the Novocherkassk authorities. At its founding the AGDH declared that it possessed "complete authority" throughout the Don Territory. In early May, as its forces radiated outward, it issued the following order: "Since the Cossack Circle has entrusted complete political authority to the Don ataman, all local organs that have emerged in the course of the civil war and that have appropriated power for themselves are to be liquidated."[86] Where insurgencies had reinstated stanitsa atamans on their own and were prepared to recognize the legitimacy of Cossack organs, the AGDH had little problem. If the Novocherkassk authorities approved of the candidates, they simply reappointed the district atamans originally elected by independent insurgent congresses. In three of ten districts, however, the atamans elevated by local insurgences were unacceptable. Krasnov then simply appointed his own candidates. These new district atamans then submitted the names of community atamans to Krasnov for approval.

When stanitsa atamans proved unwilling to pursue Novocherkassk's program, military commanders were granted the authority to remove them. Where entire communities proved uncooperative, such as in Bukanovskaia stantisa (again), the Don command instituted direct military rule.[87]

Yet while all insurgents may have been "anti-Soviet" in the sense of being opposed to the policies of the national Soviet government, many remained committed to some form of elective authority at the local level. In many places the local congresses of soviets had been the ones to overthrow "Soviet power." Golubintsev was more calculating than most, but even he recognized the appeal of local soviets. The AGDH proved unwilling, however, to accept even those local soviets that had raised insurgencies against Soviet power. It insisted that all Cossack communities abandon soviets, regardless of their political views, and return to a system of atamans. Golubintsev secretly corresponded with the AGDH leadership, plotting how to choreograph recognition of the Novocherkassk government. He informed the population that he was postponing a congress of soviets summoned to discuss the best way to constitute authority in order to focus all efforts on fighting the Red Guards.

At the same time, however, Golubintsev was surreptitiously corresponding with Krasnov, asking the Novocherkassk government to dispatch delegates immediately so that when the congress did meet, it would not "diverge from the program of the Cossack government." Such government delegates, suggested Golubintsev, could "*direct* the congress to follow the line of the Cossack government."[88] When a congress of insurgent communities finally met, it was chaired by Pavel Ageev. Ageev, the leading "leftist" among those dedicated to the Cossack corporate political program, had been a major figure in Kaledin's 1917 Cossack government. Elected to the Constituent Assembly on Kaledin's Cossack slate, he had taken refuge in Ust'-Medveditsa District after the Soviet seizure of power. Under his chairmanship the congress voted to recognize the Novocherkassk government as the region's authority and to pass local power to a district ataman. Declaring that "the defense of one's native region from Red Guard bands is a holy duty of all Cossacks of the Don Cossack community," the gathering voted to exclude from the Cossack estate any Cossacks who refused to serve in the insurgent ranks and to hand them over to a court-martial. It then mobilized the entire male population aged eighteen to fifty for compulsory public work.[89] So ended the Soviet of Free Cossack Communities and Settlements.

Cossack insurgents of course did not blindly reinstate their "traditional" atamans and embrace the Cossack leadership's claim to represent their collective interest. Against those who did not share its orthodoxy, the Novocherkassk government employed the tools that had proved so successful in the lower Don. The gunboats used so effectively against the reluctant Cherkassk stanitsas moved up the Don River to Romanovskaia and Kargal'skaia stanitsas.[90] Cossack Captain Gavrilov's punitive detachment secured Khoper District, in the north, for the Cossack leadership. Gavrilov did so by "pulling the population out of its neutrality." He presented Cossack community assemblies with a categorical choice: "for us, or for the Reds." When the populace still expressed a desire to be neutral, Gavrilov threatened to open fire: "either you are for the Cossacks, or against them."[91] Gavrilov made this ultimatum to a Cossack assembly. To be "for the Cossacks, or against them" meant to be for or against the authorities behind Gavrilov. Similarly, Lieutenant Lazarev's punitive detachment won Ust'-Medveditsa District for the AGDH. The detachment "quickly arrived and reimposed order in the Cossacks' disorganized ranks." The AGDH Department of Intelligence noted that "the mood of the Cossacks, formerly unsteady, has improved with the arrival of Lieutenant Lazarev's punitive detachment. Incidents of disobedience and desertion have ceased."[92]

Regional courts-martial were established soon after the arrival of the Don Army. Through these organs the Novocherkassk authorities tutored the populace in its discourse and expectations. The central Court for the Defense of the Don had been created in May 1918, and later that same month local court-martial branches were operating in both the Donets and the First Don Districts. By June one was operating in Khoper District; by July—in Ust'-Medveditsa, home of the Soviet of Free Cossack Communities.[93] In the period that Krasnov served as ataman, from May 1918 to February 1919, AGDH punitive organs sentenced nearly 25,000 people to death.[94] While the number of actual executions was undoubtedly less, owing to amnesties and pardons, the figure indicates the extent of official violence.

As the AGDH extended its control over other insurgent regions, punitive detachments and courts-martial were only the bluntest instruments for shaping public discourse and ordering life. Such measures were, by definition, extraordinary. To regularize its control, the AGDH command ordered each Cossack community to form a thirty-man "watch detachment" [*karaul'nye komandy*] and each Cossack settlement—a ten-man one. They were to be staffed by Cossacks who were "politically reliable," and their commanders were subject to approval by district officials.[95] These watch commands demonstrate how even counterrevolutionary movements came to employ institutions born of the revolutionary maelstrom. Staffed by the criteria of political reliability, they had little foundation in Old Regime institutions. Their precedent was instead the militia detachments proposed in October 1917 by the revolutionary Provisional Government, also to be staffed by "politically reliable" soldiers.[96]

The Novocherkassk government also consolidated control by shaping the parameters of public discussion. Even before the convocation of the Circle for the Salvation of the Don, the insurgent leadership established an "information department" [*osvedomitel'nyi otdel*], responsible for informing the population about the government's activity, and for reporting conditions throughout the territory to the government.[97] Having provided a source of "official" information, the government outlawed any information that conflicted with the official version as "rumors" and ordered the arrest of those spreading them.[98] Here, too, the counterrevolutionary leadership was adopting measures that had initially been fashioned for the First World War and then been reworked by the Provisional Government.[99]

Ideology alone did not produce the violence of the Russian civil wars. Fired by the hopes and fears of revolution, all sides operated according to wartime methods. While the anti-Soviet movements used political violence differently from their enemies, they too deployed it instrumentally.[100] Both by its projection of an official interpretation of reality (through the Information Department) and by its punishment of public speech and behavior deviating from this representation, the AGDH established the boundaries of public expression. Employing violence as a political technique, the AGDH leadership sought to make Cossacks behave in accordance with its own normative expectations of the Cossackry. The 1918 insurgency was "Cossack" less because Cossacks made it than because they were cast as the social group intended to realize it. It was this political pursuit of an idealized, imagined Cossackry that made the insurgency a "Cossack movement."

~ 6

"We Will Have to Exterminate the Cossacks"

> By means of [de-Cossackization] we hoped to render the Don healthy, to make it, if not Soviet, then at least submissive and obedient to Soviet power . . . Sooner or later we will have to exterminate, simply physically destroy, the Cossacks, or at least the vast majority of them.
> ~ I. Reingol'd, July 6, 1919

*T*he Bolshevik party-state, in contrast to the All-Great Don Host, was committed to a revolutionary program. Whereas the Cossack leadership essentially sought to firm up existing social categories, the Bolshevik leadership explicitly embraced an ideological system in at least two senses. First, it attempted to construct an idealized model of society derived from a specific revolutionary plan. That is, the Bolsheviks' ideology described for them an end (communism) and the means to achieve it (the party as instrument and class struggle as process); and it provided a timeline (capitalism-socialism-communism) and a methodology (dialectical materialism) for measuring the progress of that project. Second, all measures of the party-state had to be deemed consistent with that ideology. This proposition required the Bolshevik Party to play a "guiding role" within the Soviet state. Acting behind state organs, the party first determined official policy and then ensured (or rather attempted to ensure) that state organs consistently and systematically implemented that policy.[1]

The ideology propounded by the Bolsheviks was explicitly antagonistic, envisioning constant class war until the achievement of communism. Officials in the Provisional Government had contemplated employing state violence against their own citizens to secure grain deliveries. They had even drafted plans to do so. In addition to lacking the means to implement such policies, these officials were constrained in their efforts by a worldview that sought to bring together the various sectors of society, to achieve an inclusive and universalistic state order. The Leninist variant of Marxism, by contrast, insisted that world war be transformed into an open-ended class war. Communism was to be achieved through struggle against class enemies.

In his analysis of the French Revolution, Karl Marx had noted that Napoleon *"perfected* the *Terror* by *substituting permanent war* for *permanent revolution."*[2] Emerging out of the First World War, the Russian Revolution inverted this equation. Instead of permanent war substituting for permanent revolution, in Russia total revolution came to substitute for total war. The Bolshevik party-state, committed to the cause of the revolution as an ongoing project, adopted the practices of total war not only in its initial struggle against external enemies but also internally, in its efforts to forge a revolutionary society. The revolution thus provided a new matrix for practices that were emerging out of the First World War.

The Bolshevik Party dictated Terror. In the same text, however, Marx also observed that "ideas carry out nothing at all. In order to carry out ideas men are needed who can exert practical force."[3] Although Bolshevik ideology structured Soviet state violence, it was sustained by hostilities and resentments fostered in the late imperial period and exacerbated over the course of 1917. The ordeal of the Civil War itself—chaos, devastation, hunger, and want—embedded this violence in Soviet society.[4]

De-Cossackization: "Liquidating" the Cossackry

The Bolshevik Party made the October Revolution, but the Bolshevik party-state leviathan did not emerge until mid-1918. Through early 1918 the population of the Don Territory had no strong associations with political parties, including the Bolsheviks. All this would change by late summer 1918, when the Bolshevik Party transformed itself from one of "the two Soviet parties" into the sole party of the Soviet state. With the polarization of political life into a Soviet state, on the one hand, and an anti-revolutionary Cossack government, on the other, the middle ground disappeared from underneath the moderate socialists. Both the Menshevik and the Socialist Revolutionary parties found their members abandoning them in droves over their more conciliatory position toward the Cossack government throughout 1917 and early 1918. By mid-1918, their influence ceased to exist beyond the small number of members in the party committees.[5]

The other "soviet" party, the Left Socialist Revolutionaries, remained a vital force through the spring and summer of 1918. At the national level, there were growing conflicts between the Left Socialist Revolutionaries and the Bolsheviks over land policy and especially over the Brest-Litovsk peace, which surrendered huge swaths of territory to "German imperialism." The Soviet government's ratification of this peace caused the Left Socialist Revolutionaries to withdraw from the Soviet government. The increasing friction at the national level drew the lines more sharply for those serving in local governing organs, such as the Don Soviet Republic, the government of which was divided almost equally between Left Socialist Revolutionaries and Bolsheviks.

German forces and the Cossack insurgency had driven the officials of the Don Republic to neighboring Tsaritsyn, a revolutionary bastion. There these officials reconstituted a governing presidium. But the capture and execution of the Podtelkov expedition had dealt a catastrophic loss to the leading figures of the Left Socialist Revolutionary Party on the Don. As a result, the reconstituted seven-man presidium for the Don Soviet Republic now numbered only one Left Socialist Revolutionary among its members. In protest of the Bolshevik majority's domineering ways, even he soon resigned his position.[6] The now all-Bolshevik presidium assigned Bolsheviks to all major governmental posts.[7]

At the local and district level, however, Left Socialist Revolutionaries continued to be a potent force. In the localities, the distinction between the two parties remained, in the words of one Bolshevik observer, "imperceptible."[8] It was the Left Socialist Revolutionary uprising in Moscow (July 7–10, 1918) that led to their eclipse, both at the national level and on the Don.[9] Hoping to scuttle the peace with Germany and fire a revolutionary war, the Central Committee of the party sanctioned the assassination of the German ambassador on the eve of the Fifth Congress of Soviets and then half-heartedly moved to take over key positions in Moscow. Its goal was not to seize power but rather to force the Soviet state to change its policy. The party's Central Committee took this step without the foreknowledge of most party members. In Moscow Bolshevik control hung in the balance briefly, but the Bolsheviks brought in reliable troops and quickly put down the revolt.

The Bolsheviks gladly took advantage of the opportunity their competitors had so conveniently provided them. Circumstances contributed to the establishment of the Bolshevik monopoly on power, but it was a monopoly desired by the Bolsheviks themselves. They acted quickly to expel the Left Socialist Revolutionaries from government organs and elected soviets.[10] Lenin dispatched a telegram to Joseph Stalin in Tsaritsyn the evening following the attempted Moscow uprising, instructing him to "mercilessly crush these pathetic and hysterical adventurists, who have become a tool in the counterrevolutionaries' hands . . . be merciless with the Left Socialist Revolutionaries." Stalin assured Lenin that he would indeed be firm.[11]

In the Don Territory, however, there was little need for such firmness. In areas engaged in armed struggle with the counterrevolution, such as the Don, Left Socialist Revolutionaries rushed to proclaim their allegiance to the Soviet worker-peasant state and to denounce the actions of their own Central Committee. The Khoper District executive committee had nominated M. Ia. Makarov, the sole Left Socialist Revolutionary in the Soviet state's "Cossack section" in Moscow, as its delegate to the fateful Fifth Congress of Soviets. The day after the uprising Makarov hastily explained his Left Socialist Revolutionary affiliation to the Cossack section. He stated that he belonged to the party mainly "to acquaint the Cossack section with the direction and affairs of the [Left Socialist Revolutionary] fraction," and assured his colleagues that he had remained in the hall when the Left Socialist Revolutionary Central Committee demonstratively walked out. He concluded his report by announcing that he was withdrawing from the Left Socialist Revolutionary Party. The seven Left Socialist Revolutionaries in the Khoper District executive committee who had appointed him their delegate reacted similarly. Engaged in a struggle to the death with "Kadets" and "counterrevolutionaries" in their own district, they all condemned the Central Committee's Moscow acts as an adventure that "threatened the cause of the revolution." One of them applied immediately for transfer to the Bolshevik Party.[12]

To be sure, the Bolsheviks also resorted to repression and manipulation of the central apparatus to suppress the Left Socialist Revolutionaries in the Don Territory and elsewhere. But repression was not the primary reason for the collapse of support for the Left Socialist Revolutionaries. In this period most citizens' party identification remained amorphous. The Left Socialist Revolutionary Party found that its supporters were more committed to the cause of revolution than to questions of the specifics of revolutionary policy. With the revolution now threatened by counterrevolution, the Soviet state—and the sole party now remaining in it—became the foremost advocate and defender of that amorphous but nevertheless powerful ideal of "the revolution." By its actions on the national stage, the Left Socialist Revolutionary Central Committee unwittingly contributed to the claim of the Bolsheviks to be the sole party of the revolution.

Having emasculated their Left Socialist Revolutionary opponents, the Bolshevik leaders of the Don Soviet Republic now were confronted by a threat from another quarter. The Bolshevik Party and the Soviet state at this time were seeking to bring local bodies under stricter central control, with varying degrees of success.[13] The Don Soviet Republic had been established largely to forestall German claims to intervene on grounds of "national liberation." This gambit had proved unsuccessful, as Germans now occupied large portions of the region. Driven out of their base of operations, both party and state organs from the Don Territory depended on central funding for their continued existence, and the Soviet state's might to support their claims. For all these reasons, the central apparatus had fewer problems subordinating organs from the Don Territory than elsewhere.

The "Don Soviet Republic" had evacuated to Tsaritsyn in Saratov Province. As the linchpin for Soviet power in the south, Tsaritsyn served as the seat for the multifarious central agencies dispatched to conduct the struggle against counterrevolution. Stalin had arrived there in June 1918 as "extraordinary commissar for grain transport from the Northern Caucasus," and in July he was appointed to the military council of the Northern Caucasus Military District (NCMD). When the Tsaritsyn authorities, in a power struggle, arrested the Don government and seized its assets and print shop, Stalin ordered the officials' release. But he also took the opportunity to proclaim that "the Don Soviet Republic no longer exists, only some former members." Holding out the possibility that it might be reconstituted after the region's total liberation, he insisted that all members of "the former Don

Soviet Republic" now devote themselves fully to the Soviet state's armed struggle against counterrevolution. He indicated that the best way they could serve the cause was by transferring to the central apparatus, especially to the Red Army or the central food-supply organs. Acknowledging that its territorial base had ceased to exist, the Don Soviet Republic voted to liquidate all government affairs by early September. Believing that "the centralization of operations in the struggle to reestablish Soviet power on the Don is essential," it transferred the conduct of all military operations to the NCMD.[14] In September 1918 the Soviet government formally abolished the Don Soviet Republic.[15]

The central authorities thus increasingly subordinated local soviets to their control, at precisely the time Bolshevik control was extending over these central structures themselves. With the evacuation of the Don Soviet Republic to Tsaritsyn, the NCMD assumed power at the local level. In addition to their military tasks, NCMD officials were responsible for vetting local soviets and their military commissariats. In doing so, they aligned soviets that existed across a wide political spectrum with appropriately "Soviet" (if not yet entirely "Bolshevik") ones. To this end, Peter Moshtakov, an NCMD "organizer," sanctioned those elected military commissariats of which he approved. Whenever they displeased him, he summoned regional soviets to "elect" new ones, having first ensured that all candidates "stood for the Soviet platform." Elsewhere NCMD agents dissolved elected soviets and replaced them with all-Bolshevik military revolutionary committees.[16]

After the Left Socialist Revolutionary uprising in mid-July, the Soviet command appointed several leading Bolsheviks, including Stalin, to a newly formed NCMD military council.[17] Henceforth, this organ would seek to impart a party nature to all soviets, in addition to ensuring loyalty to central institutions. Elections to the Khoper District Congress of Soviets, meeting in mid-May 1918, returned 100 Left Socialist Revolutionary delegates and 85 Bolshevik ones. Despite the Left Socialist Revolutionary predominance at the congress, the NCMD appointed as its military commander A. G. Selivanov, the head of the district Bolshevik organization, along with a Bolshevik member of the Cossack section, Fedor Chekunov, as his aide.[18] These two central appointees then applied their own Bolshevik standards to local soviets. Chekunov penned caustic evaluations of local stanitsa soviets: "These stanitsas are for the time being on the side of soviets, but in such cases they are not Bolshevik soviets, but Menshevik and even Kadet ones, which only confuse the dark Cossackry."[19] Clearly, fighting against the Cossack insurgency and having one's own soviets were no longer enough to satisfy central authorities. A true soviet now also had to correspond to the Bolshevik-led Soviet government's image of such an organ.

Tellingly, the term "the Center" was employed increasingly to mean the Soviet state apparatus.[20] On the Don, the Center now dealt with the population through three of its own primary institutions—one civil, one military, and one party. The civil institution, the Soviet state's "Cossack Section of the Central Executive Committee," which acted as a clearinghouse for information and appeals, had little actual authority. The military institution was first the NCMD, established in May, and then its successor, the Southern Front, established on September 11, 1918. For the next two years this was the most significant and pervasive Soviet institution on the Don. The party organ, the Don Bureau of the Communist Party, was established at the end of August or beginning of September 1918.[21] Its members closely cooperated with the Southern Front's Revolutionary Military Council, all of whose members were of course Bolsheviks themselves.

The Don Bureau did not originate within the Don Territory, nor even among those fighting on its borders. While in Moscow, a group of Communists from the Don, primarily from industrial Rostov, petitioned the Communist Central Committee for permission to take over party work on the Don. They received the Central Committee's sanction and were dispatched to work alongside the Southern Front's political organs. The two most important figures were Sergei Syrtsov and Aron Frenkel', individuals who had already demonstrated an immunity to Cossack particularism, even in its Soviet forms. This group retained control of the Don Bureau even when it was broadened to include party members who called for continued institutional recognition for the Don, headed by the Cossack Viktor Kovalev. While divisions remained throughout 1919 between Syrtsov's "Russian group" and the "Cossack group" headed by Kovalev, the Center consistently backed Syrtsov's faction, thereby allowing it to retain control throughout the Civil War.[22]

Central control was exerted just as much through the Southern Front as through the Don Bureau. In autumn 1918 the Red Army took shape as an institution.[23] Previously independent military units received standardized designations and were consolidated into regular formations. At this time the Southern Front reformed the diverse units fighting on the Don into the Eighth, Ninth, and Tenth armies. Consolidation of the Red Army coincided with the extension of specifically Bolshevik control over the military. As early as July, in the wake of the Left Socialist Revolutionary uprising, the Northern Caucasus Military Commissariat had directed Communists to form party cells in their units. Given the relatively small number of local Communists and the Center's focus on the Eastern Front, this directive had little practical effect.[24] The establishment of greater party control over units of the Southern Front came only in November, when the Center shifted its attention from the Eastern Front. In October and November Lenin ordered party organizations in Moscow, Petrograd, and the central provinces to mobilize one-fifth of their members for service on the Southern Front.[25]

Mobilized party members served mainly as military commissars in units of the emerging Red Army. By mobilizing individuals through the central apparatus, the Center staffed the Southern Front with individuals sharing its orthodox views of Soviet power. All commissars appointed to the Southern Front in late November were Communist Party members. Left Socialist Revolutionaries were not accepted for service at the front. However, most commissars entered their training courses either prior to or simultaneous with entry into the Communist Party.[26] They did not become commissars because they were Communists; they became Communists because they enrolled as commissars. For them, the Bolshevik Party was first and foremost the armed defender of the Soviet state and its revolution.

By late 1918, then, the Bolshevik Party had come to dominate the organs of Soviet power at the national and local levels. Precisely at this time, Soviet power reconquered much of the Don Territory. The German Army and Cossack insurgencies had driven out Soviet power in the spring and summer of 1918, and the AGDH kept the Red Army at bay for most of the autumn. By early 1919, however, revolution in Germany and defeat in the west had removed the German Army. The Don Army, composed of forcibly conscripted Cossacks serving under often condescending and arbitrary officers, was in a state of near disintegration.[27] The combination of a reorganized Red Army and mutinies within the Don Army brought much of the Don Territory back under Soviet control. Particularly significant was the mutiny of several regiments in the Don Army in early January 1919. These units abandoned the front and returned to their communities in the Upper Don District. By allowing Soviet power to occupy large portions of the Don Territory, these Cossack regiments ironically provided the Communist Party with an opportunity to practice "de-Cossackization."

"De-Cossackization" was not a new term in 1919; indeed, it had been employed before the revolution by both the national and the local press to mean eliminating the Cossack estate as a judicial entity and leveling Cossack privileges to those enjoyed by other citizens.[28] Early in 1917, the Provisional Government had abolished all social restrictions predicated on religion, nationality, and estate. Upon taking power, the Soviet regime repeated this abolition and proclaimed that henceforth all were to be known simply as citizens of the Russian Republic.[29] From the beginning the Soviet state had decreed that Cossacks ceased to exist as a judicial estate; if they were to be identified as separate from other Russians, it must be as either an economic or a social group. The fundamental departure in the 1919 policy was that it was designed not to abolish a judicial estate or remove an economic class but rather to eliminate the Cossacks as an entire social collectivity.[30]

Cossack collective behavior certainly reinforced Soviet attitudes, but Bolshevik policies were not simply a response to some counterrevolutionary Cossack monolith. While some reports noted Cossack hostility to Soviet power, many others contain frequent mention of Cossacks welcoming it.[31] Although more Cossacks served in the anti-Soviet Don Army (more because they were forcibly conscripted than out of any freely given social support) than in the Red Army, one-fifth of all Cossacks under arms served with the latter.[32] Cossacks participated disproportionately in the ranks of *both* sides. Well through April 1919, Soviet officials continued to pass along news that "there are thirty thousand Cossacks fighting like lions in the Red Army."[33] It was a mutiny of Cossack regiments against the anti-Soviet Don command that had opened the front and made possible the Red Army's advance into the Don in early 1919.

In the face of such reports, several factors coalesced to cause the Soviet state to view Cossacks *in toto* as a counterrevolutionary force. The indisputable fact that many Cossacks were bearing arms against the revolution, willingly or not, played into a set of mutually reinforcing stereotypes. The Cossack leadership held a romanticized and paternalistic image of Cossacks as Russia's paladins of order and statehood, loyal but in need of political tutelage. This image had led the leaders of various anti-Soviet movements to seek out Cossack regions as their base of operations. To realize this idealized image of a Cossack Vendée, they then forcibly conscripted Cossacks to serve a cause presented to them as their own.

This anti-Soviet image of Cossacks as instinctive counterrevolutionaries reinforced existing Soviet views. Many in the revolutionary movement had long been conditioned to think of Cossacks as lackeys of the imperial regime. A crude form of Marxist class analysis buttressed this view with references to Cossacks' supposed land wealth. In Soviet usage, "Cossacks" came to mean only those serving in the anti-Soviet Don Army, while Cossacks serving the Soviet cause became generic "Red Army men."[34] In June 1918 Stalin had already argued that it was futile to look to the Cossacks for support, claiming, "our base in the Don Territory is the outlanders."[35]

Both sides had come to see Cossacks as an undifferentiated group. Ominously, Red and White tended to reify juridical categories and economic attributes into entirely discrete "populations." The emergence of this "population politics," as it was termed at the time, was an essential precondition for de-Cossackization. In the imperial period, a discipline termed "military statistics" had disaggregated the population into "elements" according to their purported political reliability. It had informed the tsarist regime's analyses of the country's population from the mid-nineteenth century and served as the guidelines for anti-insurgency measures in the imperial borderlands. The First World War, however, marked the watershed when the imperial state moved to the massive translation of these projections of the population into actual policies. From the very first days of the war, Russian imperial authorities oversaw the compulsory deportation of up to one million of their own subjects from the western provinces and Caucasian borderlands.[36]

Implementing "population politics" in the form of deportations, and drawing upon colonial precedents to do so, was no Russian anomaly during the First World War. The imperial regime had employed such measures in its colonial peripheries. During the war, other European states used such tactics as deportations and concentration camps against foreign foes and, to a degree, against their own national minorities. In Russia total war and then civil conflict extended these measures throughout the entire polity, where they were employed by Red and White alike. In 1918, the Don government passed a decree legally sanctioning the deportation of individuals who opposed its political agenda. The Kuban' Cossack Rada—the Kuban' equivalent of the Don Cossack Circle—went so far as to debate measures to expel all non-Cossacks; one delegate suggested instead that it would be better simply to kill off all non-Cossacks.[37] Bolshevism's penchant for anchoring all analyses in socioeconomic conditions inclined the party to such models; its Manicheism predisposed it to their ruthless implementation.

Both Red and White envisioned the Don Territory as inhabited by two distinct populations: the impoverished peasant *khokhly* (a derogatory term for Ukrainians) and the well-off, ethnically Russian Cossacks.[38] Here, too, imperial military statistics had led the way. The 1908 military-statistical overview of the Don Territory effectively conflated ethnic and estate categories, counterpoising ethnically Russian Cossacks to ethnically Ukrainian non-Cossacks, although the overlap was less than precise in both cases.[39] Thus the category of "Cossack" was no longer merely one of many administrative aggregations imposed upon a group of people. Instead it described a "population" or "element" that was irreducibly "Cossack." As Soviet forces advanced into the Don in early February 1919, the commander in chief of all Soviet forces penned an article entitled "The Struggle against the Don," in which he described the entire region as the arch-foe of the Soviet Republic, whose Cossack population had a psychology similar to "certain representatives of the zoological world."[40]

Soviet officials constructed a socioeconomic typology of an impoverished peasant and outlander population, oppressed by a wealthy and counterrevolutionary Cossackry. Such a paradigm resonated powerfully but did not correspond to actual economic relations. Soviet officials (and subsequent historical studies) have myopically focused on the aggregate amount of allotment land held by each group, to the exclusion of private landholding and land rental.[41] Cossacks undoubtedly had far more allotment land. But peasants and many outlanders, involved in market agriculture to a greater extent than Cossacks, tended to engage in more intensive forms of agriculture, employing more hired laborers and advanced agricultural equipment.[42] Among "impoverished" outlanders aligning themselves with Soviet power in early 1918 were men like Iakov Skliarov, who held nearly 240 acres of hayfields and 108 acres of sowings, eight horses, and a home valued at 25,000 rubles. He and others like him served in the ranks of the Red Army.[43] Red Army commanders themselves noted that while many peasants volunteered, far from all were impoverished. I. M. Mukhoperets, who raised peasant detachments in the dark days of 1918, later recalled:

> The masses did not follow us because of our political line. Rather, it was an elemental movement, a struggle based on the hostility between the Cossackry and the peasantry, [and] we succeeded in organizing the peasants without being too picky about their class status. We had soldiers who had over 500 acres, but they fought valiantly for us.[44]

The estate stereotype favored by the AGDH leadership itself was predicated on the preconception that all outlanders must inevitably be "Bolsheviks," driving many peasants, regardless of economic status, into the Red Army. In this way the Soviet and Don government stereotypes converged, reinforcing each other.

The stereotypes of centrally appointed Soviet officials like Stalin reinforced the views of local peasants who had suffered at the hands of Cossack insurgents. What had previously been social antagonism between peasants and Cossacks was now expressed as political conflict. One local Soviet activist warned his superiors in late summer 1918 that even those Cossacks "ostensibly dedicated to Soviet power" in fact were counterrevolutionaries. "In a word," he claimed, "the Cossack element is *unreliable*."[45] According to this view, Cossacks were innately counterrevolutionary. Acting on this view, non-Cossacks serving in the Red Army sometimes rebuffed Cossacks seeking to cross the lines and volunteer. Forced to return to their stanitsas, these Cossacks then had little choice but to join "their" Don Army.[46]

Peasants, of course, had long wished to settle accounts with Cossacks, but now they could paint their adversaries as "counterrevolutionaries" to the new revolutionary regime. In June 1918 peasants spoke of merely "cutting off the Cossacks' trouser stripes," that is, abolishing all features distinguishing Cossacks from the rest of the population.[47] (Cossacks all wore a distinguishing trouser stripe, with a specific color for each Cossack administrative community; Don Cossacks wore a red one.) By late September 1918, in conditions of civil war, some had begun to speak instead of physical extermination. Soviet officials reported that peasants had responded to Cossack calls for the total "extermination" of non-natives living on the Don with their own demand for "total extermination" of Cossacks. By December 1918, Leon Trotsky proclaimed that Soviet power was issuing a "final warning to you, Cossacks! The crimes of Krasnov have hardened the hearts of the workers and peasants. Hatred for Krasnov often extends to the Cossacks in general. More and more often we hear the voices of the workers and peasants, saying: 'we must exterminate all Cossacks, then peace and calm will come to South Russia!'"[48] By January 1919, when de-Cossackization was officially declared, it had become a truism among Soviet supporters at both the local and the national level that "the Cossack population" was counterrevolutionary and ripe for some form of elimination.

Views of Cossacks as inveterate counterrevolutionaries were an essential precondition for de-Cossackization. The Soviet state's institutional endorsement made de-Cossackization possible as policy. Subordinate organs certainly had little compunction about using terror. But it was the Center that created the environment for "excesses," both through its official sanction of violence and through establishing a command system responsible only for carrying out orders from above.

The role of central directives can be measured by contrasting Soviet policy on the Don before and after the circular decreeing de-Cossackization as official policy. On January 24, 1919, the Organizational Bureau (Orgburo) of the Bolshevik Party Central Committee issued a circular setting forth a new central policy. Until late January 1919, the Southern Front, with assistance from the Don Bureau, implemented Soviet policy on the Don. As the Red Army advanced into the Don Territory, the Southern Front had, on January 22, issued its own "Instruction to political commissars on the organization of authority in territories liberated from the Krasnovite yoke."[49] This directive was much more discriminating in its application of terror than the Central Committee circular was to be. The "Instruction" directed that

mass terror in the occupied territories is entirely undesirable and intolerable, playing into the hands of Krasnovite fear-mongering and complicating our position. Terror is to be employed against only the leading actors of the White guard camp, [while] suspicious and unreliable elements are subject to arrest and dispatch to Borisoglebsk or Balashov.

The Southern Front limited terror only to those who had demonstrated their counterrevolutionary nature through the commission of actual counterrevolutionary acts. This distinction was further elaborated in the Southern Front's "Instructions to khutor and village commissars."[50] While requiring the arrest of all those who "took an active part in the struggle against Soviet power" (officers, priests, and atamans), it distinguished between such activists and mere conscripts. As long as they were not guilty of any atrocities while in Krasnov's army, Cossack conscripts who had returned to their homes were to be treated like all other citizens.

The distinguishing feature of 1919 de-Cossackization was its use of indiscriminate terror against all Cossacks, irrespective of how they had acted previously, a policy resulting directly from a circular of January 24 issued by the party's Orgburo. The measures contained in this circular constituted "high de-Cossackization," which was pursued from early February through mid-March 1919. As the Red Army advanced into Cossack regions, Sergei Syrtsov suggested to his party superiors that they formulate a policy toward Cossack regions now coming under Soviet control.[51] Syrtsov had grown up in Rostov and graduated from a Rostov commercial school; he had then gone to St. Petersburg in 1912 to continue his studies. The following year, at the age of twenty, he joined the Bolshevik Party and was soon exiled to Siberia. With the February Revolution, he returned to the Don as the region's leading Bolshevik at the ripe age of twenty-four. From late 1918 he served as chairman of the Don Party Bureau, where he consistently pressed for the most radical form of de-Cossackization. For much of 1919 the Central Committee endorsed his views, over strong opposition from other members of the Don Bureau (notably Frenkel'), as well as from the Southern Front's Revolutionary Military Council (most prominently, Georgii Sokol'nikov).

By early 1919, however, the members of the Central Committee did not need Syrtsov to convince them that the Cossackry was congenitally counterrevolutionary. Ironically, the reason for issuing the de-Cossackization circular was the Red Army's rapid advance into Cossack regions, an advance the Central Committee knew full well was the result of Cossack units' opening the front to the Red Army. The Orgburo's circular of January 24 reads:[52]

> Recent events on various fronts in the Cossack regions—our advance to the heart of Cossack settlements and demoralization among the Cossack forces—compel us to give directions to party officials on the nature of their work in establishing and consolidating Soviet power in the specified regions. Considering the experience of a year of civil war against the Cossackry, we must recognize the only proper means to be a merciless struggle with the entire Cossack elite by means of their total extermination [*putem pogolovnogo ikh istrebleniia*]. No compromises, no halfway measures are permissible. Therefore it is necessary:
>
> (1) To conduct *mass terror* [emphasis in original] against wealthy Cossacks, exterminating them totally; to conduct merciless mass terror against all those Cossacks who participated, directly or indirectly, in the struggle against Soviet power. Toward the middle Cossackry it is necessary to take all steps that guarantee no further attempts on its part to rise against Soviet power.
>
> (2) To confiscate grain and compel storage of all surpluses at designated points, in terms of both grain and all other agricultural goods.
>
> (3) To take all measures for helping the poor who are arriving to settle [and] organizing resettlement where possible.
>
> (4) To level the nonlocal outlanders with the Cossacks in land and all other concerns.
>
> (5) To conduct total disarmament, executing anyone who is found with weapons after the date of [the weapons'] surrender.
>
> (6) To issue weapons only to reliable elements from among the outlanders.
>
> (7) To leave armed detachments in Cossack stanitsas until the establishment of total order.
>
> (8) All commissars appointed to this or that Cossack settlement are urged to demonstrate maximum firmness and implement the present instructions without deviation.
>
> The CC orders that the directive to the People's Commissariat of Land work out, in short order, practical measures for the mas-

sive resettlement of the poor to Cossack lands through relevant Soviet institutions.

—The Central Committee of the Russian Communist Party

This circular differed significantly from the Southern Front's earlier "Instruction." First, it envisioned the area coming under the control of the Red Army as "Cossack regions" rather than as "territories liberated from the Krasnovite yoke." Correspondingly, it portrayed the struggle as one against the entire Cossackry rather than against the activist core of the Krasnovite army. Second, it ordered a policy of mass terror, a policy that only two days before the Southern Front had described as "undesirable and intolerable." Third, instead of trying to win over the middle Cossackry, as the regime was trying to do at the time with the middle peasants in the rest of Russia, the Orgburo commanded that the middle Cossackry be restrained through the use of preventative terror. Finally, the circular significantly expanded the parameters of mass terror. Since the entire Cossack elite was presumed to be irreparably counterrevolutionary, it was slated for "total extermination." But while the Southern Front's "Instruction" had spared those who had been forcibly conscripted, the Orgburo circular called for "merciless, mass terror" against those who took a "direct or indirect" part in the struggle against Soviet power. Considering the Don Army's compulsory universal mobilizations, at times covering all males between the ages of eighteen and fifty, the entire male Cossack population that had remained on the Don could be said to have "indirectly" participated in counterrevolution—and hence was to be subject to "merciless, mass terror."

Before receiving the circular, the Southern Front had initiated its own policies. Then, on February 4, the Southern Front's Revolutionary Military Council (RMC) received the Orgburo circular, which it dutifully distributed down the chain of command. In its own cover letter accompanying the circular, the Southern Front RMC tried to frame the new directive in more moderate terms. Whereas the circular itself called for "maximum firmness" with "no deviations," the Southern Front directed officials to operate with the "requisite tact and caution" in the interests of furthering class differentiation among the Cossackry.[53]

However much it might introduce various interpolations, the Southern Front nevertheless had to carry out the essential points of the

Orgburo directive. On February 5, only one day after it first received the circular, the Southern Front's RMC issued Order no. 171 on the formation of revolutionary tribunals, followed the next day by Order no. 178 on district revolutionary committees. These two decrees were the essential tools for implementing high de-Cossackization. Then, on February 7, the RMC issued its own instructions on how the Orgburo's circular was to be applied.[54] During a later policy review of de-Cossackization's failure, some party officials sought to blame the RMC's instructions, rather than the Orgburo's circular, for any and all excesses.[55] Yet the instructions actually added nothing substantial to the Orgburo circular. The RMC described the categories of the population who were subject to "immediate execution": all AGDH officials; all officers of the Don Army; anyone who actively supported the counter-revolution; and "all wealthy Cossacks without exception." But, relative to the Orgburo circular, the instructions introduced a note of restraint. "However, terror against these groups," it directed, "and especially against the middle Cossackry, should not be the sole method in our struggle for strengthening the Soviet regime." Contrary to the later accusations that it was the Southern Front's instructions that were overly broad, rather than the Orgburo decree itself, the Southern Front still limited the application of terror only to those who had actively opposed Soviet power. Khutor atamans were to be subject to terror only if "they actively supported Krasnov's policies."

Terror was not some unstructured, indiscriminate slaughter; nor was it a spontaneous, terrible retribution by peasants for past Cossack abuses. Terror was policy—organized, sanctioned, and conducted by officially established institutions. Acting on the Orgburo circular and operating in close contact with the Central Committee, the Southern Front quickly established an entire network of tribunals to carry out the prescribed mass terror. Regimental tribunals, composed of the occupying unit's commissar and two other party members, were to be established in every stanitsa occupied by Soviet forces.[56] These tribunals were to operate along a unit's path of advance and at all points where it happened to quarter. Their sentences were not subject to review. Within two weeks, the Southern Front was receiving reports that its regimental tribunals were "overloaded with work."[57]

Despite its subsequent protests to the contrary, the Center was fully aware of the tribunals' activities. Through both the army and the party chain of command, central authorities diligently supervised local tribunals' actions. Indeed, central authorities regularly pressed these tribunals to be even more "energetic." In the Khoper and Upper Don Districts, military superiors became dissatisfied with the pace and severity of "regular" divisional revolutionary tribunals, even though they were showing no compunction about executing people. In their place army commanders established "extraordinary revolutionary tribunals" to review sentences already handed out and to handle all new cases.[58] Such "extraordinary tribunals" indeed proved to be significantly firmer. For the thirty-one individuals brought before it, the "regular" Khoper District revolutionary tribunal had handed down two death sentences. Its successor, the "extraordinary" tribunal, reviewed the sentences already handed out and upgraded the sentences of ten more people to execution. Over the next two weeks the "extraordinary tribunal" tried 142 defendants, sentencing 93 to death (90 for the rather elastic category of "counterrevolution"). It acquitted a mere 17. Over a one-month period in March 1919, the Khoper extraordinary revolutionary tribunal handed down a total of 226 death sentences.[59] In Morozov and Ust'-Medveditsa Districts, army-level revolutionary military councils pressed local officials to be more "energetic." The Ninth Army RMC reproached the Ust'-Medveditsa District Revolutionary Committee for its unfamiliarity with the measure of employing hostages from the civilian population "for purposes of expediency."[60] Pressure for more "energetic" prosecution, tellingly, came not from the military *per se* (it was divisional revolutionary tribunals that had proven insufficiently "energetic"), but directly from the RMCs of the Eighth, Ninth, and Tenth armies—organs appointed by and answering to central party and state organs in Moscow.

To be sure, local officials charged with carrying out de-Cossackization interpreted the directive in the broadest possible terms. Subsequent official reviews of the policy excoriated the brutality and poor quality of personnel staffing local organs. The commissar in Slashchevskaia stanitsa, one policy review reported, had declared that he intended "to drive Cossacks to their grave," a sentiment shared by some Khoper officials.[61] But central organs had insisted upon their prerogative to appoint these individuals, and had insistently refused the possibility of elected authority. Even more fundamentally, central authorities set the boundaries of acceptable behavior. By explicit directives and tacit sanction of local organs' policies, they signaled the limits of acceptable behavior.[62]

It is difficult to determine the total number of victims of de-Cossackization on the Don, as the insurgents and later the AGDH used the executions for propagandistic purposes. In the Upper Don region, the number of victims was between three and five hundred. The number would certainly have been higher had the rebellion not broken out when it did.[63] In some regions—Khoper District, Kotel'nikovo, Tsimlianskaia—revolutionary tribunals executed hundreds of people.[64] In others—Millerovo, Berezovskaia, Mitiakinskaia, Semikarakovskaia, Velikokniazheskaia, Skurishevskaia—tribunals executed only a handful.[65] In all, this highly orchestrated Soviet policy of social engineering by excision accounted for perhaps ten to twelve thousand victims throughout the Don Territory.

While terror was the most conspicuous point of the Orgburo circular, high de-Cossackization encompassed an entire complex of other measures to render Cossacks harmless to the Soviet Republic. Identifying the Don Territory with the particularistic and counterrevolutionary Cossackry, the Soviet leadership refused to grant it any form of administrative recognition analogous to that of other provinces. Instead, Soviet authorities tried to erase the Don Territory from the map altogether. Throughout January the Don Party Bureau repeatedly requested it be granted direct administration over the Don Territory, a proposal supported by the Southern Front.[66] Neither the Southern Front nor the Don Bureau yet knew of the Orgburo's January 24 circular on de-Cossackization, received by the Southern Front only on February 4. Hence they were not expecting the Central Committee's curt response to their petitions, which came on January 29 and insisted that control be concentrated in the hands of the Southern Front's RMC, with the added injunction that "there is to be no Don Executive Committee and no Don Government."[67] When the Don Bureau pressed its requests for a civilian administrative organ for the Don, the Orgburo again reiterated that the Don was to be granted no independent administrative existence.[68]

While local party officials continued to press for some civilian or party organ, they simultaneously lobbied for the elimination of all forms of distinct Cossack administration. When the Don Bureau petitioned for a territorial executive committee, it argued that such an or-

gan was necessary "to plan for the dismemberment of the Don Territory and to prepare for the creation of new administrative entities that
correspond to the economic and political needs of the moment."[69] A
program of population management drove this administrative reorganization. For much of 1919, the Soviet state planned to append portions of Tsaritsyn Province and the Donets basin, along with their populations, to the Don Territory. The explicit goal was "to dilute" the
Don's Cossack presence through the introduction of a more reliable
"element," workers and poor peasants. Indeed, the policy was intended, noted one proposal, "to tear the counterrevolution's flesh
apart," in the hope that the Cossackry would entirely "dissolve."[70]

The colonization program foreseen in the Orgburo's circular was yet
another prong in the Soviet state's program of social engineering. Colonization was expressly intended to "dilute" the Cossack "element" by
"the widespread removal of Cossacks" on the one hand, and by the introduction of "peasant elements from Central Russia" on the other.[71]
These settlers were not to be "sprinkled individually among the Cossack population," but were to be settled in compact groups.[72]

The Soviet apparatus even envisioned obliterating the distinct titles
for Cossack administrative entities within the Don Territory. Cossacks
regarded such structures as markers distinguishing them from peasants, and the Soviet regime clearly wished to remove this pillar of Cossack identity. Later Lenin, in a disingenuous attempt to displace blame
for "high de-Cossackization" from the Center onto local authorities,
portrayed this measure as a case of local officials' excessive enthusiasm,
singling out the directives of the Kotel'nikovo Revolutionary Committee in particular.[73] Regional revolutionary committees, however, had
not taken this step on their own; they were merely implementing two
orders issued earlier by the Southern Front. These orders abolished
the use of the distinctive "Cossack military districts" [*okruga*] and
"stanitsas," replacing them with the generic "region" and "county," respectively. It was these orders from the Southern Front that prompted
both the Kalach and the Kotel'nikovo revolutionary committees to
rename "stanitsas" into "counties," the act that drew Lenin's rebuke.[74]
Lenin's telegram failed to note, however, that the Kotel'nikovo committee's order had explicitly stated that the committee was merely carrying out the Southern Front's most recent order.

The Don Bureau aggressively pursued the territory's dismemberment, even over the objections of the Southern Front. At the Eighth Party Congress in March 1919, the Don Bureau argued for administrative restructuring so as to dilute the Cossack presence. The Southern Front's RMC, however, believed that the military situation made such plans premature.[75] The Don Bureau remained insistent. In April, it again petitioned the Center to oversee the dismemberment of the territory. Again, the Southern Front's RMC protested the planned dismemberment, prompting the Don Bureau to dispatch Syrtsov, its most fervent proponent of de-Cossackization, to Moscow to argue its case. Syrtsov pressed the case for dismemberment in his letter to the Central Committee on April 21, laying out plans to dilute the Cossack presence to 30 percent by detaching areas of the Don Territory to surrounding provinces.[76] The Southern Front's RMC fired off yet another protest, charging that the situation in general, and the Cossack uprising that had been prompted by these policies in particular, did not permit the break-up of existing administrative structures.[77] This opposition by the Southern Front managed to delay the territory's dismemberment until the Soviet retreat in mid-1919, making further discussion moot.

The Central Committee could forbid territorial-level organs, but it required institutional structures at some level to carry out its measures. At both the district and the stanitsa level, it sanctioned the formation of revolutionary committees. The party, however, directed that these posts be staffed only by appointment. Prior to the Orgburo's de-Cossackization circular, the Southern Front's Political Section had issued its own directive for the civil apparatus. The army would appoint revolutionary committees or temporary executive committees of soviets. But if reliable supporters of Soviet power could be found among the local population, it would allow elections under the strict supervision of the political commissar in charge.[78] Within two days, however, the Orgburo's circular on de-Cossackization superseded the Southern Front's guidelines. On February 6 the Southern Front issued Order no. 178, canceling all previous directives on administration. The Southern Front would appoint all district revolutionary committees, and they would remain subordinate both to it and to the Don Bureau. This directive would remain in force longer than any other de-Cossackization decree, outlasting both the repeal of the Orgburo's de-Cossackization circular (March 16) and cancellation of Order no. 172 on revolutionary tribunals (April 7).[79]

Order no. 178 concerned only district revolutionary committees. Among other issues, the Southern Front's February 7 "Instruction on implementing the CC directive on policy for the Don" laid down guidelines for revolutionary committees in stanitsas (for Cossack regions) and counties (for peasant ones). It explicitly established different guidelines for Cossack and peasant communities. There were to be no elections to posts in Cossack regions. Stanitsa executive committees were to be composed of three Communists from the regiment that occupied the area. If there were any trustworthy Communists or sympathizers among the local population, they could be appointed to the executive committee, but under no conditions were Communists from the occupying regiment to form less than a majority. In contrast, the instruction counseled that

> in peasant regions, considering the antagonism that has eternally existed between [peasants] and Cossacks, as well as [peasants'] more revolutionary mood, one must pursue a different policy. Elected authority is permissible, but it must be conducted in an organized manner and with the proper preparation, nominating the candidates beforehand and only then electing them at the gatherings. In general bring them to the level of the peasantry of all of Soviet Russia.[80]

Although the Southern Front obviously had no great trust in even the peasants' ability to select the correct candidate, it regarded peasants on the Don as analogous to those in the rest of the country.

The Bolshevik state did not, however, pursue an open-ended program of genocide against the Cossacks.[81] Over the spring and summer, the Center staged a gradual retreat from its original policy of "high de-Cossackization." In March a wide-scale uprising erupted in the Don's northern districts. Holding their own until June, the instigators of this rebellion—variously termed the Veshenskaia or Upper Don uprising—then linked up with the resurgent Don Army to reoccupy most of the Don. The rebellion's tenaciousness and its growing successes caused the Soviet regime to reevaluate its policies toward the Cossacks. The party abandoned de-Cossackization as physical extermination and replaced it with a policy of eliminating Cossacks as a socioeconomic class. Revolutionary tribunals did not cease their activities, but their scope was sharply circumscribed. While it continued to prescribe merciless retribution for those who raised arms against the revolution, Soviet power no longer called for the elimination of Cossacks as Cossacks. The policy shifted from punishing Cossacks for who they were to punishing them for what they had done.

The Don Bureau had never made peace with the Center's total ban on a territorial-level administrative organ. The Southern Front did not favor the ban, either. It did, however, insist on retaining control over all work in the territory, testifying not only to its reluctance to surrender authority but also to its distrust of the Don Bureau, and specifically of Syrtsov. As a result of their joint prodding, the Center finally relented somewhat. It remained opposed to the formation of a regular, provincial-level organ, either an executive or a revolutionary committee. Instead it established a "Civil Administration of the Southern Front's Revolutionary Military Council," an organ with the same name and functions as the imperial government's institution for administering territories occupied during wartime. During the First World War such organs had ruled portions of occupied Galicia and Armenia.[82] (Some anti-Soviet armies in the civil wars also looked to this precedent for administering regions under their control.)[83] These imperial organs had suffered from a lack of coordination between military and civilian branches, crippling their effectiveness. For the Soviet "Civil Administration," the Bolshevik Party conveniently, if unintentionally, served as the coordinating link between the military and civilian authorities. The Southern Front retained overall control of the region, but the new organ directly oversaw civilian administration. The Don Bureau, while disappointed at the continued dominance of the Southern Front, acceded to the Civil Administration's formation in the interests of military expediency.[84]

In the second week of March the Veshenskaia uprising broke out in protest of Soviet power and soon encompassed most of the Upper Don District. This was precisely the region that only a month and a half earlier had thrown open the front to the Red Army, an act that had prompted Soviet officials to review their policy on the Don and issue their de-Cossackization circular. The Southern Front, which had long opposed the Don Bureau's more extreme policies, invoked the uprising as an argument for a more restrained approach to the region. As a member of the Southern Front's RMC, Sokol'nikov presented a report to the Central Committee arguing that it was impossible to carry out the Orgburo's de-Cossackization orders. He proposed instead to utilize the different socioeconomic profiles of the Don Territory's northern and southern districts to foster socioeconomic differentiation "without our unnecessary interference." (Generally, the southern districts were wealthier and thus perceived to be more conservative than the northern districts). At a March 15 meeting the Orgburo decided to place the issue of the circular's annulment before the entire Central Committee. The following day the Central Committee endorsed Sokol'nikov's analysis, passing a resolution that called for an end to "actions against the Cossackry."[85]

Syrtsov forwarded news of the Central Committee's change in policy to local authorities on March 25:

> Immediately inform all responsible party and Soviet leaders of your region that the CC has reviewed its directive and directs party workers to cease the implementation of mass terror. Take absolutely no measures that might complicate relations and lead to an uprising. Economic measures—especially requisitions—should be pursued with the utmost caution and circumspection . . . Removing individual counterrevolutionaries who are harmful is of course necessary. The Veshenskaia uprising should of course be suppressed with all decisiveness and mercilessness, but repressions ought not to be extended indiscriminately to stanitsas that have not rebelled. It is of course necessary to employ more severity toward the southern Cossackry, but not to excess.[86]

Although the document is no model of humanitarianism, it nevertheless represents a major shift from "high de-Cossackization." Terror was still the order of the day—but now only for those who had engaged in counterrevolutionary acts. The Cossackry in its entirety was no longer the target. Nor was the Cossackry seen as some monolithic, counterrevolutionary bloc. The putative economic differentiation between Cossacks in the northern and southern districts was now invoked, and would continue to be invoked in the future, to explain Cossacks' counterrevolutionary tendencies.[87] Cossacks were no longer assumed simply to be congenital counterrevolutionaries; now class reasons had to be advanced to explain their behavior.

Two weeks later, another, more sweeping decree further dismantled the legal structures underpinning "high de-Cossackization." On April 5, the Southern Front issued an order annulling almost all previous orders directed specifically against Cossacks, particularly order no. 171 on revolutionary tribunals. At this time the Southern Front also cancelled its own February 7 "Instructions" to the Orgburo circular of January 24, which itself had already been annulled three weeks before. The order directed an overall change in Soviet policy on the Don:

> In place of all previous instructions concerning general policy for the Don Territory, the Southern Front's RMC orders the following be observed: suppress attempts at uprising in the rear in the most merciless manner, while simultaneously not resorting to mass terror toward peaceful regions, persecuting only active counterrevolutionaries.[88]

The shift in views on the Cossackry, visible in Syrtsov's earlier directive, is evident here as well. Not the Cossackry in its entirety, but "only active counterrevolutionaries" and those engaged in the Upper Don insurgency were now to be subject to terror. (Subsequent accounts of de-Cossackization erroneously conflate these later measures against insurgents together with the earlier and much broader de-Cossackization measures.)

The case of the Morozovskaia Revolutionary Committee demonstrates both how the Center pressed its policies and how it subsequently sought to distance itself from them. The atrocities in Morozovskaia, while not as extensive as those in other regions, crop up in almost every account of de-Cossackization.[89] We know so much about the executions (the sixty-four corpses found in the Morozovskaia barn figure in nearly every treatment) because Boguslavskii, the local commissar, became the scapegoat for the entire policy of de-Cossackization.

The Morozovskaia Revolutionary Committee, like all others, was appointed, with Boguslavskii as its head.[90] Following overall policy, Boguslavskii soon began to execute groups of people. The extent of these executions worried even local military and party officials. When a local party representative came to complain about the number of executions, Boguslavskii described his predicament. Local officials accused him of being overzealous, but a delegate from the Tenth Army had reprimanded him for being too "weak" and had instructed him to be more "energetic." Bewildered, Boguslavskii asked the local party representative whom he should obey: the local party organization protesting his "excesses," or his party and military superiors, pressing for an even more energetic application of terror? In direct response to the call for more "energetic" policies, Boguslavskii took out and executed all sixty-four people held in the prison. These are the infamous corpses later disinterred to indict Boguslavskii, and invoked in all subsequent accounts of de-Cossackization.

The winds were changing, however. The Center repudiated high de-Cossackization in late March. In April the Morozovskaia district party organization arrested Boguslavskii, informing the Don Bureau of its action. In order to appease public opinion, the Ninth Army's revolutionary tribunal tried Boguslavskii and two colleagues publicly for "their" crimes. The trial was closely orchestrated. The Don Bureau—which had initiated the de-Cossackization policy and then pressed for the most aggressive implementation of it—gave its approval to the investigation, dispatched a representative to supervise the case, and closely monitored its course. Despite protestations by Boguslavskii and his two codefendants that they were merely carrying out orders from their superiors, all three were sentenced to death. Upon confirmation by the CC, the sentence was carried out on May 8.[91]

Boguslavskii was undoubtedly guilty of the violations with which he had been charged. But he also had not been acting on his own. Boguslavskii paid for the policies he had been pressured to carry out. Holding him responsible for the "excesses" of de-Cossackization allowed all subsequent critics of the policy to cite Morozovskaia as an example of how the policy had been "misapplied" by over-zealous local officials. The ubiquitous discussion of Morozovskaia in the subsequent reviews by party officials (reviews that have served as historians' most basic source for de-Cossackization) ensured that Morozovskaia entered the historical literature as the paradigmatic example of the failed policy.

Yet, while forced to abjure the more extreme variant of de-Cossackization, many party officials retained their belief in its fundamental correctness. Syrtsov, for instance, placed all responsibility for its failure not on the policy itself but on the Southern Front's inability or unwillingness to carry it out. (Indeed, the Don Bureau continued to protest through the summer of 1919 against the Southern Front's attempts to come to some "accommodation with the Cossacks.")[92] The Don Bureau's continued intransigence, spearheaded by Syrtsov, was evident in its April 8 "Resolution on policy toward the Cossacks." Issued only three days after the Southern Front had cancelled the essential decrees of "high de-Cossackization," the Don Bureau's policy statement opens with a proclamation that "the existence of the Don Cossackry stands before proletarian power as a constant threat of counterrevolutionary rebellion." The Cossack threat therefore

> makes vital the question of the complete, immediate, and decisive destruction of the Cossackry as a specific cultural [bytovoi] and economic group, the destruction of its economic foundations, the physical elimination of the Cossack bureaucrats and officers (indeed, of the entire counterrevolutionary Cossack elite), the dispersal and neutralization of the rank-and-file Cossackry, and the formal liquidation of the Cossackry.

While conceding that terror should be employed only as a "justified retribution" for counterrevolutionary actions, the resolution argued for the confiscation of land from Cossacks and the imposition of "contributions" and special taxes. Its primary recommendation, however, was for the Soviet state to pursue a policy of massive resettlement "of peasant elements from Central Russia" to the Don, a program that had already been proposed in the Orgburo circular and restated in the Southern Front's "instructions" that accompanied it.[93]

Clearly, Syrtsov's view of Cossacks and the measures necessary to neutralize them had changed little. His hard-line approach caused a split within even the Don Bureau. While four members led by Syrtsov supported the resolution's firm line, two others (led by Frenkel') accused the majority of failing to adopt the Center's new, less extreme policy.[94] Syrtsov took his case to the Central Committee, traveling personally to Moscow and submitting a lengthy policy proposal there on April 21. In his proposal he argued for the dismemberment of the Don Territory and suggested that the regime rely only on the peasantry in pursuing the elimination of the Cossackry.[95]

The Don Bureau's continued insistence on hard-line measures, together with its charge that the army was to blame for de-Cossackization's failure, brought the bureau into conflict with the Southern Front's RMC. On behalf of the Southern Front, Sokol'nikov exchanged recriminations by telegraph with the Don Bureau. The Southern Front, aware that Syrtsov was traveling to meet the Central Committee, sent a telegram of its own. In it Sokol'nikov ridiculed the Don Bureau's charge that de-Cossackization had failed because the army had failed to implement it. As proof he cited figures confirming the "broad implementation" of the directive in the area currently seized by the Upper Don rebellion. He then went on to charge that the Don Bureau had "not changed its policy at all, which entirely corresponds to its view that the original directive had simply not been given a chance to work."[96] Syrtsov's trip to Moscow, however, paid dividends. The Central Committee gave its approval to the Don Bureau's "Resolution on the Cossackry." Over the continued objections of the Southern Front and a minority of the Don Bureau, the Orgburo endorsed Syrtsov's plan for a coordinated colonization program and entertained plans for the immediate dismemberment of the Don province.[97]

Following Syrtsov's advice, on April 24 the Council of People's Commissars decreed that "the starving urban and rural proletariat" should be resettled in the Don Territory and ordered the Commissariat of Agriculture to supervise the resettlement of peasants from six northern provinces to "the former Don Territory." The following month, as the first parties of settlers were about to arrive, the Southern Front ordered that military and civilian institutions should use all means at their disposal to further the program.[98] By May the first parties of settlers began arriving on the Don, where they were directed to the Kotel'nikovo and Millerovo regions. At this very time, however, the Red Army began a slow retreat from the Don Territory. Fearing retribution, the settlers began refusing the land slated for them. Several months later, a White newspaper article did not so much condemn the settlers as find them pathetic. Uninformed as to their final point of destination, they had been scattered along the railway line. When local farmers, racing to harvest their fields, attempted to employ them, they found the settlers entirely incompetent at the type of fieldwork required in southern regions.[99]

Like the Southern Front's Civil Administration, the Soviet colonization program for the Don extended preexisting state practices. The imperial state's Ministry of Agriculture had pursued its own resettlement program. Sergei Chirkin, the leading official in the tsarist Ministry of Agriculture's Resettlement Bureau, continued his duties under the Soviets.[100] Tsarist military officials also had extensively theorized about colonization programs. They implemented them too, largely in the empire's colonial peripheries of the Caucasus and Central Asia. In the course of 1914–1917, the imperial regime had extended these measures to wide swaths of the front, deporting populations deemed "unreliable." In the aftermath of the widespread 1916 uprising in Central Asia, tsarist military authorities drafted a systematic colonization and deportation program for the region. Only the February Revolution had prevented its realization. Nor was Russia alone in pursuing such measures. German and Austro-Hungarian forces employed analogous tactics, particularly in their operations in the East.[101]

With the civil wars, combatants now extended these techniques, perfected in colonial spaces and widely expanded during the First World War, to the entire political space of the empire. The anti-Soviet AGDH engaged in sporadic expulsions from individual communities, and some officials discussed expelling non-Cossacks altogether. Yet Bolshevik ideology, emphasizing the endemic and ongoing nature of class war, raised these measures from the realm of military practice to one of permanent state policy. Bolshevik officials such as Syrtsov envisioned de-Cossackization measures not as the outgrowth of military operations but rather as a central and continuing goal of Soviet power, to be pursued in war or peace. In early July I. I. Reingol'd, a member of the Don Revolutionary Committee formed in early May to replace the Civil Administration, wrote a report for the Central Committee entitled "On the Issue of Our 'Cossack Policy' on the Don." Reingol'd proposed the formation of a civilian Don Soviet government and criticized the tactless behavior of revolutionary committees over the past six months. Nevertheless, de-Cossackization itself had not been a mistake:

> By means of [de-Cossackization] we hoped to make the Don healthy, to make it, if not Soviet, then at least submissive and obedient to Soviet power . . . Indisputably, our doctrinal view that Cossacks are an element alien to communism and to the Soviet idea was correct. Sooner or later we will have to exterminate, sim-

ply physically destroy the Cossacks, or at least the vast majority of them, but for this we will need enormous tact and huge caution . . . Only under the banner of a Soviet Don Government will we be able to conduct Red Terror against the Cossack counterrevolution, by means of arms, propaganda, and an agrarian-resettlement policy.[102]

Reingol'd was no lone fanatic. In an analysis entitled "Why We Suffered a Defeat on the Southern Front," written in early August 1919, Iosif Khodorovskii, a member of the Southern Front's RMC, postulated that "we must once and for all recognize that we are conducting a struggle not for the Cossackry but against the Cossackry, [that] before us stands the task of the Don's complete conquest and extinction [*zamiranie*]." This analysis was circulated, among others, to Lenin and Trotsky.[103]

Even critics of de-Cossackization within the party were not opposed to its violence and terror. They argued that the policy had simply failed to target the appropriate group. While on the Don Bureau, Frenkel' had vainly fought Syrtsov's excesses in de-Cossackization. During a review of the failed policy in July 1919, he wrote to the Central Committee that "the struggle between estates, between the Cossackry and the peasantry (outlanders), should, in my view, be conducted within the parameters of class struggle and not degenerate into an amorphous zoological struggle." Valentin Trifonov, a plenipotentiary dispatched from Moscow, similarly condemned the policy not because it was violent but because the violence had been deployed in a "non-Marxist" fashion.[104]

Here the role of official state endorsement for particular policies becomes evident. The Bolshevik Party's culture of centralism created an ethos in which official policy overrode the reservations of individual party members or even entire structures, such as the Southern Front RMC. Not a few officials in key positions (Frenkel', Trifonov, and especially Sokol'nikov) had opposed the portrayal of all Cossacks as inveterate counterrevolutionaries. The Southern Front had vigorously protested the Don Bureau's continuing enthusiasm for de-Cossackization. Their views made little difference once the Orgburo issued its de-Cossackization circular. Conversely, many (such as Syrtsov, Khodorovskii, and Reingol'd) retained their distrust of each and every

Cossack even after the renunciation of high de-Cossackization. But once the Center had introduced a more discriminating approach, they were no longer able to translate their more extreme views into policy.

Normalizing the Cossacks

Through April the Center continued to act upon Syrtsov's recommendations. As summer approached, the Red Army failed to bring the Veshenskaia rebellion under control and was soon forced to begin a retreat from the Don. With Soviet forces in retreat, central agencies engaged in an extensive review to determine why they had lost the Don. On May 12, the Republic's Revolutionary Military Council again granted Cossacks the right to bear arms in defense of the republic.[105] The Council of People's Commissars on May 24 then ordered a study of whether the rights of the Cossack population should be made equal with those of the rest of the Soviet Republic's laboring population, and if so, what steps should be taken.[106] Here was a major shift in perception: though separate, Cossacks now were considered equal to the rest of the population.

The effects of this shift were felt almost immediately. At the end of May Vitalii Larin, the chairman of the Khoper District Revolutionary Committee, issued a broadsheet proclaiming that only provocateurs could be spreading rumors about the Soviet state's alleged intention to exterminate the Cossackry. (The Veshenskaia insurgents had been using captured Soviet de-Cossackization directives as agitational material to great effect. Khoper District bordered on the rebellious Upper Don District.) No, argued Larin: the Eighth Party Congress (March 18–23, 1919), at which the party had reversed its policy in the countryside and had called for accommodation with "the middle peasant," also had decreed punishment for any Communist who harmed a middle Cossack or middle peasant. Larin's May interpretation was entirely retrospective. The turn to the middle peasant was implemented after March in the rest of Russia, but at that time it had not been extended to the Don Territory. Larin now threatened punishment for any officials who abused the "middle peasantry," meaning primarily Cossacks, who had just been retroactively included under this category.[107]

This shift in strategy made evident the Center's role in sanctioning the previous policy's pervasive violence. Local officials testified that upon receipt of directives from above to moderate policy, the rate of executions dropped precipitously. One Soviet official noted that, upon receiving a directive to temper political and economic policy on the Don, "the executions ceased within a day or two, and now over a period of three weeks such incidents hardly ever occur."[108] Even where the Center had not directly ordered executions, it had indicated its tolerance of them. As soon as it communicated its nonacceptance, "local excesses" ceased.

It was at precisely this time that Lenin sought to attribute responsibility for the renaming of Cossack settlements to the excessive enthusiasm of local officials. Several days later, Elena Stasova, the Central Committee's secretary, attempted to shift the blame for the entire policy of de-Cossackization from the Party Orgburo to the Soviet state's Cossack section. Under the outraged protests of the Cossack section, Stasova withdrew her accusation, but she pointedly failed to indicate who in fact had been responsible for the policy.[109] Lenin's and Stasova's attempts to distance central authorities from their failed policies foreshadowed Stalin's analogous attempt, with his March 1930 "Dizzy with Success" article, to blame local officials for the "excesses" in carrying out the Center's own wildly unrealistic collectivization program.

The Center's review of overall policy generated a flood of reports evaluating what was already recognized as a failed initiative.[110] The reports' authors wrote with the knowledge that de-Cossackization had been repudiated, a fact that inevitably shaped their presentation of it. Facing Cossack rebellions and a reinvigorated Don Army, the Center moved to "normalize" both the Cossacks and the Don Territory. Because it was viewed as especially malevolent—unlike other, "normal" provinces—central authorities in early 1919 had refused to grant the Don Territory a provincial-level civil organ. Even after the Center had repudiated the Orgburo's "mass terror" circular in March, Moscow's suspicion of the region remained so great that it permitted only the Civil Administration, modeled upon organs intended for military rule of occupied enemy regions. In late April, however, a review of policy toward Cossack regions concluded that the administration of the Don could not entirely be left in the hands of the military; it thus called for administration of the territory to pass to Soviet civil organs of provinces bordering the Don.[111] Soon afterward the Central Committee did much more than that: in the first days of May it reorganized the Civil

Administration into a five-man Don Revolutionary Committee "along the lines of a provincial executive committee" as existed in other provinces.[112]

Change at the territorial level also meant changes at the local level. Gerasimov, one of the five members of the new Don Revolutionary Committee, argued on May 21 that the time when all district revolutionary committees were appointed had finally passed, and that "the time had come to create democratic soviets—even artificially—in areas liberated from the opponent."[113] The change from appointed revolutionary committees to soviets, even artificially elected ones, testified to a major shift in attitude to the Cossacks and toward the Don in general. It was in this period that the Commissariat of Internal Affairs discussed "the question of equaling the rights of the Cossack population with the rest of the laboring population," and the Khoper Revolutionary Committee issued its order threatening to punish Communists who harmed "middle Cossacks or middle peasants."

With the Soviet retreat from the Don Territory, these issues became academic. The legacy of de-Cossackization did not even end then. In order to rally Cossacks to the Soviet cause, Soviet military and political authorities sanctioned the formation of a separate "Don Corps," to be commanded by Filipp Mironov, the leading pro-Soviet Cossack commander. Mironov had kept much of the northern districts Soviet through 1918. Owing to the tactlessness of his unit's political commissars and lingering Cossack resentment, however, Mironov led the unit into mutiny. Indicting Bolsheviks for imperiling the revolution and for waging indiscriminate war against all Cossacks, Mironov attempted to lead his mutinous units to the front—not against the Red Army but against the counterrevolutionaries. Within a week the Red Army seized him and his followers.[114]

With the Upper Don uprising and the mutiny of Mironov, the Soviet state now tried to win over Cossack support. On August 28, just as the Mironov mutiny was unfolding, the Center dissolved the Civil Administration and replaced it with the Don Revolutionary Committee. On September 3 the Orgburo met to discuss what form civil authority for the Don should take and, in stark contrast to its earlier January circular, approved the formation of appointed soviets, with the possibility of partial elections in the foreseeable future. Later that same month the Don Revolutionary Committee took the symbolically significant step of renaming itself the "Provisional Don Executive Committee," with the corresponding change in name of local organs from "district revolutionary committees" into "provisional district executive committees." Even stanitsa, village, and khutor revolutionary committees now were to bear the title of "soviets." And while district executive committees were still to be appointed, elections would be permitted for khutor and stanitsa soviets.[115] To be sure, these changes were often nominal (the change in title from "revolutionary committees" to "provisional executive committees" did not change their composition), and any elections would be strictly controlled. But what is important here is that the mechanism and degree of control in the Don Territory would now be the same as for any other, "normal" province.

The complete rehabilitation of the Cossacks and the Don came in September 1919. A September 4 article in the Ninth Army's newspaper foretold the official shift. Written while Mironov's mutiny was still ongoing, the article provided the following instructions for soldiers:

> While it is true that a certain portion of the Don Territory's population is counterrevolutionary for reasons of an economic nature, this is far from the majority. And this entire remaining section of the population could become our ally. Why, then, haven't they? One can't blame everything on ignorance and benightedness. We must admit that we repeated the same story on the Don that we had earlier in Siberia and Central Russia. Quite some time ago we came to recognize our mistake in Siberia, and even earlier [at the Eighth Party Congress in March] we recognized our mistake toward the middle peasant in central Russia. Now it's the Don's turn. It is entirely understandable that in the heat of battle, particularly after such a fierce one, one cannot expect special kindness from warriors to their foes, but we are entitled to demand a strict distinction between friend and foe . . . *Be attentive, comrades, to the Don middle Cossack.*[116]

The new line entirely contradicted the official policy of early 1919. Vatsetis, in his January 1919 article "on the struggle with the Don," had argued that the Don Cossacks represented almost an entirely different species. Now in September a Red Army newspaper declared that the Cossacks themselves were not solely to blame for their behavior;

Soviet "mistakes" had played no small role in shaping Cossacks' response to Soviet power. Cossacks, it transpired, were not incorrigible counterrevolutionaries. Given the proper policy, even they could be won over to Soviet power. One week later, Trotsky issued an order with new principles for civilian administration of the Don Territory. Soviet power in the Don Territory was to establish "local soviet power founded upon the principles of the Soviet Constitution."[117]

The new line received official formulation soon after. On September 16 Trotsky convened a conference in Balashov to discuss political work among the Cossacks. On the basis of this gathering he composed "Theses about Work on the Don," which, after receiving approval from the Orgburo, appeared in *Izvestiia* on September 30. The article argued that Soviet power should win Cossacks over through agitation rather than through force. It postulated that political groupings within the Cossackry corresponded to poor, middle, and well-off categories present among the peasantry in general.[118] In early October, a special military tribunal tried Mironov and his comrades in arms and sentenced them to death for their mutiny. The Soviet state immediately pardoned them, with the explicit goal of employing them as an "interlocutor" with the Cossack population. By the end of the month the Soviet state had appointed Mironov to the newly established Don Executive Committee.[119] Soviet policy toward the Don Cossacks had come full circle. In January 1919 Cossacks were presumed counterrevolutionary by nature, despite acts on behalf of Soviet power. In September they were considered potential allies, barring any outright opposition. The Soviet state even strove to find extenuating circumstances for Cossack rebellion.

Triumphantly pursuing the defeated anti-Soviet armies, which in autumn had pushed toward Moscow, Soviet forces swept into the Don Territory in late 1919 and early 1920. Retreating to the Black Sea ports, the anti-Soviet armies embarked on ships and sailed off to make their final stand in the Crimean peninsula. As they advanced through the Don, the Red Army found many Cossack areas almost entirely bereft of males. Sixty percent of Cossack males in Khoper District and 40 percent of the entire Cossack population of Ust'-Medveditsa District abandoned their homes before the advancing Red Army. Soldiers wrote home that "in Cossack-land there are absolutely no Cossacks, they have all left . . . on the streets you see only women and children."[120]

By late 1919 the Soviet state had moderated its policy toward Cossacks. It now defined Cossack behavior as the product of class relations. Nevertheless, many Communists continued to view Cossacks as a particularly suspect segment of the population. Those Cossacks who remained in their communities scrupulously avoided implicating themselves in politics of any kind. Soviet commentators unanimously noted their passivity and apathy in the face of the Red triumph. It seemed that only those Cossacks with relatives in the Red Army welcomed the arrival of Soviet power.[121]

Military developments brought Cossack males streaming back to the Don in the spring of 1920. During the retreat of the anti-Soviet armies in March 1920, General Denikin had ordered the Don Army to provide a screen for the Volunteer Army while ships evacuated the volunteers from the Black Sea ports to the Crimea. As a result, most of the Don Army—23,000 of 38,000 troops—remained behind, watching the ships sail away. This experience left its mark on the political sympathies of the returning Cossacks, who understandably felt that the anti-Soviet cause had simply abandoned them. The more recent the returnees, reported Soviet officials, the more disillusioned they were with the White cause.[122]

Soviet authorities allowed Cossacks who had served in the anti-Soviet armies to return to their homes, but ordered that they be kept under strict surveillance. Organs of the Cheka—the Soviet political police—however, were to send all returning officers to "concentration camps."[123] Press reporting on British measures during the Boer War had acquainted Russians with both the term and the concept of "concentration camps." Several combatant powers during the First World War had employed such camps, especially for "enemy aliens."[124] Thus "concentration camps" already were a recognized means for dealing with perceived threats from supposedly unreliable populations. Soviet authorities shifted their axis of analysis from citizenship and ethnicity to class, and vastly expanded the use of such camps. Military commissariats in two districts interned not only officers but all Cossack returnees. Indeed, some Soviet authorities arrested even Cossacks who had not retreated with the anti-Soviet forces simply because they were Cossacks.[125]

Returning Cossacks therefore also tended to shun political activity. One Cossack, who returned home after serving in the Don Army only to be conscripted into the Red Army, expressed the general sense of resignation. Punning on the Cossack expression "Put up with it, Cossack, and you'll become an ataman," he wrote to his relatives: "What can you do? Now the Cossack simply has to put up with it and become Red."[126] Pervasive Soviet suspicions about Cossacks, while officially renounced, had a long-lasting effect on the degree to which Cossacks participated in Soviet political life. Throughout the rest of the decade, Cossacks would be conspicuously under-represented among delegates to Soviet and party congresses and as members of Soviet administrative organs.

Discriminated against and terrorized under Cossack rule, non-Cossacks welcomed the advancing Red Army as liberators.[127] Both this reception and longstanding preconceptions led Soviet officials to view peasants as their natural pillar of support in the Don Territory. Three years after a supposedly socialist revolution, Soviet officials continued to speak in terms of estate. Semen Budennyi, the famed commander of the Red Army's cavalry army and himself an outlander peasant from the Don Territory, counseled that "the Cossack population is hostile toward the peasant population and counterrevolutionary toward the Red Army, and is anti-Soviet as well. I consider it necessary to pursue a course based not upon the Cossacks but upon the peasantry."[128] He held this view despite the fact that the bulk of Red cavalry formations were composed of Cossacks, with the possible exception of his own corps, recruited from among Don peasants.[129] Wherever Soviet officials allowed local participation, peasants staffed local organs. Regardless of their actual prerevolutionary economic status, peasants had become the face of Soviet power throughout the Don Territory by early 1920.

Political Violence as Political Culture

Adrian Lyttelton has noted that the First World War marked a watershed in Italian political life. "Before [the First World War]," he writes, "political violence was either associated with 'protest,' or with repression by state organs; its deliberate, large-scale use by a party to further political aims, was something which most prewar politicians, even revolutionaries, did not seriously contemplate." Fascism exemplified this transformation in Italian political culture. But, argues Lyttelton, the emergence of fascism was "the most important but not the only manifestation" in the "general growth of violence in postwar Italy." Richard Bessel similarly observes for Germany that "the violence in German politics after 1918 was both qualitatively and quantitatively different." Domestic politics after the war was not peacetime politics: it was instead a form of "latent civil war."[130]

In Russia, as in Italy and Germany, the war experience alone did not cause this shift; revolution was a necessary component. Russia had been at war since 1914, but only in the aftermath of 1917 did violence become a regular and constitutive feature of everyday political life. While the Bolsheviks employed violence more instrumentally and more consciously than did their competitors, it had become an enduring feature of the post-1917 Russian political landscape. Bolshevik violence took place within this broader tectonic shift in Russian—indeed European—political culture. If war and revolution were the crucial components, the experience of civil war provided the necessary catalyst. These policies did not result from the abstract unfolding of ideology or from the exigencies of civil war; rather, the practices of the governing and the governed crystallized in a concrete experience of civil war. Utopian dreams fused with an experience of want, fear, devastation, and brutalization.[131] It was not simply Bolshevik measures that summoned forth violence from the Soviet state's opponents. Indeed, to see the tactics of the Bolsheviks as the cause of their opponents' violence is to miss this larger shift.[132] Red political violence did not cause White violence, or vice versa. Rather, they were twin strands, inextricably intertwined, emerging out of the 1914–1921 maelstrom of war, revolution, and civil wars.

Russia's prerevolutionary crisis and, even more so, people's lived experience in the 1914–1921 continuum of crisis made such Manichaeism plausible and even appealing. Contemporaries themselves noted how the revolutions of 1917 had woven together an ethos of violence emerging out of the First World War with a belief in the revolution's promise to remake the world.[133] Political actors turned wartime practices and institutions to political ends: deportation and colonization programs; "watch detachments"; the control of public discourse through state information organs; and military-controlled civil organs such as the Southern Front's Civil Administration. Many of the tools that have been identified as intrinsically "Bolshevik," then, in fact owed their emergence to the nexus forged between practices of violence developed during the First World War and the hopes and fears generated by revolution. The practices provided the means; the revolution's hopes and fears—the ends.

The AGDH and the Soviet party-state both employed violence as a technique for forging "social" movements posited by their respective political worldviews. Those who experienced the repressive measures of both testified that "the Volunteer Army and Bolsheviks resorted to entirely identical measures: burning down villages, requisitioning property, persecuting families, executions."[134] Forged in the same civil war context, these insurgent "green" movements, arraying themselves against Red and White, also inhabited the common political culture of their opponents. In pursuing their ends, greens employed many of the same practices used by their opponents, including "people's courts," "special" punitive detachments, and mandatory labor conscription.[135]

Yet while all sides in the Russian civil wars engaged in violent practices and coercive measures, there were crucial differences in how they employed such violence. Hannah Arendt argues that "violence is by nature instrumental; like all means, it always stands in need of guidance and justification through the end it pursues."[136] Pursuing different ends, Red violence and White violence were *not* homologous.[137] Bolshevism was distinct not so much because it employed practices of violence but rather because of the ends this violence was meant to serve. Unlike the violence of its predecessors and competitors, Soviet violence was not a temporary and extraordinary tool intended for use only during a circumscribed period of civil conflict. Rather, for the Bolshevik party-state, political violence was a regular and calculated program. Many of the features we presume to be Stalinist in fact were inscribed into the Soviet system at precisely this period.[138]

The foundation of all new political entities requires violence. Once established, however, most polities shift from this violence of foundation to a more mundane and routine violence—legitimized violence, or force—for upholding the newly established order.[139] Revolution, for the Bolsheviks, was not simply the foundation event but an ongoing project. Rather than maintaining a particular political order, they pursued the revolutionary transformation of society. After its political establishment the Bolshevik party-state therefore did not abandon the violence of foundation even as it built a system of more routinized and legitimized force. Here Arendt's analytic distinction between violence and terror is useful: "Terror is not the same as violence; it is, rather, the form of government that comes into being when violence, having destroyed all power, does not abdicate, but, on the contrary, remains in full control."[140] Throughout the following decades—with varying intensity, to be sure—the Soviet state would employ this more naked violence of foundation as part of its open-ended project to shape a revolutionary, harmonious, and integrated socialist society.

De-Cossackization therefore was not simply a policy pursued during civil war. In discussing de-Cossackization, party officials were quite explicit about its goals: not just to conquer the region but to make the region once and for all Soviet and socialist. The officials of the anti-Soviet AGDH never articulated such an overarching plan for their violence; they never had an institution so total as the Bolshevik Party to plan and carry it out. It was therefore not the use of specific practices—deportations, executions, military courts—that distinguished the Bolshevik regime, but rather the ends that those practices were to serve. What distinguished the Bolsheviks was the extent to which they turned tools originally intended for total war to the new ends of revolutionary politics, both during the civil wars and especially after their end. During the extended period of war, revolution, and civil wars the Bolshevik regime's reliance on particular practices remained at the outer reaches of comparison with other states. With the end of Europe's crisis period, this quantitative difference in Bolshevik violence became a qualitative difference. After 1921, the Bolshevik regime's continued use of wartime measures to pursue its revolutionary project fundamentally set it apart from most other European states.

~ 7

"Psychological Consolidation"

> We must shift the center of attention in our understanding of the state
> away from the external attributes of territory and the sum of the
> population, and toward a psychology of the state's members.
> ~ Maks Lazerson, "The State without Territory," *Russkaia mysl'*,
> February 1915

The Bolsheviks and their foes in the civil wars did not rely only on force; nor did they simply seek to coerce people into accepting their rule. White generals and their Kadet advisors, just as much as Bolshevik commissars, defined their task as forging committed and enlightened citizens out of obedient but passive subjects. A burgeoning historical literature demonstrates the Soviet state's massive investment in state surveillance.[1] These works, however, invariably ascribe the emergence of state surveillance solely to Bolshevik ideology or the Bolsheviks' hunger for power. Such an analysis leaves unexplained how and why the Soviets' opponents constructed similar institutions to keep track of the population's political attitudes.

The term "surveillance" can refer to the techniques for keeping subjects under observation. For those who originated it, however, it was more than a technology—it was a manifestation of a specific concept of power.[2] Surveillance was the ethos that motivated state officials and public activists to gather information for the purpose of observing and then shaping the population's attitudes. In Russia and throughout Europe, policing was a concern of public order, whereas surveillance was used to gather knowledge in order to foster the full potential of the citizen and society. Policing in Russia involved "oversight" [*nadzor*] as carried out by the tsarist "security police," whose very title denotes its negative agenda of safeguarding an extant society from threats.[3] Russians employed a different term [*osvedomlenie*] for surveillance, which went far beyond the purely negative program of policing. Whereas policing gathered data on delinquents, malcontents, and revolutionaries, surveillance sought information on the whole population. Unlike "oversight," surveillance almost invariably meant a two-way circuit of information, its collection and dissemination. Surveillance, in Russia and throughout Europe, sought to transform hierarchically ordered and passive subjects into self-directed and autonomous agents. Before the 1905 Revolution, the security police gave little thought to the attitudes of citizens, provided they did not support the revolutionary movement or threaten the proper ordering of society.[4] Like the pre-Reformation Catholic Church, the imperial state aggressively suppressed heresy but otherwise demonstrated little concern for inculcating doctrinal orthodoxy within each individual.[5]

In its policing efforts the imperial state relied upon perlustration of the mails. Perlustration—the surreptitious opening and reading of certain letters passing through the post—was a widespread practice among continental European states.[6] The agencies charged with this task, deriving their title "black offices" from the French prototype, reported their findings to the security police. Operating with a list of specific individuals and addresses to target, these officials concentrated their attention only on suspected revolutionaries and opponents of the regime. In 1904 the list of addresses subject to perlustration numbered one thousand. After 1905, the security policy extended its focus beyond the revolutionary movement and court opinion to include Duma deputies and oppositionist parties and figures. It increasingly sought to probe the "mood" of zemstvo and industrial circles through a network of secret reporting. Still, the goal of these efforts was primarily policing and intelligence. In 1913 the total number of officials employed in such "black offices" throughout the entire Russian Empire was only fifty individuals. On average, they opened 380,000 letters a year.[7]

The shift from security policing to surveillance occurred during the course of the Great War. Surveillance was embedded within a broad spectrum of public activities seeking to mobilize society, first for total war and then for revolution. Both conducting the war and forging revolution relied upon this *self*-mobilization of society, albeit under the aegis of the state. That some segments of the population willingly mobilized for war does not mean all segments did so equally. In Russia the intelligentsia, a narrow but active sector seeking to bring Russian society into being, played a particularly prominent role first in the wartime and then in the revolutionary project of surveillance.

The Mobilization of Enthusiasm

The First World War radically expanded the institutional foundations of surveillance and extended its scope. With the outbreak of war, the imperial government enacted a "Temporary Statute on Military Censorship," covering both press and postal controls.[8] Such censorship was introduced, as the statute itself proclaimed, as "an extraordinary measure," although the tactics it sanctioned were to become part of the power structure for the next seventy-five years. The statute extended postal censorship in varying degrees to the entire empire. Total implementation covered areas of the front and entailed the interception of all correspondence. Partial implementation, covering the rest of the empire, encompassed all letters from the armed forces, all letters directed to newspapers and to nonpermanent addresses such as post office boxes, as well as all outgoing letters of enemy POWs held in Russia and incoming letters from Russian POWs in captivity. In addition, partial censorship mandated the interception of correspondence of individual suspects and, soon afterward, the correspondence of entire groups deemed to be potentially unreliable, such as Jews, Balts, Germans, and Poles.[9]

These measures marked both a quantitative and a qualitative increase over the peacetime activity of the security police. Instead of focusing only on specific suspects who had been previously identified, the state was now opening whole categories of mail. Military censorship offices, attached to staffs of each front and to each military district throughout the empire, reviewed tens of thousands of letters each week.[10] Before 1914 the security police had processed 380,000 letters per year; during the war, the military censorship commission for just one military district processed more than that number *in three days*.[11] To meet staffing demands for these new organs, the military impressed postal employees and Ministry of Internal Affairs officials. In April 1916 the demand for staff had become so great that the authorities revoked a previous ban on hiring women and allowed them to perform this sensitive duty.[12]

As in all other combatant countries, military censors in Russia were supposed to prevent the circulation of defeatist sentiments and possible military secrets. Equally important, however, military censors were set the task of describing and explaining popular attitudes. They compiled weekly summaries of the mail's overall content. Here policing shifted into surveillance. These summaries included representative passages from particular letters and a statistical breakdown of the week's mail into categories of patriotic, apathetic, and dissatisfied letters.[13] From the end of 1915, in the aftermath of the Great Retreat, censors were instructed to focus not simply on issues of military security but also on questions of a general political nature.[14]

Soldiers, of course, became aware that authorities had a newfound interest in their letters. Some tried to outwit the military censor by using the civilian post or complained in their correspondence about the interception of their letters. Others addressed the censors directly in addenda to their letters.[15] Surveillance had begun to establish the limits of permissible written expression, even for private correspondence. Before 1914 the state had been interested in a small circle of political activists. With the war, its interest expanded to much of the rest of the population. At the same time, this surveillance suggested to everyday people that their views—whatever they might be—mattered to the authorities.

During the course of the war the government also established a system of routine reporting on the mood of the population. Beginning in March 1915 the Police Department began to require its officials to submit not only the usual reports on individual events but also regular monthly reports on the activities of revolutionary parties and the opposition movement.[16] Still, surveillance was limited to the negative function of policing. But in October 1915, in the aftermath of the Great Retreat and with the activization of oppositionist sentiment, the Ministry of Internal Affairs ordered provincial and district police officials to compile regular monthly reports on the population's "moods" and issued a standardized set of questions to be addressed.[17] For nearly the next eighty years, police agencies of the imperial, Provisional, and Soviet governments would continue the standardized reporting begun at this time.

In the summer of 1915, in the face of a military crisis and dangerously low morale, the Russian imperial state introduced surveillance.

Most other states would not resort to similar measures until mid-1916, in the second, more intensive phase of "remobilization" for total war.[18] Germany was the next to institute such measures. The political police in Germany had sporadically collected aggregate information on political attitudes from the 1850s, but here, as in Russia, the First World War marked a qualitative shift.[19] In Germany, however, with the war's outbreak this task passed directly to the military. Beginning in November 1915 the War Ministry directed the generals in charge of military districts throughout the Reich to report on the general situation in their districts. Four months later, in March 1916, the command ordered them to report explicitly on the morale of the population. The first category in these standardized reports was to be "the mood of the civilian population." The following month, the German military postal censorship offices also began compiling standardized reports on popular moods.[20]

Yet the organization of morale during the First World War depended on more than government measures. Throughout Europe, total mobilization saw the emergence of a hybrid "parastatal complex" that managed to elicit society's broad and willing participation in conducting the war.[21] In Russia and other combatant countries, this self-mobilization of society enabled the state to extend its reach deeper into society. Without such self-mobilization, states would never have been able to achieve the revolutionary reordering of society necessary in wartime. But because the Russian autocracy had so limited the role of public organizations in the prewar period, the formal organization of many of the structures aspiring to the role of civil society was telescoped into this brief war period. In Russia, wartime self-mobilization provided the matrix for the formation of many public organizations, and not simply their reorganization.

Before the war, zemstvos had counterposed themselves to the autocracy, and the autocracy in turn had viewed their activities with much suspicion. Not unlike Krivoshein and the Ministry of Agriculture, zemstvo activists saw the war as an opportunity to realize their long-standing aspirations to transform the countryside. On the eve of the First World War, zemstvo activists in Ufa had struggled to establish a program for peasant education and enlightenment in order to make peasants into citizens. The war provided an opportunity to pursue these programs. By 1915 demand for reading material and lectures was so great that the provincial zemstvo established a network of "reading huts." The Ufa zemstvo also organized lectures and courses on the war and its meaning. Central government funding augmented zemstvo allocations to pay for these measures. As one scholar has noted, the zemstvo activists aspired to play a role analogous to that of French schoolteachers in the years before and during the First World War.[22] Unlike Russian zemstvo activists, however, French *instituteurs* had been accepted by the French state as participants in patriotic efforts long before the war. They could rely, in addition, upon a firmly established network of republican institutions, well-integrated with existing state structures.[23] Harassed by some government officials, short on funds, and hampered by a fraying zemstvo network, the Russian adult-education program was in crisis by the time the Old Regime collapsed.

Yet as the autocracy turned to public organizations to help with the war effort, the previous barrier between the state and nonstate spheres became increasingly permeable.[24] Public organizations embraced the opportunity to aid the war effort within the narrow parameters permitted to them. The semiofficial Skobelev Committee produced postcards, newsreels, and patriotic films.[25] In Petrograd, another committee placed receptacles throughout the city for used newspapers, which were then shipped to the front to be read secondhand by the soldiers, thereby assuring informed—and thus presumably self-motivated—citizen-soldiers.[26] On the eve of the February Revolution one observer noted that "a hitherto rare and most interesting form of poster has emerged during the war, the purpose of which was not the personal profit of the entrepreneur . . . but the interests of the state and society." The poster's new function was to serve as "the agitator and organizer of the masses."[27]

"Sociopolitical Enlightenment"

The war radically expanded the previously limited scope of existing institutions and provided a matrix within which many new fused state-public organizations had emerged. The 1917 Revolution created a new focus for the activities of such organs and expanded them even more. As public organizations that had grown up in wartime transferred their focus to revolutionary politics, they inevitably conflated the once-distinct military and civilian realms. This conflation did not so much produce "militarization"—the colonization of the civilian realm by the military—as transform the parameters and substance of *both* the civilian and the military realms. In Russia a peculiar civilian-military hybrid emerged, in which there was as much a "societalization" of the military as a militarization of society.

The Provisional Government's "Bureau for Sociopolitical Enlightenment" exemplifies how public activists sought to appropriate the military, first during the war and especially in 1917, as an instrument for their own programs. During the war Russia's technical and engineering societies had formed, on their own initiative, a "Committee for Military-Technical Assistance" to aid the war effort. With the outbreak of the February Revolution, this committee formed a "Bureau for Organizing Morale," which set itself the task of securing the revolution's achievements by enlightening Russia's new citizens. It immediately began conducting large meetings and holding courses to train lecturers on new political topics. Its earlier wartime work, in the bureau's own eyes, prepared it for its work in 1917.

For the men staffing it, the bureau represented an opportunity to anchor their prewar agendas in the revolutionary state. The bureau was meant to combat "the popular masses' sociopolitical illiteracy," which derived, they charged, from "the tsarist regime's criminal refusal to grant the people light and knowledge." Later, in petitioning the Provisional Government for funds, the committee stated that "its task will be achieved only if broad segments of the democratic intelligentsia will be drawn to its work." It was to serve as a structure for "organizing the Russian intelligentsia" in pursuing these tasks.[28]

The Bureau for Organizing Morale was committed to dual power as a program rather than simply as a compromise. Among its members were luminaries of the moderate left and future stalwart defenders of dual power and the Provisional Government: Lev Deich, Nikolai Chaikovskii, V. F. Pekarskii, and Peter Pal'chinskii. All had been involved in the revolutionary movement for decades but had become outspoken Defensists during the war, propounding the need to defeat Germany before overthrowing the regime. The bureau's secretary was Dr. Sergei Chakhotin, a Kadet and biophysicist. After his expulsion from Moscow University for his role in the 1902 student unrest, Chakhotin had studied under Wilhelm Conrad Röntgen in Germany. He returned to Russia in 1912 at the insistence of I. P. Pavlov.[29] During the war Chakhotin served as the general secretary of the Committee for Military-Technical Assistance, the same post he held in 1917 for the Bureau for Organizing Morale.

Born out of a wartime parastatal organization, the bureau recast its main objective after the February Revolution in a fundamentally political direction: to enlighten the population so that it would, of its own accord, support the Provisional Government as guarantor of revolution. The democratic army, these public men argued, provided the best surrogate for Russia's nonexistent civic institutions. Its members identified the greatest threat to "the motherland and the revolution" as coming from "those dark elements of the popular masses who lack consciousness and who are armed"—in other words, Russia's soldiers. But if the army represented a threat, it also represented an unparalleled opportunity. The bureau argued that "the country's cultural forces" ought to focus their efforts on the army because it represented "the fastest way to implant knowledge in the country." The army, the bureau argued, concentrated Russia's new citizens in one establishment and provided the ideal tools for working with them, tools lacking elsewhere in Russian society. Believing it did not have the "authority" and the necessary institutional framework to act on its own, the bureau petitioned the Provisional Government to incorporate it into the Political Directorate of the War Ministry. With Alexander Kerensky as war minister, the Provisional Government rechristened the bureau "the Committee for Sociopolitical Enlightenment" and incorporated it into Kerensky's new "Cabinet of the War Minister."[30] From mid-summer the committee organized courses to train lecturers, sponsored lectures and performances in army regiments, and compiled daily summary reports for the War Ministry's Political Directorate. In this latter capacity it traced the Provisional Government's declining popularity.[31]

The Russian Revolution occurred at a critical moment in the world conflict, just as all combatants were "remobilizing" their societies for total war, seeking new, more intensive techniques for conducting it. In several respects, the origins and initial goals of the Provisional Government's Committee for Sociopolitical Enlightenment mirrored the French "Union des Grandes Associations contre la Propagande Enemie" (UGACPE), which held a "national oath" at the Sorbonne in early March 1917 as an act of rededication for war. The UGACPE derived its greatest impetus from the Ligue de l'Enseignement. Like the

Committee for Military-Technical Assistance, the Ligue was a voluntary body. Unlike the Russian committee, however, the Ligue had existed for several decades. It was part of the republican establishment
that had crusaded for the secularized primary school system, the foundation of the French republican political order. From November 1916,
the Ligue had established a network of local committees and issued
calls for "intellectual mobilization." While the Ligue was already
deeply embedded in the structure of French society, its Russian counterpart was committed to summoning that structure into being. The
Ligue could rely on a thick network of preexisting republican institutions, not least the republican school system; its English counterpart
turned to the structures of the political parties as its conduit.[32] In contrast, the Russian analogue was very much an organ of the post-February political elite, keenly aware of the lack of any such web of institutions permeating society. Ominously for the proponents of the
Committee for Sociopolitical Enlightenment, by October it had established local branches in only sixteen large cites outside of Petrograd.
(Among these was Novocherkassk, the capital of the Don Territory.)
Even the more active branches, such as that in Ivanovo-Voznesensk,
depended entirely on the Petrograd office for funding. By September
the central office was on the verge of collapse itself, and had to turn to
the Provisional Government for an immediate infusion of 200,000
rubles. The Political Directorate of the War Ministry and the Special
Council for State Defense both interceded on the central committee's
behalf and highly praised its efforts.[33]

     This conflation of the military and civilian realms was not just a re-
sult of the committee's own aspirations. Indeed, the restructuring of institutions in the course of the revolution played a crucial role in this
process. Until February 1917, the war minister in Russia had always
been a career military man; under the Provisional Government, the
war minister was a civilian. From early May until the end of the Provisional Government, the man in charge of the military was not just a civilian but a self-styled revolutionary democrat: Alexander Kerensky.
From mid-summer his ministerial posts blurred the boundaries between the military and the civilian realms. From the time he became
prime minister in the second coalition (July 25–August 27) until the
collapse of the Provisional Government, he united supreme civilian authority with leading military posts. In the second coalition Kerensky

served as both prime minister and war minister. In the aftermath of the Kornilov affair he surrendered the post of war minister, but took over the post of supreme commander in chief. He united this post with his continued role as prime minister until the demise of the Provisional Government.

As war minister and supreme commander in chief, Kerensky introduced new, specifically political, organs into the army. Owing to the occupation of enemy territories and the proclamation of vast swaths of Russian territory under military rule, beginning in October 1914 the Russian army had established a "Chancellery for Civilian Administration." This organization involved itself with ruling the population rather than engaging it. Upon taking up the post of war minister in May 1917, Kerensky established a new "Cabinet of the War Minister." The "cabinet" bearing this nondescript title contained a political department, a surveillance department, and a department for liaison with the troops. In early August the political department of this cabinet was made into a separate "Political Directorate of the War Minister," existing alongside the Cabinet of the War Minister. After the Kornilov affair, with Kerensky simultaneously occupying the post of prime minister and supreme commander in chief, the Provisional Government reformed the Cabinet of the War Minister into a "Military Cabinet of the Prime Minister and Commander in Chief." Kerensky thus carried the War Ministry's cabinet with him when he left that post. The Political Directorate of the War Minister was then made into an entirely independent entity within the War Ministry. Thus the prime minister gained a military cabinet, and the war minister—a political directorate. Both were dissolved after the October Revolution, but the Soviet state reformed the directorate of civilian administration, which had continued to exist after 1914, into its own "Military-Political and Civilian Directorate under the Commander in Chief."[34]

These organs did not represent the military's expansion into politics so much as the expansion of politics into the military. Kerensky did not appoint career military men to head the War Ministry's new political directorate. Instead he selected public men who had become officers only in the course of the war, such as V. B. Stankevich (a lecturer in criminal law and a political activist prior to 1914) and his replacement, Fedor Stepun (a lecturer in idealist philosophy before the war). By late summer 1917 the political directorate had become, in the words of its directors, "one of the most significant posts in the system of military administration," "a quite solid state institution." Among its primary functions was to ensure the promotion of officers loyal to the Provisional Government and to coordinate the government's military commissars, yet another extension of civilian political control over military affairs.[35] In April 1918 the Bolshevik regime would follow this precedent and establish an "All-Russian Bureau of Military Commissars," later subordinated to the Red Army's own "Political Directorate."[36]

Kerensky and the Provisional Government placed great hopes on the army's June 1917 offensive. They anticipated that the offensive would both help end the war and rally support for the government. In the weeks leading up to it, Kerensky as minister of war renamed the Bureau for Organizing Morale as the "Central Committee for Sociopolitical Enlightenment" and incorporated it into his politicized Cabinet of the War Minister. In this function the committee prepared daily information summaries for the Political Cabinet of the War Minister and actively proselytized on behalf of both the offensive and the government. Emerging from a public organization seeking to aid the war effort (the Committee for Military-Technical Assistance), the Committee for Sociopolitical Enlightenment had, at its own request, been absorbed into the military itself.

Kerensky did not have to force his vision of a politicized army on the military. True, some officers opposed the politicization of the army, symbolically represented by the Petrograd Soviet's "Order no. 1," establishing soldiers' committees throughout the army and giving the soviet oversight of military affairs. Many officers opposed to the committees and "Order no. 1," however, were not hostile to politicization *per se*, but rather to the fact that it was the Petrograd Soviet rather than the Provisional Government that was conducting it. Many officers welcomed the revolution as an opportunity to transform Russia's obedient but passive troops into committed citizen-soldiers, something many had been advocating since the army's defeat in the Russo-Japanese War.[37] Such officers not only did not fear politics; they positively sought to inject it into the army.

The establishment of "political departments" in the army demonstrates how such military men sought to suffuse the military with political efforts. As early as mid-March 1917 the Moscow military district established its own "Political-Civic Department." Its founder, serving in the directorate of the General Staff, argued in July 1917 for the extension of such "civic-political departments" to all military districts in the rear. "The immensity of the unfolding events," he argued to his superiors, "has advanced the public element to prime significance in state construction." Closely paralleling the attitudes of the nonmilitary public activists, this officer argued from the military side that "the War Ministry cannot and *must not* evade this development. The necessity for the very closest ties between military and civilian life can no longer be subject to any doubts and ought not to meet any opposition." In order to manage this amalgamation of the civilian and military spheres, he further insisted, "We must have the liveliest contact with active public forces, on the one hand, and on the other hand we must have precise and regular information on the internal life of our units, on their moods, and on the currents of sociopolitical thought that are acting in their milieu." He closed by suggesting the formation of a special political organ under the War Ministry, a proposal realized less than one month later with the creation of the War Ministry's separate political directorate.[38]

By September military-political departments had been established in the Moscow and Petrograd military districts, and plans had been drawn up for introducing them to other internal military districts. The General Staff argued that these departments were so important that they should be created for the front regions as well. The explicit goal of these organs was to identify and track popular sentiments in the army, and then to direct them. They were to have two subsections: one for liaison with public organizations, and one for "surveillance (cultural enlightenment)."[39] In September, while still at war, the War Ministry's Political Directorate introduced universal compulsory adult education throughout the army and established a department for distributing popular literature and organizing libraries.[40] Similar to the civilians in the Central Committee for Sociopolitical Enlightenment, the officers had come to see the army as the surrogate for an educational infrastructure that the autocracy stood accused of neglecting. After 1917, the Red Army's own "political departments" would engage in a nearly identical "cultural-enlightenment" endeavor.[41]

From February onward, information and knowledge became the coin of the new political realm, for the military as for everyone else. In July the Provisional Government issued revised instructions on censorship of the press and mails, on the basis of the 1914 temporary statute. Throughout 1917 military postal-censorship departments continued to operate, reporting on the mood of the troops and their civilian correspondents.[42] In addition to this source, beginning in late summer A. T. Kuz'min-Karaev, the head of the War Ministry's Commissariat, directed Provisional Government military commissars attached to army units to submit "detailed weekly summaries" on the troops' mood and their attitudes to the government, and provided a standardized form for these reports. (Like so many other military specialists, Kuz'min-Karaev later entered service in the Red Army.) Two weeks later, the political directorate ordered staffs to coordinate the submission of their summaries on soldiers' moods with the reports of the Provisional Government's military commissars, and soon after provided detailed instructions regarding when and how staffs were to submit such reports. In October the army command clarified that the reports should seek to identify the underlying "reasons causing events" in the military.[43]

This practice of submitting regular reports on the troops' moods continued without regard for the Bolshevik takeover in October. In December 1917 the new revolutionary command complained that it was receiving reports submitted according to forms composed prior to the seizure of power. Bolshevik authorities continued to receive information from commissars of the now-deposed Provisional Government and data on the number of cases tried by the now-abolished military-revolutionary courts. The Soviet command therefore directed staffs to continue to submit regular reports on moods, but not to constrain themselves to the parameters of the previous questionnaire. In early January 1918 the military-political department finally issued new, Soviet guidelines, with standardized categories on the "removal of counter-revolutionary elements," "liquidation of the old and organization of new local courts," and "democratization."[44] The categories had changed, but the practice of such regular reporting—and many of the personnel responsible for carrying it out—carried over from the more generalized 1917 revolutionary environment.

Civilian organs similarly expanded their interest in public moods. Since October 1915 the security police had been compiling regular monthly reports on the population's mood according to a standardized form issued by the Ministry of Internal Affairs. With the collapse of the

Old Regime in February, the Provisional Government had abolished the hated police network. In the place of the former police, the Provisional Government's new Ministry of Internal Affairs directed its provincial commissars to report by telegraph on any outstanding events in their localities until new standardized directives could be issued. Three days later, provincial commissars were charged to complete the information circuit by informing the population of the government's decrees and acts.[45] By mid-April the Provisional Government issued its own directives for routine reporting on life in the localities. The Ministry of Internal Affairs collated these reports into synthetic summaries, arranged into sixteen thematic categories. These summaries then served as the principal source on the dynamics of the "peasant movement" first for the Provisional Government and then subsequently for historians of 1917.[46] With the July days in Petrograd, the Ministry of Internal Affairs directed commissars henceforth to submit reports not to the Ministry of Internal Affairs, but rather to the Information Department of the Main Directorate of the Militia, the new government's designation for the police.[47] Thus the Provisional Government resurrected its predecessor's practice of having the police, rather than the Ministry of Internal Affairs in general, collect information on public moods, an institutional practice that would carry over into the ensuing seventy-five years of Soviet power.

The militia was interested in surveillance and not simply policing. The Petrograd authorities attempted to inculcate this ideal in their regular informants, the provincial commissars. In mid-August the head of the militia directorate issued a circular to them. Noting that since July they had been charged with submitting weekly reports on political life and on the agrarian movement, he complained that "the majority of reports do not touch upon sociopolitical life in the province." His telegram then noted that "it is highly desirable that you indicate the causal linkage between events and trends in sociopolitical life." Similarly, the army's Political Directorate repeatedly lectured those compiling regular reports on the state of the troops to include not only facts but also the underlying causes for these more general phenomena.[48] Under the Provisional Government, both civilian and military authorities had come to operate with the assumption that particular events were significant not so much in their own right, but rather as manifestations of larger sociopolitical processes.

Clearly, the Provisional Government's program, especially in light of Kerensky's gamble on the failed June offensive to unite the cause of revolution and that of the war effort, must be seen within the more general "remobilization" of combatant societies for the war effort. The strains of war in this same period led to attempts by other states to mobilize their own homefronts as well. Beginning in late 1916 German military authorities had been arguing for "enlightenment activities" to inculcate willing and informed support, rather than just obedience, in the troops and the civilian population. These proposals led to the development of a program of "enlightenment activity," carried out by the commands of military districts for their own troops as well as for the civilian population, and from late July 1917 to the establishment of "patriotic instruction" in the Germany army.[49] To coordinate film propaganda more effectively, Erich Ludendorff advocated the consolidation of the German film industry into the conglomerate UFA. The German Army's "enlightenment officer" [*Aufklärungsoffizer*], conducting both indoctrination and more generalized adult education, might thus be seen as the German analogue to the Provisional Government's commissars. However, in Germany, unlike Russia, the old-time military oversaw the extension of surveillance and propaganda, leading to a militarization of the sociopolitical realm, but without the corresponding civilianization of the military realm.

But developments in Russia were not simply an epiphenomenon of the Great War. From 1917 the relationship between war and revolution became reciprocal. Russia's revolution politicized the discussion of the war's aims and conduct in all combatant societies. The Russian example heightened concerns among all combatant powers about how committed to and informed about the struggle their own populations were, and this led authorities to increase surveillance and propaganda efforts directed at their own citizens. Other combatants' wartime mobilization efforts emerged not only from wartime exigencies but also as a response to the political threat represented by the Russian Revolution. For much of the rest of Europe such fears in fact proved greater than any reality. Yet this fear caused governments to initiate particular policies to address the perceived threat of revolution.

Inspired partly by the German prototype, the Austro-Hungarian military overcame its devotion to an entirely apolitical army and introduced its own "patriotic instruction" in March 1918. This program was to be conducted by the "Enemy Propaganda Defense Agency," whose purpose was to counter domestic war-weariness, oppose enemy propaganda, and combat the threat of Bolshevism. In arguing for its establishment, the minister of war cited the cautionary example of the Russian Army, which (he argued) had disintegrated because its "educational organs" had proved unable to counteract the revolutionary agitation. Austro-Hungarian authorities had reason for concern. In April 1917 the central censorship agency ordered censorship bureaus to compile special reports on the impact of Russia's February Revolution. These reports indicated that the Russian Revolution was the first event to have a broad political resonance throughout all of Austro-Hungarian society. In the aftermath of the Bolshevik Revolution in November, the Austro-Hungarian Army's censorship departments found that a large proportion of letters expressed the hope of receiving peace directly from Russia or from a revolution at home, or from some combination of the two.[50]

In Britain, the bastion of liberalism, security organs by the beginning of 1917 had progressed "from counter-espionage to political surveillance," devoting special attention to industrial unrest. In 1918 they became increasingly concerned about the spread of Bolshevik propaganda. From the close of 1917 until the start of 1920, the British army was responsible for monitoring unrest. Meanwhile, a new wartime ministry, the "Ministry of Information," promoted Britain's cause abroad, but increasingly also devoted its efforts to rallying the homefront.[51] In France, "even before the Russian Revolution the vulnerability of its citizen armies was the dominant preoccupation among commanding officers and their political masters; after the collapse of the Russian Armies it became an obsession." French postal censorship had first introduced systematic quantitative and comparative analyses beginning in 1916, but the mutinies of spring 1917 and the cautionary example of Russia had led both military and civilian authorities to give heightened attention to identifying public moods. From mid-1917 the French Army General Staff's central intelligence section took to compiling regular "confidential bulletins on internal morale," drawing primarily upon materials generated by postal censorship boards at the front and throughout the country.[52] The surveillance measures of Russia's Provisional Government thus must be seen as emerging out of the more generalized 1917–1918 remobilization of wartime societies. But the Russian Revolution, both as a cautionary example and in terms of the ideological challenge it self-consciously presented to all other combatants, itself contributed significantly to defining the nature and extent of this more generalized remobilization throughout Europe.

"Surveillance and Agitation" under the Anti-Soviet Movements

All sides in the Russian civil wars elaborated upon a common heritage of wartime and revolutionary practices of surveillance. To be sure, there were important differences between Soviet and anti-Soviet practices. But both "represented essentially a radical extension, rather than revolutionary break, with the past."[53]

The Volunteer Army had abandoned the Don Territory in late January 1918 and departed on its storied "Ice March," finally finding safe refuge in the Kuban' region by mid-summer. There it became the core of the anti-Bolshevik "Armed Forces of South Russia" (AFSR), headed by General Anton Denikin. This force is often portrayed as an unalloyed reactionary institution. Yet it did not return to the principles of the pre-February army. In early June 1918 the Volunteer Army established its own "military-political department," an institution that had emerged out of the revolutionary reorganization of the army in 1917. Beginning in August 1918, this political apparatus issued appeals to the population in areas under its control and published a two-page periodical for distribution among its own soldiers.[54] The Volunteer Army therefore established its own military-political organs at least as early as the Red Army, a fact that seems less surprising if one views them both as emerging out of the revolutionary army of 1917.

By the autumn of 1918, Denikin had also established a civilian face for his movement, termed "the Special Council." Kadets played a dominant role in this organization.[55] In early September 1918, the Volunteer Army transferred the responsibilities of its military-political department to the Special Council. The government's civilian surveillance organization became known as "OSVAG," an acronym for the "surveillance and agitation branch." However, all officials of OSVAG continued to be rated as "officials in the ranks of the Volunteer Army." Meanwhile, the Volunteer Army's military-political department was made into a "special department" of the supreme commander in chief.

The AFSR General Staff continued to maintain its own political chancellery.[56]

Originally, OSVAG was subordinated to the Special Council's Foreign Affairs Department. This institutional arrangement, however, did not mean that OSVAG concerned itself primarily with foreign powers. The Foreign Affairs Department oversaw relations with all former Russian provinces. As soon as it ceased to serve this function, OSVAG was placed under a separate Political Chancellery. OSVAG was charged with completing the now standard information circuit: informing the population of the government's plans and measures, and reporting the population's attitude to the government. OSVAG was to carry out this task of surveillance and agitation in all territories under control of the Volunteer Army, including the area of the All-Great Don Host, which also had its own surveillance and agitation agency.[57] Over the course of its existence, from September 1918 through March 1920, OSVAG had four directors. But for the very last, all were prominent Kadets: Sergei Chakhotin (September 1918–January 1919); Nikolai Paramonov (January 1919–late March 1919); and Konstantin Sokolov (March–December 1919).

The Whites are often accused of underrating agitation and propaganda, and political affairs generally.[58] While the content and execution of their endeavors can certainly be criticized, there can be no doubt that the anti-Soviet movement in South Russia recognized the importance of agitation. Chakhotin, OSVAG's first director, obviously did not begin his surveillance and agitation efforts in 1918 under Denikin. He had earlier helped establish the Provisional Government's Central Committee for Sociopolitical Enlightenment. Many of OSVAG's measures, such as its "maps of political meteorology," grew directly out of previous measures for the Provisional Government, as Chakhotin himself testified.[59] Recognizing the need to expand its activities, OSVAG in December 1918 established a network of information points, expanding upon local offices originally organized by the army's military-political department. Their purpose was primarily "ideological." The directors of these points, vetted and funded by the local military centers, were to submit regular reports on their activities and the state of their regions.[60] While the area under the control of the anti-Bolshevik AFSR would expand and contract in dramatic fashion, this network continued to function throughout.

Still not satisfied with these efforts, in January 1919 the Special

Council created a separate Department of Propaganda. Headed by Nikolai Paramonov, it absorbed Chakhotin's OSVAG. For the first and last time, the anti-Bolshevik Special Council deigned to summon a civic activist from the Cossack territories. In part, the Special Council was responding to the suggestions of Colonel Keyes, a British officer serving with General Poole, the head of the British mission to the Caucasus. Keyes had argued that the struggle now was to win over peoples rather than just their governments, and hence propaganda efforts had to be pursued on the very broadest scale.[61] One year before, in February 1918, Britain had initiated its first broad-scale domestic "information" campaign under Lord Beaverbrook. Paramonov, not unlike Beaverbrook, was a leading industrialist and press magnate, as well as a prominent Rostov Kadet. During the war he had served as head of the important Rostov military-industrial committee and in February 1917 had been summoned by the city's head to constitute the new political order in Rostov. Under Paramonov's direction, OSVAG moved from Ekaterinodar to Rostov, which had greater technical and production resources.

Anti-Soviet surveillance practices demonstrate that these movements did not seek the restoration of the pre-February order, but rather grew organically out of the post-February ecosystem. Paramonov saw his task as winning over a broad spectrum of democratic and progressive opinion to the cause of Russian state consciousness, the pillar of the anti-Bolshevik movement's program. To this end, he advocated incorporating socialists and other democratic activists who supported the program of Denikin's AFSR. He proposed that Denikin issue a political declaration that would be broadly "democratic, without demonstrating any fear of moving too far to the left." The movement's main task, argued Paramonov, should be restoring order, a cause dear to the hearts of Denikin's officer base. But the movement should also repudiate any restoration of the monarchy and promise the introduction of "land and other social reforms, and also a review of worker legislation."[62]

Paramonov's two assistants demonstrated that Russia's wartime self-mobilization of the public had carried over into the civil war, and in fact became even more extensive under the Whites. Fedor Kriukov was a well-known Don Cossack author whose publications before the war had appeared predominantly in the democratic publication *Russkoe bogatstvo*, the editorial board of which was dominated by Popular Socialists. He had been elected to the First Duma as an oppositionist delegate. Kriukov, who in August 1918 had been elected secretary of the Don Cossack Circle, was appointed as Paramonov's aide in part to satisfy the demands of Don Ataman Peter Krasnov, who extracted the promise of a Cossack appointee in return for allowing Denikin's Department of Propaganda to work out of Rostov. Paramonov's other key aide was Sergei Svatikov, a well-known Don civic activist and historian. Svatikov was a longstanding critic of the autocracy, having collaborated with Peter Struve in the 1903–1905 liberal oppositionist periodical *Osvobozhdenie*. In 1917 the Provisional Government had dispatched Svatikov to Europe to oversee the liquidation of the autocracy's secret police operations abroad. In November 1917 Svatikov arrived on the Don and lived through the Soviet occupation of Rostov. Paramonov also convinced Vladimir Amfiteatrov-Kadashev, a budding author who had been serving as the editor of the Don government's official organ, *Donskie vedomosti*, to head the cinematography section of the new Department of Propaganda. Ivan Bilibin, a well-known Art Nouveau graphic artist and designer of opera sets, also worked for the OSVAG propaganda effort. The OSVAG endeavor was, without doubt, a program supported by and driven by the Russian intelligentsia.[63]

In addition to surveillance agencies set up by governments, the right-wing political activist and newspaper publisher Vasilii Shul'gin established Azbuka, his own intelligence agency in the service of the White cause.[64] By 1919, one OSVAG official noted that "now in Rostov there is not one person who has not set up his own OSVAG or his own counterintelligence agency." The multitude of agencies hindered the common cause. OSVAG officials in Rostov attempted, without success, to prevent an unofficially organized anti-Bolshevik "agitational theatrical performance."[65] Surveillance during the civil wars was not simply a state project, imposed from above; indeed, it resulted at least as much from the self-mobilization of society, albeit along a very narrow spectrum.

Within Paramonov's Department of Propaganda, Chakhotin continued to head the OSVAG section in Rostov. Having become a devotee of Taylorism in the workplace while in Germany, he sought to introduce the most up-to-date methods of personnel and time management at the micro-level, in an agency itself dedicated to shaping the population's psyche at a macro-level. Within the Rostov OSVAG building, employees wore color-coded badges signifying their degree of access to supervisors, and semaphore flags hung over office doors to indicate whether messengers could enter that office or not.[66] This system actually hindered rather than helped efficiency, and officials in the more distant parts of the building tried to ignore it. Paramonov, meanwhile, advocated running OSVAG "like a commercial enterprise rather than a bureaucratic institution." Propaganda, in his view, should imperceptibly permeate all spheres of life, aiming to find a broad social basis. To this end Amfiteatrov-Kadashev's cinematography section in the Department of Propaganda sought to make three types of films: newsreels; comedies playing on the idiocy of everyday life in the Soviet zone; and "big, American-style films" with a strong anti-Bolshevik thrust. Paramonov's commercial sensibilities, however, ran counter to Denikin's own sense of the purity of his struggle. Even before Paramonov's appointment, Denikin had "categorically" opposed the enlistment of private film companies in the cause of propaganda. Commercial pursuits, he declared, "do not correspond to the foundations of the Volunteer Army."[67]

Paramonov's tenure as head of the Department of Propaganda highlights certain tensions within the anti-Bolshevik movement. While the Russian officer corps as a whole was far from reactionary, those who found their way into the anti-Bolshevik armies were, by process of self-selection, the most unabashed antirevolutionaries. As head of his Special Council, Denikin had appointed General A. M. Dragomirov, a fervent monarchist. Paramonov's commercial program and "turn to the left" brought him into conflict with these officers. Paramonov's appointment of Svatikov, a "socialist," outraged many of them, who refused to carry out any directives signed by him. Within the department, Konstantin Sokolov, a Kadet lawyer of far more conservative views, conducted an outright campaign against Paramonov, accusing him of employing Jews and socialists. Charging Paramonov with pursuing too independent and leftist a policy in Rostov, the authorities in Ekaterinodar replaced him with the more conservative Sokolov. Svatikov, Chakhotin, and Kriukov promptly resigned. Chakhotin and Kriukov, however, simply transferred from OSVAG, under Denikin's Special Council, to the Don government's Department of Surveillance.[68]

Even under Sokolov, OSVAG continued its enlightenment mission. Throughout the civil wars, OSVAG's network of information points submitted increasingly standardized regular summaries, invariably listing the "mood of the population" as their first category of analysis.[69] The anti-Soviet surveillance project, like its Soviet counterpart, was concerned as much with thought as with action. Describing the attitudes of the population in one region recently liberated from Soviet control in August 1919, Lieutenant Fedorov of the AFSR Intelligence Department noted that the "broad masses" welcomed the arrival of the anti-Soviet forces. While grateful for their delivery from Bolshevik violence, the population had an entirely passive attitude to their "liberators": "there was not that anticipated uplift in the national spirit of patriotism." Such feelings were found only "among the intelligentsia and bourgeois circles in liberated cities."[70] Fedorov clearly felt the need to shift from seeking subjects' obedient submission to generating citizens' active support. Yet his report captured the dilemma found in the intelligentsia's attempt to employ agitation and surveillance in the civil wars to achieve its prewar aspirations. The Russian Revolution had not, as anticipated, bridged the gulf between "people" and "society," but rather had exacerbated it.

Precisely to implant a sense of state consciousness and patriotism, the task of surveillance was not limited to gathering data about the population. It equally encompassed attempts to engage the population politically, to elevate citizens to the proper level of consciousness through state-sponsored enlightenment measures. Invoking the latest branch of the human sciences, anti-Soviet surveillance technocrats attempted to probe the "psychological condition of the peasant masses" and aspired to the "psychological consolidation of newly occupied territory."[71] OSVAG had a dual task. It sought to "pass information 'up' (to the authorities) and pass information 'down' (into the population).[72] To proselytize their political message, *de rigueur* in the new-style politics predicated on popular sovereignty and an enlightenment project, the Whites engaged in many of the same "cultural-enlightenment measures" practiced by the Soviet side. Anti-Soviet "information departments" employed a network of reading huts containing newspapers and political pamphlets (published, of course, by the information departments); agitational steamships and agitational trains (OSVAG eventually had four at its disposal); official journals and newspapers;

and even the use of agitational plays and films.[73] These examples clearly demonstrate that the common presentation of the White movement as hopelessly reactionary in contrast to the progressive Soviet state stands in need of serious revision. OSVAG's reliance on agitational films extended the efforts of the Skobelev Committee during the First World War and had obvious parallels with UFA, the German film conglomerate formed by Ludendorff. Red and White not only employed agitational posters and placards extensively, but there were striking similarities in their formal style and content.[74]

The All-Great Don Host was first allied with and, from January 1919, subordinated to Denikin's "Armed Forces of South Russia." Hence the Special Council's OSVAG operated throughout the Don Territory. But OSVAG was not the only surveillance and agitation agency operating there. When Sokolov replaced Paramonov as head of OSVAG, Paramonov's compatriots Chakhotin and Kriukov simply left OSVAG and joined the AGDH's own surveillance and agitation agency. One of the very first acts of the anti-Soviet Don government in the spring of 1918 had been to establish this "Don Surveillance Department." The government described the new agency as having a twofold task: it was to inform the population about the government's activity and the government—about the population's sentiments.[75] Like the 1917 Russian Provisional Government, the 1918 Don Provisional Government placed its hopes on Russia's intelligentsia as *Kulturträger* to the benighted countryside. The new organ was to inform the population and serve generally as "the center and focus of all cultural and educational endeavors of the government in all spheres of activity."[76]

The Don Surveillance Department had two primary conduits for maintaining contact with the population: its traveling agents and branch offices established in the localities. Agents were drawn from among members of Russia's educated society, individuals who saw their task as dispelling the common people's ignorance. As the department's own reports indicated, educated society responded warmly to the surveillance department's enterprise, in contrast to much of the rest of the population.[77] Once they had signed on, agents received a crash "instructional-organizational course," similar to those offered a year before by both the Committee for Sociopolitical Enlightenment and the Don Food-Supply Committee to their student agitators. By mid-June 1918, within a month of its establishment, the department had graduated four classes of such agitators. By early summer, the surveillance department was already reporting that "more thorough reports are beginning to arrive from agents who have returned from missions and turned in reports."[78] In larger population centers the surveillance department established a regular presence through its network of "offices," which carried agitational literature and official newspapers.

In early 1919 Denikin's Special Council moved OSVAG from Ekaterinodar to Rostov and appointed several leading figures from the Don (Paramonov, Kriukov) to head it. In this period, during which much of the territory was occupied by Soviet forces, OSVAG supplanted the activities of the Don Surveillance Department. In April 1919, with the removal of leading Don figures such as Paramonov from OSVAG as well as the liberation of much of the Don Territory, the Don government established a reinvigorated surveillance organ of its own, the Don Department of Surveillance (DDS). The reorganized DDS was structured hierarchically. A central administration in Novocherkassk oversaw nine district departments, each of which in turn supervised six to ten centers, around which six to ten subcenters were grouped. By August 1919 the entire network encompassed the central administration, nine district departments, sixty centers, and roughly two hundred subcenters. The method of conducting surveillance remained much the same as in 1918. Agents traveled undercover throughout the territory in the guise of actors, refugees, students, railway workers, teachers, and even obstetricians. Others traveled openly as lecturers, communicating the government's activities to remote communities.[79]

These traveling agents and the officers in the field compiled regular reports on the population, which then passed up the bureaucratic chain to the central administration. The central administration then collated these reports into daily summaries.[80] In contrast to the 1918 summaries, which lacked any regular structure, the 1919 DDS summaries were organized by topic, each of which was assigned a letter. Among the routine topics of reporting were local administration, the land issue and responses to the AGDH's land reform, and economic conditions. But the first and most common category, assigned the letter "A," was that on "the mood of the population."

Having identified societal moods, the DDS set itself the task of cultivating them in a more enlightened and state-conscious direction. To this end, OSVAG and the DDS each published several of their own newspapers and controlled the content of all other press reporting.[81] Both the central OSVAG administration as well as its local Don branch published separate daily newspapers in Rostov. The DDS did not content itself with informing the territory's population through central organs alone. In order to bring news of government activity to an even broader circle of readers, it also published three district newspapers, two in the remote northern Upper Don and Ust'-Medveditsa Districts.

By 1919 anti-Soviet surveillance agencies took an active role in scripting the news. All newspapers drew their information from a central press bureau. While the Volunteer Army was advancing, editors were permitted to select themes for articles, although the articles were then subject to censorship. But when the tide turned against the Whites, the head of OSVAG's Information Department convened daily meetings at which journalists were assigned topics for their articles.[82] In addition, almost every newspaper carried a section entitled "Out and about the Territory," containing short reports on life in the localities. Unbeknownst to most readers, this section drew almost exclusively on information from the DDS, which distributed its daily summaries in edited form to the newspapers for publication. Between April and August 1919, the DDS had placed more than four hundred such articles, representing the closure of the information circuit.[83] The surveillance agency gathered information on the population's views, edited it into edifying form, and then broadcast it back to the population.

In many communities the DDS established a more permanent presence through its centers and subcenters. Termed "reading huts," these offices served the same function as the wartime zemstvo organs. Kamenskaia stanitsa had two separate "reading huts": one established by the DDS and another by OSVAG.[84] Even the small community of Chuevka had its own reading hut. From it the inhabitants of Chuevka learned that the AGDH had passed a decree upholding the fees that non-native peasants were to pay for living in Cossack settlements. Outraged, they stormed the reading hut and tore it apart.[85] In an ironic way, the Chuevka reading hut had achieved its purpose. While the inhabitants disapproved of the government's measure, they had learned of it. Even more significantly, in the public's eye the reading hut had become the locus of central government authority.

That the anti-Soviet movements attempted to secure the "psychological consolidation" of the masses did not mean they succeeded in their efforts. While "cultural forces" proved eager to aid the government in this endeavor, other segments of the population, even in Cossack communities, were hostile to it. As a result, people became increasingly reluctant to express their views publicly. The surveillance agencies dutifully noted that the population "fears to express its views openly," "engages in political discussions only very reluctantly," and "expresses itself with great reserve, unwillingly, and cautiously."[86] People had not stopped talking about politics, but they had come to realize that the authorities were now listening to what they had to say. The anti-Soviet movement failed spectacularly at winning widespread popular support. It had succeeded, however, in changing the parameters of political life. Whether the population detested or welcomed surveillance and agitation, there would now be no escaping it.

The surveillance efforts of the anti-Soviet movements cannot be termed antirevolutionary. Many of their programs grew directly out of post-February institutions and practices. Much like the Provisional Government, these movements proceeded from the assumption that Russia's existing educated elite—intelligentsia, quasi-intelligentsia, and students—would staff such "progressive" efforts.[87] The sociological profile of the anti-Bolshevik surveillance effort in fact undercut the very goals it was seeking to achieve by giving it a class face. The surveillance program of both the Provisional Government and the anti-Bolshevik movements represented an extension and reworking of the Russian intelligentsia's prewar, anti-autocratic agenda. With the collapse of the monarchy, and with the tools provided to members of the intelligentsia by wartime mobilization, they believed that at last they had the opportunity to enlighten the benighted countryside. Opposition to the autocracy had inspired the breadth of their aspirations; but the autocracy also bequeathed them few networks that penetrated into the population they wished to uplift. When they finally had an opportunity to act on their visions, they found that the gulf between "society" and "democracy" remained. Surveillance for the Provisional Government and the anti-Bolshevik movements, paradoxically, proved much more effective at mobilizing the intelligentsia to participate in its dream of transforming the population than it ever did in actually winning over the population to its views.

Soviet Surveillance

The prerevolutionary intelligentsia's enlightenment ethos also under-
lay the Bolshevik agenda, and the first Soviet surveillance structures
emerged directly out of Provisional Government organs.[88] Not surpris-
ingly, these were military structures. The Russian Army after October
1917 continued the surveillance programs it had been pursuing under
the Provisional Government, although the categories had to be
changed. When the Soviet state dissolved the old Russian Army in January 1918, it reinscribed (albeit with some delay) these practices into its
new Red Army, an institution unabashedly identified with the cause of
social revolution. Unlike its predecessors and competitors, the Soviet
state disentangled its revolutionary effort from the prerevolutionary
bearers of this ideal, the Russian intelligentsia.

After the October Revolution, the Russian Army continued collecting information on soldiers.[89] In January 1918, however, the Soviet
state did away with the old army, and along with it the army's military
censorship departments, which had served as one of the main conduits
of information on the population. Through autumn 1918 the Soviet
government did not have any official organs for vetting the mail or
perlustration of anything but international correspondence. By the end
of 1918 the staff of the Petrograd Military-Censorship Bureau had
shrunk almost by a factor of ten, from 2,000 to 250 officials. (This decline was relative: before 1914 the St. Petersburg Censorship Office
had a staff of 11 people.)[90]

As part of its overall effort in the autumn of 1918 to consolidate the
Red Army, the Soviet leadership in September established a "Revolutionary-Military Council of the Republic," within which there was a
"field headquarters." In the headquarters' "registration secretariat" the
Soviet state formed a "military censorship department" in October
1918.[91] The task and structure of the Soviet military-censorship organs
did not differ fundamentally from those of their prerevolutionary predecessors; in fact many of the personnel carried over. In mid-1918 both
the head of the Moscow Military Postal-Telegraph Control Bureau and
his aide had been serving there since 1916. Forty-eight percent of their
staff had been working in that office since before the Soviet seizure of
power.[92] Soviet military censors, like their predecessors, copied out excerpts from all letters typifying in any way the author's political atti-

tudes, whether they were positive, negative, or simply apathetic. These excerpts were then collated and served as the source for regular bi-monthly thematic and regional reports. The Red Army prepared regular desertion summaries, supply summaries, and summaries on abuse of office. The most common, however, was the political summary, providing an overview of the "moods" of the troops and their civilian correspondents.[93] Postal censorship departments included interpretative analyses of the content of these summaries as an accompanying cover letter.[94] In 1915 even the Russian Imperial Army became interested in "political topics" in a rudimentary way. But Soviet interpretive categories were of course predicated on Marxist analysis. Owing to Marxism's more expansive definition of the political sphere, Soviet surveillance encompassed a much broader spectrum of issues than had the tsarist regime.

The Red Army did not rely solely on its military-censorship departments for information on public moods. It relied equally on its political departments, which were expressly charged with conducting "political (party) and cultural-enlightenment work."[95] These organs were direct descendants of the Provisional Government's own military-political project to plumb the moods of the population. From June 1918 onward, political departments in Red Army field formations compiled regular summaries on the mood of the troops and the population of the front, while military commissariats did the same throughout the rest of the republic. Although Soviet military commissariats did not complete the institutionalization of their system for collecting information until mid-1920, henceforth they would refract popular moods through this spectrum of analytical categories ("clearly counterrevolutionary"; "apathetic"; "wavering"; "inclined toward the revolution"; "reliably revolutionary").[96] In addition, Red Army political commissars regularly reported on moods to the "Political Directorate of the Revolutionary-Military Council of the Republic" (PUR). PUR had been established in February 1919 and became the key political organ of the Red Army for the next several decades. Like its antecedents under the Provisional Government—the War Ministry's Political Directorate and the government's military commissars—PUR pursued the dual task of surveillance and "cultural-enlightenment."[97]

Such measures were not unique to Russia or the Bolshevik regime during Europe's 1914–1921 "Time of Troubles." What distinguished the Soviet regime was that it carried over such methods, forged during a particular period of remobilization during the First World War, from wartime into peacetime. In doing so, the regime also acted on the Russian tendency to "civilianize" these practices. As the civil wars wound down, responsibility for military as well as civilian surveillance passed from the army to the "Cheka," the "All-Russian Extraordinary Commission for Combating Counterrevolution, Speculation, and Abuse of Office."[98] A state rather than a party institution, the Cheka was charged with defending the revolution, albeit in the form defined by the Communist Party. The Cheka's own information network also had begun to emerge in the second half of 1918. This network built upon previous practical experience of the People's Commissariats of Internal Affairs and of Military Affairs. Both continued the reporting methods of the Provisional Government.[99] In August 1918 the Cheka began publishing its own regular bulletins, and in the autumn it started issuing a "weekly report," employing the terminology that would become characteristic of later reports.

In June 1919, the Third All-Russian Conference of Chekas further systematized this endeavor, placing the collection of all political information in the hands of secret departments of local Cheka organs. Congress delegates were issued an "Instruction to Provincial Chekas," which contained directions for compiling standardized summaries. Like the Provincial Government's Militia Department before it, the Cheka was interested not only in events but also in the underlying sociopolitical reasons for behavior. It took some time for this network to gain a purchase. In June 1919, only 10 percent of local Chekas submitted their required reports, although the figure rose to 40 percent the next month. The central agency, however, found many of these reports to be overly superficial and evaluated only 38 percent of them as "satisfactory." The central organs insisted on "satisfactory" information "so that the Secret Section, by means of statistical analysis, might clarify the actual causes of the current situation in the RSFSR." In order to obtain the proper form of information, beginning in October 1920 the Don Cheka circulated critiques of incomplete reports, indicating the specific shortcomings and what was expected in the future. In its critique, circulated to all other district-level politbureaus, the Don Cheka sternly admonished the local organs that it was insufficient merely to identify attitudes. It demanded that local officials also "indicate what explains this difference in views." As a national Cheka circular instructed, only on the basis of such material could the central organization "establish the regularity and consistency of events, and make corresponding conclusions."[100] As a result of these efforts, by the end of 1919 the Cheka's information-gathering system had taken on its systematic and secret nature, even in such recently conquered areas as the Don Territory.[101]

Whereas the surveillance and agitation organs of the Provisional Government and the anti-Soviet movements were staffed largely by students and members of the intelligentsia, only 14 percent of those staffing local Cheka departments had completed even secondary school. Fully 64 percent had received no more than education at the elementary school level. What they lacked in traditional education, however, they made up for in "consciousness": more than three-quarters were members of the Communist Party.[102]

By mid-1920 the Soviet state began to transfer information-gathering from the military to the Cheka. Early in August 1920 the army's agencies of postal-telegraph control were turned over to "special departments," Cheka organs within the Red Army. With the end of the civil wars one year later, the department of military censorship was not abolished but rather passed to the Cheka as a subdepartment of the Cheka's own preexisting Information Department.[103] Thus in the aftermath of the civil wars responsibility for perlustration of letters passed from military postal boards to purely "political" organs, first the Cheka and then subsequently the information departments of the "State Political Directorate" (GPU) and its successor, the "Unified State Political Directorate" (OGPU). This transfer of wartime-style surveillance to a civilian agency had profound consequences. Rather than transient wartime measures bracketed within military structures, these wartime practices and institutions now became deeply embedded within the everyday and routine structure of the Soviet state.

The Communist Party of course had its own internal information apparatus.[104] In March 1921, however, just as the Soviet state declared its turn to the New Economic Policy (NEP), a joint circular from the government and the Communist Party directed both local executive committees and local party committees to inform the Soviet leadership of the political situation through the organs of the Cheka, not the party. One month later, the Cheka ordered the formation of state information troikas in the localities, and in May it issued directives on the forms to be employed for such summaries. In September 1921 an "Instruction for State Information Summaries" reiterated that information reporting was the responsibility of the Cheka. This same instruction criticized summaries submitted by local troikas that recited facts but failed to indicate their underlying causes. In early 1922, with the civil wars now over, the Soviet state reformed the Cheka, the "Extraordinary Commission," into the GPU. The Soviet state thus came to incorporate an "extraordinary" structure, born of revolution and employing instruments of war, as part of its regular structure. Now both the Soviet state (with the GPU) and the Red Army (with PUR) each had its own separate "political directorates." Surveillance had become one of the essential modes of Soviet power.[105]

The Culture of Revolutionary Enlightenment

Soviet surveillance institutions and their reports are not unique.[106] Rather, such practices and institutions emerged directly from wartime mobilization practices common to other European states. In Russia, however, such measures emerged within a political system that had long denied "society" any role in policy formation. Even during the war years, the autocracy remained ambivalent and half-hearted about harnessing society to its war effort. For its part, educated society could not commit itself unambiguously to a war effort headed by the autocracy.

For men like Sergei Chakhotin and Fedor Stepun, the February Revolution abolished the autocracy—and hence any ambivalence they might have felt about mobilizing for the state—and provided them with the opportunity finally to carry out their longstanding enlightenment mission with regard to Russia's benighted masses. For them, the revolution represented the triumph of their prewar ideals. With the revolution occurring during the Great War, they could now harness new state institutions and practices forged for the war to their long-desired ends. Hence early in the February Revolution the civilian academic Chakhotin helped establish the Bureau for Organizing Morale, a nonstate organization, and then agitated for it to be subsumed under the War Ministry. Stepun, a popular lecturer on idealistic philosophy before the war, eagerly served as the head of Kerensky's new Political Directorate of the War Ministry.

The program of state surveillance closely corresponded to the anti-autocratic prewar aspirations of Russia's educated classes. The surveillance efforts of both the Provisional Government and the anti-Bolshevik movements were staffed disproportionately by members of the Russian intelligentsia: Stankevich, Stepun, Paramonov, Kriukov, Svatikov, and Sokolov. All had opposed the autocracy before the war and greeted its fall with enthusiasm. While antirevolutionary in the sense of opposing the Bolsheviks' vision of revolution, they were hardly reactionary. Writing in emigration in 1921, Chakhotin paid tribute to the Soviet state, his erstwhile foe, precisely because it served as a vehicle for his own progressive ideals. The Bolshevik victory "guaranteed the impossibility of any return to the past," wrote the devotee of Taylorism: "now there is the possibility of laying a new edifice of Russian statehood, on new rational principles." When he asked himself how best to help Russia, Chakhotin responded characteristically: "The first task is to aid, by all our efforts, the enlightenment of the popular masses."[107] The involvement of such men in "surveillance" institutions therefore was not accidental. Surveillance, in Russia as in other wartime states, was not simply the passive and surreptitious reporting on public moods. Surveillance technocrats sought to know the collective psyche in order to mold and uplift it. Although this activist side of surveillance is often termed "propaganda," the actual term many states employed was "enlightenment."[108]

In addition to its enlightenment agenda, surveillance equally exemplified the emergence of a technocratic ideal for governing.[109] The Provisional Government's Militia Department and the War Ministry's Political Directorate both insisted that reports demonstrate "the causal linkage between events and trends in sociopolitical life." This outlook obviously continued to dictate the agenda of Soviet surveillance technocrats. The Cheka also demanded that officials indicate the underlying "causes" of events. Surveillance had come to mean less the haphazard reporting of specific events than the analysis of such events as markers pointing to underlying socioeconomic patterns and regularities. When OSVAG employed the term "psychology" for describing its surveillance task, it only demonstrated the breadth of this technocratic conceit to identify the true *zakonnomernosti*—structural regularities—of sociopolitical life. Surveillance, in the minds of OSVAG operatives, was a science analogous to psychology, and hence equally capable of diagnosing and treating the population's collective psyche.

Bolshevik ideology established the direction the Soviet state would take; the state structure itself, however, crystallized out of a particular moment of war and revolution. Seen from this perspective, Soviet measures were not a radical departure from previous Russian practices, nor did they fundamentally set the Bolshevik regime off from the more general European wartime ecosystem. Victory in the civil wars permitted the Soviet state to pursue surveillance more fully and within its explicitly Marxist framework. Yet the practices themselves had been elaborated by the imperial state in its total-war manifestation and constituted a common heritage for all movements in the civil wars. The ten thousand people devoted to perlustration for the Soviet state in 1920 had their roots less in the fifty people pursuing that task in 1914 than in the massive expansion of the surveillance enterprise during the war.[110] The shift from policing to surveillance, and the foundations for this burgeoning surveillance structure, can be found in the war as much as in the revolutions of 1917. Indeed, this link between European measures for wartime mobilization and Bolshevik practices extended beyond the war proper. Soviet surveillance not only emerged out of the Great War; the Soviets continued to refract their study of surveillance efforts through the general European war experience. Soviet works in the 1920s and early 1930s frequently invoked the writings of European authors (especially Germans) on wartime propaganda to demonstrate the efficacy of state measures for "working on public opinion."[111]

Yet the surveillance project underscores certain structural features specific to Russia. The Russian Empire lacked any developed web of institutions that penetrated into society, such as the French Republican school system or the British party structure. The absence of such institutions not only dulled the effects of the Russian professional class's surveillance program after February but also accounted for this class's embrace of military and state institutions to serve as surrogates for missing civil institutions. "State consciousness" in part derived precisely from this reliance on the state in the absence of other civic structures.

Russian political culture across the 1917 divide also tended to subordinate the military to civilian control more generally. This tendency was evident during the war in both food-supply issues and surveillance.[112] Even in wartime Russia, reporting on popular moods—under the imperial government, Provisional Government, White regimes, and Soviet state—was a civilian operation, usually conducted under the aegis of the Ministry of Internal Affairs and by the political police (be it the tsarist security section, the Provisional Government's militia, or the Soviet Cheka). Thus it would be incorrect to speak simply of the "militarization" of Russian political life. Rather, the years of war and revolution produced a hybridized politico-military realm in military and political institutions alike.

Yet while Soviet surveillance efforts emerged out of the general European wartime context, they became refracted through the experience and expectations of millenarian revolution. The Russian political class's attempt to employ wartime surveillance as a proxy for its longstanding mission as *Kulturträger* failed. This class understood "revolution" as a structural opening for its preexisting dream to enlighten the masses. This vision clashed with a more expansive vision of revolution as ongoing project for social justice embraced precisely by those whom Russia's political class wished to tutor as citizens. Russia's workers and peasants viewed surveillance efforts, not incorrectly, as embodiments of the prerevolutionary intelligentsia's aspirations, which they had by now passed beyond. Wartime and revolutionary state efforts at surveillance thus benefited from the self-mobilization of the Russian intelligentsia. But these efforts failed precisely because they found no purchase with the aspirations and lived experience of those for whom they claimed to speak.

Soviet surveillance thus differed in important ways from its competitors. While equally motivated in the abstract by the Russian intelligentsia's enlightenment mission, its sociological profile reflected less the old intelligentsia than the new revolutionary enlightenment institution—the Communist Party. Soviet state surveillance, for better or worse, was identified not with the prerevolutionary intelligentsia but with the revolutionary regime's own institutions: the Cheka, the Red Army, and the Communist Party.

Within a European context, what most distinguished Soviet surveillance was not the actual practice of surveillance itself—it was nearly ubiquitous during the war period—but the fact that the Soviet state so completely carried it over into "peacetime." This continued institutional mobilization based on a wartime model should come as no surprise. Bolshevik ideology insisted that "the history of all hitherto existing societies is the history of class struggle." Lenin had called for the transformation of the world war into ongoing class war. In this sense, the Soviet Union never really demobilized from "total mobilization." Soviet surveillance was not a set of practices limited to wartime, but rather an institution that became embedded within the new state's permanent civilian structures. Russian society's "remobilization" for war ended in 1917. The remobilization of society for revolution continued for several decades longer.

~ 8

The Revolution as Orthodoxy

> We must put an end to the kulak feast from the moment this
> conference closes. The mobilization of Communists and trade unions
> should bring the dictatorship of the proletariat there and force them to
> surrender all that we need. We should shoot malicious kulaks and
> confiscate from nonmalicious kulaks.
> ~ Comrade Miller, head of the Don Food-Supply Committee,
> August 1920

The Red Army reconquered the Don Territory in early 1921. Victory now meant that the Soviet state could impose its version of revolution. The revolution, however, remained an amorphous ideal. Its vagueness in part accounted for its broad appeal. In the Don Territory, this testing of aspirations against actual policy coincided with the receding of any real military threat from the counterrevolution. Citizens could no longer rationalize Soviet measures as driven by the exigencies of Civil War. Would supporters of "the revolution" recognize Soviet orthodoxy as their own?

In mid-summer 1920 Soviet power had replaced its previous model of political support based on estates with Marxist class analysis. The First Don Party Conference, meeting in the first week of June 1920, signaled the new turn. It debated at length the question of whether Cossacks were a monolithic counterrevolutionary bloc, or whether they too were divided by class differentiation. Syrtsov, who had pressed so strongly for de-Cossackization throughout 1919, argued that the line dividing Soviet supporters and foes continued to run between Cossacks and peasants, rather than between rich and poor, as it did in the rest of European Russia. In making this argument, Syrtsov committed the heresy of suggesting that conditions on the Don differed from those in European Russia. Semen Vasil'chenko presented the argument for a class-based approach, extending arguments found in Trotsky's "Theses about Work on the Don." Vasil'chenko did not so much remove suspicion from the Cossacks as extend it to the entire rural population:

> I will not contrast the peasant and Cossack population, for they are both equally wealthy and kulak. Is this segment of the population interested in good Soviet power? Of course not . . . On which elements can the proletariat rely in the stanitsas? None . . . We must have a different idea: the dictatorship of the proletariat must be practically implemented by relying on Red Army and even Communist units.[1]

Vasil'chenko argued that Soviet power could dependably rely on neither Cossacks nor peasants. The Second Don Congress of Soviets, meeting two weeks later, publicly proclaimed the new line, albeit with a more positive emphasis. It explained that while "not so long ago it seemed to many that the Cossacks were a hopelessly anti-Soviet element," now only the Cossack elite continued to harbor hostility to the worker-peasant state. The laboring Cossacks "have manifestly and undoubtedly become Soviet."[2]

Attitudes did not change overnight. In January 1921 the Don Executive Committee felt the need to lecture again on the question of "whether Cossacks represent a monolithic, impermeable, petty bourgeois mass, or whether they are characterized by the same groupings as are found among the peasantry of the central provinces (poor peasants, middle peasants, kulaks)." "The essence of class policies in the village," its circular to district executive committees proclaimed with doctrinal certainty, "remains precisely the same as . . . in central provinces."[3] Subsequent party and Soviet gatherings reiterated the class line. The true enemy was the Cossack elite, together with the peasant kulaks and village bourgeoisie.[4]

Repudiating the view that all Cossacks were counterrevolutionary necessarily entailed a reevaluation of their socioeconomic standing. Party and Soviet functionaries continued to maintain that before the revolution Cossacks had occupied a privileged economic position. Increasingly, however, they came to the conclusion that whatever their prior wealth may have been, the civil wars had utterly devastated Cossack economies. One speaker at the Second Don Party Conference, in October 1920, expressed an emerging consensus. "The Cossackry as it once existed has been destroyed," he asserted. Political allegiance now ran "not between peasants and Cossacks, but between various groupings of the peasantry and Cossacks."[5] Of course, Cossack economies *were* devastated. The civil wars had transformed the Don from one of the regions richest in livestock to one of the poorest.[6] Although generalized impoverishment had been the case in 1919 and early 1920 as well, in mid-1920 Cossack destitution provided a convenient explanation for this shift from estate criteria to class criteria.

Extracting Grain "No Matter What"

There were two immediate causes for this shift in perception: the end of military operations and the emphasis on gathering much-needed grain. As the military struggle receded, Soviet authorities no longer depended on peasant recruits to combat the White armies and no longer confronted Cossacks as an armed opponent. At the same time, the proletarian dictatorship desperately needed grain from the grain-producing regions, among which the Don figured prominently. Indeed, one observer saw the shift from an estate policy to a class policy solely as a means for securing grain collections from the only segment of the population with any reserves left: "Where could [the assessment] be gotten? The Cossacks were ruined . . . All attention moved to the peasant population. It had it!"[7]

The shift from an estate analysis to a class one indeed occurred immediately prior to Soviet power's first major food-supply campaign on the Don. But the decision was not the result of a cynical calculation. In mid-1920, Soviet power confronted the rift between the putative economic condition it had ascribed to various social groups—proletarian peasants and wealthy Cossacks—and actual socioeconomic relations in the Don countryside. In addition to finding that not all Cossacks were wealthy, Soviet officials also learned that not all peasants were impoverished laborers. True, before the revolution the amount of peasant allotment land paled next to Cossack holdings. But peasants had purchased and rented vast amounts of land, and they engaged in much more intensive forms of agriculture upon it than did the Cossacks.

They were, in fact, more likely than Cossacks both to employ hired labor and to use modern agricultural implements.[8] If the Soviet state
wanted grain, it would have to squeeze it from peasants as well as from
Cossacks.

In order to "extract grain" Moscow relied upon a civilian apparatus
that was staffed largely by soldiers and, even more significantly, was itself subject to military discipline. When the Don was first occupied,
civil administration had officially passed to the Don Executive Committee, with the Don Party Committee operating behind it. Unofficially, however, the army continued to exercise great control over civilian administration. Given the weakness of the nominal party and
state organs, passing army units were the primary agents for establishing Soviet power. Passing divisions and regiments formed local soviets
and often assigned the officials to staff them.[9] Where the army found
soviets formed by the local population, it frequently reconstituted
them, replacing elected office-holders with its own political workers.[10]
The Don Party Committee openly admitted to the Central Committee
that it relied on the army's political apparatus to staff the civilian administration. By mid-1920, the Don party organization numbered
barely five thousand members, in a region with a population of one and
a half million people.[11] Army political organs became a surrogate for
the Communist Party itself.

As the front moved further away from the Don, Soviet authorities
sought to replace temporary revolutionary organs with the more enduring institutions of Soviet power. In a change of policy from the year
before, the Don Party Committee in mid-1920 permitted elections to
local soviets, albeit highly orchestrated elections. From the debates at
the First Don Party Conference, it was clear that party members had
little faith in either peasants or Cossacks. Owing to tight control over
the election process, such as vetting of candidates and controlling the
timing of elections, the composition of the "elected" soviets differed
little from that of the earlier, appointed ones. Most members of the
Soviet apparatus in fact continued to be drawn directly from army service.[12]

Nonetheless, Soviet officials felt it was necessary to hold elections.
Local soviets remained the essential building blocks of the new revolutionary order, extending the reach of the Communist Party far beyond
its own narrow membership. They were meant to elicit greater popular

participation in the Soviet order. Elections were to be "celebratory and demonstrative, with mass participation from the localities."[13] As one party representative put it, the goal was "to demonstrate . . . that Soviet power is constructed by the population itself." Another expressed the hope that elections would transform citizens from passive observers to active participants in "Soviet construction."[14] This meticulous orchestration of popular participation would become a constituent feature of Soviet political culture. In this manner, Soviet power attempted to institutionally freeze the revolutionary ecosystem of 1917 in the form of a new orthodoxy.

During 1920, just as it was establishing "Soviet power," the Soviet state was also single-mindedly pursuing the "extraction" of grain from the Don countryside. It did so as the military struggle on most fronts had ended. The Bolsheviks were not alone in retaining wartime food-supply measures after military operations had ceased. Although studies of the First World War end customarily with the Armistice in November 1918 or at the peace making at Versailles in the summer of 1919, most of Europe did not return to any degree of normalcy until 1921 or even 1923. Britain maintained rationing and food-supply controls through the end of 1920, France—until August 1921.[15] Germany, entirely for its own reasons, pursued policies that most closely paralleled those of the Soviet state. After 1918, the German government chose to subordinate agriculture to industry, in order to reconquer former markets and to reabsorb returning soldiers. After the war, the wartime measures of *Zwangswirtschaft*—control over grain production, price controls, and prosecution of food-supply violations—continued in the countryside. The "War Food Office," established in May 1916, became after the war's end the "Reich Food Office." In 1921, the same year that NEP was introduced in Russia, the German government instituted a system of "levies," establishing target figures for each state government to meet by dividing this centrally determined figure among producers. These levies were met, but only with the aid of military force. Only in the summer of 1923 did the German government abandon official controls over agriculture.[16]

For the Bolsheviks, food-supply campaigns were both a means to extract grain and a political instrument. As in postwar Germany, the Soviets subordinated agriculture to industrial development. Food-supply campaigns secured, by force if necessary, the surplus required for development programs. But that was not all. Along with Russia's non-Bolshevik modernizers and agrarian specialists, the Bolsheviks saw their food-supply operations as an instrument for transforming Russia's backward peasant into a more enlightened citizen.[17] For Soviet officials, as for their predecessors in Krivoshein's Ministry of Agriculture and the Provisional Government's Ministry of Food Supply, the Don Territory loomed large in their plans.

The Soviet state's emphasis on food supply, and its reliance on force to acquire it, built upon a preexisting legacy. Rittikh, the tsarist regime's last minister of agriculture, had introduced a grain levy. Shingarev, the Provisional Government's first minister of agriculture, had introduced the grain monopoly, which remained in force from March 1917 all the way through March 1921. Peshekhonov and Prokopovich, ministers of food supply for the Provisional Government, had issued directives for the use of force to secure grain. Immediately after the Bolshevik seizure of power, local food-supply committees—often headed by holdovers appointed by the Provisional Government—continued requesting armed force, both to compel peasants to turn over grain and to combat the black-market trade in grain.[18] The use of violence in this period, from November 1917 through January 1918, was not a Bolshevik innovation but rather a radicalization along an existing continuum.

Such developments derived not only from the dynamics of revolution but also from a particular wartime conjuncture. During late 1917 and early 1918, both Germany and Austria-Hungary employed armed force to secure food supplies from their own rural populations. The Soviet state, by contrast, was unable to deploy any real armed force at this point. In response to the flood of requests for military support from civilian food-supply organs throughout the country, the army command simply responded that it could offer none, as the army itself was disintegrating.[19]

The Soviet food-supply apparatus grew directly out of the Provisional Government's Food-Supply Ministry, and it retained many of the Provisional Government's guiding directives. Through June 1918 Lenin continued publicly to defend the grain monopoly introduced by the Kadet Shingarev in March 1917.[20] A decree from May 13, 1918, established a "food-supply dictatorship," conferring extraordinary powers on the Commissariat of Food Supply.[21] This decree reiterated the grain monopoly and fixed prices, demanded that grain producers turn over all surpluses to the state, and sanctioned the use of armed force to fulfill the food-supply campaign. All these measures merely consolidated earlier legislation from the Provisional Government.

In all this, Soviet policy remained a recognizable part of a broader Russian political culture. Like their Kadet and moderate socialist predecessors, Soviet officials held that the local population was incapable of transcending its parochial views. The Soviets shared the suspicions voiced by Viktor Anisimov in September 1917: the common people were simply not yet capable of recognizing *raison d'état*. Local organs were, he charged, "by their very nature too close to the interests of the population." A circular of December 1918 from the People's Commissariat of Food Supply instructed Soviet officials to see the world in terms of a binary contrast between state necessity and parochial local interests. "First," it directed, "the food-supply cause is of paramount importance to the state; and second, in order to implement food-supply policies, local organs must distance themselves from local needs and interests and take a point of view that considers the whole state."[22]

The statist planning ethos, fostered in the Great War, thus was endemic to nearly all movements in the Civil War. Anti-Soviet food-supply specialists denounced "speculation" and decried the market's anarchy just as much as their Bolshevik counterparts did. Following yet another First World War precedent, the Don government passed a law to fight inflation and speculation and established local committees for combating these evils.[23] General Anton Denikin's anti-Soviet government in the South of Russia implemented a tax-in-kind on grain and introduced compulsory requisitioning. A member of Denikin's government later observed that it "established on its territory an economic policy of an essentially Soviet character, and in 1919 it was forced to introduce the very same type of agricultural tax that the Bolsheviks . . . introduced in 1922 [*sic*], under the very same resistance of the agricultural population . . . Of course, it is to the 'White' government's credit that its 'Instructions' were immeasurably more humane."[24]

Without doubt, the policies of the Soviet state were less humane than those of its opponents. Whereas the Provisional Government had believed that it was compelling benighted peasants to become good citizens, Soviet power cast its policies as an extension of the class struggle. According to the decree establishing the "food dictatorship," peasants were not hoarding grain; "kulaks" were. The goal was no longer to implant state consciousness and tutor citizens but "to unite immediately in a merciless struggle against the kulak." Since at least 1916 a gulf had opened in Russia between producers and consumers, as it also had in Germany and Austria-Hungary during the First World War. But under the Soviet regime this conflict took an explicitly ideological form, as "class struggle."[25]

By refracting food supply through the lens of revolution, the Soviet state rallied support for measures that the Provisional Government had posited but proved unable to carry out. Rather than relying on the army, the Soviet regime in May and August 1918 authorized worker detachments to carry out food-supply campaigns in the countryside. The Commissariat of Food Supply had its own "food-supply army," which it deployed on the "food-supply front." Nikolai Kondrat'ev, a Socialist Revolutionary and leading food-supply specialist, noted that "Soviet power to a significant degree realized the reforms begun by the Provisional Government's [food-supply] ministry." The Soviet state had, however, "introduced its own original principle of 'political reliability' for food-supply workers." Even more significantly, by harnessing social dissatisfaction the Soviet state managed to provide the coercive means to implement its programs. "Under Soviet power," continues Kondrat'ev, food-supply measures "had changed radically both qualitatively and in their relative significance. As much as the Provisional Government had envisioned the moment of freedom and persuasion, Soviet power extends the feature of compulsion by an unprecedented degree."[26]

Soviet food-supply policy took its definitive form between August 1918 and January 1919. According to the grain monopoly (in force since March 1917), all surplus grain was the property of the state. A precondition for obtaining this "surplus" grain was an inventory of each and every producer to determine the stocks needed for consumption and sowing. This inventory required an infrastructure that simply did not exist under either the Provisional or the Soviet governments. Beginning in August 1918 the Soviet state therefore abandoned the goal of taking grain from each producer, and instead administratively assigned each district a levy to meet. The district authorities were made responsible for meeting this levy by distributing it among counties; counties then distributed it among villages; and villages—among households. Should local officials fail to obtain the levy, they would suffer the consequences. To back up these demands, the state dispatched armed detachments.[27]

These were the policies that Soviet power would bring to the Don Territory in 1920. In this case, however, Soviet officials would be demanding grain from a devastated region. Conscription by all sides and heavy casualties had produced a serious labor shortage in the territory. Heads of households begged their relatives serving in the Red Army to desert and return home, since "there is absolutely no one to do the work."[28] The weather dealt a further blow: a drought in the summer damaged the harvest. The northern districts that had suffered in 1917—Ust'-Medveditsa, Khoper, Upper Don, and Second Don—were yet again the hardest hit in 1920.[29] The fighting and requisitions had left a desperate shortage of draft animals. Then, as the Red Army passed through, its requisitions further impoverished the region. This constellation of factors led to a sharp decrease in sown territory. The sowings for 1920 dropped precipitously even in comparison with the preceding tumultuous years. They were half that of 1917, and below the average even for the civil war years.[30]

The Soviet Republic, which had relied upon the central provinces for two and a half years, had virtually stripped them bare. In 1920 the Red Army finally reacquired Russia's traditional grain-producing regions: the Northern Caucasus, including the Don Territory; Ukraine; and Siberia. Soviet planners eagerly anticipated siphoning off these regions' supposedly vast reserves, rather than again trying to pump grain from those producing regions that had prostrated themselves during the civil wars. A 1920 handbook for training military and party cadres mobilized for the "food-supply front" identified the grain-rich peripheries as the "source of life" for Soviet Russia. Iurii Larin, the leading Soviet expert on German wartime food-supply measures and guiding force behind War Communism, lectured that "around 125 million people now live under Soviet power; of them almost 80 million are found in Soviet Russia proper, in its essential core, that is, in European Russia without Ukraine, the Don Territory, without the Caucasus and Minsk province."[31] The Don Territory, in this view, was not part of "Soviet Russia proper, its essential core."

As a result of such views, Soviet planners reduced the levies for the fall 1920 food-supply campaign on the central provinces by 80 million poods of grain (2,880 million pounds). Newly conquered Siberia and the Northern Caucasus (including the Don Territory) were slated to provide more than half the country's entire grain assessment. Soviet officials thus viewed the Don Territory, impoverished or not, as absolutely crucial to the success or failure of the 1920 campaign as a whole. The Don Territory was assigned a levy of 20 million poods (720 million pounds) of grain and seed, larger than any other province outside of Siberia or the Northern Caucasus. This amount, in fact, was roughly the same size as the levy that the imperial food-supply apparatus had assigned the Don Territory for the 1916–1917 campaign.[32] But the imperial government had managed to collect only a tiny portion of that assignment, and by 1920 the situation in the countryside was much worse. Sowings alone had dropped by half compared with 1917.

Throughout the autumn, winter, and spring of 1920–1921, central authorities bombarded officials in the Don Territory with a blizzard of orders directing them to fulfill the assigned food-supply levy at any cost.[33] Receiving these instructions, local authorities laid down a firm line: no retreat from the republic's needs in favor of petty local concerns.[34] Reiterating the Soviet state's general levy system for food supply, officials in the Don Territory decreed the following in May 1920:

> We will not proclaim the entire assessment by household. We don't care about Ivan Ivanovich or Peter Petrovich; we don't care about specific individuals. The entire responsibility will rest on the food-supply commissars, it will rest on the district and county chairmen of soviets. They ought to institute unflinchingly the policies in order to obtain grain for the Center.[35]

Given this predilection for privileging central demands and dismissing local concerns, the Soviet Center predictably blamed local organs when the food-supply campaign began to fall drastically behind the appointed pace in late autumn 1920. A whole welter of decrees placed local officials under military discipline and made them legally responsible for meeting their assigned targets.[36] The Soviet Republic placed tremendous pressures on local organs to extract centrally assigned assessments at any cost. Such pressure, combined with the tendency of local officials to see the population as either hopelessly self-interested or malevolently disposed against the republic, resulted in a predisposition to resort to overt force.

From May through September 1920, "food-supply agents" were the officials responsible for attempting to get the population to surrender the "surpluses" it was supposed to have. Entrusted with this all-important task and answering only to superiors in the food-supply apparatus, they cajoled, threatened, and bullied communities. Acting with a sense of impunity, they engaged in all sorts of violations. When agents alone failed to secure the assigned targets, the Don food-supply commissar next dispatched "special agent–plenipotentiaries" to prod the apparatus to greater exertions. These officials tended to get into even more conflicts with local officials than the agents had.[37]

Producers actually were willing to hand over grain—so long as they could receive essential goods such as oil and salt in return. One peasant delegate at a June 1920 Congress of Soviets declared, "We don't even need set prices, take all we have—only give us what we need to live."[38] Yet the Soviet state in 1920 faced the same problem that had confronted the tsarist state in 1916 and the Provisional Government in 1917: it simply could not provide individual producers with "what they needed to live." Following national policy, Don authorities sparingly doled out the meager amount of goods they did have to those communities that had managed to meet their assessments.[39] But they did not have enough manufactured goods to barter for all the grain they needed.

This food-supply "campaign" soon began to take its toll on popular sympathies. Throughout the summer of 1920, Cossacks and an increasing number of peasants complained of the actions of food-supply agents in letters to relatives serving in the Red Army.[40] From such intercepted letters one military censorship board in July 1920 drew the disturbing conclusion that "what is remarkable is that not only Cossacks but even peasants in such a revolutionary district as Sal' . . . engage in uprisings and express dissatisfaction with Communists."[41]

As a result of these practices, estate categories increasingly receded and the Soviet class categorization of poor, middle, and rich peasants took form in concrete policies. A barrage of directives from Moscow and from the Don Food-Supply Committee instructed local officials to implement class policies in the countryside. Kulaks were to bear the overwhelming share of the region's grain assessment. Local officials were instructed to prosecute kulaks for failure to meet their levy, but to treat violations by poor and middle peasants leniently. Kulaks alone were to be taken as hostages or subjected to confiscations.[42] By late

1920, the Soviet apparatus applied the same class prism to the Don as it did to the rest of Russia.

Looking out on their impoverished charges, though, many local Soviet officials came to the conclusion that their communities were "homogeneous—there are no kulaks or moneybags, but predominantly middle and poor peasants."[43] Others reported that poor peasants stubbornly refused to play their appointed political role, remaining "in close contact with the middle and better-off peasants."[44] Asserting orthodoxy in the face of such reports, the Don Executive Committee issued a circular telegram declaring that such claims "were absolutely not true." At the Third Don Congress of Soviets in May 1921, one speaker drove the point home: "There are individuals who affirm that in their areas there is no division between the poor and kulaks. This is fiction and phrase-mongering."[45]

Soviet class principles, however, clashed with the overriding state imperative to extract grain at any cost.[46] Several speakers at the Second Don Party Conference in October 1920 reported that peasants had become even more anti-Soviet than Cossacks. Food-supply operations in peasant counties, they reported, proceeded far worse than in Cossack communities.[47] Military censors reading letters from the Don countryside noted the shift: by winter "even peasants" were growing dissatisfied with Soviet power.[48] Meteorological conditions and the poor harvest soon introduced yet more grounds for popular unease over Soviet food-supply policy. Farmers had begun to plead for relief as early as June, citing the fear of drought and lack of surpluses, but such requests became endemic in August as the extent of the harvest failure became evident.[49] Yet central authorities directed all provincial and local organizations to maintain a firm line. Drought or not, there would be no delays or concessions in meeting state obligations.

Already privileging imperatives of state over any and all local concerns, Bolshevik planners tended to place greater faith in published target figures than in local reports. Kadets, moderate socialists, and Bolsheviks alike viewed rural Russia as backwards, and all placed their hopes on the state as virtually the only tool for acting upon this backwardness. World War I, and especially Germany's *Kriegswirtschaft*, had seemingly provided an empirical demonstration of the state's efficacy. Having placed such faith in the rationality and power of the state, Russia's political class shrank from faulting its own planning mentality when these initiatives failed. Rather, they displaced their frustrations onto those who had somehow "failed" to carry out these plans. One plenipotentiary mobilized for the grain campaign on the Don attributed the peasantry's tendency to hide grain to its lack of state consciousness: "The peasant . . . is still far from accepting the statist idea for socially engineering a new life . . . He schemes by any means necessary to make himself secure for the future."[50] Bolshevik authorities, unconstrained by concerns of legality or any usual checks on executive power, were particularly prone to resort to naked force as a means for achieving these supposedly "rational" goals.

In the grips of this worldview, Soviet authorities asserted the existence of grain surpluses in the face of their evident absence. In September Moscow instructed local organs that even drought did not justify any concessions or delays in fulfilling levies.[51] Meeting in October 1920, the Second Don Party Conference proclaimed that the Don Territory would meet the state's twenty-million-pood levy "no matter what," asserting that "its fulfillment will be the military task of the day." "No matter what" was a common formulation of this period, expressing—in the definition of a contemporary study of revolutionary language—"a categorical imperative in a military situation."[52] The head of the Don Food-Supply Committee was even blunter: "The condition of the republic requires twenty million poods, and therefore we can't worry about how much is left to the [local] population . . . We should shoot malicious kulaks and confiscate from the nonmalicious kulaks."[53] Local officials petitioned for delays and partial cancellations in their regions' assignments owing to the drought. These requests only confirmed suspicions within the Soviet apparatus that local authorities were incapable of grasping the collective good. Therefore in late October the Don Executive Committee, the Don Party Committee, and the Don Food-Supply Committee issued a joint decree establishing "food-supply councils of five" in each district and "food-supply councils of three" in each stanitsa and county. In addition to the local food-supply official, these boards included representatives from the local executive committee, the local party committee, and the the local military commissariat.[54] The food-supply apparatus would provide the infrastructure; the party would give guidance and stiffen backbones; and the military commissariat would supply the means to fulfill the plan.

In the population's inability to meet its levies the Soviet apparatus saw not its own inflated expectations but rather the self-interest of the petty-bourgeois peasantry. If grain was not flowing out of the country-side, it was not because there was none there; the grain, asserted Soviet authorities, *was* there. The task, then, was to find means to extract it forcibly. Military force had been an integral part of food-supply operations in other parts of Soviet Russia during War Communism.[55] For the Don, however, the autumn of 1920 represented the first extensive experience with Soviet food-supply methods, an experience exacerbated by the fact that it came during the first harvest in peacetime conditions, after the Whites had been driven from the region.

The Soviet use of force differed from that of the Whites in both quantitative and qualitative terms. With a military-command administrative hierarchy and no pretensions of "bourgeois" democracy or legality, overt force became a constitutive feature of Soviet policies. Kondrat'ev emphasized the particular nature of violence in Bolshevik initiatives:

> This compulsion manifested itself in the form of requisitions, which became a real armed struggle for grain. But this was not simply requisitions, nor was this simply compulsion. This was a compulsion that penetrated the entire food-supply policy and that tinged this policy. A particular ideological form enveloped it.[56]

The role assigned to the Don Territory in the national campaign and the resulting pressure from Moscow predisposed local authorities on the Don in particular to use violence for acquiring grain from the countryside "no matter what." In late August 1920 the Council of Labor and Defense ordered the intensification of food-supply work in the Northern Caucasus and dispatched food-supply detachments there. The next month the commander of forces in the Don Territory, following central instructions, ordered all local military commissariats to work closely with district food-supply commissioners to secure the delivery of the assigned levies.[57] As it became clear in mid-November that actual deliveries were still lagging far behind target figures, the Soviet government placed the entire food-supply apparatus on a military footing and ordered that all levies were to be delivered by January 1921.[58]

The central government thus provided local organs not only with the authority to use force but also with the means to do so. Local publications lectured in bold letters that "the food-supply front is a continuation of the military front."[59] In August, the Council of Labor and Defense dispatched special internal defense units to the Don Territory, and throughout the autumn the Soviet command shifted food-supply detachments and units of the food-supply army from the central provinces to the grain-rich peripheries.[60] District food-supply committees had hundreds of armed men under their command. The Khoper District committee had at its disposal 567 men in two internal defense battalions, while the Rostov committee had 570 men in a detachment that arrived in September from the Soviet-Polish front.[61] Local military forces were also released for food-supply work. Of the six food-supply detachments active in Rostov District, food-supply agents made up only two of them, while Red Army men from the Rostov District military commissariat constituted the other four.[62]

In mid-November the Don Food-Supply Conference laid down further coercive measures. It established "shock groups" and ordered the dispatch of roving circuit sessions of the Don Revolutionary Tribunal to the localities.[63] "Shock groups" were an *ad hoc* tool of coercion made up of Red Army men, trade unionists, and party and Komsomol members. They were sent to areas that had not met their assessments, where they conducted searches and closed down mills until the assessment was met in full. Delinquent communities had to supply food and provide housing to "shock groups" for the duration of their stay. In the face of flagging deliveries, the Khoper District food-supply council intended to carry out its task by "physical coercion with the aid of military force." This, however, was beyond the powers of the 95 Red Army men transferred for the purpose from the military commissariat. Consequently, the district plenipotentiary for procurement requested a 500-man force to requisition grain. The military department of the Don Food-Supply Committee permitted Khoper authorities to form four shock groups, to be composed of food-supply agents, Red Army men, and mobilized party and Komsomol workers. Each shock group numbered between 70 and 100 men.[64] By mid-December 19 shock groups, numbering more than 2,000 bayonets, were operating throughout the Don Territory.[65]

Yet even this amount of force did not secure fulfillment of the Don Territory's levy. The Don leadership, under great pressure from Moscow, therefore declared December to be "Red Food-Supply Month." Arguing that all efforts at "agitation" had failed to secure the necessary grain, the Don leadership ordered the introduction of punitive measures. Even more infantry and cavalry detachments were dispatched to areas that failed to meet their targets. Those who "refused" to turn over grain were now subject to total confiscation.[66]

On paper, such coercive measures brought impressive results. In several districts grain deliveries jumped sharply during December.[67] These figures, however, reflected a focus on results at all costs. Military units were granted great latitude so long as they secured the grain. In Kotel'nikovo, a region long identified with support for Soviet power, shock group no. 26 beat women, insulted party members, and arrested six local executive committees. It acted so imperiously that the community's party cell issued a formal complaint against its commander. Don authorities, however, exonerated the shock group. Local Communists had not cooperated with the requisitions, and the shock group's methods had managed to extract more grain in three weeks than had been delivered over the previous three months.[68]

This insistent demand for results, together with the sanction to employ military force, predisposed local officials to use armed force as the solution to any and all obstacles. Having gathered only 2 percent of the district's assigned levy by December, the Upper Don District food-supply commissar called for the introduction of what he termed "machine gun agitation." He assured his superiors that he could meet the district's levy if he were given 100 bayonets and a cavalry detachment to post in *each* stanitsa. (There were twelve stanitsas in the district). This force was to be in addition to the 925 men in shock groups already under his control.[69] Facing a similar situation, the Khoper District food-supply council of five decided to employ "coercion with the aid of military force." Shock groups, the district food-supply commissar noted, "increased productivity, and it would have been expedient if they had existed from the very beginning of the assessment campaign, since agents alone cannot deal with our population."[70] In point of fact, grain deliveries in both districts actually *dropped* during December, "Red Food-Supply Month."[71] Local officials' faith in naked force was a flight into the only option permitted them, rather than a result of any study of its actual efficacy.

Judicial Coercion

But the Soviet apparatus relied on more than brute force. Rather than simply bullying the population into compliance, the authorities attempted to frame this compliance in terms of legitimacy. Judicial coercion, operating in conjunction with naked force, communicated the official interpretation of reality. Early in its existence, Soviet authorities had legally defined failure to meet levy quotas as a serious criminal offense. Whereas the Provisional Government had also established obligations, its directives had not detailed punishments for failure to meet them. The Provisional and anti-Soviet governments only punished farmers for failing to turn over surpluses they actually had; Soviet policy punished farmers for failing to meet targets, regardless of whether the grain was there or not. A Soviet decree of May 14, 1918, defined those who failed to meet state obligations as "enemies of the people" and ordered them "to be tried by a Revolutionary Court."[72]

Before the establishment of roving circuit sessions of the central Don Revolutionary Tribunal in November 1920, district politburos had tried cases of "malicious" noncompliance with requisitioning assessments, together with cases of counterrevolutionary agitation and abuse of office.[73] In October, the Rostov District food-supply commissar urged the creation of local revolutionary tribunals to prod local soviets into complying with their assignments.[74] He did not have to wait long. On November 19 the Soviet government ordered that "the judicial-executive apparatus be activated, achieving continuous functioning of roving circuit sessions of the revolutionary tribunals."[75] By early December the Don leadership had constituted and dispatched such circuit sessions to the countryside.[76] In early January the Soviet state ordered all food-supply operations on the Don to be completed by mid-February, again indicating that this should be done "in a military manner." In order to accomplish this task, the plenipotentiaries assigned to the Don by the Justice and Food Supply Commissariats in Moscow again pressed local officials to rely extensively on such circuit sessions.[77] Clearly, the Soviet leadership assigned great significance to these organs of revolutionary justice.

Roving circuit sessions of the revolutionary tribunal, acting in conjunction with shock groups, were active in all but the two northernmost districts of the Don, both of which had suffered total harvest failure.[78] Circuit sessions invariably accompanied shock groups, providing judicial justification for the punishment visited upon citizens.[79] They also prosecuted those members of local soviets who had failed to implement directives issued as military orders. The members of the Kagal'nitskaia stanitsa executive committee, which had failed to meet its assessment, were put on trial as "an example" to others.[80] In addition to confiscating goods, circuit sessions had the authority to order executions and to dispatch "delinquent" or "recalcitrant" citizens to concentration camps. In one month, the First Don District Circuit Session sentenced 91 people to a concentration camp for food-supply violations alone.[81]

The impact of these circuit sessions, however, extended far beyond the circle of those who were brought directly before them. They were also intended to serve as a didactic tool. In December 1919, the Commissariat of Food Supply had sent out circular telegrams directing all provincial food-supply committees to publicize their prosecutions. In Tambov province, the telegram noted, this practice had "produced wonderful results" in speeding up grain deliveries. (Tambov province would be seized by a major rebellion in the autumn of 1920.) A second telegram instructed provincial committees to "widely publiciz[e] . . . repressive actions against those who decline to turn over grain."[82] When it dispatched circuit sessions to the localities in December 1920, the Don Food-Supply Conference issued instructions entitled "The Revolutionary Tribunal as a Means of Agitation and Repression."[83] The local press, under firm control of the local party, broadcast far and wide the cautionary tale of the circuit sessions' activity.

The Second Don District Circuit Session invested much effort to communicate its activities. Upon arriving in the district, it had found grain collection lagging far behind schedule. Members of the revolutionary tribunal decided that it was necessary to provide a strong cautionary reproof to "kulaks" and so ordered two people executed. Afterward, "the results of the circuit session's activity became manifestly evident": daily grain deliveries more than tripled. To ensure awareness of its activity, the tribunal ordered its sentences to be read at village gatherings. It even printed up several hundred broadsheets of its sentences for wide public dissemination and ordered that they be read aloud at public gatherings.[84]

Soviet authorities, however, viewed revolutionary justice as more than simply a blunt tool for securing compliance from the population. They intended circuit sessions to impress upon the population the regime's evaluation of justice and social relations. As their sentences make clear, circuit sessions required citizens brought before them to recognize and accept the Soviet state's categorization of their behavior. Defendants frequently asserted that they had committed no wrong. The tribunals would have none of this, and insisted when handing down sentences that defendants recognize their wrongs and abjure them. In commenting upon several sentences handed down by the circuit sessions, the Don Food-Supply Committee's official organ declared that if individuals "fulfill the assessment and become honest citizens, they avoid heavy penalties." This identical point was emphasized in broadsheets circulated by roving revolutionary tribunals.[85]

This declaration was not mere rhetoric; such was the policy in practice. Of seventeen citizens of Bogoiavlenskaia stanitsa brought before a revolutionary tribunal for concealing grain, all but three had their sentences commuted once they "confessed before the court" and revealed their concealed grain. Of the three others who received sentences, one got fifteen years hard labor for counterrevolutionary activity and another received ten years for abuse of office in his post in the local soviet. Ivan Nazarov, however, was sentenced to death "for concealing grain, for not revealing all of his concealed grain, for signing a declaration that he had no more concealed grain—and yet he stubbornly refused to admit to the circuit sessions of the Don Territorial Revolutionary Tribunal that he knew of the concealed grain."[86] Nazarov's "stubbornness" thus brought a harsher sentence than either counterrevolutionary activity or abuse of office. Throughout the Don, revolutionary tribunals regularly reduced or commuted sentences for those who proffered "heartfelt admissions" and "sincere repentance."[87] At the same time, those who "stubbornly" and "maliciously" refused to acknowledge their acts in the language of the revolutionary tribunals routinely received the harshest sentences.[88]

Prosecutions of food-supply violations revealed two clear lessons. First, class proved to be a poor barometer for determining actual political behavior. Second, class nevertheless remained the essential prism through which the Soviet state perceived and prosecuted such acts. Soviet tribunals faced the conundrum of somehow differentiating be-

tween the often identical behavior of poor peasants and kulaks. They
did so by formulating a distinction at the level of consciousness and intent. If poor peasants happened to have committed crimes alongside
"kulaks," Soviet courts peremptorily decreed that the poor peasants
had acted "under the influence" of their "kulak exploiters."[89] Reports
on the Aleksandrovskoe trial, the regional show trial on food-supply violations, described the defendants as rich, middle, and even poor peasants. The court, however, summarily dismissed the charges against the
poor peasants and aggressively prosecuted only "kulaks." Only kulaks,
the courts claimed, had committed their crimes in full consciousness
and out of maliciousness.[90] Revolutionary tribunals regularly pardoned
or commuted the sentences of "non-kulak" transgressors, while punishing to the full letter of the law kulaks convicted of the same crimes.[91]
Prosecutions and the copious reportage on them served as primers on
how the authorities chose to read rural relations. While Soviet power
ran roughshod over its proclaimed class principles in its desperate efforts to "extract" grain, its methods of judicial coercion reintroduced
the primacy of class analysis.

"Policies Conducted on the Principles of a Dictatorship"

In the face of growing resistance and flagging deliveries in late 1920
and early 1921, the Soviet government issued order after order asserting that "grain from the Caucasus is the primary, almost solitary, source
of grain for Central Russia."[92] Popular desperation reached new
heights in December as local officials began transferring grain assembled in local state barns to centralized grain-storage points. Farmers—
peasants as much as Cossacks—tried to prevent the transfer, blocking
the barns.[93] The wave of unrest first passed through the two northern
districts, Khoper and Ust'-Medveditsa, both of which had experienced
harvest failure. Several communities drove out food-supply workers.[94]
Unrest then passed to the neighboring Upper Don and Donets Districts, where citizens proved willing to take up arms against food-supply detachments. The Upper Don District was isolated from rail lines
and administrative centers, making it difficult for authorities to pre-
empt any incipient unrest. An uprising in Sukhoi Donets grew to more
than one thousand armed participants before it was put down in late
November 1920.[95]

In late December 1920 Comrade Chebotarev, a party member who had been dispatched on food-supply assignment, pointed to the failed harvest and particularly the Soviet regime's intransigent response to it as causes for the rebellions in Donets District. Even so, Chebotarev managed in the end to fault the peasantry itself. Unable to view the situation from a statist perspective, he charged, peasants thought only about their own grain reserves. The dispatch of shock groups to those regions that had fallen behind in meeting their levies had led to uprisings in virtually every county where they had been sent. Even though peasants recognized the hopelessness of their cause, the flames of unrest spread rapidly from community to community. These rebellions staged in despair were not entirely one-sided affairs, as Chebotarev himself could attest. Comrade Burovtsev, whom the Don Party Committee had dispatched on food-supply duties together with Chebotarev, perished along with his entire detachment. Another comrade barely escaped with serious wounds when insurgent peasants annihilated the food-supply detachment he commanded. Of the 170 Red Army men sent to save that detachment, only 60 returned.[96] It was more than a Soviet rhetorical flourish to describe the food-supply front as a "continuation of the military front."

By January 1921 popular unrest was so widespread in the Don Territory that the regional leadership requested a change in official policy. A joint plenum of the Don Party Committee, the district party committees, and the presidium of the Don Executive Committee met in early January. The plenum discussed an order from the central authorities for requisitioning to continue for another month past the previously announced date of January 15, until all assessments were met in full. In place of this order, the plenum proposed that requisitioning cease by January 20 in areas that had fulfilled 75 percent of their assessment, and end altogether by February 10, even for those areas that had fulfilled less than half of it. Rather than stripping the entire Don of grain until the centrally established target figures were met, the plenum argued that a minimum of the harvest should be reserved for local sowing needs. Soon afterward, a joint gathering of the presidium of the Caucasus Party Bureau, the Don Party Committee, and the presidium of the Council of Trade Unions seconded the plenum's call for the cessation of requisitioning within one month. The Don Executive Committee, the region's top civil organ, immediately telegraphed Lenin and

Mikhail Kalinin, informing them of its decision but noting that it would wait for a response before announcing the resolution.[97]

The Don leadership received its answer five days later. Kalinin peremptorily cancelled the plenum's resolution, thereby overruling the region's leading civil and party organs and siding instead with the Don food-supply commissar, Comrade Miller. The requisitions, Moscow directed, would continue as long as it took to fulfill 100 percent of assessments. In the face of assertions to the contrary from virtually the entire regional apparatus up through the regional party leadership, Moscow again dictated that the twenty million poods were indeed out there. The Soviet government then publicly reprimanded the Don Executive Committee, together with the Samara Provincial Executive Committee, for proposing measures that undercut the food-supply campaign.[98]

Soviet policy was clearly ruinous. Although ignorance, inefficiency, and corruption were endemic throughout the hierarchy, Soviet food-supply policy was not the product of individual failings. Rather, it derived from the Soviet state's specific ethos and its form of administrative hierarchy. Officials at the local and regional level operated within an administrative system that both expected and enforced ruthless discipline—military discipline, in fact—in carrying out central directives. As Communist Party members, they had elected to embrace this command structure and the worldview underpinning it. Even where they saw its empirical failings, individuals staffing regional organs shared a culture that privileged the transcendent demands of state and revolution over parochial local needs.

This military-command principle extended down through the entire administrative edifice. From the very first, local food-supply commissars answered directly to their district food-supply commissar, not to their own elected local executive committees. The chairman of the Don Executive Committee explained why: "The policies of the district food-supply committees must be conducted on the principles of a dictatorship."[99] In early February 1921, Don Food-Supply Commissar Miller issued order no. 42, directing the Upper Don District to ship 400,000 poods of seed grain to the needy northern provinces. The Upper Don, however, had only 135,000 poods of seed grain at hand and faced its own shortage for the spring sowing. For these reasons, the district party and soviet chairmen both refused to sign Miller's order. District Food-Supply Commissar Murzov printed it anyway.[100] The district executive committee then passed a resolution to carry out this order only after the Upper Don District's own seed reserves had been set aside. The district party committee summoned a district-wide party conference, and both the committee and the conference endorsed the resolution opposing fulfillment. District Food-Supply Commissar Murzov, however, continued to insist upon the full and immediate implementation of the order. At the meeting of the district food-supply conference several days later, Murzov raised the issue of order no. 42 yet again. He insisted that if greater pressure were brought to bear on the population, the grain would appear. (It was Murzov who in December 1920 had called for "machine gun agitation" and requested 100 troops to station in each stanitsa.) One speaker argued that from a purely administrative point of view, they ought to carry out the order. He noted, however, that the Don Food-Supply Committee should be informed that its figure of 400,000 poods was "an illusion." Another speaker insisted that as party members they owed their loyalty to the party and not to Miller, the territorial food-supply commissar. An emergency session of the district food-supply council of five decided not to transport the grain, again over the sole opposition of Murzov.[101]

Soon the Don Party Bureau and the Presidium of the Don Executive Committee, which itself had just been censured for obstructing food-supply work, dispatched a plenipotentiary to the district to resolve the dispute. He found that there indeed was no possible way the Upper Don District could ship 400,000 poods of seed grain to Khoper and Ust'-Medveditsa Districts, as this amount simply did not exist. Instead he ordered the immediate shipment of all seed material at hand, nearly 200,000 poods.[102] As a result, the Upper Don District was left with absolutely no grain for sowing. Partly in response to this episode, the cavalry squadron stationed in Veshenskaia, the district capital, rebelled two weeks later, joined by one-third of the local party cell. Party members, it transpired, *did* owe their loyalty more to the territorial food-supply commissar than to any abstract party principles.

Despite petitions for moderation from much of its party and Soviet apparatus on the Don, Moscow continued to press for full delivery of its assigned target figure. Under insistent pressure from Moscow and confronted with increasing popular opposition, local officials responded in the only way open to them: they resorted to ever more force. The number of soldiers operating in shock groups jumped from 2,147 in December 1920 to more than 8,500 in January 1921.[103] In addition to these forces, field units of the Red Army also continued to participate in the campaign. These forces were channeled to the areas where the food-supply campaign was lagging behind its target figures. In January regional officials declared both the entire Donets and the Upper Don Districts to be "recalcitrant." To address this "recalcitrance," the commander of forces in the Don Territory instructed units there to move ahead with the "decisive extraction of grain." In Donets District alone there were 6,500 soldiers involved exclusively in food-supply operations.[104] In this myopic pursuit of the mythical target figure, circuit sessions of the Don Revolutionary Tribunal also intensified their activity.[105]

Not until April 1921 did Soviet authorities declare an end to the 1920 food-supply campaign in the Don Territory. Despite all the violence, the region had secured only 45 percent of its target figure.[106] Yet the results of meeting even less than half of this phantasmagoric target figure were catastrophic. Many areas, especially in the northern districts, were left with no seed grain for the spring sowing. Some were already facing famine by late winter.[107] While several factors contributed to the famine of 1921, the Soviet food-supply policy itself was a major cause.

NEP in Theory and NEP in Practice

The end of the 1920 food-supply campaign in April 1921 coincided with the introduction of the New Economic Policy, formally adopted at the Tenth Party Congress in early March 1921 and officially proclaimed by the Soviet government in central newspapers on March 23, 1921. Studies of the Civil War usually point to NEP as the key event in a Soviet shift toward accommodating the countryside.[108] The Bolshevik Party itself viewed NEP as a "concession" to the peasantry. For many rural dwellers, especially in the central provinces, NEP certainly was a welcome relief.

But while the Soviet government immediately replaced the levy system with a tax-in-kind throughout most of the country, it retained the levy for the grain-rich peripheries: the Don, the Northern Caucasus, Ukraine, and Siberia.[109] On the Don, in fact, the declaration of NEP was immediately followed by the proclamation of a one-million-pood "one-time, extraordinary grain consignment." This additional assignment was meant to bridge the grain shortfall throughout the republic that had resulted from the disappointing 1920 food-supply campaign countrywide.[110]

Rural dwellers in one of the Soviet Republic's premier grain regions thus learned of NEP but saw little evidence of it. In Sal' District, many citizens charged that NEP was nothing more than the old requisitioning "only under a different sauce." Given the evident gulf between officially proclaimed policy and local practice, one Don newspaper felt the need to publish an editorial entitled "There Is No Deception."[111]

In fact, there was little difference between the collection methods under the old requisitions and those under the new "one-time, extraordinary consignment." NEP was declared in late March, but in April the Commissariat of Food Supply plenipotentiary in the Northern Caucasus, M. I. Frumkin, requested the dispatch of twenty-five battalions to the region.[112] Circuit sessions of the revolutionary tribunal continued to prosecute "malicious and recalcitrant" citizens for failing to meet the one-time consignment, just as they had punished those who failed to meet their levy assessments. Throughout June and July 1921—more than three months after the announcement of NEP—circuit sessions continued to rove throughout the districts, holding trials for "violations" of the grain consignment.[113] Looking back in December on the failure of the 1921 campaign, the chairman of the Don Executive Committee concluded that "the food-supply campaign bore all the characteristics of requisitioning . . . It is abundantly clear that we extended this requisitioning to excess."[114]

On July 3, more than three months after the declaration of NEP, the Don Food-Supply Committee issued order no. 343, instructing district officials to cease requisitioning on all products. In addition, it finally recalled all agents working in food-supply detachments for preparatory classes on the tax-in-kind, and instructed the heads of shock groups to return their personnel to the various Soviet and party institutions from which they had been mobilized. Implementation of even this order was not immediate, however. The official newspaper of one northern district published it only on July 31.[115]

This extension of requisitioning long after the announcement of NEP eroded faith in the tax-in-kind, intended to be the pillar of the new policy.[116] But even when it was finally introduced, the tax-in-kind did not placate popular opinion as planned. NEP's tax structure had been constructed with the paradigm of central European Russia in mind, the Russia of three-field, communal agriculture with individual allotments. A tax built with this agricultural world in mind poorly matched conditions on the Don. Unable to rely on communal allotments as their guideline for determining citizens' individual tax obligations, local officials instead took as their basis the amount of territory assigned as "obligatory sowings." The Soviet state in December 1920 had taken upon itself the management of the 1921 spring sowing campaign by establishing "sowing committees." Regardless of local conditions, the Soviet government simply decreed that the sown territory in 1921 was to be no less than that of 1916. Under tremendous pressure from above to secure a large harvest for the following year, these committees set impossibly high target figures for each community and assigned fantastic obligatory sowings to individuals.[117] While in the grips of this planning mania, the Soviet state then proved incapable of returning to communities the required amount of seed grain, which it had forcibly extracted from them during the fall and winter of 1920–21. Farmers in 1921 sowed even less territory on the Don than in 1920, meaning that the sown territory was less than half of what it had been as recently as 1917.[118] But the Soviet state was assessing communities as if it were collecting a harvest from those previously "good" years. With the decision to base NEP's tax-in-kind on the "obligatory sowing," individual farmers now owed the state a portion of an imaginary harvest based on these wildly inflated figures. Sowing committees in Cherkassk District assigned an obligatory sown area that was ten times the actual sown territory. Thus, when it came time to deliver the tax-in-kind, many farmers on the Don found that it exceeded the amount that had been seized under previous requisitions. The situation was similar in Siberia.[119]

With fulfillment of "tax assessments" proceeding no better than the levy targets a year earlier, the Don Food-Supply Committee in early September 1921 began employing "coercive measures" once again, this time against "delinquent taxpayers." When the available armed detachments proved insufficient to secure an "immediate improvement," the Don food-supply commissar ordered out Red Army units that had been placed at his disposal.[120] Indeed, regional authorities employed certain repressive measures during the supposedly "conciliatory" 1921 food-supply campaign earlier than they had in the previous year. Whereas in 1920 Soviet power had waited until November to dispatch "shock groups" and until December to send out circuit sessions of the revolutionary tribunal, in 1921 local officials introduced both in September.[121]

True, the "shock groups" of 1920 no longer existed. For the 1921 campaign they were supplanted by "assistance detachments."[122] This change in names certainly testified to an attempt by the regime to portray itself in a more conciliatory manner, but in practice the new organs differed little from the ones they had replaced. A community in default had to support the "assistance detachments" sent to prod it into compliance. If the community remained "recalcitrant," the detachment declared an "economic blockade," closing the local market, all mills, and slaughterhouses, and banning all trade and transport of goods. If this too failed, the unit then began arresting individual citizens.[123]

Nor were the tools of judicial coercion altered much. The introduction of the tax-in-kind led to the reformation, not the elimination, of the Don Revolutionary Tribunal. "Under NEP," declared the Don Department of Justice, "judicial organs will take on new importance." The revolutionary tribunal now added a tax department, which was empowered, predictably, to dispatch roving circuit sessions.[124] As the food-supply campaign again stalled in late 1921, roving circuit sessions intensified their "repressive measures." Ten sessions operated in five districts. As throughout the Soviet Republic, the overwhelming majority of sentences concerned "tax evasion."[125]

So the struggle began again. The Soviet apparatus mobilized party members and trade unionists to form its detachments, and sent Red Army men to fill them out. Six assistance detachments operated in the First Don District, eight in Donets District, and five more in Morozov District.[126] In all, thirty-five assistance detachments, numbering 2,092 armed men, were operating throughout the Don Territory by the beginning of October 1921. Such decisive measures brought some results. As the collection predictably slowed again in mid-October, however, the authorities declared a "two-week shock period." Circuit sessions worked "intensively," trying more citizens and handing down harsher sentences. Again, collections spiked upward during this period, only to drop precipitously immediately afterward.[127]

By this point the food-supply apparatus was attempting to squeeze blood from a stone. The drought, seed shortage, and poor harvest had left the population with nothing left to give. Soviet officials frankly admitted that military force was necessary because citizens refused to believe the tax would be collected from them when they had nothing to offer. One party member compared collecting the tax-in-kind to asking the chairman of the Don Executive Committee "to give me 100,000 rubles by tomorrow when he only has 100 rubles on him. Of course he won't be able to turn it over."[128]

Because of the way NEP was introduced in the Soviet Republic's grain-rich regions, it led to an increase, rather than a decline, in popular unrest.[129] Studies of the widespread unrest in this period have ascribed it to the visceral reaction of peasants who had accepted the Bolshevik regime only so long as it was fighting against the landlords. Having retreated into its "age-old shell," the peasantry is supposed to have rejected the Communist regime as an urban and foreign interloper into the rural world. The Bolshevik assault on the countryside, in these analyses, produced a "peasant war."[130] Despite differences in emphasis, these analyses all suggest that political action was largely the expression of underlying social structures. The political program of the 1921 insurgencies then becomes merely the extension of ingrained peasant mentalities or the instinctive eruption of popular rage. Furthermore, such analyses draw a sharp distinction between the peasants' aspirations and the regime's illegitimate and intolerable political demands.

The peasantry certainly withdrew into autarkic economic relations. That peasants retreated into an economic shell does not mean, however, that they eschewed politics on a broader plane. By 1920–1921 people had incorporated the revolutionary schematic into their worldview; they had come to order the world through it and situated themselves within it. The political ideals of the revolution provided the legitimating framework not only for Soviet authority but also for many of its opponents. The crisis confronting Soviet power in 1920–1921 came less from those who had repudiated Soviet power than from those who had embraced it. Anti-Soviet insurgents, leaders and participants alike, more often than not had previously served the revolution at length and with distinction. Such life histories were no anomaly, but rather the very motivation for the actions of these individuals in 1921.

Soviet press accounts at the time routinely dismissed anti-Soviet insurgents as "kulaks" and "bandits." Yet the supposedly implacable and congenital opponents of Soviet power were not the primary participants in anti-Soviet unrest. To be sure, some Cossacks were active in banditry. But their participation had less to do with their Cossack background than with difficulties in readjusting to civilian life after seven years of warfare. As throughout Europe, the extended war experience had transformed the lives of those who had taken part in it.[131] Many had come to see violence not as a means to some other end but rather as a mode of being. A Cheka study of the organization's struggle against banditry in Siberia from 1920 through 1922 noted that "the seven-year experience of war [1914–1921] has had a marked impact upon the insurgent movement."[132] On the Don, many Red and White Cossacks alike felt out of place upon demobilization and returned to banditry because they had become accustomed to that lifestyle. One "bandit," a Cossack, explained how he found his way to "banditry." Returning home on leave from the Red Army, he had discovered that his parents had died, his wife had left him, and his boyhood enemy had become chairman of the khutor soviet. Unable to humble himself before his adversary, he slipped away and joined a marauding band.[133] Cossacks like this one, whose defining life experience had been warfare, represented a war generation more than a monolithically hostile Cossack estate. Most Cossacks simply bowed their heads to the new order. They believed that they had known what to expect from Soviet power, had fought and lost, and now their expectations were largely being realized.

As Soviet power was consolidated, it was not those groups "known" to be anti-Soviet (Cossacks and kulaks) but the putative pillars of the new order who were most active in anti-Soviet revolts. Requisitioning sorely tried the loyalty of those who had embraced Soviet power. Their dissatisfaction with Soviet power derived not so much from its violating peasant notions of property and moral economy as from the regime's failure to deliver on its promises. In their frantic efforts to meet inflated targets, food-supply agents indiscriminately requisitioned supplies, thereby failing to observe the class distinctions they were supposed to uphold. Such actions harmed poor peasants much more than wealthy ones, thereby undermining their faith in Soviet power's declared backing of them.[134] Initial support for the Soviet regime among poor peasants was further eroded by its inability to deliver on promises to help them, leading some even to take up arms.[135]

The winter and early spring of 1920–1921 marked a watershed in popular attitudes to the new order. In both Rostov and Khoper Districts, the methods of requisitioning eroded the relatively broad support for Soviet power that had initially existed there.[136] Peasants in previously pro-Soviet regions increasingly attacked and even murdered food-supply agents. In Zhlobinskaia, one such county, some peasants made a gory statement against official policies. Having murdered three food-supply agents, they cut open their stomachs and stuffed them with wheat.[137] Shock groups operating in Donets District were concentrated overwhelmingly in peasant counties, the very same counties that had been bastions of Soviet power in 1918 and 1919.[138] By the spring of 1921, the peasant about-face on Soviet power was complete. Soviet officials throughout the Don reported that peasants rather than Cossacks were the primary pillar of support for numerous marauding bands throughout the region.[139]

The uprising in Efremevo-Stepanovskaia county was the most significant anti-Soviet revolt in the Don Territory in 1920–1921. Ten thousand native Don peasants inhabited this isolated county in the middle of the Donets District. Like many other peasants in this region, they suffered from land shortage, with most holding only a paltry allotment of about three and a half desiatins.[140] From 1917 the community endured the Cossack government's antipeasant policies. During the 1918 Cossack insurgency, German troops had occupied the county and disarmed its inhabitants for the Cossacks. Throughout the civil wars, anti-Soviet intelligence agencies consistently portrayed its population as precociously "pro-Bolshevik."[141]

Support for Soviet power, however, did not spare Efremovo-Stepanovka from the demands of the food-supply campaign. Food-supply agents took control of the county's mill in September 1920, prosecuting peasants who brought "unauthorized" grain for milling. (Soviet officials allowed citizens to mill their grain only after the county had delivered its state levy.) In late November a shock group, with 130 bayonets and one machine-gun, stopped in the county seat. The next sources in the archives are military dispatches reporting the county seat's capture from insurgents and reports of Soviet investigative commissions.[142]

The investigative commissions reconstructed the course of the revolt. A disorganized protest by roughly 500 peasants on December 12 had been the spark setting off the uprising. The region's isolation and the disjointed response by Soviet authorities allowed the protest to grow into a full-blown peasant rebellion. On December 15 the rebels routed two separate Soviet detachments sent against them and two days later drove back another unit. These initial successes led the insurgents to believe that they had recast the boundaries of the possible. Soon the number of rebels grew to more than 2,000. By now the insurgent peasant army was organized into companies and platoons. Their greatest victories came on December 20, when they clashed with the Soviet Third Special Regiment, numbering 1,300 men. (Units designated as "special" were those considered particularly reliable and thus entrusted with especially sensitive internal duties.) The insurgents routed the special regiment, killing more than 500 men and capturing both machine guns and artillery. That very same day they drove off another unit consisting of 450 bayonets and 120 sabers. These setbacks shocked the Soviet command into organizing a concerted operation against the insurgents, including the dispatch of two armored trains. On December 25 Soviet forces occupied the county seat. Three days later they decisively crushed the insurgents, killing or wounding 500 of them. The uprising had lasted sixteen days.

On December 31 an "extraordinary commission for consolidating Soviet power and combating banditry" arrived in Efremevo-Stepanovka. It found no constituted authority. All male peasants were in hiding. Once it had assembled what citizens it could find, the commission appointed a revolutionary committee. The occupying Soviet regiment then conducted a house-to-house search and arrested those peasants suspected of participating in the rebellion. Many of the rebellion's major officials were seized, including the head of the insurgents' "provisional government" and the military chief of staff. Soviet troops also captured the peasant army's communications officer, who had been the county organizer for Communist Party cells. Soviet investigators were particularly interested in establishing the "social base" of the uprising. While they dutifully pilloried kulaks for creating the preconditions of the rebellion, they nevertheless concluded that "what is characteristic about the Stepanovka uprising is the fact that the poor peasants participated in it."[143]

The participation of poor peasants in such unrest was indeed "characteristic." In several communities of Sal' District, which was reputed to be the most "proletarian," crowds of peasants broke into state warehouses and distributed grain among the needy and poor.[144] Among the defendants brought before the circuit session of the revolutionary tribunal in Rostov District were poor peasants and former Red Army men. They were accused not only of evading their taxes but also of actively opposing attempts to collect them. One defendant had urged Red Army men engaged in food-supply operations to drop their weapons, because he himself had served in the Red Army for three years and "knew what bloodsuckers were in power." While the court sentenced five defendants to death in this case, it immediately commuted all their sentences in recognition of their previous service in the Red Army and in consideration of their sincere repentance and "lack of consciousness."[145]

Popular unrest in this period, then, was not simply a peasant repudiation of Soviet policies, a war between city and countryside.[146] The intransigence of Soviet policies was the critical catalyst. But the fault line between those who rebelled and those who did not ran along more of a political than a socioeconomic divide. Cossacks, who were "peasants" by any socioeconomic measure, generally did not participate in uprisings during this period. Unrest was concentrated rather precisely among those who had previously been the most ardent proponents of Soviet power. Rebellion was essentially a *political* phenomenon of dashed expectations and resulted from a feeling of betrayed loyalties.

The Red Army man, another supposed pillar of Soviet power in the countryside, also proved to be highly volatile.[147] Most Soviet officials in the countryside had served in the Red Army, but so too had many anti-Soviet insurgents. Carrying over the political-enlightenment program begun under the Provisional Government, the Red Army invested vast amounts of time and energy inculcating the Soviet worldview in its recruits. Soldiers and former soldiers contrasted the idealized portrait of Soviet power that they had received in the Red Army with the actual form it took in the countryside, and found it wanting.[148] The political consciousness cultivated in the army established a yardstick of what Soviet power was supposed to be. Owing to this indoctrination, former soldiers proved to be more politically active, both for *and* against the new order, than other segments of the population.

The food-supply campaign tested the expectations for Red Army men as much as for everyone else. One brigade commander in the Fourth Cavalry Division reported to his superiors that "in discussions with Red Army men returning from home, and from reading their relatives' letters to them, I have become convinced that all is not well on the Don . . . In these letters they write that food-supply organs . . . very often protect the bourgeoisie, kulaks, and veterans of Denikin's army, while they seize nearly all food products, cattle, and even clothes from the families of Red Army men." Demobilized Red Army men complained, "There you go—we fought for Red power [*sic*], and then Soviet power goes off and does the type of things that are entirely unacceptable." Soviet officials dismissed this latter view as "a petty-bourgeois deviation."[149] But these soldiers found Soviet policy unacceptable not by any "petty-bourgeois" criteria, or by those of some rural moral economy, but rather by the regime's own standards as taught to them in the Red Army.

The intensive food-supply campaigns in the Don Territory coincided with the mass demobilization of the Red Army after the conclusion of the Soviet-Polish War. The returning wave of demobilized Red Army men further destabilized the situation.[150] Indeed, government reports on political sentiments from late 1920 onward singled out demobilized soldiers as the most politically volatile group, figuring much more prominently as instigators of unrest than as pillars of support. Such men were often those responsible for breaking into state barns to distribute grain among the hard-pressed local population.[151]

The 1920–1921 food-supply campaign even caused the Red Army to fear for its own integrity. By January 1921, the commander of forces in the Don Territory reported that military units frequently interfered with food-supply work and agitated against food-supply policies. Some units went so far as to demand the execution of food-supply plenipotentiaries who were operating in regions where they were quartered.[152] Soldiers detached for food-supply duty increasingly turned against the grain dictatorship and the methods used to implement its policy. In doing so, they justified their opposition within the terms of Soviet political culture, asserting that "it is not Soviet power but the Communists who thought up this requisitioning."[153] Such sentiments led the Red Army command to become circumspect in employing military units for food-supply duties. Red Army commanders warned against dispatching units to politically volatile areas. By October 1921 the Northern Caucasus military district scolded the Don food-supply commissar for using soldiers as "bodyguards" for food-supply agents, as such tasks inevitably "led to demoralization of the units."[154] As during the collectivization campaign in 1929–1930, the army attempted to limit its involvement and to curb the more extreme excesses of Soviet agrarian policy out of fear that they would destabilize the armed forces.[155]

Unrest in the winter of 1920–1921 had largely taken the form of community-wide rebellions. Beginning in early 1921 this type of unrest was replaced by "banditry," with groups of mounted and heavily armed men roving through the countryside. The most significant "bands" emerged as a result of mutinies led by revolutionary commanders against food-supply policies.[156] The leaders of all major anti-Soviet rebellions in the Don Territory throughout 1921—K. T. Vakulin, G. S. Maslakov, I. P. Kolesov, and Ia. M. Fomin—were Red commanders with impeccable revolutionary credentials. Vakulin, Maslakov, and Kolesov had formed some of the earliest pro-Soviet detachments on the Don, raising them before the Red Army even came into existence. More often than not, active or demobilized Red Army men filled the insurgent ranks. The Cheka itself declared that the bands operating throughout the Don in the spring of 1921 were "constituted mostly from among former Red Army men."[157]

Soviet food-supply policies on the Don led all four men—Vakulin, Maslakov, Kolesov, and Fomin—to raise mutinies between December 1920 and March 1921. All but Maslakov were serving at the time of their mutinies as commanders of garrisons or squadrons in their home regions. Maslakov led his regiment into mutiny while stationed in Tauride province, and then led it back to the Don Territory. All followed a political trajectory similar to that of Iakov Efimovich Fomin. A native of Elanskaia stanitsa in the Upper Don District, he had led the defection of Upper Don units from the anti-Soviet Don Army in January 1919.[158] He then served in the Red Army and advanced to the rank of unit commander in Filipp Mironov's Don Corps, taking part in that unit's August 1919 "mutiny" in Saransk. The man to whom Mironov and Fomin formally surrendered in Saransk was none other than Maslakov. A revolutionary tribunal sentenced Mironov and Fomin to death, but the Soviet government amnestied them, ostensibly for their services to the revolution but in fact as part of a campaign to win over Cossack support. Thereafter Fomin, like Mironov, returned to service in the Red Army. By late 1920 he commanded the cavalry squadron stationed in Veshenskaia stanitsa, the same site as his January 1919 exploits.

Fomin's mutiny took place against the backdrop of the general intensification of Soviet requisitions. It also grew out of the fierce struggle among Upper Don District officials over whether to obey orders to ship the district's seed grain to other districts. The garrison itself was composed of local Cossacks who were directly affected by requisitioning policies. In mid-March, two weeks after a plenipotentiary had ordered all seed grain shipped out of the district, the garrison mutinied under the slogans "Down with requisitioning! Down with nonlocal Communists!" In Veshenskaia it met with near-universal support. The garrison's party cell sided with the revolt, as did one-third of the Veshenskaia stanitsa party cell.[159] In many of these uprisings, in fact, local party members organized or sided with the revolt.

When Soviet forces drove Fomin and his followers out of Veshenskaia, the previously Soviet "garrison" became an anti-Soviet "band." It changed locations daily. As he passed through peasant and Cossack communities, Fomin summoned assemblies and proclaimed that he was fighting against Communists but not against Soviet power. By late spring, Soviet forces managed to push him and his followers into Voronezh province with heavy losses. But Fomin returned to his old haunts in autumn 1921, enjoying much sympathy among the local population. He gained new recruits and routed several Soviet detachments sent against him. He continued issuing appeals to "citizen Cossacks and peasants, Red Army men in the front-line units of our glorious Red Army!" Condemning the bloodthirsty policies of the "Communist" regime, he called for "citizens" to rise up and reestablish "the true power of the whole laboring people!" Concerned that local recruits were swelling Fomin's "band," the Soviet command in November and December 1921 dispatched a special unit of the Don Cheka, a regular army regiment, and even "assistance detachments" against him. In February 1922 they finally caught up with Fomin and his followers and wiped them out. Fomin had been active for one year.[160]

Fomin was no exception. The "bands" of all these former Red commanders cut down food-supply officials and party members, broke open state grain-storage centers, and "requisitioned" goods and cash. In communities through which they passed, the insurgent leaders addressed the population in the language of the revolution. Vakulin proclaimed to village assemblies that "just like you, I am an ordinary peasant. I fought for the entire Civil War on the Red fronts against the bourgeoisie—I cherish the achievements of our great Revolution." He called for *"liberté, egalité, fraternité"* [*svobodu, ravenstvo, bratstvo*]. In his wake Vakulin left behind not traditional village assemblies but rather "Soviets of Five" and "Soviets of Three."[161]

Before the First World War, Grigorii Maslakov had been a poor peasant who had worked as a paid laborer on the horse estates in the Sal' steppes. Early in 1918 he raised a detachment to fight for Soviet power, and later rose to command a cavalry brigade in the Red Army. Outraged by letters reporting food-supply violations on the Don, he led his brigade into mutiny and took it to the Don. As he passed through communities in the territory, "Uncle Maslak" organized agitational assemblies. There he proclaimed, "We march not against Soviet power but for it . . . We march not against our comrade Communists who proceed along the proper path and help the workers, but against the bourgeois Communists." Rather than doing away with soviets, he urged villagers "to purge the Soviet institutions of their vermin." A Soviet agent explained what Maslakov meant by "vermin": "all those honest and conscientious functionaries of the republic who religiously fulfill the decrees concerning requisitioning." His unit released Red Army men it had captured, unless they were Communists or food-supply workers.[162] These he had executed. Next he broke open the state grain warehouses, distributed grain to the citizens, and appealed for volunteers. Recently demobilized Red Army men proved especially susceptible to his call.[163]

Soviet policies had caused widespread dissatisfaction in the Don Territory by early 1921, but unrest did not reflect a generic "peasant" repudiation of Soviet power. The standards by which the regime fell short in the insurgents' eyes cannot be separated out from the general political ecosystem of the revolution. The insurgents communicated with and appealed to their fellow citizens in this political language. Operating within such a matrix, the insurgents in fact replicated many of the underlying features of Soviet power even in their protest against it. Their tropes of legitimacy, means of mobilization, and Manichean political universe remained recognizably part of this common revolutionary ecosystem.

If NEP is taken to mean actual concessions to the rural population, it did not arrive on the Don until the end of 1921. In late autumn Moscow lowered the Don's original assessment, which in conditions of harvest failure was recognized as "utterly unrealizable."[164] The introduction of more lenient policies coincided with a decline in "banditry." But it was no NEP-instituted social contract that overcame popular unrest; indeed, Soviet power used methods other than economic policies to confront discontent, even after the introduction of NEP.

In the course of the Civil War the Soviet state came increasingly to use the term "banditry" as a catchall category to criminalize and pathologize political action. By conflating political opposition and criminal deviance, this concept suggested that resistance was merely antisocial behavior from which society must be protected. To address this challenge, the Soviet government in late January 1921 formed a "Central Interdepartmental Commission for Combating Banditry."[165] Several days later, the Don Executive Committee devoted an entire meeting to the issue of banditry, and in late February it held a special plenum to discuss banditry in the localities.[166] Local military officials could do little to pursue these mobile bands without cavalry units, and in the spring of 1921 these were concentrated against Makhno in Ukraine and Antonov in Tambov.[167] But in May the Central Interdepartmental Commission for Combating Banditry focused on eliminating the problem in the Ukraine, the Northern Caucasus, and Siberia, and dispatched to these regions Cheka forces and special units composed entirely of Communists.[168]

But neither the dispatch of these forces nor the proclamation of NEP led to a decrease in "banditry" by the summer of 1921. In July 1921 party officials established a "Don Territorial Military Assembly for Combating Banditry" (DTMA), subordinate to the republic-wide commission of the same name and identical to other such regional assemblies set up in Ukraine, Tambov, and later Central Asia.[169] The personnel heading this organ, all national-level party and military figures, testified to its significance: Aleksandr Beloborodov, Andrei Bubnov, Semen Budennyi, and Kliment Voroshilov. At first the Don assembly tried a policy of amnesties. When this approach failed, and with bandits reported to control 30 percent of the territory, the DTMA in September 1921 shifted to a "punitive policy," meaning executions and hostage-taking.[170] These measures had earlier been tested with success during the Antonov rebellion in Tambov province. The commission issued an "Instruction on the Application of Punitive Measures" to local officials. Among the suggested measures were collective punishment of communities for the actions of bandits; the seizure of hostages from among the civilian population; and the execution of bandits.[171] Voroshilov instructed members of the district military assemblies, "You can execute any bandits you seize, but if you have arrested them, be so kind as to conduct an investigation first." In other words, either shoot them on the spot or arrest them and then try them—don't arrest them and then simply shoot them.[172] Those who were not shot out of hand were either dispatched to one of the three concentration camps operating in the Don Territory or exiled "to the north."[173]

The Soviet leadership defined "banditry" not so much as an act but as an underlying social phenomenon. Rather than merely seeking to reimpose order, Soviet authorities understood their struggle against "banditry" to mean "removing and exterminating the bandit element." Once the symptom of banditry revealed the presence of dangerous elements, "cleansing" was required whether the insurgency itself had continued or not. Therefore, military operations were conducted explicitly "to remove and eliminate the bandit element" and "to cleanse those regions infected with banditry."[174] The chairman of the Don Military Assembly's northern sector described how he saw his duties:

> To destroy totally banditry's manpower, as well as all forces that aid and abet it . . . In order to accomplish this [task], we must use all means at our disposal: 1) to capture all individuals who have participated directly in bands, as well as all those who have offered any aid to individual bands, and 2) then to eliminate a portion of them without mercy, and to resettle the remainder beyond the boundaries of the Don Territory.[175]

From the beginning of 1921 Soviet authorities relied increasingly on "special detachments," units composed entirely of party members, rather than regular army units to combat "banditry." Not coincidentally, the party had issued its "Instruction on Special Detachments"— described as "an irregular army, the party's closest and most reliable foundation"—in the immediate aftermath of NEP.[176]

Reports from the end of 1921 and early 1922 noted with satisfaction that these measures had brought about a sharp decline in "banditry." By May Day 1922 newspapers proclaimed that "political banditry" on the Don had ceased to exist. What NEP and the amnesty campaign had failed to do, repression and military force had accomplished.[177] In addition, the consolidation of Soviet power itself had eliminated other conceivable political options, thereby undercutting the grounds for opposition. By the autumn of 1921 the Whites had been defeated and the war with Poland had ended. Soviet reports noted the existence of continued widespread dissatisfaction but predicted that there would be no uprisings so long as the population saw no viable alternative to Soviet power.[178]

One final factor put an end to widespread resistance to the new order: the famine of 1921–1922. While Soviet authorities did not plan or intend the famine, their actions certainly contributed to it. Coercion had succeeded in extracting grain and keeping the regime in power; it also shaped peasant strategies. Famine was the result of Soviet miscalculations and the state's repressive measures toward the rural population.[179] By spring 1922, 85 percent of the entire population in the Don Territory, once Russia's wheat basket, was facing starvation. Large numbers of people abandoned their homes in search of food in neighboring provinces. Contagious diseases further ravaged the population. Over the course of 1922–1923, more than one-third of the population in Khoper District was suffering from malaria. People were physically incapable of offering any further resistance. In addition, Soviet policy—while less successful than it had hoped—had nevertheless succeeded in concentrating seed grain and grain reserves in the hands of the state. Whatever their opinion of the new order, citizens could now look only to the Soviet state for succor.[180]

Revolutionary Orthodoxy

In early 1917, Vladimir Vernadskii had decried the fact that Russia "now had democracy, but without the political organization of society." After four years of civil war, the Soviet state had managed to impose a "political organization" in the form of an orthodox interpretation of the revolution. However, the other half of Vernasky's equation—"democracy"—remained a crucial component of official political culture, albeit in domesticated form. The revolution had not simply provided a new point of state legitimacy; it had sanctioned, indeed insisted upon, popular political engagement. In 1921 former Soviet commanders who raised rebellions against Soviet power convened agitational gatherings and issued broadsides not just to win over recruits but because their cause was to proselytize and institute the revolution. In their declarations, these revolutionaries against the Soviet revolution invariably drew a sharp contrast between their passive lives before 1917 and their active political engagement after it. They stressed that the cathartic impact of 1917 activated them as political subjects.[181] The widespread unrest of 1920–1921, then, was not just a "peasant" repudiation of Soviet policies, as it is commonly portrayed. Rather, it testified to the deep and abiding political impact of the revolutionary ideals of 1917, ideals that extended widely beyond the boundaries of official Bolshevik interpretation.

Yet by the end of 1921, the Soviet state and Communist Party had managed to impose their vision of the revolution as an official orthodoxy. The Soviet state did not just proselytize its new orthodoxy; it communicated it through a whole set of concrete policies. The Communist party-state pursued its program in the face of massive popular opposition and the loss of many onetime supporters. In pursuing this orthodoxy, Soviet power often employed naked force. But it also attempted to provide legitimate grounding for its use of force. Circuit sessions served both as an instrument of repression and as a didactic tool, a "means of agitation and repression." They provided a primer in the meaning of Soviet power by framing certain behavior as illegal and providing a justification for state violence. Through its selective application of violence and its use of revolutionary justice, the Soviet state conveyed to the population its form of Marxism as ideology.

The new regime succeeded in imposing this orthodoxy, at the cost of alienating not only much of the population but also many of its erstwhile supporters. By 1921 the Bolshevik Party organization in the Don Territory truly was a drop in the ocean, especially in the countryside. True, it had grown from 5,000 members in mid-1920 to nearly 12,000 by the year's end. But the party continued to harbor suspicions of the Don population's loyalties. In the party purges following the Civil War, the Don organization lost 45 percent of its members, double the national average. By 1924 the Bolshevik Party organization in the Don Territory numbered only 6,224 people, only slightly more than it had in mid-1920.[182]

The revolutionary conjuncture of 1917–1921 had been defined by the lack of any authoritative definition of political authority. NEP and the establishment of a definitive Soviet political order coincided with the more generalized postwar consolidation throughout Europe. Yet other European states were attempting to reconstitute some type of order and normalcy, to "recast" a bourgeois political and social order.[183] The Soviet state, on the contrary, pursued a highly specific form of "political organization." Soviet measures in 1920–1921 redefined revolution from its original structural definition—the contestation for legitimacy—into political orthodoxy. By 1921, revolution as event had ended. For the Soviet state and its supporters, revolution as ongoing state project, as a work-in-progress, was just beginning.

Conclusion: The Emergence of the Soviet State

$\mathcal{B}$y the end of 1921, the Bolsheviks were the indisputable masters of the Don Territory, and of Russia. But Frederick Engels, in a letter to Vera Zasulich, one of the founders of Russian Marxism, had presciently warned that "people who boast that they have *made* a revolution see . . . that a revolution *made* does not in the least resemble the one they would have liked to make."[1] As the Bolsheviks raised their heads and cast a glance around, they must have been sobered by what they saw. The Don Party organization looked out on a scene of unrelieved ruin.

The population of the Don Territory had suffered grievous losses in the seven-year stretch of war, revolution, and civil war. Five percent of the countryside's population had perished in those years, and a further 2.5 percent had been made invalids. Among those aged twenty to thirty-nine, there were nearly two women for every man; in several districts—Sal', Upper Don—the ratio was three to one.[2] The Civil War was disproportionately responsible for these losses. Throughout the Don countryside, deaths during the Civil War were three times greater than during the First World War. Nagavskaia stanitsa (Second Don District) puts these losses in some perspective. The community had six dead and thirty wounded in the First World War; during the Civil War it suffered 270 dead, and 80 percent of the surviving male population was wounded.[3]

Given such grievous losses among the population, agriculture faced daunting prospects. The Don Territory simply ceased to be one of the granaries of the European continent. In 1917, three years into the First World War, the average household sowing was 10.2 desiatins; by 1922 the average sowing had collapsed to less than one-third that size. And the sown territory continued to contract each year *after* the fighting had ended, testifying both to the ruinous nature of Bolshevik policies and to emerging famine conditions. By 1921 the region's livestock, decimated in ceaseless requisitions and driven off by retreating armies, had contracted by a factor of four, transforming what had been one of the Russian Empire's richest livestock regions into one of the Soviet Union's poorest ones. Drought and famine then followed. In one typical region, the sown territory in 1924 was 74 percent less than it had been in 1917, itself a year of war and revolution; the number of cows—44 percent less; and draft animals—67 percent less.[4] The Bolsheviks had won. But they ruled a ruined and devastated countryside, with agriculture continuing to decline even after their "victory."

Yet among all the pretenders to power in the Civil War, the Bolsheviks alone emerged victorious out of this maelstrom. Two longstanding explanations for the origin of the Soviet society emphasize either radical continuity or radical rupture. Proponents of the Russian *Sonderweg* thesis have identified the Soviet experience as a more ruthless variant of eternal and enduring traits of Russian life.[5] Advocates of a Marxist *Sonderweg* argue, on the contrary, that the Bolshevik seizure of power marked a fundamental and absolute rupture in Russian history.[6] This study has emphasized instead the 1914–1921 period as a specific conjuncture, a continuum of intensified but historically conditioned change.

Bolshevik Russia was a product neither of pure ideology nor simply of the circumstances of 1914–1921. Throughout this period, the state had attempted to impose a definitive order on society. Such efforts failed, but as a consequence "a successive series of social forms accumulated, each constituting a layer that covered all or most of society without altering the older forms lying under the surface."[7] The structure of imperial society, and the ambitions for change generated by it, formed the framework within which both wartime change and revolutionary restructuring emerged. Officials in the Russian state bureaucracy had long held an almost mythic faith in the efficacy of the state. Educated society also came to idolize the state as an ideal in its own right and an instrument for achieving all its own fondest dreams. Opponents of the autocracy often looked to the state not simply as a tool of repression but also as the only available instrument for overcoming backwardness. The struggle, therefore, was less between "state and society" than between autocracy and society over how best to employ the state to transform Russian reality.[8]

The autocracy's jealous protection of its prerogatives had prevented the emergence of a true civil society in imperial Russia. This situation fostered attitudes within the Russian public that were at least as important as the missing institutions themselves. Educated society's political impotence and its sense of social obligation produced among the Russian political class an unusually strong commitment to reforming both the political order and society. Many in educated society had come to see the state as both a tool and an ideal for "consciousness" to channel the masses' "spontaneity" toward progress and enlightenment. This transformationist and tutelary ethos of *étatisme* was an enduring feature of Russian political culture, within which wartime and revolutionary agendas emerged. As Tocqueville observed for the French Revolution, a "great many of the practices we associate with the Revolution had precedents in the treatment of the people by the government in the last two centuries of the monarchy. The old régime provided the Revolution with many of its methods; all the Revolution added was a savagery peculiar to itself."[9]

The autocracy finally allowed institutional structures for realizing the goals of the public, but only in a supercharged wartime context. Total mobilization in Russia took place, then, against the background of a longstanding and powerful critique of the existing order. This was the first phase of telescoped development in the 1914–1921 period. Rather than a civil society existing autonomous of the state, a specific wartime parastatal complex emerged in Russia. This parastatal complex and its mobilizational techniques provided a common heritage for all political movements after 1917.

Wartime forged the tools of future political action and suggested new horizons of possibility for state intervention in society. The February Revolution provided a new focus both for society's preexisting aspirations and for the new instruments forged in war. Educated society initially held out much hope for the organic development of consciousness and enlightenment among the masses. Its members turned to the state as the necessary instrument, in Vladimir Vernadskii's words, to "impose political order" upon a chaotic "democracy." But when the masses failed to proceed along the lines scripted for them, the public looked increasingly to the state, and its wartime practices, as the tool necessary to impose consciousness on the population. Here was the second telescoped stage of development. The implementation of wartime policies overlapped with, and was harnessed to, the revolutionary reordering of the political system and society.

The events of 1917 caused Russia's political class to despair over the people's capacity for self-development, predisposing many to side with the tutelary program of the Soviet state, even when they did not sympathize with Bolshevism as an ideology. Following the collapse of their initial post-February hopes, non-Bolshevik technocrats such as Kondrat'ev, Groman, Anisimov, and Chaianov all came to work for the Soviet state. Vladimir Vernadskii, a member of the Kadet central committee, continued his scientific efforts under the Soviet regime well into the Stalinist years. While Vernadskii was critical of some aspects of the Stalinist system, his continued service "rested on an ethos of social transformation and scientific utopianism which the scholar shared with the political architects of the Soviet regime."[10] There existed a strong current of statism within Russian society itself, an ethos conditioned by the lack of prewar institutions, strengthened by the war experience, and infused with new urgency by the collapse of tsarism. The entire political class shared a common transformatory agenda to create a new society through the power of the state. The Bolshevik program for conflating state and society thus mapped onto an important preexisting current in Russian political culture.

The war experience alone did not shape the Soviet state; revolution was an equally crucial component. Russia had been at war since 1914, but only in the aftermath of 1917 did violence become a regular and constitutive feature of everyday political life. What distinguished the Soviet regime from other wartime societies was that it carried over such wartime methods, forged during a particular period of remobilization during the First World War, from wartime into peacetime. This specificity was a result of the Soviet state's revolutionary project. To be sure, other European powers during the First World War had incorporated institutions and practices of total mobilization into their societies and governments. But in most societies these wartime practices were appended to an existing political or social order, which could shed them once the war was over. In revolutionary Russia, by contrast, the institutions and practices of total mobilization became the building blocks of both a new state and a new socioeconomic order. In 1917 public organizations that had grown up in wartime transferred their focus to revolutionary politics, thereby inevitably conflating the once-distinct military and civilian realms. By autumn 1917 the Provisional Government had embraced a mobilizational form of politics. Certainly, its aspirations were far greater than its actual results. But this form of politics constituted the legacy inherited by the Soviet regime and all its competitors.

So the war had a profound impact on both the Russian state and Russian society. But war did not so much "militarize" the Soviet state and Russian society as tranform the parameters and substance of both military and civilian realms.[11] It produced a specific civilian-military hybrid. This hybrid was not solely the product of Bolshevism, but resulted at least as much from the particular historical conjuncture out of which the Soviet state emerged. Unlike other combatants—Germany, Hungary, or Italy—Russia's revolution came *during* war, not after it. Consequently, Russia amalgamated the phases of war and domestic restructuring. In Russia, the revolution wove together an ethos of violence emerging out of the First World War with an insistent demand for remaking Russian society. To emphasize only the impact of war on the Soviet system overlooks the profound ways in which revolution also shaped its emergence. Total war and total revolution in Russia thus acted upon each other in a reciprocal way.

The Bolshevik regime looked more similar to other mobilized European states than has often been appreciated. Yet by 1921 the Soviet Union viewed itself, and was viewed by other societies, as radically different. This gulf was real. Unlike other European states, Soviet Russia carried wartime practices over into "peacetime," absorbing them as part of its regular state apparatus. The Soviet state, and Soviet society, never really shifted away from "total mobilization," but rather transferred its axis from war to revolution. The different goal of mobilization—a socialist society, rather than waging war—distinguished the Soviet Union from other regimes that mobilized during wartime.

Circumstances of origin can explain the shape and form of the Soviet state but cannot explain the further course of Soviet history. While noting that many revolutionary practices originated within the Old Regime, Tocqueville equally insists that the revolutionary regime then transforms them, imbuing them with a "peculiar"—and ongoing— "savagery." Bolshevism as ideology provided a particular explanation for the slaughter, ruin, and devastation of war, revolution, and civil war. This ideology—Marxism-Leninism—was explicitly antagonistic, envisioning a constant and unremitting struggle of classes until the achievement of communism. Bolshevik ideology, sustained by resentments fostered in the late imperial period and exacerbated by the events of 1917, came to structure Soviet state violence. The attitudes prevalent in Russia's prerevolutionary society, and the manner in which they became transformed in people's lived experience in war and civil wars, made such Manicheism plausible, and even appealing. Violence, then, was not simply the degradation of everyday life or an atavism inherent in backward Russian behavior. As fantastic, utopian dreams fused with an experience of devastation and brutality, those employing violence invested it with a redemptive and purifying significance.[12] If war and revolution were the components necessary for forging a violent and brutal Soviet society, the experience of civil war provided the crucial catalyst. The ordeal of the Civil War—chaos, devastation, hunger, want, and violence—embedded itself into the practices of the ruling as well as the behaviors of the governed. In the concrete experience of civil war, forms of future conduct crystallized for both the governing and the governed.[13]

This mobilization and violence continued after "warfare" ostensibly ended. The Bolshevik Party understood "revolution" not simply as a historical foundation-event; indeed, it cast "revolution" as its own ongoing political project.[14] Rather than upholding a particular social or political order, the Communists sought the revolutionary transformation of society. After its political foundation, the Bolshevik party-state therefore did not abandon the violence of foundation even as it established a system of more routinized and legitimized force. What distinguished the Bolsheviks was the extent to which they turned tools originally intended for total war to the new ends of revolutionary politics, during the civil wars but especially after their end. Whereas other European states employed many of these measures in conditions of total war, they ceased to employ them extensively once the war and subsequent crises had passed. Similarly, White violence, while profligate, was much less open-ended than Bolshevik violence. During the extended period of war, revolution, and civil wars the Bolshevik regime's reliance on practices of mobilization and violence remained within the outer reaches of comparison with other states. With the end of Europe's crisis period, this quantitative difference in Bolshevik violence became a qualitative one. After 1921, the Bolshevik regime's continued use of wartime measures to pursue its revolutionary project set it fundamentally apart from other European states.

Note on Sources

A full bibliography for this book can be found at http://www.arts. cornell.edu/history/faculty/holquistbibliography.htm. Citations for all the published sources in this work are found in the endnotes. Much of this account, however, is based on archival materials. As the abbreviations for the archives and collection numbers give the reader no sense of the nature of the material cited, here I provide a description of the archival holdings employed in this study.

This study is based on the archival holdings of the competing contenders for political power from 1914 to 1921. For policy at the national level, I worked in four central archives in Moscow: the State Archive of the Russian Federation (GARF); the Russian State Military Archive (RGVA), covering the post-1917 period; the Russian State Military-Historical Archive (RGVIA), covering the period before October 1917; and the Russian State Archive of Sociopolitical History (RGASPI), formerly the archive of the Communist Party. The collections of the imperial government are mostly found in the Russian State Historical Archive (RGIA) in St. Petersburg.

The collections in these central archives illuminated the attempts of succeeding regimes to impose a political order on the chaos of the 1914–1921 period. For the imperial period, I relied on the holdings of RGIA, especially those of the Council of Ministers (RGIA, f. 1276), the Agriculture Ministry's army food-supply chancellery (RGIA, f. 456), and the Special Council for Food Supply (RGIA, f. 457); and the holdings of various military organs in RGVIA. Memoirs of administrators and the national press were very useful.

Materials on the Provisional Government in 1917 were found primarily in GARF and RGVIA. My account is based on materials found among the holdings of the Provisional Government's Ministry of Food Supply (GARF, f. 1783), Ministry of Internal Affairs (GARF, f. 1788), and Main Administration for the Militia (GARF, f. 1791), as well as holdings of the Central Committee for Sociopolitical Enlightenment (GARF, f. 9505). RGVIA, the pre-1918 military archive, were particularly valuable for shedding light on how the Provisional Government planned to secure its goals. I relied on the collections of the Military Cabinet of the Prime Minister (RGVIA, f. 366), the Directorate of the Chief Quartermaster (RGVIA, f. 499), the Supreme Commander's Military-Political and Civil Directorate (RGVIA, f. 2005), and the Special Delegate of the Ministry of Food Supply (RGVIA, f. 2009).

I consulted three separate types of archive in order to analyze Soviet policy in the Civil War: the archive of the Soviet state; that of the Red Army; and that of the party itself. In order to understand the Communist Party's role as "coordinator" of state policy, I utilized the holdings of RGASPI, which contained records of the party's Central Committee (RGASPI, f. 17) and its subordinate Don Bureau (RGASPI, f. 554). Holdings of Soviet state institutions included those of the People's Commissariat of Internal Affairs (GARF, f. 393), the Cossack section of the All-Russian Central Executive Committee (GARF, f. 1235), and the personal collection of Vladimir Antonov-Ovseenko, detailing his role as commissar for suppressing counterrevolution in the South in 1917–1918 (GARF, f. 8415). Since the Red Army for much of 1918–1920 was the face of Soviet power in the Don Territory, the collections of the Russian State Military Archive were especially important. For the Civil War period, I relied on the holdings of the Southern Front (RGVA, f. 100); the three armies constituting that front which were active in the Don Territory (the Eighth, Ninth, and Tenth Armies: RGVA, ff. 191, 192, 193); and Filipp Mironov's Twenty-third Rifle Division, recruited from and active in the Don Territory (RGVA, f. 1304). For the 1920–1921 period, the collections of the Headquarters for Forces in the Don Territory (RGVA, f. 28087) and the Military Council of the Northern Caucasus Military District (RGVA, f. 40435) were invaluable.

A crucial aspect of this study has been the analysis of how, and to what degree, central policies gained traction in local contexts. Thus the holdings of local institutions were a critical aspect of this research. The collections of many of these organs were found in the State Archive of Rostov Territory (GARO) and the Center for Documentation for Modern History of the Rostov Region (TsDNIRO, formerly the Party Archive of the Rostov Region, PARO). In addition, the central archives in Moscow house the holdings of many local agencies and organs. In particular, materials of the anti-Soviet Don Cossack government— evacuated abroad at the end of the Civil War—after 1945 were incorporated into Soviet central archives after the Red Army seized the Russian Foreign Historical Archive in Prague.

For examining the interplay of policy and practice in the 1914–1917 period, I relied largely on the reports of the Don Territory's local plenipotentiary and the territorial special council on food supply (RGIA, ff. 456 and 457), as well as the local press. During 1917, the Provisional Government's pretensions to dictate to the Don Territory were undercut by the fracturing of political authority. In tracing this process, I relied on the holdings of the Don Territorial Executive Committee (GARO f. 863) and the collections of the Cossack organs that rose to challenge it: the Don Cossack government under Kaledin (GARF f. 1255, GARO f. 864) and the Don Cossack Circle (GARF f. 1258). The personal collections of Nikolai Mel'nikov (Columbia University, Bakhmeteff Archive) and I. V. Denisoff (Cornell University Archives) provided an individual perspective on developments during 1917. My account for 1917 also relies extensively on the local and national press.

To follow the further fracturing of authority during the Civil War, one must piece together the collections of the myriad movements and institutions. My account of the Soviet side of the story for 1918 is based on holdings of the military council of the Northern Caucasus military district (RGVA, f. 25896); the Don Territorial Military Revolutionary Committee (GARO, f. 3440); and the Central Executive Committee of the short-lived Don Soviet Government (GARO, f. R-4071).

For the policy and practices of the anti-Soviet Don Cossack government during the Civil War, I relied upon the holdings of the Cossack Circle (GARF f. 1258, GARO, f. 861); the Cossack "unified" parity government of late 1917 (GARO, f. 864); and the Provisional Cossack government and Circle for the Salvation of the Don of spring 1918 (GARF, f. 1257). The Don Cossack government's various departments contained an untapped wealth of information on the anti-Soviet zone in 1918–1919: the department of internal affairs (GARF, f. 1260); the department of agriculture and land consolidation (GARF, f. 1262); the department of food supply (GARF, f. 1265); the chancellery of the ataman (GARO, f. 46); and the holdings of the Don government's various surveillance organizations (GARF, f. 113; GARF, f. 452; GARO, f. 861; the Wrangel Military Archive, Hoover Institution). Given the degree of coercion in this period, the holdings of the Staff of the Don Army and General Fitskhelaurov's expeditionary force were also invaluable (RGVA, ff. 39456, 40116). The Wrangel Military Archive, Hoover Institution, contains material on the other anti-Soviet movements in the South. Yet the most useful source proved to be the voluminous holdings of the district-level atamans (GARO, f. 856), which detail how policy was actually applied and enforced.

Material on the consolidation of Soviet power at the local level in 1920–1921, as with that at the national level, is found in three types of repositories. The Communist Party directed and coordinated policy in the newly conquered Don Territory: its role may be traced in the holdings of the Don Committee of the Communist Party (TsDNIRO, f. 4), the party's district committees (TsNIRO, f. 6), the party archive's collection of documents (TsDNIRO, f. 12), and the holdings of Istpart, the party agency charged with documenting the party's achievements (TsDNIRO, f. 910). Local administrative agencies were charged with implementing policy: my account is based on the collections of the Don Soviet Executive Committee (GARO, f. R-97), its department of justice (GARO, f. R-1220), and the Don territorial food-supply committee (GARO, f. R-1891). The military was crucial to this consolidation, both as coercive force and as staffing institution. For these questions I relied upon the holdings of military agencies based in the Don Territory (RGVA 28087, 40435).

Archival Collections Cited in This Work

Gosudarstvennyi arkhiv rossiiskoi federatsii, Moscow (GARF)
f. 113	Surveillance [*osvidomitel'noe*] Bureau of the Cossack government
f. 393	Commissariat of Internal Affairs, Soviet of People's Commissars
f. 452	Don Department of Surveillance for the All-Great Don Host
f. 1235	All-Russian Central Executive Committee
f. 1255	Cossack government of the Don Cossack Community [*voisko*]
f. 1257	Provisional Cossack government
f. 1258	Cossack Circle of the All-Great Don Host

f. 1260	Department of Internal Affairs, All-Great Don Host
f. 1262	Department of Agriculture and Land Improvement, All-Great Don Host
f. 1265	Department of Food Supply, All-Great Don Host
f. 1783	Ministry of Food Supply, Russian Provisional Government
f. 1788	Ministry of Internal Affairs, Russian Provisional Government
f. 1791	Main Directorate for Militia Affairs, Russian Provisional Government
f. 8415	Personal Collection of Vladimir Antonov-Ovseenko
f. 9505	Central Committee for Sociopolitical Enlightenment

Rossiiskii gosudarstvennyi voennyi arkhiv, Moscow (RGVA)

f. 100	Directorate for the armies of the Southern Front (Soviet)
f. 191	Eighth Army (Soviet)
f. 192	Ninth Army (Soviet)
f. 193	Tenth Army (Soviet)
f. 1304	First Ust'-Medveditsa Rifle Division (later, the Twenty-third Rifle Division) (Soviet)
f. 25896	Military Council of the Northern Caucasus Military District (Soviet, 1918)
f. 28087	Headquarters for Armed Forces for the Don Territory (Soviet, 1920–1921)
f. 39456	Headquarters for the All-Great Don Host
f. 40116	Headquarters for the Armed Forces of the northern detachment of General Fitskhelaurov (Don Army)
f. 40435	Military Council of the Northern Caucasus Military District (Soviet, 1920–1921)

Rossiiskii gosudarstvennyi voenno-istoricheskii arkhiv, Moscow (RGVIA)

f. 366	Military Cabinet of the Prime Minister and Political Directorate of the War Minister, Russian Provisional Government
f. 499	Directorate of the Main Quartermaster
f. 2003	Headquarters of the Supreme Commander in Chief (STAVKA)
f. 2005	Military-Political and Civil Directorate for the Supreme Commander in Chief
f. 2009	Special plenipotentiary of the Minister of Food Supply, Russian Provisional Government
f. 2048	Western front (1914–1918)
f. 13216	Governor-General for the Territories of Austria-Hungary occupied by right of war
f. 13227	Governor-General for the Territories of Turkish Armenia and other areas of Turkey occupied by right of war
f. 13841	Tsaritsyn military-censorship point

Rossiiskii gosudarstvennyi arkhiv sotsial'no-politicheskoi istorii, Moscow (RGASPI)

| f. 17 | Central Committee of the Russian Communist Party (Bolsheviks) |
| f. 554 | Don Bureau of the Russian Communist Party (Bolsheviks) |

Rossiiskii gosudarstvennyi istoricheskii arkhiv, St. Petersburg (RGIA)

| f. 456 | Chancellery of the main commissioner for army grain purchases |

f. 457   Special Council for discussing and coordinating measures for food
              supply
f. 1276   Council of Ministers
f. 1278   State Duma
f. 1282   Chancellery for the Minister of Internal Affairs

Gosudarstvennyi arkhiv rostovskoi oblasti, Rostov (GARO)
f. 46   Chancellery of the Appointed Cossack Ataman for the Don
              Territory
f. 213   Territorial office for peasant affairs
f. 856   Administrations of the district atamans
f. 861   Cossack Circle of the Territory of the Don Cossacks/Cossack
              Circle of the All-Great Don Host
f. 863   Don Executive Committee/Don Territorial Executive Committee,
              Russian Provisional Government (1917)
f. 864   Cossack Government of the Don Cossack Territory/Provisional
              United Cossack Government (1917–1918)
f. 3441   Don Territorial Military Commissariat (Soviet)
f. R-97   Don Executive Committee (Soviet, 1920–1922)
f. R-1220   Department of Justice, Don Executive Committee (Soviet)
f. R-1891   Don Territorial Food-Supply Committee (Soviet, 1920–1921)
f. R-4071   Central Executive Committee of the Don Soviet Republic (1918)

Tsentr dokumentatsii noveishei istorii rostovskoi oblasti, Rostov (TsDNIRO)
f. 4   Don Committee of the All-Russian Communist Party (Bolsheviks)
f. 6   District party committees
f. 12   Istpart (collection on history of the party)
f. 910   Collections of the archive

Hoover Archive on War, Revolution, and Peace (HIA), Stanford University
Nikolai Akaemov, "Kaledinskie miatezhi" (unpublished manuscript)
I. Bykadorov Collection
Donskaia armiia (Don Army)
Golovin Collection
Litoshenko Collection
Shishkin Collection
Wrangel Military Archive (WMA)

Hoover Library on War, Revolution, and Peace, Stanford University
Osobye zhurnaly Soveta Ministrov, 1914–1916
Zhurnaly zasedanii Vremennogo Pravitel'stva, 1917

Bakhmeteff Archive (BAR), Columbia University
N. M. Mel'nikov Collection
V. V. Shapkin memoir
M. A. Svechin memoir

Cornell University Archives
I. V. Denisoff Collection

University of California-Berkeley: Russian Émigré Oral History Collection
George Guins, "Professor and Government Official"

Abbreviations

AFSR	Armed Forces of South Russia
AGDH	All-Great Don Host
BAR	Bakhmeteff Archive, Columbia University
CC	Central Committee
DDS	Don Department of Surveillance
DL	*Donskaia letopis'*, 3 vols. (Vienna: Izd. donskoi istoricheskoi komissii, 1923–1924)
DTMA	Don Territorial Military Assembly for Combating Banditry
Ek. Pol.	*Ekonomicheskoe polozhenie Rossii nakanune velikoi oktiabr'skoi revoliutsii*, ed. A. L. Sidorov, 3 vols. (Moscow-Leningrad: Izdatel'stvo Akademii nauk-"Nauka," 1957–1967)
GARF	Gosudarstvennyi arkhiv rossiiskoi federatsii, Moscow
GARO	Gosudarstvennyi arkhiv rostovskoi oblasti, Rostov
HIA	Hoover Institution Archive on War, Revolution, and Peace, Stanford University
HIA WMA	Hoover Institution Archive, Wrangel Military Archive
Izvestiia DOPK	*Izvestiia donskogo prodovol'stvennogo komiteta* (later, *Izvestiia donskogo oblastnogo prodovol'stvennogo komiteta*)
NCMD	Northern Caucasus Military District
NEP	New Economic Policy
PUR	Political Directorate of the Revolutionary-Military Council of the Republic *(Politicheskoe upravlenie revvoensoveta Respubliki)*
RGASPI	Rossiiskii gosudarstvennyi arkhiv sotsial'no-politicheskoi istorii, Moscow
RGIA	Rossiiskii gosudarstvennyi istoricheskii arkhiv, St. Petersburg
RGVA	Rossiiskii gosudarstvennyi voennyi arkhiv, Moscow
RGVIA	Rossiiskii gosudarstvennyi voenno-istoricheskii arkhiv, Moscow
RMC	Revolutionary-Military Council *[revvoensovet]*

RPG	*The Russian Provisional Government*, 3 vols, eds. Robert Browder and Alexander Kerensky (Stanford: Stanford University Press, 1961)
SOGD	*Stenograficheskie otchety gosudarstvennoi dumy*
SOVDSK	*Sbornik Oblasti voiska Donskogo statisticheskogo komiteta*
TsDNIRO	Tsentr dokumentatsii noveishei istorii rostovskoi oblasti, Rostov
TsGIA RB	Tsentral'nyi gosudarstvennyi istoricheskii arkhiv respubliki Bashkortostan, Ufa

Notes

Introduction

1. Stéphane Courtois et al., *The Black Book of Communism: Crimes, Terror, and Repression*, trans. Jonathan Murphy (Cambridge, Mass.: Harvard University Press, 1999). On the October Revolution as a narrative marker, see Frederick Corney, "Rethinking a Great Event," *Social Science History* 22, no. 4 (1998): 12–28.

2. John Horne, "Remobilizing for 'Total War,'" in *State, Society, and Mobilization in Europe during the First World War*, ed. John Horne (Cambridge, England: Cambridge University Press, 1997).

3. "Razmyshleniia o russkoi revoliutsii," *Russkaia mysl'*, no. 1–2 (1921): 6–37, here at p. 6.

4. There are several works that follow this chronology: George Yaney, *The Urge to Mobilize: Agrarian Reform in Russia, 1861–1930* (Urbana, Ill.: University of Illinois Press, 1982); Lars Lih, *Bread and Authority in Russia, 1914–1921* (Berkeley: University of California Press, 1990); Alessandro Stanziani, *L'économie en revolution: le cas russe, 1870–1930* (Paris: A. Michel, 1998); Joshua Sanborn, "Drafting the Nation: Military Conscription and the Formation of a Modern Polity in Tsarist and Soviet Russia, 1905–1925" (Ph.D. dissertation, University of Chicago, 1998).

5. B. V. Anan'ich et al., *Krizis samoderzhaviia, 1895–1917* (Leningrad: Nauka, 1984); Norman Stone, *The Eastern Front, 1914–1917* (New York: Penguin, 1998); Raymond Pearson, *The Russian Moderates and the Crisis of Tsarism, 1914–1917* (New York: Barnes and Noble, 1977). There has been a renewed interest in Russia's World War I experience: Peter Gatrell, *A Whole Empire Walking: Refugees in Russia during World War I* (Bloomington: Indiana University Press, 1999); Eric Lohr, "Enemy Alien Politics in the Russian Empire during World War One" (Ph.D. dissertation, Harvard University, 1999).

6. Alexis de Tocqueville, *The Old Regime and the French Revolution* (New York: Doubleday, 1983).

7. I borrow the term "political class" in this context from Lih, *Bread and Authority*, p. 5.

8. "Total Mobilization," in *The Heidegger Controversy*, ed. Richard Wolin (New York: Columbia University Press, 1991), pp. 119–139, here at p. 123.

9. Richard Bessel, *Germany after the First World War* (New York: Clarendon Press, 1993), p. 262.

10. Laura Engelstein, *Keys to Happiness: Sex and the Search for Modernity in Fin-de-Siècle Russia* (Ithaca: Cornell University Press, 1992), pp. 129–130. The Russian term *obshchestvo* in this period meant the "informed, civic-minded public." I have used the terms "educated society" and "the public" interchangeably to capture the meaning of *obshchestvo*, which sociologically was broader than the concept of the intelligentsia. It stood in contradistinction to Russian officialdom, on the one hand, and to the people *(narod)* on the other. See William G. Wagner, "Ideology, Identity, and the Emergence of a Middle Class," in Edith W. Clowes, Samuel D. Kassow, and James L. West, eds., *Between Tsar and People: Educated Society and the Quest for Public Identity in Late Imperial Russia* (Princeton: Princeton University Press, 1991), pp. 149–150.

11. Michael Geyer, "The Stigma of Violence, Nationalism and War in Twentieth Century Germany," *German Studies Review*, special issue (1992): 75–110, here at p. 84.

12. On the ecosystem/ecology metaphor, see Michael David Fox, *Revolution of the Mind: Higher Learning among the Bolsheviks, 1918–1929* (Ithaca: Cornell University Press, 1997), pp. 190–191; Katerina Clark, *Petersburg: Crucible of Cultural Revolution* (Cambridge, Mass.: Harvard University Press, 1995), pp. ix–28.

13. Keith Baker, *Inventing the French Revolution* (New York: Cambridge University Press, 1990), pp. 158, 238–243; William Sewell, "Ideologies and Social Revolutions," *Journal of Modern History* 57, no. 1 (1985): 57–85, esp. p. 77.

14. On the Civil War and its impact, see Donald Raleigh, *Experiencing Civil War: Politics, Society, and Revolutionary Culture in Saratov, 1918–1922* (Princeton: Princeton University Press, forthcoming).

15. John Bushnell, *Mutiny amid Repression: Russia's Soldiers in the Revolution of 1905–1906* (Bloomington: Indiana University Press, 1985), p. 225.

16. Tocqueville, *The Old Regime*, p. vii.

17. For other local studies, see Donald Raleigh, *Revolution on the Volga: 1917 in Saratov* (Ithaca: Cornell University Press, 1986); Orlando Figes, *Peasant Russia, Civil War: The Volga Countryside in Revolution, 1917–1921* (Oxford: Clarendon Press, 1989); Theodore Friedgut, *Iuzovka in Revolution, 1869–1924*, 2 vols. (Princeton: Princeton University Press, 1989 and 1994).

18. Peter Kenez, *Civil War in South Russia, 1918* and *1919–1920*, 2 vols. (Berkeley: University of California Press, 1971 and 1977).

19. See I. P. Khlystov, *Don v epokhu kapitalizma* (Rostov: Izdatel'stvo rostovskogo universiteta, 1962); Robert McNeal, *Tsar and Cossack, 1855–1914* (New York: St. Martin's Press, 1987); Shane O'Rourke, *Warriors and Peasants: The Don Cossacks in Late Imperial Russia* (New York: St. Martin's Press, 2000).

20. Aleksandr Kozlov, *Na istoricheskom povorote* (Rostov: Izdatel'stvo rostovskogo universiteta, 1977), p. 32.

21. *Alfavetnyi spisok naselennykh mest Oblasti voiska donskogo* (Novocherkassk: Oblastnaia tipografiia, 1915), table preceding p. 1.

22. A. M. Grekov, "K istorii zemel'nogo voprosa na Donu," *SOVDSK*, vol. 7 (1907): 71–97, here at pp. 95–97; *Statistika zemlevladeniia 1905 g: Svod dannykh.* (St. Petersburg: M. Ia. Minkov, 1907), pp. iv–v, xii–xiii, xlii–xliii, 138, 144, 193–194.

23. GARF, f. 1258, op. 1, d. 81, ll. 138–149.

24. *Donskoi statisticheskii ezhegodnik na 1924* (Rostov: 3-ia gosudarstvennaia tipografiia, 1924), p. 90; also, GARF, f. 1258, op. 1, d. 81, ll. 140, 143–146; M. A. Kushnyrneko-Kushnyrev, *Polozhenie sel'sko-khoziaistvennogo promysla v Oblasti voiska Donskogo* (Novocherkassk: Donskoi pechatnik, 1913), pp. 37–38; D. Iablokov, "Rezul'taty vyborochnogo ucheta zemli v 1922 godu," *Donskoi statisticheskii vestnik*, book 2, nos. 4–6 (1923): 30–39, here at p. 33.

25. GARF, f. 1258, op. 1, d. 81, ll. 143–146; *Litso donskoi derevni k 1925: Po materialam obsledovaniia DKK i DonoRKI* (Rostov-on-Don, 1925), pp. 5–6.

26. F. Kriukov, "O kazakakh," *Russkoe bogatstvo*, no. 4 (1907): 25–47, here at pp. 36, 38; *Trudy mestnykh komitetov o nuzhdakh sel'sko-khoziaistvennoi promyshlennosti* (St. Petersburg: Tip. V. Kirshbauma, 1903), vol. 50, pp. 9, 39, 214, 236, 295, 304, 313, 343, 378.

1. Russia at War

1. Richard Wortman, *Scenarios of Power: Myth and Ceremony in the Russian Monarchy*, 2 vols. (Princeton: Princeton University Press, 1995 and 1999), vol. 2; David McDonald, *Foreign Policy and United Government in Russia* (Cambridge, Mass.: Harvard University Press, 1992).

2. On the rise of these parties, see Terence Emmons, *The Formation of Political Parties and the First National Elections in Russia* (Cambridge, Mass.: Harvard University Press, 1983); on the Kadets, see William Rosenberg, *Liberals in the Russian Revolution: The Constitutional-Democratic Party, 1917–1921* (Princeton: Princeton University Press, 1974), pp. 11–38.

3. Wortman, *Scenarios of Power*, vol. 2; McDonald, *United Government*. For the desacralization of the monarchy, see Orlando Figes and Boris Kolonitskii, *Interpreting the Russian Revolution: The Language and Symbols of 1917* (New Haven: Yale University Press, 1999), chap. 1.

4. Leopold Haimson, "The Problem of Social Stability in Urban Russia, 1905–1917," in *Structure of Russian History*, ed. Michael Cherniavsky (New York: Random House, 1970), argued for "dual polarization"; Wortman, *Scenarios of Power*, suggests the third axis, between Nicholas and his government.

5. Laura Engelstein, *The Keys to Happiness: Sex and the Search for Modernity in Fin-de-Siècle Russia* (Ithaca: Cornell University Press, 1992), pp. 6–8.

6. Leopold Haimson, *The Russian Marxists and the Origins of Bolshevism* (Boston: Beacon Press, 1966), pp. 209–210; Engelstein, *Keys*, pp. 129–130.

7. Leon Trotsky, *The Russian Revolution*, 3 vols. (New York: Simon and Schuster, 1932), 1: 4–6; Laura Engelstein, "Combined Underdevelopment: Discipline and the Law in Imperial and Soviet Russia," *American Historical Review* 92, no. 2 (1993): 338–353, here at p. 343.

8. Trotsky, *The Russian Revolution*, 1: 5.

9. Engelstein, "Combined Underdevelopment," p. 344; also Engelstein, *Keys*, p. 6. For the widespread hostility toward the "bourgeoisie" across the political

spectrum, see Boris Kolonitskii, "Anti-Bourgeois Propaganda and Anti-*'Burzhui'* Consciousness in 1917," *Russian Review* 53, no. 2 (1994): 183–196.

10. B. V. Anan'ich, "Rossiiskaia burzhuaziia na puti k 'kul'turnomu kapitalizmu,'" in *Rossiia i pervaia mirovaia voina*, ed. N. N. Smirnov (St. Petersburg: Dmitrii Bulanin, 1999), esp. p. 111.

11. John Hutchinson, *Politics and Public Health in Revolutionary Russia, 1890–1918* (Baltimore: Johns Hopkins University Press, 1990), pp. xix–xx; Yanni Kotsonis, *Making Peasants Backward: Agricultural Cooperatives and the Agrarian Question in Russia, 1861–1914* (New York: St. Martin's Press, 1999), p. 94.

12. Rosenberg, *Liberals*, pp. 12–32.

13. Geoffrey Hosking, *The Russian Constitutional Experiment: Government and Duma, 1907–1914* (New York: Cambridge University Press, 1979), pp. 182–242; Haimson, "Social Stability," p. 396.

14. Haimson, "Social Stability," p. 369; Bernard Pares, *The Fall of the Russian Monarchy* (New York: Vintage, 1961), p. 118.

15. Raymond Pearson, *Russian Moderates and the Crisis of Tsarism, 1914–1917* (New York: Barnes and Noble, 1977), pp. 10–21.

16. Hosking, *Constitutional Experiment*, pp. 243–246.

17. Alexis Antsiferov et al., *Russian Agriculture during the War* (New Haven: Yale University Press, 1930), pp. 93, 100, 109–110; M. K. Bennett, *Wheat and War, 1914–1918 and Now* (Stanford: Stanford University Press, 1939), charts 2, 8, 9 and Table 3.

18. Peter Gatrell, *The Tsarist Economy, 1850–1917* (London: Batsford, 1986), pp. 98–140. The 1917 agricultural census determined that 99 percent of the 13,127,253 agricultural households in 39 provinces were "of a peasant type" (*Tsentral'nogo statisticheskogo upravleniia*, [hereafter *Trudy Ts. S. U.*], 5, no. 1, p. 42).

19. Nikolai Kondrat'ev, *Rynok khlebov i ego regulirovanie vo vremia voiny i revoliutsii* (Moscow: Nauka, 1991), pp. 94–95.

20. Krivoshein was the head of the Main Administration of Agriculture and Land Improvement (GUZZ), which was reformed into the Ministry of Agriculture on October 26, 1915. For reasons of brevity, however, I employ "Ministry of Agriculture" throughout.

21. RGIA, f. 1276, op. 10, d. 800, ll. 2–3; *Sovet ministrov rossiiskoi imperii v gody pervoi mirovoi voiny: Bumagi A. N. Iakhontova*, ed. B. D. Gal'perna (St. Petersburg: Dmitrii Bulanin, 1999), pp. 26–27, 30, 367 n. 55.

22. Kirill A. Krivoshein, *A. V. Krivoshein: Ego znachenie v istorii Rossii nachala XX veka* (Paris: PUIF, 1973), pp. 221–222; *Osobyi zhurnal soveta ministrov*, 1915, no. 155 (March 6, 1915).

23. Kimitaka Matsuzato, "Obshchestvennaia ssypka i voenno-prodovol'stvennaia sistema," *Acta Slavica Iaponica*, no. 15 (1997): 17–47, here at p. 27.

24. V. I. Gurko, *Cherty i siluety proshlogo: Pravitel'stvo i obshchestvennost' v tsarstvovanie Nikolaia II v izobrazhenii sovremennika* (Moscow: Novoe literaturnoe obozrenie, 2000), pp. 607–611; Krivoshein, *Krivoshein*, pp. 109, 148–150, 175, 222–224, 236; Peter Struve, ed., *Food Supply in Russia during the War* (New Haven: Yale University Press, 1930), pp. 4–5.

25. David A. J. Macey, *Government and Peasant in Russia, 1861–1906: The Prehistory of the Stolypin Reforms* (Dekalb, Ill.: Northern Illinois University Press, 1987), pp. 44–53.

26. Kotsonis, *Peasants,* pp. 48–52, 58, 116–119, 146.

27. Boris V. Anan'ich et al., *Krizis samoderzhaviia, 1895–1917* (Leningrad: Nauka, 1984), pp. 421–428, 443–447. See also Krivoshein, *Krivoshein,* pp. 163–193.

28. Krivoshein, *Krivoshein,* pp. 290–292; also Anan'ich, *Krizis samoderzhaviia,* pp. 443–445.

29. Gurko, *Cherty i siluety,* p. 610; Macey, *Government and Peasant,* pp. 155, 246; Kotsonis, *Peasants,* p. 94.

30. S. Margolin, "Khlebnaia torgovlia, elevatory, i kooperativy," *Vestnik kooperatsii,* no. 1 (1915): 11–20. See also Kotsonis, *Peasants,* pp. 57–93.

31. V. M., "Kooperatsiia i narodnyi uchitel'," *Vestnik kooperatsii,* no. 1 (1915): 20–38, here at pp. 21–22.

32. George Yaney, *The Urge to Mobilize: Agrarian Reform in Russia, 1861–1930* (Urbana, Ill.: University of Illinois Press, 1982), p. 405; Lars Lih, *Bread and Authority in Russia, 1914–1921* (Berkeley: University of California Press, 1990), pp. 7–8.

33. Anan'ich, *Krizis samoderzhaviia,* pp. 421–422, 426, 428, 446; Kotsonis, *Peasants,* pp. 62–68.

34. Krivoshein, *Krivoshein,* p. 208.

35. Kondrat'ev, *Rynok,* p. 187 (emphasis in original); RGIA, f. 1276, op. 10, d. 800, ll. 2–2ob.

36. Lih, *Bread,* p. 8; RGIA, f. 456, op. 1, d. 203, l. 7; V. M., "Kooperatsiia i narodnyi uchitel'," pp. 21–22; for such views in the immediate prewar period, see Kotsonis, *Peasants,* p. 173.

37. George Yaney, *The World of the Manager: Food Administration in Berlin during World War I* (New York: Peter Lang, 1994), p. 35; Niall Ferguson, *The Pity of War: Explaining World War I* (New York: Basic Books, 1999), pp. 257–261; José Harris, "Bureaucrats and Businessmen in British Food Control, 1916–1919," in *War and the State: The Transformation of British Government, 1914–1919,* ed. Kathleen Burk (London: George Allen and Unwin, 1982), here at p. 137.

38. Struve, *Food Supply,* pp. 4–5; Lih, *Bread,* pp. 7–8.

39. A. V. Sypchenko, *Narodno-sotsialisticheskaia partiia v 1907–1917 gg.* (Moscow: ROSSPEN, 1999), pp. 188–189.

40. A. Merkulov, "Kooperativnoe dvizhenie v 1914 godu," *Vestnik kooperatsii,* no. 1 (1915): 59–80, citations at p. 59; Professor A. A. Isaev, "Kooperatsiia v dele vozrozhdeniia russkogo narodnogo khoiaistva," *Vestnik finansov, promyshlennosti, i torgovli,* no. 17 (1916): 163–164. See also Alessandro Stanziani, *L'économie en revolution: le cas russe, 1870–1930* (Paris: A. Michel, 1998), pp. 71–72; and Yaney, *Urge,* pp. 443, 454.

41. Michael Geyer, "The Stigma of Violence, Nationalism and War in Twentieth Century Germany," *German Studies Review,* special issue (1992): 75–110, citation at p. 84.

42. For the argument that wartime mobilization *did* form the "underpinnings of civil society," see Thomas Porter and William Gleason, "Democratization of the Zemstvo during the First World War," in *Emerging Democracy in Late Imperial Russia,* ed. Mary Conroy (Boulder: University Press of Colorado, 1998), p. 239; *contra,* Leopold Haimson, "The Problem of Social Identities in Early Twentieth Century Russia," *Slavic Review* 47, no. 1 (1988): 1–20, here at p. 2.

43. Antsiferov, *Russian Agriculture during the War,* p. 213; Kondrat'ev, *Rynok,* pp. 188–189.

44. Lih, *Bread*, pp. 12–13; Kondrat'ev, *Rynok*, pp. 188–192.

45. Kondrat'ev, *Rynok*, pp. 196, 198–199.

46. Kondrat'ev, *Rynok*, pp. 229–231, 163; for the Don Territory, see RGIA, f. 456, op. 1, d. 203, ll. 6–7, 209.

47. *Reguliruiushchie meropriiatiia pravitel'stvennoi i obshchestvennoi vlasti v khoziaistvennoi zhizni za vremia voiny* (Petrograd: Amerikanskaia skoropechatnaia, 1917), p. 7; for criticism, see Aleksandr Chaianov, *Prodovol'stvennyi vopros* (Moscow: [n.p.], 1917), p. 8.

48. Stanziani, *L'économie*, pp. 154, 156, 157.

49. *Osobye zhurnaly soveta ministrov*, 1915, no. 72 (January 31 and February 3); *Birzhevye vedomosti*, February 6, 1915; Struve, *Food Supply*, p. 7 (War Ministry's support); *Rech'*, February 5 and 6, 1915.

50. Kondrat'ev, *Rynok*, p. 231; *Obzor deiatel'nosti Osobogo Soveshchaniia dlia obsuzhdeniia i ob"edineniia meropriatii po prodovol'stvennomu delu, 17 avg. 1915–17 fev. 1916* (Petrograd: Ekaterininskaia tipografiia, 1916), p. 2.

51. RGIA, f. 457, op. 1, d. 12, ll. 36–36ob.; Kondrat'ev, *Rynok*, pp. 192, 197–199.

52. Kondrat'ev, *Rynok*, pp. 95, 313–314, 328–331.

53. Kondrat'ev, *Rynok*, p. 106; P. Popov, *Proizvodstvo khleba v R.S.F.S.R. (khlebnaia produktsiia)* (Moscow: Godusarstvennoe izdatel'stvo, 1921), p. 16.

54. *Materialy po prodovol'stvennomu planu: Urozhai khlebov v Rossii v 1916 godu* (Petrograd: Ekaterininskaia tipografiia, 1916), p. xi; Kondrat'ev, *Rynok*, cartograms 2 and 3.

55. *Urozhai khlebov v 1916 godu*, pp. 76–77; *Predvaritel'nye itogi vserossiiskoi sel'sko-khoziaistvennoi perepisi 1916 goda*, 3 vols. (Petrograd: [n.p.], 1916), 1:520–525, 628–633; *Trudy Ts. S. U.* 5, no. 1, pp. 42, 48.

56. I. P. Khlystov, *Don v epokhu kapitalizma* (Rostov: Izdatel'stvo rostovskogo universiteta, 1962), pp. 16, 70–77, 110, 237; Kondrat'ev, *Rynok*, pp. 324–335.

57. John Bushnell, *Mutiny amid Repression: Russia's Soldiers in the Revolution of 1905–1906* (Bloomington: Indiana University Press, 1985), pp. 109–111, 194–196.

58. F. Kriukov, "O kazakakh," *Russkoe bogatstvo*, no. 4 (1907): 25–47; Shane O'Rourke, "The Don Cossacks during the 1905 Revolution," *Russian Review* 57, no. 4 (1998): 583–598.

59. Robert McNeal, *Tsar and Cossack, 1855–1914* (New York: St. Martin's Press, 1987), chap. 4; *Prologue to Revolution: Notes of A. N. Iakhontov on the Secret Meetings of the Council of Ministers, 1915*, ed. Michael Cherniavsky (New York: Prentice Hall, 1967), pp. 63, 66, 71.

60. Emmons, *The Formation of Political Parties*, pp. 320–321; McNeal, *Tsar and Cossack*, pp. 129–131.

61. "Proekt vyborov v V gos. dumu," in *Monarkhiia pered krusheniem, 1914–1917*, ed. V. P. Semennikov (Moscow-Leningrad: Gosizdat, 1927), p. 233.

62. "Proekt," p. 233.

63. *Sovet Ministrov*, pp. 139–142.

64. RGIA, f. 456, op. 1, d. 202, ll. 1, 4.

65. RGIA, f. 456, op. 1, d. 206, l. 36; d. 203, l. 221.

66. RGIA, f. 456, op. 1, d. 202, ll. 28, 34, 44, 51–53.

67. RGIA, f. 456, op. 1, d. 202, ll. 98, 104, 109.

68. RGIA, f. 456, op. 1, d. 205, ll. 23–24ob., 26.

69. RGIA, f. 456, op. 1, d. 202, ll. 5, 7; similarly, *Priazovskii krai*, August 12, 1915.

70. RGIA, f. 456, op. 1, d. 205, ll. 182, 187, 211, 234, 270.

71. Norman Stone, *The Eastern Front, 1914–1917* (New York: Penguin, 1998), p. 195; also Haimson, "Social Stability," pp. 372, 396. On these organs, see W. Gleason, "The All-Russian Union of Zemstvos in World War I," in *The Zemstvo in Russian History*, eds. Terry Emmons and Wayne Vucinich (Cambridge, Mass.: Harvard University Press, 1982); Thomas Fallows, "Politics and the War Effort: The Union of Zemstvos and the Organization of Food Supply," *Slavic Review* 37, no. 1 (1978): 70–91; Lewis Siegelbaum, *The Politics of Industrial Mobilization, 1914–1917: A Study of the War-Industries Committees* (New York: St. Martin's, 1983); Peter Gatrell, *A Whole Empire Walking: Refugees in Russia during World War I* (Bloomington: Indiana University Press, 1999).

72. N. G. Dumova, *Kadetskaia partiia v period pervoi mirovoi voiny i fevarl'skoi revoliutsii* (Moscow: Nauka, 1988), pp. 30–32, 34, 37, 51; V. V. Shelokhaev, "Liberaly i massy v gody pervoi mirovoi voiny," in *Politicheskie partii i obshchestvo v Rossii, 1914–1917*, ed. Iu. I. Kir'ianov (Moscow: INION RAN, 2000), pp. 77–78; Sypchenko, *Narodno-Sotsialisticheskaia partiia*, pp. 188, 193, 196; Mark von Hagen, "Discussion," in *Rossiia i pervaia mirovaia voina*, ed. N. N. Smirnov (St. Petersburg: Dmitrii Bulanin, 1999), pp. 447–448.

73. Iakov Bukshpan, *Voenno-khoziaistvennaia politika: Formy i organy regulirovaniia khoziaistva za vremia mirovoi voiny, 1914–1918* (Moscow-Leningrad: Gosizdat, 1929), pp. 377–378; Lih, *Bread*, pp. 16–19.

74. Cherniavsky, ed., *Prologue to Revolution*, pp. 77–84, 87–99, 109–111, esp. pp. 112–117, 143–145; Pearson, *Moderates*, chap. 3.

75. A. N. Naumov, *Iz utselevshikh vospominanii, 1868–1917*, 2 vols. (New York: Russian Printing House, 1955), 2: 364, 484–486.

76. Bukshpan, *Voenno-khoziaistvennaia politika*, pp. 377–378; Struve, *Food Supply*, pp. 10–13; Taisia Kitanina, *Voina, khleb, i revoliutsiia* (Leningrad: Nauka, 1985), pp. 136–149; Richard Pipes, *Struve: Liberal on the Right, 1905–1944* (Cambridge, Mass.: Harvard University Press, 1980), pp. 219–221.

77. Kondrat'ev, *Rynok*, p. 357.

78. Struve, *Food Supply*, p. 375; RGIA, f. 457, op. 1, d. 683, ll. 22–23, 33, 38, 47–48.

79. RGIA, f. 457, op. 1, d. 683, ll. 44, 52, 57–59.

80. RGIA, f. 457, op. 1, d. 683, ll. 79, 81.

81. *Filipp Mironov: 'Tikhii Don' v 1917–1921*, ed. Viktor Danilov (Moscow: "Demokratiia," 1997), pp. 27–28.

82. RGIA, f. 457, op. 1, d. 683, ll. 203–203ob., 206–207.

83. RGIA, f. 457, op. 1, d. 683, ll. 79ob.–80ob.; also ll. 158, 166, 169; *Protokoly tsentral'nogo komiteta konstitutsionno-demokraticheskoi partii*, vol. 3 (1915–1920) (Moscow: ROSSPEN, 1998), p. 350.

84. *Rossiia v mirovoi voine 1914–1918 goda (v tsifrakh)* (Moscow: [n.p.], 1925), p. 21; Stanislas Kohn and Alexander Meyendorff, *The Cost of the War to Russia* (New Haven: Yale University Press, 1932), pp. 13–31.

85. Kondrat'ev, *Rynok*, p. 122; *Russkoe slovo*, July 23, 1916.

86. *Urozhai khlebov v Rossii v 1916 godu*, pp. xii–xiii; *Russkoe slovo*, October 20, 1916; *Ek. Pol.*, 3: 151–156.

87. *Pouezdnye itogi vserossiiskoi sel'skokhoziaistvennoi i pozemel'noi perepisi 1917 g.,* in *Trudy Ts. S. U.,* t. 5, vyp. 2 (Moscow, 1923), p. 33; *Ek. Pol.* 3, doc. 71.

88. Kondrat'ev, *Rynok,* p. 127; Yaney, *Urge,* p. 409; Pavel Volobuev, *Ekonomicheskaia politika Vremennogo pravitel'stva* (Moscow: Izdatel'stvo Akademii Nauk, 1962), pp. 384–387.

89. Struve, *Food Supply,* p. 128.

90. Kondrat'ev, *Rynok,* pp. 136–137; *Reguliruiushchie meropriiatiia,* pp. 1–2.

91. Stone, *Eastern Front,* pp. 205, 297. For complaints about the rail system at the imperial level, see RGIA, f. 457, op. 1, d. 12, ll. 25ob.–26; *Obzor deiatel'nosti,* p. 32. For complaints regarding its functioning on the Don, see RGIA, f. 457, op. 1, d. 684, ll. 46, 165–66, 181; *Russkie vedomosti,* October 9, 1916; *Russkoe slovo,* October 9, 20, 24, 1916.

92. Kimitaka Matsuzato, "Interregional Conflicts and the Collapse of Tsarism," in *Emerging Democracy in Late Imperial Russia.*

93. *Reguliruiushchie meropriiatiia,* p. 44; Lev N. Litoshenko, "Agrarian Policy of Soviet Russia" (unpublished ms., Hoover Institution Archives, Litoshenko collection, box 1), p. 111; *Rossiia v mirovoi voine,* Tables 40–42; Emily Pyle, "Village Social Relations and the Reception of Soldier's Family Aid Policies in Russia, 1912–1921" (Ph.D. dissertation, University of Chicago, 1997).

94. Struve, *Food Supply,* p. xx; also Chaianov, *Prodovol'stvennyi vopros,* p. 18; *Reguliruiushchie meropriiatiia,* pp. 1–2, 44–45; Litoshenko, "Agrarian Policy," pp. 114, 117–119; Kondrat'ev, *Rynok,* p. 132.

95. E. M. H. Lloyd, *Experiments in State Control at the War Office and Ministry of Food* (Oxford: Humphrey Milford, 1924), p. 331; Gerd Hardach, *The First World War, 1914–1918* (Berkeley: University of California Press, 1977), p. 131.

96. Robert Moeller, "Dimensions of Social Conflict in the Great War: The View from the German Countryside," *Central European History* 14, no. 2 (June 1981): 142–168, here at pp. 157–158.

97. Horst Haselsteiner, "The Habsburg Empire in World War I: The Mobilization of Food Supplies," in *East Central European Society in World War I,* ed. Béla Király and Nándor Driwsziger (Boulder, Colo.: Social Science Monographs, 1985), pp. 96–97; Richard Plaschka, Horst Haselsteiner, and Arnold Suppan, *Innere Front: Militärassistenz, Widerstand u. Umsturz in d. Donaumonarchie 1918* (Vienna: Verlag für Geschichte und Politik, 1974), pp. 209–233.

98. For a similar situation in Germany, see Moeller, "Social Conflict," p. 151.

99. Roger Chickering, *Imperial Germany and the Great War, 1914–1918* (Cambridge, England: Cambridge University Press, 1998), pp. 43–45, citation at p. 43. Overall, see Gerald Feldman, *Army, Industry, and Labor in Germany, 1914–1918* (Providence, R.I.: Berg, 1992), pp. 97–116; August Skalweit, *Die deutsche Kriegsernährungswirtschaft* (Stuttgart-Berlin: Deutsche Verlag, 1927), pp. 171–173.

100. Yaney, *World of the Manager,* pp. 24–25, 28.

101. Lloyd, *Experiments in State Control,* p. 365; similarly, p. 367.

102. William H. Beveridge, *British Food Control* (London: Oxford University Press, 1928), pp. 73–74.

103. Harris, "Bureaucrats and Businessmen," p. 142.

104. Pierre Pirot, "Food Supply," in Michel Augé-Laribé and Pierre Pinot, *Agriculture and Food Supply in France during the War* (New Haven: Yale University Press, 1927), pp. 158, 169, 311; Joseph Redlich, *Austrian War Government* (New

Haven: Yale University Press, 1929), pp. 114, 117–118, 123; Hans Loewenfeld-Russ, *Die Regelung der Volksernährung im Kriege* (Vienna: Hölder-Pischler-Tempsky, 1926), pp. 74–84.

105. On government regulation of milling, see Naum Iasnyi, *Opyt regulirovki snabzheniia khlebom* (Petrograd: Anderson i Loitsianskii, 1917), pp. 106–109; Struve, *Food Supply*, pp. 32–34, 83–88; Kitanina, *Voina*, 149–158.

106. Ahmed Emin, *Turkey in the World War* (New Haven: Yale University Press, 1930), pp. 121–124; Feroz Ahmad, "War and Society under the Young Turks, 1908–1918," in *The Modern Middle East: A Reader*, eds. Albert Hourani, Philip Khoury, and Mary Wilson (Berkeley: University of California Press, 1993), pp. 134–138.

107. Kondrat'ev, *Rynok*, pp. 191–192; Lih, *Bread*, pp. 12–13.

108. Lih, *Bread*, pp. 22–24; more generally, see Stanziani, *L'économie*, chap. 7.

109. Kondrat'ev, *Rynok*, p. 170; similarly, pp. 188–189; Struve, *Food Supply*, pp. xv, 89.

110. Lih, *Bread*, p. 24; Kondrat'ev, *Rynok*, p. 250.

111. Anan'ich, *Krizis samoderzhaviia*, pp. 205–210, 468, 601–602; Bukshpan, *Voenno-khoziaistvennaia politika*, p. 117.

112. RGIA, f. 456, op. 1, d. 202, ll. 49–50, 98, 125; d. 203, l. 127; *Priazovskii krai*, March 31, 1915.

113. *Russkoe slovo*, August 27, September, 1, 2, 3, 4, 7, 16, 17, 20, 30, 1916; *Russkie vedomosti*, October 2, 28, November 29, 1916.

114. *Ek. Pol.*, 3:166–167; Kitanina, *Voina*, pp. 172–175; Lih, *Bread*, pp. 24–25.

115. *Russkie vedomosti*, August 27, October 5, 12, 1916; *Vestnik Evropy* 51, no. 8 (August 1916), pp. 328–329.

116. *Russkoe slovo*, September 16–17, 20, 30, 1916; *Russkie vedomosti*, October 2, 28, 1916; *Izvestiia osobogo soveshchaniia po prodovol'stviiu*, no. 29 (November 1916), pp. 2–4.

117. *SOGD*, sozyv 4, sessiia 5 (December 5, 1916), columns 741–762.

118. *SOGD* (December 5, 1916), columns 754–758; (February 14, 1917), column 1281; "Zhurnal no. 144," in *Zhurnaly osobogo soveshchaniia obsuzhdeniia i ob"edineniia meropriiatii po oborone gosudarstva*, 4 vols. in 12, ed. L. G. Beskrovnyi (Moscow: Institut istorii AN SSSR, 1975–1980), 1917, vol. 2: 215–229; *Protokoly tsentral'nogo komiteta Konstitutsionno-demokraticheskoi partii*, vol. 3 (1915–1920), p. 339.

119. As cited in Kitanina, *Voina*, p. 301.

120. Esther Kingston-Mann, *In Search of the True West: Culture, Economics, and Problems of Russian Development* (Princeton: Princeton University Press, 1999), pp. 160–161; Anan'ich, "Rossiiskaia burzhuaziia."

121. Michael Geyer, "The Militarization of Europe," in *Militarization of the Western World*, ed. John Gillis (New Brunswick: Rutgers University Press, 1989).

122. Struve's articles for this period are assembled in *P. B. Struve: Collected Works in Fifteen Volumes*, ed. Richard Pipes, vol. 11 (Ann Arbor: University Microfilms, 1970); Pipes, *Struve: Liberal on the Right*, pp. 219–230.

123. Many of Larin's articles from the war years are republished in Iurii Larin, *Gosudarstvennyi kapitalizm voennogo vremeni v Germanii* (Moscow-Leningrad: Gosudarstvennoe izdatel'stvo, 1928).

124. Naum Jasny, *To Live Long Enough: The Memoirs of Naum Jasny, Scientific*

Analyst (Lawrence, Kans.: University of Kansas Press, 1976), p. 30. Jasny [Iasnyi] was Groman's aide at the time.

125. "Monopolizatsiia khlebnoi torgovli," *Russkoe slovo*, August 30, 1916. For a modified project, not mentioning the grain monopoly but insisting that private trade be subordinated "to the overall state interest," see "Vvedenie," *Izvestiia osobogo soveshchaniia po prodovol'stvennomu delu*, no. 28 (October 10, 1916), pp. 1–4, here at p. 2. On the gestation of this plan, see Bukshpan, *Voenno-khoziaistvennaia politika*, pp. 391–392; Iasnyi, *Opyt regulirovki*, pp. 36–37.

126. Bukshpan, *Voenno-khoziaistvennaia politika*, pp. 391–392, n. 2; Pipes, *Struve: Liberal on the Right*, p. 220.

127. Kitanina, *Voina*, p. 175; Lih, *Bread*, p. 29.

128. Robert Moeller, *German Peasants and Agrarian Politics, 1914–1924: The Rhineland and Westphalia* (Chapel Hill: North Carolina University Press, 1986), chap. 3.

129. Macey, *Government and Peasant*, pp. 62–68; Anan'ich, *Krizis samoderzhaviia*, pp. 615–621.

130. Lih, *Bread*, pp. 48–56; Struve, *Food Supply*, pp. 89–96.

131. *SOGD*, February 14, 1917, columns 1268–1269; similarly, *Zhurnaly osobogo soveshchaniia po oborone gosudarstva*, 1917, vol. 2, p. 221 (no. 144, meeting of February 15, 1917).

132. Kondrat'ev, *Rynok*, p. 203; also Iasnyi, *Opyt regulirovki*, chap. 8.

133. Anan'ich, *Krizis samoderzhaviia*, pp. 609–649; Orlando Figes, *A People's Tragedy: The Russian Revolution, 1891–1924* (New York: Penguin, 1997), chap. 7.

134. Kimitaka Matsuzato, "Prodrazverstka A. A. Rittikha," *Acta Slavica Iaponica* 13 (1995): 165–183, here at p. 173; A. S. Salazkin (Kadet Duma deputy from Riazan', Duma plenipotentiary to the Nizhnii Novgorod conference on food supply) reported in *Russkoe slovo*, October 17, 1916; Karazin (Octobrist Duma deputy from Khar'kov, serving as army grain purchasing commissioner for Khar'kov), *Russkoe slovo*, February 16, 1917.

135. Kitanina, *Voina*, pp. 257–258; E. Iashnov, "Itogi," *Izvestiia po prodovol'stvennomu delu*, no. 1 (32) (May 1917), p. 10; RGIA, f. 457, op. 1, d. 684, ll. 165–166, 180.

136. RGIA, f. 456, op. 1, d. 206, ll. 242, 258.

137. Kondrat'ev, *Rynok*, p. 419.

138. Matsuzato, "Obshchestvennaia ssypka," p. 36.

139. *Russkoe slovo*, July 23, 1916; *Russkoe slovo*, August 20, 1916; *Russkoe slovo*, October 9, 1916.

140. *Priazovksii Krai*, January 11, 1917, February 11, 1917.

141. *Russkoe slovo*, June 17, 1916, June 28, 1916, July 2, 1916, July 6, 1916, July 21, 1916, August 17, 1916; *Russkie vedomosti*, September 2, 1916, all reporting on events in the Don Territory.

142. *Russkoe slovo*, September 23, 1916.

143. *Russkoe slovo*, June 28, 1916, July 24, 1916, September 23, 1916.

144. Lih, *Bread*, p. 53; the citation is to Chaianov, *Prodovol'stvennyi vopros*, p. 22. See also Rosenberg, *Liberals*, pp. 44–45.

145. *Priazovksii Krai*, January 3, 18, 1917; *Russkie vedomosti*, January 19, 25, 1917.

146. RGIA, f. 457, op. 1, d. 684, ll. 197–198; *Priazovskii krai*, February 20, 21, 22, 1917; *Russkoe slovo*, February 28, 1917.

147. Jacques Sapir, "La guerre civile et l'économie de guerre: Origines du système soviétique," *Cahiers du monde russe* 38, no. 1–2 (1997): 9–28.

148. Stone, *Eastern Front*, p. 284; also, pp. 9–11, 15, 208–209.

149. Struve, *Food Supply*, p. xx; similarly, Yaney, *Urge*, p. 424.

150. Geyer, "Militarization of Europe, 1914–1945," pp. 79–80, 75; John Horne, "Mobilizing for Total War, 1914–1918," in *State, Society and Mobilization in Europe during the First World War*, ed. John Horne (Cambridge, England: Cambridge University Press, 1997), pp. 2, 5.

151. Ahmad argues for a similar situation in Turkey ("War and Society," pp. 139–140).

2. *"Radiant Days of Freedom"*

1. Rex Wade, *The Russian Revolution, 1917* (New York: Cambridge University Press, 2000), chaps. 2–3; Orlando Figes, *A People's Tragedy: The Russian Revolution, 1891–1914* (New York: Penguin, 1998), chaps. 8–9.

2. Leopold Haimson, "The Problem of Social Identities in Early Twentieth Century Russia," *Slavic Review* 47, no. 1 (1988): 1–20, here at pp. 3–4.

3. Sergei Sergeevich Luk'ianov, "Revoliutsiia i vlast'," in *Smena vekh: Sbornik statei*, 2nd edition (Prague: Otto Elsner, 1922; original, 1921), p. 72.

4. Sergei Chakhotin, "V Kanossu!" in *Smena vekh*, p. 150. For Chakhotin's role in the wartime parastatal organs and then the Provisional Government, see Chapter 7.

5. "Obiazannost' kazhdogo," *Rech'*, May 3, 1917.

6. V. I. Vernadskii, *Dnevniki, 1917–1921*, 2 vols. (Kiev: Naukova dumka, 1994), 1: 88 (November 10, 1917).

7. Tsuyoshi Hasegawa, *The February Revolution: Petrograd, 1917* (Seattle: University of Washington Press, 1981), chaps. 26–27.

8. William Rosenberg, *Liberals in the Russian Revolution: The Constitutional-Democratic Party, 1917–1921* (Princeton: Princeton University Press, 1974), pp. 52–59, 70–71, 134–136, 234–235; William Rosenberg, "Social Mediation and State Construction(s) in Revolutionary Russia," *Social History* 19, no. 2 (1994): 168–188, here at pp. 174–175.

9. Rosenberg, "Social Mediation"; Ziva Galili, "Commercial-Industrial Circles in Revolution: The Failure of 'Industrial Progressivism,'" in *Revolution in Russia: Reassessments of 1917*, eds. Edith Rogovin, Jonathan Frankel, and Baruch Knei-Paz (Cambridge, England: Cambridge University Press, 1992).

10. L. G. Protasov, *Vserossiiskoe uchreditel'noe sobranie: Istoriia rozhdeniia i gibeli* (Moscow: ROSSPEN, 1997), pp. 42, 135; Rosenberg, *Liberals*, pp. 17–18, 64–65.

11. On "social representation," see Keith Michael Baker, *Inventing the French Revolution* (New York: Cambridge University Press, 1990), pp. 238–250.

12. *Priazovskii krai*, March 1, 2, 1917; GARF, f. 1788, op. 2, d. 95, ll. 3–4; G. Ianov, "Revoliutsiia i donskie kazaki," and K. Kakliugin, "Organizatsiia vlasti na Donu v nachale revoliutsii," in *DL*, 2: 20–32, 63–89.

13. For reasons of clarity in English I have replaced the term "host" [*voisko*] with "Cossack." Rather than "host" [*voisko*], "host administration" [*voiskovoe pravlenie*], and "host government" [*voiskovoe pravitel'stvo*], I employ "corporate Cossack community," "Cossack administration," and "Cossack government," respectively.

14. Robert McNeal, *Tsar and Cossack, 1855–1914* (New York: St. Martin's, 1987), pp. 143–153.

15. GARF, f. 1783, op. 6, d. 41, ll. 10–14; *Priazovskii krai*, March 5, 1917.

16. Aleksandr Kozlov, *Na istoricheskom povorote* (Rostov: Izdatel'stvo rostovskogo universiteta, 1977), p. 201.

17. *Priazovskii krai*, March 4, 1917; *Russkoe slovo*, March 3, 1917.

18. HIA WMA, box 38, item 23, pp. 1–11; V. N. Sergeev, *Bankrotstvo melkoburzhuaznykh partii na Donu* (Rostov: Izdatel'stvo rostovskogo universiteta, 1979), p. 43.

19. See Chapter 1. On the war's impact on state structures, see Daniel Orlovsky, "Professionalism in the Ministerial Bureaucracy," in *Russia's Missing Middle Class*, ed. Harvey Balzer (Armonk, N.Y.: M. E. Sharpe, 1996).

20. Charles Maier, "Between Taylorism and Technocracy," *Journal of Contemporary History* 5, no. 2 (1970): 27–61. For Russia, see Alessandro Stanziani, *L'économie en revolution: le cas russe, 1870–1930* (Paris: A. Michel, 1998), chap. 7; and Rosenberg, "Social Mediation."

21. Stanziani, *L'économie*, chap. 8.

22. GARF, f. 1788, op. 2, d. 95, ll. 4–5.

23. GARF, f. 1788, op. 2, d. 95, ll. 4, 6; Ianov, "Revoliutsiia i donskie kazaki," *DL*, 2: 24; Kakliugin, "Organizatsiia," *DL*, 2: 82.

24. Kakliugin, "Organizatsiia," *DL*, 2: 82.

25. Kakliugin, "Organizatsiia," *DL*, 2: 80–82; G. P. Ianov, "Revoliutsiia i donskie kazaki," *DL*, 2: 33.

26. *RPG*, 1: 243.

27. Sergeev, *Bankrotstvo*, p. 22.

28. Daniel Orlovsky, "Reform during Revolution: Governing the Provinces in 1917," in *Reform in Russia and the USSR: Past and Prospects*, ed. Robert Crummey (Urbana, Ill.: University of Illinois Press, 1989).

29. "Organizatsiia prodovol'stvennogo dela," *Rech'*, March 8, 1917; *Izvestiia donskogo prodovol'stvennogo komiteta*, no. 1 (May 5, 1917), p. 10; *Zhurnaly zasedanii vremennogo pravitel'stva* (Petrograd, 1917), no. 11 (March 8, 1917), point 12b.

30. For example, neither Sergeev, *Bankrotstvo*, nor Iu. K. Kirienko, *Revoliutsiia i donskoe kazachestvo* (Rostov: Izdatel'stvo rostovskogo universiteta, 1988), discusses Voronkov's activity in food supply.

31. William Sewell, "Ideologies and Social Revolutions," *Journal of Modern History* 57, no. 1 (1985): 57–85, here at p. 77.

32. Keith Michael Baker, "Introduction," in Baker, ed., *The Political Culture of the Old Regime* (New York: Pergamon Press, 1987), p. xiii.

33. Haimson, "Problem of Social Identities," p. 5.

34. GARO, f. 863, op. 1, d. 25, l. 28.

35. G. A. Gerasimenko, "Obshchestvennye ispolnitel'nye komitety v revoliutsii 1917 g.," in *Fevralskaia revoliutsiia: ot novykh istochnikov k novomu osmysleniiu*, ed. P. V. Volobuev (Moscow: RAN, 1997); Orlovsky, "Reform during Revolution"; V. Buldakov, *Krasnaia smuta: Priroda i posledstviia revoliutsionnogo nasiliia* (Moscow: ROSSPEN, 1997), pp. 178–181.

36. Sergeev, *Bankrotstvo*, pp. 15, 17, 20, 23.

37. As asserted in Gerasimenko, "Obshchestvennye ispolnitel'nye komitety," and Buldakov, *Krasnaia smuta*, p. 178.

38. GARF, f. 1788, op. 2, d. 95, l. 33; GARO, f. 863, op. 1, d. 25, ll. 7, 16, 23, 28.

39. RGIA, f. 1278, op. 5, d. 1307, ll. 53, 41, 5; GARO, f. 863, op. 1, d. 25, l. 43; GARO, f. 863, op. 1, d. 12, l. 92; GARO, f. 863, op. 1, d. 7, ll. 110–111; GARO, f. 863, op. 1, d. 4, l. 18.

40. Rosenberg, "Social Mediation," pp. 174–176. For this sentiment in the Don Territory, see GARO, f. 863, op. 1, d. 28, l. 9.

41. Orlovsky, "Reform during Revolution," p. 106.

42. "Instructions," *RPG*, 1: 243. See also the Provisional Government's March 25 directives for establishing local food-supply committees, which similarly sought to legislate how "society" was to be represented (*RPG*, 2: 620).

43. RGIA, f. 1278, op. 5, d. 1307, ll. 2, 88, 16, 64, 56, 59, 65.

44. Baker, *Inventing*, pp. 240–243.

45. GARO, f. 863, op. 1, d. 12, l. 92.

46. GARO, f. 863, op. 1, d. 12, ll. 38–42.

47. "The Organization of Volost Committees," *RPG*, 1: 244.

48. GARO, f. 863, op. 1, d. 4, l. 40.

49. GARO, f. 863, op. 1, d. 12, l. 37.

50. For example, GARO, f. 863, op. 1, d. 144, l. 110.

51. Bakhmeteff archive (Columbia University), N. M. Mel'nikov collection, box 3, V. M. Kuznetsov, "Biograficheskie svedeniia o . . . Nikolae Mel'nikove," pp. 1–3.

52. RGIA, f. 1278, op. 5, d. 1307, ll. 11–12; N. M. Mel'nikov, "Chto proiskhodilo v Nizhne-Chirskoi," *Rodimyi Krai* (Paris), no. 37 (1961): 11–16.

53. GARF, f. 1788, op. 2, d. 95, l. 14.

54. RGIA, f. 1278, op. 5, d. 1307, ll. 18–19, 35, 37, 39. 49.

55. RGIA, f. 1278, op. 5, d. 1307, ll. 58, 66; GARF, f. 1788, op. 2, d. 95, l. 16.

56. Orlovsky, "Reform during Revolution," describes similar sentiments throughout the rest of Russia.

57. GARO, f. 863, op. 1, d. 25, l. 74.

58. Kakliugin, "Organizatsiia," *DL*, 2: 86.

59. GARO, f. 864, op. 1, d. 10, l. 82; GARO, f. 863, op. 1, d. 4, l. 40.

60. V. N. Sergeev, *Sovety Dona v 1917 godu* (Rostov: Izdatel'stvo rostovskogo universiteta, 1987), appendix.

61. See also Donald Raleigh, *Revolution on the Volga: 1917 in Saratov* (Ithaca: Cornell University Press, 1986), p. 75.

62. Orlovsky, "Reform during Revolution," pp. 108–109; Sergeev, *Sovety*, pp. 127–128.

63. GARO, f. 864, op. 1, d. 10, l. 83.

64. GARF, f. 1788, op. 2, d. 95, l. 14.

65. For example, Sergeev, *Sovety* and *Bankrotstvo*, and Kirienko, *Revoliutsiia*; Peter Kenez, *Civil War in South Russia, 1918* (Berkeley: University of California Press, 1971), pp. 37–44.

66. McNeal, *Tsar and Cossack*, pp. 127–153, 219–223.

67. A. M. Grekov, "K istorii zemel'nogo voprosa na Donu," *SOVDSK*, vol. 7 (1907), pp. 88–89; F. Kriukov, "O kazakakh," *Russkoe bogatstvo*, no. 4 (1907): 25–47, here at pp. 36–38.

68. John Bushnell, *Mutiny amid Repression: Russia's Soldiers in the Revolution of*

1905–1906 (Bloomington: Indiana University Press, 1985), pp. 109–111, 194–196; Shane O'Rourke, "The Don Cossacks during the 1905 Revolution," *Russian Review* 57, no. 4 (1998): 583–598; S. Ia. [Arefin], "Donskie kazaki," *Russkoe bogatstvo,* no. 12 (1906); F. Kriukov, "O kazakakh," pp. 36–38.

69. Hubertus Jahn, *Patriotic Culture in Russia during World War I* (Ithaca: Cornell University Press, 1995), pp. 23–24, 160.

70. On the promotion of rank-and-file Cossacks to officer positions during the First World War, see Kozlov, *Na istoricheskom povorote,* p. 125, and Ivan M. Kalinin, *Pod znamenem Vrangelia* (Rostov: Rostovskoe knizhnoe izdatel'stvo, 1991), p. 17.

71. "The Abolition of Estates and Ranks" (May 9, 1917), in *RPG,* 1: 210–211.

72. GARF, f. 1791, op. 6, d. 401, ll. 58–72, 117–130; GARF, f. 9505, op. 2, d. 10. See also General Basil Gurko, *Memories and Impressions of War and Revolution in Russia, 1914–1917* (London: John Murray, 1918), p. 315.

73. GARO, f. 856, op. 1, d. 75, l. 63; I. N. Oprits, *Leib-gvardii kazachii ego Velichestva polk v gody revoliutsii i grazhdanskoi voiny* (Paris: Izd. V. Siial'skogo, 1939), p. 16.

74. Ianov, "Revoliutsiia i donskie kazaki," *DL,* 2: 33–35.

75. "Reorganization of the Civil Administration of the Cossacks," *RPG,* 2: 868–869.

76. GARO f. 863, op. 1, d. 4, l. 21; Kakliugin, "Organizatsiia," *DL,* 2: 82, 89.

77. Telegram reprinted in Kakliugin, "Organizatsiia," *DL,* 2: 82.

78. Gregory Tschebotarioff, *Russia: My Native Land* (New York: McGraw-Hill, 1964), p. 98. On the emergence of national and ethnic units in the Russian Army in 1917, see M. Frenkin, *Russkaia armiia i revoliutsiia, 1917–1918* (Munich: Logos, 1978), chap. 4.

79. Oprits, *Leib-gvardii kazachii polk,* pp. 22–23; also Kirienko, *Revoliutsiia,* p. 24.

80. *Ust'-Medveditskaia gazeta,* June 8, 1917 (on an event of early May).

81. GARO, f. 863, op. 1, d. 4, ll. 7, 10–11.

82. A. N. Grekov, "Soiuz kazach'ikh voisk v Petrograde," *DL,* 2: 229–283, here at pp. 229–230; Iu. Kirienko, *Revoliutsiia,* pp. 27–34.

83. Bakhmeteff archive (Columbia University), N. M. Mel'nikov collection, box 3, N. M. Mel'nikov, ed., "Mitrofan Bogaevskii," appendix; K. P. Kakliugin, "M. P. Bogaevskii: kharakteristika," and A. P. Bogaevskii, "Detstvo i iunost'," in *DL,* 1: 43–60 and 2: 200–205, quote at p. 201.

84. GARO, f. 863, op. 1, d. 144, ll. 73–4; similarly, GARO, f. 864, op. 1, d. 10, l. 163.

85. GARO, f. 864, op. 1, d. 10, l. 163.

86. GARO, f. 864, op. 1, d. 10, l. 137.

87. *Postanovleniia voiskovogo kazach'ego s"ezda voiska Donskogo* (Novocherkassk: Oblastnaia voiska donskogo tipografiia, 1917); GARO f. 861, op. 1, d. 3, ll. 43–50.

88. *Postanovleniia kazach'ego s"ezda,* pp. 4–6, 11–13; GARO, f. 863, op. 1, d. 31, l. 8.

89. *Postanovleniia kazach'ego s"ezda,* pp. 2–4.

90. On the host circle as institution and ideal, see S. G. Svatikov, "Donskoi voiskovoi krug," *DL,* 1: 169–265.

91. *Postanovleniia kazach'ego s"ezda,* pp. 5–6, 14.

92. *Voiskovoi krug na Donu, 8–20 dekabria 1909 goda: voiskovoe soveshchatel'noe*

sobranie (Rostov-on-Don: Donskaia rech', 1910); McNeal, *Tsar and Cossack*, pp. 141–143.

93. Wade, *Russian Revolution*, pp. 80–86.

94. *Ust'-Medveditskaia gazeta*, May 25, 1917.

95. GARO, f. 864, op. 1, d. 13, ll. 15, 37, 65, 76, 91; GARO, f. 861, op. 1, d. 30, ll. 8, 10, 24, 29, 31, 40, 42, 45, 53, 64, 69, 74.

96. For example, the delegates from Veshenskaia: GARO, f. 864, op. 1, d. 13, l. 76.

97. On a similar profile of Cossack electors in elections to the First Duma in early 1906, see Terence Emmons, *The Formation of Political Parties and the First National Elections in Russia* (Cambridge, Mass.: Harvard University Press, 1983), p. 175.

98. Semen Nomikosov, *Statisticheskoe opisanie oblasti voiska Donskogo* (Novocherkassk: Oblastnoe pravlenie Voiska Donskogo, 1884), pp. 15, 40–43, 298–300; *Ocherki geografii vsevelikogo voiska Donskogo* (Novocherkassk: Izdatel'stvo otdela narodnogo prosveshcheniia, 1919), pp. 256–262.

99. On concentration of nobles in the lower districts, see V. V. Lobachevskii, *Voenno-statisticheskoe opisanie oblasti voiska Donskogo* (Novocherkassk: Oblastnaia v. D. tipografiia, 1908), p. 322; for complaints that Novocherkassk ignored the needs of the northern districts, see *Trudy mestnykh komitetov o nuzhdakh sel'sko-khoziaistvennoi promyshlennosti* (St. Petersburg: Tip. V. Kirshbauma, 1903), vol. 50, p. 313.

100. Emmons, *Formation*, p. 321.

101. Kakliugin, "Organizatsiia," *DL*, 2: 97–98.

102. *Ust'-Medveditskaia gazeta*, no. 25 (June 23, 1917).

103. *Postanovleniia donskogo voiskovogo kruga—pervyi sozyv* (Novocherkassk: Oblastnaia tipografiia, 1917); GARO, f. 861, op. 1, d. 3, ll. 28–42. Also, Kirienko, *Revoliutsiia*, pp. 50–62; N. M. Mel'nikov, "A. M. Kaledin," and Kakliugin, "Organizatsiia," *DL*, 1: 15–19, 97–107.

104. N. M. Mel'nikov, "A. M. Kaledin," *DL*, 1: 18–19.

105. Anton Denikin, *Ocherki russkoi smuty*, 5 vols. (Moscow: Nauka, 1991), vol. 1, part 2: 9.

106. Gurko, *Memories and Impressions*, pp. 315–316.

107. Mel'nikov, "Kaledin," *DL*, 1: 18; vote figures in Kirienko, *Revoliutsiia*, p. 59.

108. *Postanovleniia kruga—pervyi sozyv*, p. 4; Kakliugin, "Organizatsiia," *DL*, 2: 112.

109. *Priazovskii krai*, June 14, 1917; Sergeev, *Bankrotstvo*, pp. 36–37.

110. Sergeev, *Sovety*, p. 141; GARO, f. 863, op. 1, d. 144, l. 89.

111. *Postanovleniia kruga—pervyi sozyv*, pp. 4–5; *Priazovskii krai*, June 14, 1917; Sergeev, *Bankrotstvo*, p. 36.

112. *Statistika zemlevladeniia 1905 g.: Svod dannykh* (St. Petersburg: M. Ia. Minkov, 1907), p. 138.

113. *Postanovleniia kruga—pervyi sozyv*, pp. 24–25.

114. GARF, f. 1258, op. 1, d. 81, ll. 140, 143–146; *Litso donskoi derevni k 1925: Po materialam obsledovaniia DKK i DonoRKI* (Rostov-on-Don, 1925), pp. 5–6.

115. GARF, f. 1791, op. 2, d. 181, ll. 11–12, 31–32, 34–34ob., 35; ibid., d. 153b, ll. 80–80ob; GARO, f. 863, op. 1, d. 16, ll. 33–35, 43–45, 155.

116. GARO, f. 864, op. 1, d. 10, l. 236; similarly, GARO, f. 863, op. 1, d. 16, ll. 8a, 57–58, 63, 68–69.

117. McNeal, *Tsar and Cossack*, chap. 4; N. Borodin, "Zemel'nyi vopros na Donu," *Russkaia mysl'*, no. 7 (1907): 108–117.

118. GARO, f. 864, op. 1, d. 16, l. 19; analogous and nearly identically worded resolutions: ibid., ll. 26, 27, 29, 31, 39; GARO, f. 861, op. 1, d. 19, ll. 8, 61; resolutions from military units, GARO, f. 864, op. 1, d. 16, ll. 26, 34, 37.

119. *Ust'-Medveditskaia gazeta*, June 1, 1917.

120. Iu. D. Grazhdanov, *Vsevelikoe voisko donskoe v 1918 godu* (Volgograd: VAGS, 1997), p. 119; Kirienko, *Revoliutsiia*, p. 242. In Veshenskaia, votes for the Cossack slate in October were three times the number of votes for delegates to the First Circle.

121. GARO, f. 863, op. 1, d. 31, l. 8; ibid., d. 5, ll. 5–7; GARO, f. 864, op. 1, d. 4, l. 163.

122. *Novyi put'* (Rostov), 1917, no. 9/10: 31.

123. GARF, f. 1255, op. 1, d. 8, l. 38.

124. Kirienko, *Revoliutsiia*, p. 26; Frenkin, *Russkaia armiia*, p. 408.

125. Sergeev, *Sovety*, pp. 141–142; Mel'nikov, "Chto proiskhodilo v Nizhne-Chirskoi," pp. 15–16. For similar developments elsewhere, see *Ust'-Medveditskaia gazeta*, June 25, 1917, July 2, 1917; TsDNIRO, f. 12, op. 3, d. 1370, l. 3.

126. Mel'nikov, "Chto proiskhodilo v Nizhne-Chirskoi," pp. 15–16; Kuznetsov, "Biograficheskie svedeniia," pp. 2–3.

3. Persuasion and Force

1. Rex Wade, *The Russian Revolution, 1917* (New York: Cambridge University Press, 2000), chap. 7.

2. *Priazovskii krai*, July 21, 1917.

3. *Priazovskii krai*, June 24, 1917; similarly, GARO, f. 863, op. 1, d. 31, l. 8.

4. GARF, f. 1788, op. 2, d. 95, l. 77; K. P. Kakliugin, "Organizatsiia vlasti na Donu v nachale revoliutsii," in *DL*, 2: 84. The government in fact generally failed to fund civic organizations (GARF, f. 1788, op. 2, d. 178, ll. 132–133ob.).

5. *Priazovskii krai*, June 24, July 21, September 20, 1917.

6. GARF, f. 1788, op. 2, d. 95, ll. 27, 28, 29, 35; GARF, f. 9505, op. 2, d. 4, l. 209 (quote).

7. GARF f. 1788, op. 2, d. 184, l. 24.

8. GARF, f. 1788, op. 2, d. 95, ll. 52–56, 73, 73ob.

9. Alexander Rabinowitch, *The Petrograd Bolsheviks and the July 1917 Uprising* (Bloomington, Ind.: Indiana University Press, 1967); Iu. K. Kirienko, *Revoliutsiia i donskoe kazachestvo* (Rostov: Izdatel'stvo rostovskogo universiteta, 1988), pp. 83–96.

10. GARF, f. 9505, op. 2, d. 10, ll. 5, 10, 29, 56, 58–59, 62–63. While these "maps of political meteorology," compiled on the basis of clippings from the centrist press, give a good idea of the government's sense of its support, they poorly reflect its actual levels.

11. *Priazovskii krai*, July 8, 1917.

12. V. N. Sergeev, *Sovety Dona v 1917 godu* (Rostov: Izdatel'stvo rostovskogo universiteta, 1987), pp. 142–143.

13. GARF, f. 1788, op. 2, d. 95, ll. 87–88.

14. *Priazovskii krai,* August 5, 1917.

15. GARO, f. 863, op. 1, d. 16, ll. 8a, 33, 35, 43–44, 57–58, 63, 68–69, 122, 152, 155.

16. GARO, f. 864, op. 1, d. 10, l. 236; GARO, f. 863, op. 1, d. 144, ll. 33–34.

17. GARF, f. 1255, op. 1, d. 92, ll. 27, 61; *Priazovskii krai,* August 4, 1917; GARF, f. 1788, op. 2, d. 95, ll. 52–56.

18. GARO, f. 863, op. 1, d. 144, l. 34; William Rosenberg, *Liberals in the Russian Revolution: The Constitutional Democratic Party, 1917–1921* (Princeton: Princeton University Press, 1974), pp. 205–207.

19. Sergeev, *Sovety,* chap. 3.

20. *Priazovskii krai,* August 27, 1917; Kakliugin, "Organizatsiia vlasti," *DL,* 2: 102–103; *RPG,* 1: 311.

21. Ia. N. Raienko, *Khronika istoricheskikh sobytii na Donu, Kubani i Chernomor'e,* vol. 1, March 1917–March 1918 (Rostov, 1939), pp. 55, 62.

22. *Bor'ba za vlast' sovetov na Donu, 1917–1920,* ed. I. M. Borokhova (Rostov: Rostovskoe knizhnoe izdatel'stvo, 1957), pp. 67–69, 82–86; V. N. Sergeev, *Bankrotstvo melkoburzhuaznykh partii na Donu* (Rostov: Izdatel'stvo rostovskogo universiteta, 1979), p. 43.

23. GARO, f. 863, op. 1, d. 144, ll. 73–75, 76.

24. *Ust'-Medveditskaia gazeta,* August 27, 1917.

25. TsDNIRO, f. 12, op. 33, d. 118, l. 3; ibid., d. 1074, l. 2.

26. GARO, f. 861, op. 1, d. 13, l. 33.

27. GARO, f. 863, op. 1, d. 15, ll. 8–9, 18; ibid., d. 40, ll. 21–22, 29.

28. GARO, f. 863, op. 1, d. 31, l. 8; Sergeev, *Bankrotstvo,* p. 53 (citation).

29. GARO, f. 863, op. 1, d. 194, l. 1.

30. Cited in Sergeev, *Sovety,* p. 141.

31. GARF, f. 1788, op. 2, d. 95, l. 8, responding to the September 23 query from the Ministry of Internal Affairs (GARF, f. 1788, op. 2, d. 95, ll. 73, 73ob.).

32. October 7, 1917, circular, reprinted in *Krest'ianskoe dvizhenie v 1917 godu,* eds. K. G. Kotel'nikov and V. L. Meller (Moscow-Leningrad: Gosudarstvennoe izdatel'stvo, 1927), pp. 422–423; translated in *RPG,* 3: 1649.

33. Anton Denikin, *Ocherki russkoi smuty,* 5 vols. (Moscow: Nauka, 1991), vol. 1, part 2: 118–119.

34. Kirienko, *Revoliutsiia,* pp. 88–90.

35. *Rech',* May 24, 1917.

36. *Protokoly tsentral'nogo komiteta k.-d. partii, 1915–1920,* vol. 3, book 1 (1915–1920), ed. O. N. Lezhneva (Moscow: ROSSPEN, 1998), pp. 394–395; *S"ezdy i konferentsii konstitutsionno-demokraticheskoi partii, 1915–1917,* ed. O. N. Lezhneva (Moscow: ROSSPEN, 2000), p. 748.

37. L. G. Protasov, *Vserossiiskoe uchreditel'noe sobranie: Istoriia rozhdeniia i gibeli* (Moscow: ROSSPEN, 1997), pp. 133–135.

38. Rosenberg, *Liberals,* pp. 205–206, 214; *Rech',* August 4, 1917.

39. *Priazovskii krai,* August 5, 6, 1917.

40. *Ust'-Medveditskaia gazeta,* August 13–18, 1917.

41. *Rech',* August 5, 8, 10, 1917; GARO, f. 861, op. 1, d. 5, ll. 6–13; Kirienko, *Revoliutsiia,* pp. 114–119.

42. N. M. Mel'nikov, "A. M. Kaledin," *DL,* 1: 24–25.

43. Iakov Iakovlev, ed., *Gosudarstvennoe soveshchanie* (Moscow: Gosudarst-

vennoe izdatel'stvo, 1930), pp. 73–77; portions of Kaledin's speech can be found in *RPG*, 3: 1478–1480.

44. Pavel Miliukov, *Istoriia vtoroi russkoi revoliutsii*, 3 vols. (Sofia: Rossiisko-bolgarskoe izdatel'stvo, 1921–1924), 2: 138, 140.

45. For example, the speech of Nagaev, Cossack delegate from the Caucasus front (*Gosudarstvennoe soveshchanie*, pp. 288–291).

46. *Ust'-Medveditskaia gazeta*, August 13, 23, 1917; Ianov, "Revoliutsiia," *DL*, 2: 15; Kakliugin, "Voiskovoi Ataman Kaledin," *DL*, 2: 123.

47. Kirienko, *Revoliutsiia*, pp. 126–128.

48. Orlando Figes, *A People's Tragedy: The Russian Revolution, 1891–1924* (New York: Viking, 1997), pp. 438–455.

49. *RPG*, 3: 1573; *DL*, 2: 297–298.

50. *Revoliutsionnoe dvizhenie v Rossii v avguste 1917*, ed. D. A. Chugaev (Moscow: Izdatel'stvo Akademii Nauk SSSR, 1959), pp. 447, 462, 469.

51. The degree of Kaledin's actual knowledge is a point of dispute: see Miliukov, *Istoriia vtoroi russkoi revoliutsii*, 2: 272–273; Kirienko, *Revoliutsiia*, pp. 143–152; *RPG*, 3: 1584–1585.

52. Kirienko, *Revoliutsiia*, pp. 143–145.

53. Kakliugin, "Voiskovoi Ataman Kaledin," *DL*, 2: 134.

54. Miliukov, *Istoriia vtoroi russkoi revoliutsii*, 2: 272.

55. *Bor'ba za sovetskuiu vlast' v voronezhskoi gubernii, 1917–1918*, ed. M. G. Chechuro et al. (Voronezh: Voronezhskoe knizhnoe izdatel'stvo, 1957), pp. 135, 138, 140–141; *Revoliutsionnoe dvizhenie v Rossii v avguste 1917*, pp. 462–464.

56. RGVIA, f. 366, op. 2, d. 28, ll. 365–366, 367, 369–371; Kirienko, *Revoliutsiia*, p. 149.

57. I. N. Oprits, *Leib-gvardii kazachii ego Velichestva polk v gody revoliutsii i grazhdanskoi voiny* (Paris: Izd. V. Siial'skogo, 1939), p. 43; similarly, M. Frenkin, *Russkaia armiia i revoliutsiia, 1917–1918* (Munich: Logos, 1978), p. 431; *Revoliutsionnoe dvizhenie v Rossii v avguste 1917*, p. 535.

58. *Ust'-Medveditskaia gazeta*, September 6, 8, 1917.

59. GARF, f. 1788, op. 2, d. 95, l. 54.

60. *Postanovleniia vtorogo bol'shogo voiskovogo kruga, 5–14 sentiabria 1917* (Novocherkassk: Oblastnaia tipografiia, 1917), in GARO, f. 861, op. 1, d. 5, ll. 1–5; also Kakliugin, "Voiskovoi Ataman Kaledin," *DL*, 2: 138–145.

61. *Priazovskii krai*, September 13, 1917.

62. GARF, f. 1788, op. 2, d. 95, ll. 87–88.

63. *Postanovleniia vtorogo kruga*, p. 12; *Russkie vedomosti*, September 17, 1917; Kirienko, *Revoliutsiia*, p. 171.

64. *Russkie vedomosti*, September 17, 1917; *Postanovleniia vtorogo kruga*, p. 13.

65. GARF, f. 1255, op. 1, d. 92, l. 58.

66. *SOGD* (December 5, 1916), columns 754–758 (Voronkov); Iakov Bukshpan, editorial in *Izvestiia po prodovol'stvennomu delu*, May 27, 1917, p. 1; Aleksandr Chaianov, *Prodovol'stvennyi vopros* (Moscow: [n.p.], 1917), pp. 15, 20.

67. *Zhurnaly zasedanii Vremennogo pravitel'stva*, no. 4 (March 4, 1917); no. 5 (March 5, 1917).

68. *Russkoe slovo*, May 4, 1917; *Izvestiia po prodovol'stvennomu delu*, no. 1 (32), May 1917, p. 32.

69. "Iz protokola," *Izvestiia DOPK*, no. 1 (May 5, 1917), pp. 7–10; *Novyi Put'*, no. 3–4 (1917), p. 16; GARF, f. 1783, op. 6, d. 41, ll. 4–5.

70. "Organizatsiia prodovol'stvennogo dela," *Rech'*, March 8, 1917.

71. *Zhurnaly zasedanii vremennogo pravitel'stva* (Petrograd, 1917), no. 11 (March 8, 1917), point 12b. For those provinces with zemstvos, the chairmen of provincial zemstvo boards became government commissars. At this meeting the government appointed commissars to both Siberia and the Don, areas lacking zemstvos.

72. GARF, f. 1783, op. 6, d. 42, l. 14ob.

73. Iakov Bukshpan, *Voenno-khoziaistvennaia politika: Formy i organy regulirovaniia khoziaistva za vremia mirovoi voiny, 1914–1918* (Moscow-Leningrad: Gosizdat, 1929), pp. 148, 509; Naum Jasny, *To Live Long Enough: The Memoirs of Naum Jasny, Scientific Analyst* (Lawrence: University of Kansas Press, 1976), p. 29; *Otchet o vserossiiskom prodovol'stvennom s"ezde v Moskve, 20–26 maia 1917 goda*, vol. 2 (Moscow: Mosk. gorodskoi prodovol'stvennyi komitet, 1617 [*sic*]), p. 19 (Peshekhonov's speech). Some members of the Provisional Government opposed this measure (Pavel Volobuev, *Ekonomicheskaia politika Vremennogo pravitel'stva* [Moscow: Izdatel'stvo Akademii Nauk, 1962], pp. 393–396), but all members of the food-supply commission regarded it as a self-evident necessity.

74. Bukshpan, *Voenno-khoziaistvennaia politika*, pp. 148, 509. For a Provisional Government study of German and Austrian food-supply measures, see GARF, f. 1783, op. 6, d. 166, ll. 1–6.

75. Decree found in *Izvestiia po prodovol'stvennomu delu*, no. 1 (32); for an edited version in English, see *RPG*, 2: 618–621. On this measure, see Lars Lih, *Bread and Authority in Russia, 1914–1921* (Berkeley: University of California Press, 1990), pp. 58–66.

76. Chaianov, *Prodovol'stvennyi vopros*, p. 34.

77. Peter Struve, ed., *Food Supply in Russia during the War* (New Haven: Yale University Press, 1930), p. 106; Nikolai Kondrat'ev, *Rynok khlebov i ego regulirovanie vo vremia voiny i revoliutsii* (Moscow: Nauka, 1991), p. 59.

78. Kondrat'ev, *Rynok*, pp. 222, 186. For the Bolsheviks' later policies, see Chapter 8.

79. *Izvestiia po prodovol'stvennomu delu*, 1 (32); Volobuev, *Ekonomicheskaia politika*, pp. 393–394; *Otchet o vserossiiskoom prodovol'stvennom s"ezde*.

80. *Izvestiia DOPK*, 2 (1917): 12; *Izvestiia DOPK*, 1 (1917): 10–18.

81. "Enlistment of Cooperatives . . . in the Work of Purveying Grain and Fodder," *RPG*, 2: 626; also "Doklad 'O poriadke sbora . . .'" (ca. April 18–May 5), *Ek. Pol.*, 3: 191–195. For opposition to involving the private trade apparatus, see *Izvestiia po prodovol'stvennomu delu*, no. 1 (32) (1917): 93–94; Volobuev, *Ekonomicheskaia politika*, p. 425; Lih, *Bread*, pp. 58–66.

82. *Russkoe slovo*, April 11, 1917; *Ek. Pol.*, 3: 191–195; *Izvestiia po prodovol'stvennomu delu*, 1 (32), pp. 63–64; *Priazovskii krai*, May 18, 1917; *Vestnik vremennogo pravitel'stva*, May 20, 21, 1917.

83. *Rech'*, May 24, 1917; *Vestnik vremennogo pravitel'stva*, May 19, 20, 21, 1917; *Priazovskii krai*, May 18, 1917.

84. *Priazovskii krai*, May 18, 1917.

85. "Rech' ministra zemledeliia," *Izvestiia po prodovol'stvennomu delu*, no. 1 (32) (1917), p. 65.

86. *Vestnik vremennogo pravitel'stva*, May 19, 21, 1917; *Priazovskii krai*, May 18, 1917.

87. *Izvestiia po prodovol'stvennomu delu*, no. 1 (32) (May 1917), Official Section,

p. 54; Kondrat'ev, *Rynok,* pp. 213–214; G. G. Shvittau, *Revoliutsiia i narodnoe khoziaistvo v Rossii (1917–1921)* (Leipzig: Tsentral'noe kooperativnoe izdatel'stvo, 1922), pp. 112–113. Chaianov's lectures were published as the pamphlet *Prodovol'stvennyi vopros.*

88. *Sistematicheskii sbornik dekretov i rasporiazhenii pravitel'stva po prodovol'stvennomu delu,* 4 vols. (Nizhnii Novgorod–Moscow: Narkomprod, 1919–1920), 1: 18–25; GARF, f. 1783, op. 6, d. 162, ll. 1–5.

89. *Izvestiia DOPK,* 1: 12; *Izvestiia DOPK,* 2: 10.

90. Wade, *Russian Revolution,* pp. 131–133; for the gulf between state and market prices, see Kondrat'ev, *Rynok,* pp. 401–402.

91. RGVIA, f. 499, op. 1, d. 1657, l. 6; I. V. Denisoff collection, Cornell University, box 4, pp. 171–176.

92. GARF, f. 1783, op. 2, d. 420, ll. 94–99.

93. GARF, f. 1255, op. 1, d. 16, ll. 10–11; ibid., l. 6; *Ust'-Medveditskaia gazeta,* June 23, 1917, August 2, 1917.

94. GARF, f. 1791, op. 6, d. 401, ll. 152ob.–155; more generally, see Lih, *Bread,* pp. 71–72.

95. GARO, f. 863, op. 1, d. 4, l. 42; GARF, f. 1255, op. 1, d. 16, ll. 10–11.

96. *Ust'-Medveditskaia gazeta,* June 16, 1917.

97. GARF, f. 1791, op. 6, d. 401, ll. 168–170ob.

98. *Russkie vedomosti,* June 27, 1917.

99. *Ust'-Medveditskaia gazeta,* June 28, 1917; see also ibid., June 23, 1917. For similar measures in Rostov, see *Russkie vedomosti,* June 27, 1917. Such actions were typical of "food-supply excesses" throughout the country (GARF, f. 1791, op. 6, d. 401, ll. 168–168ob.).

100. *Ek. Pol.,* 2: 280–291.

101. Cited in Taisia Kitanina, *Voina, khleb, i revoliutsiia* (Leningrad: Nauka, 1985), p. 328.

102. E. E. Pisarenko, "A. D. Tsiriupa v gody voiny i revoliutsii," in *Oktiabr'skaia revoliutsiia: Ot novykh istochnikov k novomu osmysleniiu,* eds. S. V. Titiutkin et al. (Moscow: RAN, 1998), p. 289; *RPG,* 2: 563–565.

103. RGVIA, f. 2005, op. 1, d. 88, l. 106; reissued on July 31 (*Ek. Pol.,* 3: 249–250, 489, n. 141).

104. RGVIA, f. 499, op. 1, d. 1657, l. 4.

105. GARO, f. 863, op. 1, d. 16, l. 33 (June); similarly, ibid., ll. 43–45, 63, 122 (June), ll. 57, 58, 68–69 (July), ll. 152, 155 (August).

106. GARO, f. 863, op. 1, d. 144, ll. 33–34; *Priazovskii krai,* August 8, 1917.

107. GARF, f. 1255, op. 1, d. 92, l. 27.

108. *Priazovskii krai,* August 4, 1917.

109. The following is based on the reportage in *Priazovskii krai,* August 23, 1917.

110. *Priazovskii krai,* August 25, 1917; *Russkoe slovo,* August 23, 1917; *Russkie vedomosti,* August 23, 1917.

111. "Doubling of Fixed Prices," *RPG,* 2: 641–642; Volobuev, *Ekonomicheskaia politika,* p. 433.

112. RGVIA, f. 499, op. 1, d. 1657, l. 102.

113. "Guarantee of Government Not to Raise Fixed Prices" (August 4), *RPG,* 2: 641. On Peshekhonov's resignation, see his statement in *RPG,* 3: 1640–1641.

114. RGVIA, f. 499, op. 1, d. 1657, l. 66.

115. *Ek. Pol.*, 3: 489, note to document 141.

116. RGVIA, f. 2005, op. 1, d. 88, ll. 120–124; ibid., d. 87, l. 9. On Gavrilov, see Naumov, *Iz utselevskhikh vospominanii, 1868–1917*, 2 vols. (New York: Russian Printing House, 1955), 2: 388–390.

117. This conflation is examined more closely in Chapter 7.

118. GARF, f. 1791, op. 2, d. 148, ll. 1–2, 11, 13.

119. Sergei Chakhotin, "V Kanossu!" *Smena vekh*, 2nd ed. (Prague: Otto Elsner, 1922), pp. 151–152. Both Chakhotin and Anisimov term educated society's embrace of democracy in February as a "wager" *(stavka)*; see also Vladimir Vernadskii's description of his disillusionment with his February ideals (chap. 2).

120. RGVIA, f. 499, op. 1, d. 1657, ll. 234–235. On Anisimov, see A. V. Sypchenko, *Narodno-sotsialisticheskaia partiia v 1907–1917 gg.* (Moscow: ROSSPEN, 1999), pp. 190–191, 246; *Politicheskie partii Rossii, konets XIX-pervaia tret' XX veka: Entsiklopediia*, eds. V. V. Shelokhaev et al. (Moscow: ROSSPEN, 1996), s.v. Anisimov, V. I.

121. *Russkie vedomosti*, October 1, 1917.

122. GARF, f. 1783, op. 6, d. 157, ll. 26–27.

123. RGVIA, f. 366, op. 1, d. 94, ll. 81–82.

124. "Rech' ministra prodovol'stviia Prokopovicha," *Ek. Pol.*, 3: 353–369, citations at 357, 368. An edited version of this speech in English can be found in *RPG*, 2: 647–652.

125. For the exchanges of telegrams over October 19–21, 1917, see *RPG*, 2: 653; 3: 1651–1652; *Revoliutsionnoe dvizhenie v Rossii nakanune oktiabr'skogo vooruzhennogo vosstaniia*, ed. G. E. Reikhberg (Moscow: Izdatel'stvo Akademii nauk, 1962), pp. 459–460.

126. *RPG*, 3: 1645; GARF, f. 1791, op. 2, d. 153b, ll. 59–60.

127. Alan Wildman, *The End of the Russian Imperial Army*, 2 vols. (Princeton: Princeton University Press, 1980 and 1987), 2: 78, 125–127, 134–141, 146; V. B. Stankevich, *Vospominaniia, 1914–1919* (Berlin: Ladyzhnikov, 1920), pp. 165–166, 257; Fedor Stepun, *Byvshee i nesbyvsheesia*, 2nd ed. (St. Petersburg: Aleteiia, 2000; original ed., New York, 1954), pp. 392–394, 401–402.

128. For example, RGVIA, f. 2005, op. 1, d. 88, ll. 40–41; RGVIA, f. 499, op. 1, d. 1657, l. 250; RGVIA, f. 2003, op. 4, d. 26, l. 38; GARF, f. 1791, op. 2, d. 153b, ll. 138, 193; GARF, f. 1791, op. 2, d. 181, l. 59; *Russkoe slovo*, September 13, 1917.

129. For example, N. A. Orlov, *Prodovol'stvennoe delo v Rossii vo vremia voiny i revoliutsii* (Moscow: Izdatel'skii otdel narodnogo komissariata po prodovol'stviiu, 1919); Kondrat'ev, *Rynok khlebov i ego regulirovanie vo vremia voiny i revoliutsii*. Lih, *Bread*, underscores this continuity.

130. *Russkie vedomosti*, October 3, 1917.

131. GARF, f. 1788, op. 2, d. 95, l. 81 (see notes 31–32 above on this exchange).

132. *Ek. Pol.*, 3: 361.

133. GARF, f. 1255, op. 1, d. 92, l. 61; GARF, f. 1783, op. 6, d. 42, l. 23.

134. GARF, f. 1783, op. 6, d. 42, ll. 22–22ob; similarly, GARF, f. 1783, op. 6, d. 157, ll. 26–27.

135. Kondrat'ev, *Rynok*, p. 222; also p. 186.

136. RGVIA, f. 2009, op. 2, d. 20, ll. 95–98; RGVIA, f. 2009, op. 2, d. 105, ll. 6–

8, 12, 16–16ob., 96–97, 105–106, 129–130, 138–139, 157–158, 181, 183, 197; RGVIA, f. 2009, op. 2, d. 107, ll. 13, 18.

137. RGVIA, f. 2009, op. 2, d. 105, l. 184. With the establishment of the Soviet government, commissariats had replaced ministries. Tellingly, however, throughout January 1918 telegrams from the "interfront commission" continued to use the wartime and Provisional Government term, "ministry."

138. Alessandro Stanziani, "Le Narkomprod, l'armée, et les paysans, 1918–1921," *Cahiers du Monde russe* 38, no. 1–2 (1997): 83–116. The *Prodarmiia* was established in late May 1918; by November it numbered 42,000 troops.

139. *Izvestiia DOPK*, no. 18 (November 17, 1917); GARF, f. 1255, op. 1, d. 92, ll. 84, 133–134.

140. For example, John Bradley, *Civil War in Russia* (London: B. T. Batsford, 1975), p. 40; Peter Kenez, *Civil War in South Russia, 1918* (Berkeley: University of California Press, 1971), pp. 37–44; Iu. K. Kirienko, *Krakh Kaledinshchiny* (Moscow: "Mysl'," 1976), pp. 14–30.

4. Toward Civil War

1. "Obiazannost' kazhdogo," *Rech'*, May 3, 1917.

2. For the supraparty political culture in 1917, see Michael Melancon, "The Syntax of Power: The Resolutions of Local Soviets and Other Institutions, March–October 1917," *Russian Review* 52, no. 4 (1993): 486–505; Rex Wade, *The Russian Revolution, 1917* (New York: Cambridge University Press, 2000), pp. 53–86, 209–213. For the continuation of this phenomenon in the post-1917 period, see Orlando Figes, *Peasant Russia, Civil War: The Volga Countryside in Revolution, 1917–1921* (Oxford: Clarendon, 1989), pp. 40–47, 61–83; Donald Raleigh, *Experiencing Civil War: Politics, Society, and Revolutionary Culture in Saratov, 1918–1922* (Princeton: Princeton University Press, forthcoming), chap. 5.

3. GARF, f. 1255, op. 1, d. 92, ll. 71–74; James Bunyan and H. H. Fisher, eds., *The Bolshevik Revolution, 1917–1918: Documents and Materials* (Stanford: Stanford University Press, 1934), p. 404.

4. *RPG*, 3: 1804–1805.

5. Iu. K. Kirienko, *Revoliutsiia i donskoe kazachestvo* (Rostov: Izdatel'stvo rostovskogo universiteta, 1988), p. 205.

6. *Filipp Mironov: 'Tikhii Don' v 1917–1921*, ed. Viktor Danilov (Moscow: "Demokratiia," 1997), p. 29.

7. GARO, f. 864, op. 1, d. 19, l. 26; Petr Krasnov, "Na vnutrennem fronte," *Arkhiv russkoi revoliutsii*, vol. 1 (1922), 97–190.

8. GARF, f. 1255, op. 1, d. 92, l. 78; GARO, f. 864, op. 1, d. 19, ll. 14–15, 18.

9. GARO, f. 864, op. 1, d. 13, l. 102; *Proletarskaia revoliutsiia na Donu*, 4 vols. ([Rostov-on-Don]: Donskaia komissiia po istorii revoliutsionnogo dvizheniia i RKP(b), 1922–1924), 2: 120; 4: 91.

10. GARO, f. 863, op. 1, d. 15, l. 24; Ibid., d. 40, l. 22; *Novyi put'* (Rostov), no. 13–14.

11. GARO, f. 863, op. 1, d. 36, ll. 3–5.

12. GARF, f. 1255, op. 1, d. 92, l. 81.

13. *Bor'ba za vlast' sovetov v Donbasse: Sbornik dokumentov i materialov*, eds. V. E. Vilisova et al. (Stalino: Oblastnoe izdatel'stvo, 1957), pp. 170–171, 188, 209.

14. Oliver Radkey, *Russia Goes to the Polls: The Elections to the All-Russian Constituent Assembly*, revised edition (Ithaca: Cornell University Press, 1990), pp. 52, 72–77, 114.

15. Ibid., pp. 148–155; Kirienko, *Revoliutsiia*, pp. 208–218 and appendix one.

16. Nikolai Akaemov, "Kaledinskie miatezhi" (unpublished manuscript, Hoover Institution Archives), p. 126; "V verkhov'iakh Dona," *Donskaia volna*, no. 47 (May 12, 1919). Generally, see L. G. Protasov, *Vserossiiskoe uchreditel'noe sobranie: Istoriia rozhdeniia i gibeli* (Moscow: ROSSPEN, 1997), pp. 224–239.

17. GARF, f. 1791, op. 6, d. 401, ll. 36–45, here at l. 37; also GARF, f. 9505, op. 2, d. 1, l. 51.

18. Until October, the Rostov Soviet was dominated by Mensheviks. The elections on October 19 produced 112 delegates who were Bolsheviks or Bolshevik sympathizers; 63 Mensheviks; and 31 Socialist Revolutionaries. Bolsheviks controlled the new executive committee: V. N. Sergeev, *Sovety Dona v 1917 godu* (Rostov: Izdatel'stvo rostovskogo universiteta, 1987), pp. 189, 219.

19. D. Chernoiarov, "Ocherki revoliutsionnoi zhizni na Donu," *DL*, 2: 40–62; Iu. K. Kirienko, *Krakh kaledinshchiny* (Moscow: Mysl', 1976), pp. 76–108.

20. *Proletarskaia revoliutsiia na Donu*, 2: 37–41, 43–44, 53–58, 84; 4: 49–53.

21. GARO, f. 864, op. 1, d. 13, l. 102.

22. "Pokhod Kaledina na Rostov," *Donskaia volna*, no. 4 (July 1, 1918); V. Dobrynin, "Vooruzhennaia bor'ba Dona s bol'shevikami," *DL*, 1: 96; A. Padalkin, "Donskie partizanskie otriady," *Rodimyi krai*, no. 50 (1964), 2–21.

23. Pavel Miliukov, *Istoriia vtoroi russkoi revoliutsii*, 3 vols. (Sofia: Rossiisko-bolgarskoe izdatel'stvo, 1921–1924), 3: 306–307.

24. Vladimir Got'e, *Time of Troubles: The Diary of Iurii Vladimirovich Got'e, Moscow, July 8, 1917 to July 23, 1922*, trans., ed., and intro. by Terence Emmons (Princeton: Princeton University Press, 1988), pp. 77, 84, 90, 108; Alexis Babine, *A Russian Civil War Diary: Alexis Babine in Saratov*, ed. Donald J. Raleigh (Durham: Duke University Press, 1988), pp. 24, 29.

25. Letter in *Bor'ba za vlast' sovetov na Donu, 1917–1920* [hereafter *Bor'ba na Donu*], ed. I. M. Borokhova (Rostov: Rostovskoe knizhnoe izdatel'stvo, 1957), p. 236.

26. Peter Kenez, *Civil War in South Russia, 1918: The First Year of the Volunteer Army* (Berkeley: University of California Press, 1971), pp. 54–58, 68–85; William Rosenberg, *Liberals in the Russian Revolution: The Constitutional-Democratic Party, 1917–1921* (Princeton: Princeton University Press, 1974), pp. 308–313.

27. V. I. Vernadskii, *Dnevniki, 1917–1921*, 2 vols. (Kiev: Naukova dumka, 1994), 1: 33, 49; K. N. Sokolov, *Pravlenie generala Denikina* (Sofia: Rossiisko-bolgarskoe knigoizdatel'stvo, 1921), pp. 3–4.

28. S. Efron, "Oktiabr'," *Na chuzhoi storone* 11 (1925): 137–162, here at 160–170.

29. N. Belogorskii [pseud.], "V dni Kaledina," *Beloe delo* 4 (1928): 39–70. Although Belogorskii was not a Cossack, he had served in Kaledin's Twelfth Cavalry Division during the First World War.

30. Natalia Reshetova, *Intelligentsiia Dona i Revoliutsiia* (Moscow: ROSSPEN, 1998), p. 21.

31. K. G. Serezhnikov, "Vospominaniia donskogo ofitsera," *Arkhiv russkoi*

revoliutsii, vol. 18 (1926): 208–236, at 209–210; Gregory Tschebotarioff, *Russia: My Native Land* (New York: McGraw-Hill, 1964), p. 141.

32. Bunyan and Fisher, eds., *The Bolshevik Revolution*, pp. 407–409.

33. *Lenin o Done i severnom Kavkaze*, ed. L. I. Berz, V. N. Perelygina, L. A. Etenko (Rostov: Rostovskoe knizhnoe izdatel'stvo, 1967), pp. 144–145; *Bor'ba na Donu*, p. 180.

34. Edward M. Dune, *Notes of a Red Guard*, trans. and ed. Diane Koenker and S. A. Smith (Urbana: University of Illinois Press, 1993), pp. 17, 53, 69; also *Bor'ba na Donu*, pp. 198, 200–201; Rex Wade, *Red Guards and Worker Militias in the Russian Revolution* (Stanford: Stanford University Press, 1984), pp. 227, 269.

35. Ia. Kirpichev, "Tretii voiskovoi krug," *DL*, 4: 17; Akaemov, "Kaledinskie miatezhi," p. 152.

36. GARO, f. 864, op. 1, d. 13, ll. 15, 37, 65; *Bor'ba na Donu*, pp. 187, 192; *Proletarskaia revoliutsiia na Donu* 4: 101.

37. Peter Holquist, "From Estate to Ethnos: The Changing Nature of Cossack Identity in the Twentieth Century," in *Russia at a Crossroads: Historical Memory and Political Practice*, ed. Nurit Schleifmann (London: Cass, 1998), 89–123.

38. GARF, f. 8415, op. 1, d. 4, ll. 145–152; *Priazovskii krai*, January 5, 1918.

39. GARO, f. 863, op. 1, d. 4, l. 55.

40. GARO, f. 863, op. 1, d. 13, l. 43.

41. GARF, f. 9505, op. 2, d. 4, l. 205.

42. GARF, f. 1255, op. 1, d. 92, l. 73.

43. V. N. Sergeev, *Bankrotstvo melkoburzhuaznykh partii na Donu* (Rostov: Izdatel'stvo rostovskogo universiteta, 1979), p. 83; *Proletarskaia revoliutsiia na Donu*, 2: 104–106.

44. GARO, f. 863, op. 1, d. 15, ll. 29–35.

45. *Izvestiia VTsIK*, December 29, 1917.

46. *Priazovskii krai*, January 6, 1918; *Proletarskaia revoliutsiia na Donu*, 4: 201–203; G. Ianov, "Paritet," *DL*, 2: 170–199, here at 180–181.

47. Kakliugin, "Voiskovoi ataman Kaledin," *DL*, 2: 16–62; Anton Denikin, *Ocherki russkoi smuty*, 5 vols. (Moscow: Nauka, 1991), 2: 187–194.

48. GARF, f. 113, op. 1, d. 1, ll. 4, 12–13, 17; Dobrynin, "Vooruzhennaia bor'ba," *DL*, 1: 96; *Proletarskaia revoliutsiia na Donu*, 2: 68–72, 78; 4: 91, 101–106.

49. Belogorskii, "V dni Kaledina," p. 54.

50. I. N. Oprits, *Leib-gvardii kazachii ego Velichestva polk v gody revoliutsii i grazhdanskoi voiny* (Paris: Izd. V. Siial'skogo, 1939), pp. 53–55.

51. Danilov, ed., *Filipp Mironov*, pp. 25–31, 34–38.

52. Kirienko, *Krakh kaledinshchiny*, chap. 5.

53. S. Syrtsov, "Nakanune i vo vremia s"ezda," *Proletarskaia revoliutsiia na Donu*, 4: 124.

54. *Bor'ba na Donu*, p. 220.

55. Mandel'shtam, "Obryvki," *Proletarskaia revoliutsiia na Donu*, 4: 157.

56. Antonov Ovseenko, *Zapiski o grazhdanskoi voine*, 3 vols. (Moscow: Vysshii voennyi redaktsionnyi sovet, 1924), 1: 206–207.

57. GARF, f. 8415, op. 1, d. 22, ll. 1–4; variants of the protocols were published in both *Donskaia volna*, no. 27 (December 16, 1918), and *DL*, 2: 306–318.

58. Antonov-Ovseenko, *Zapiski*, 1: 211; GARF, f. 8415, op. 1, d. 22, l. 49.

59. The portrayal in Mikhail Sholokhov, *And Quiet Flows the Don* (New York: Vintage, 1940), is historically quite plausible.

60. *Proletarskaia revoliutsiia na Donu*, 4: 99, 107, 123; Oprits, *Leib-gvardii kazachii polk*, pp. 78–81.

61. *Proletarskaia revoliutsiia na Donu*, 4: 108; Oprits, *Leib-gvardii kazachii polk*, p. 75; A. I. Tret'iakov, "Iz bor'by," *Rodimyi Krai*, no. 70 (1967): 29.

62. GARO, f. 861, op. 1, d. 30, l. 31; Ibid., d. 15, ll. 7, 9, 16, 17, 35, 37, 89, 91, 108, 140, 144.

63. Documents in *Donskaia volna*, no. 4 (July 1918); reprinted in *DL*, 2: 319–322.

64. GARF, f. 8415, op. 1, d. 17, l. 73.

65. *Bor'ba na Donu*, p. 240; GARF, f. 8415, op. 1, d. 17, l. 17.

66. GARF, f. 393, op. 2, d. 30, l. 26.

67. For example, GARF, f. 8415, op. 1, d. 17, l. 56.

68. John W. Wheeler-Bennett, *Brest-Litovsk: The Forgotten Peace, March 1918* (New York: Norton, 1971), pp. 149–204; E. H. Carr, *The Bolshevik Revolution*, 3 vols. (New York: Norton, 1980–1981), 3: 3–58.

69. Vladimir Lenin, *Polnoe sobranie sochinenii*, 5th ed., 55 vols. (Moscow: Gosudarstvennoe izdatel'stvo politicheskoi literatury, 1958–1965), 50: 34–35; similarly, 50: 44.

70. For German goals in this period, see Fritz Fischer, *Germany's Aims in the First World War* (New York: Norton, 1967), pp. 475–509, 534–582, here at 479–480, 502–503; for the Don in particular, see Udo Gehrmann, "Germany and the Cossack Community in the Russian Revolution," *Revolutionary Russia* 5, no. 2 (1992): 147–171.

71. Lenin, *Polnoe sobranie sochinenii*, 35: 580; 50: 46.

72. Ibid., 50: 365–366.

73. I. I. Mints, ed., *Imperialisticheskaia interventsiia na Donu i severnom kavkaze* (Moscow: Nauka, 1988), pp. 88–89; also Fischer, *Germany's Aims*, p. 536.

74. I. Borisenko, *Sovetskie respubliki na severnom kavkaze v 1918 godu*, 2 vols. (Rostov: "Severnyi Kavkaz," 1930), 1: 80–81; see also *Bor'ba na Donu*, pp. 285–287.

75. RGASPI, f. 17, op. 4, d. 36, ll. 4–5; *Rabochee slovo*, February 23, 25, 1918.

76. HIA, Nicolaevsky collection, box 6, folder 2, typescript of A. Lokerman, *74 dnia sovetskoi vlasti: iz istorii diktatury bol'shevikov v Rostove-na-Donu* (Rostov: Izdanie donskogo komiteta Rossiiskoi sotsial-demokraticheskoi rabochei partii, 1918), pp. 32–36.

77. Typescript of Lokerman, *74 dnia sovetskoi vlasti*, pp. 43–44.

78. HIA WMA, box 38, item 23, pp. 5–6, 10; Typescript of Lokerman, *74 dnia sovetskoi vlasti*, pp. 46, 60, 101, which reports these facts but still terms the period "the Bolshevik dictatorship."

79. GARO, f. 861, op. 1, d. 102, ll. 11–14.

80. J. L. H. Keep, *The Russian Revolution: A Study in Mass Mobilization* (New York: Norton, 1976), pp. 436–463; Figes, *Peasant Russia*, pp. 40–47, 61–83.

81. Borisenko, *Sovetskie respubliki*, 1: 77–79.

82. For the Volga region, see Figes, *Peasant Russia*, pp. 66–67.

83. M. Ch., "Krasnaia stanitsa," *Donskaia volna*, no. 44 (April 1919), pp. 11–13; *Proletarskaia revoliutsiia na Donu*, 4: 79–80; *Priazovskii krai*, May 25, 1918; TsDNIRO, f. 12, op. 3, d. 1074, ll. 2–3.

84. _Proletarskaia revoliutsiia na Donu,_ 4: 80, 83; similarly, 2: 74; 4: 76–77.

85. GARO, f. 856, op. 1, d. 75, ll. 63, 65–67, 82, 89–90, 93–95.

86. A. I. Tret'iakov, "Iz bor'by donskikh kazakov s bol'shevikami," _Rodimyi krai_ (Paris), no. 69 (1967): 25–29; no. 70 (1967): 28–33; no. 71 (1967): 29–32; no. 72 (1967): 32–38; here at no. 70, p. 33, and no. 71, p. 29. For similar accounts, see "V verkhov'iakh Dona," _Donskaia volna,_ no. 47 (May 1919): 13–15; G. P. Ianov, "Don pod bol'shevikami," _DL,_ 3: 18; [S. V.] Denisov, _Zapiski: grazhdanskaia voina na iuge Rossii, 1918–1920_ (Constantinople: Pressa, 1921), p. 45.

87. TsDNIRO, f. 12, op. 3, d. 13, ll. 9–10; GARO, f. 46, op. 1, d. 4156, l. 136.

88. GARF, f. 393, op. 2, d. 30, l. 26.

89. TsDNIRO, f. 12, op. 3, d. 13, ll. 9–10.

90. _Donskaia pravda_ (Uriupinskaia), February 24, 1918.

91. "Bol'shevistskie organizatsii nakanune VII s"ezda RKP(b)," _Istoricheskii arkhiv,_ no. 4 (1958): 25–37, here at 33; _Perepiska sekretariata TsK RSDRP(b) s mestnymi partiinymi organizatsiiami,_ 8 vols. (Moscow: Gosudarstvennoe izdatel'stvo politicheskoi literatury, 1957–1974), 3: 233.

92. GARF, f. 8415, op. 1, d. 25, ll. 4–9; similarly, GARO, f. R-4071, op. 1, d. 9, ll. 1–2.

93. [Aleksei Vasilevich] Golubintsev, _Russkaia vandeia_ (Munich: [n.p.], 1959), p. 57; O. Vladimirov, "Nachalo skitanii," _Kazach'i dumy,_ no. 16 (1923), pp. 2–7; GARO, f. 46, op. 1, d. 4156, ll. 172–173.

94. The intervention of the well-disposed Red Cossacks in the Novocherkassk garrison is a _de rigueur_ feature of émigré Cossack memoirs: I. A. Poliakov, _Donskie kazaki v bor'be s bol'shevikami_ (Munich: [n.p.], 1962), pp. 142–144; Tscherbotarioff, _Russia,_ p. 181; Ianov, "Don pod bol'shevikami," _DL,_ 3: 21; A. I. Tret'iakov, "Iz bor'by," _Rodimyi krai,_ no. 70 (1967): 30; Oprits, _Leib-gvardii kazachii polk,_ pp. 78–82; "Dva kazaka," _Donskaia volna,_ no. 7 (July 1918): p. 6.

95. Andrei Venkov, _Donskoe kazachestvo v grazhdanskoi voine_ (Rostov: Izdatel'stvo rostovskogo universiteta, 1992), p. 24.

96. GARF, f. 393, op. 2, d. 30, l. 52.

97. GARO, f. 4071, op. 1, d. 10, ll. 21–31. See also "Trudovoe kazachestvo o brestskom mire i zashchite Sovetskoi strany," _Krasnyi arkhiv_ 75 (1936): 185–188; _Bor'ba na Donu,_ pp. 310–315; Borisenko, _Sovetskie respubliki,_ 1: 84–90.

98. Among the Left Socialist Revolutionaries in attendance were Boris Kamkov; V. A. Karelin; I. Shteinberg; S. D. Mstislavskii; Iurii Sablin; Iakov Moiseevich Fishman; and A. V. Severo-Odoetskii (_Partiia levykh sotsialistov revoliutsionerov: dokumenty i materialy, iiul' 1917–mai 1918,_ ed. Ia. V. Leont'ev [Moscow: Rosspen, 2000], pp. 22–23).

99. Cited in Borisenko, _Sovetskie respubliki,_ 1: 85.

100. Danilov, ed., _Filipp Mironov,_ pp. 34–37 (emphasis in original).

101. _DL,_ 2: 308.

102. _Bor'ba na Donu,_ p. 272; also Lokerman, Typescript of _74 dnia sovietskoi vlasti,_ p. 39.

103. Danilov, ed., _Filipp Mironov,_ pp. 25–44.

104. "Trudovoe kazachestvo o brestskom mire"; similarly, GARO, f. R-4071, op. 1, d. 9, l. 7.

105. "Trudovoe kazachestvo o brestkom mire"; Borisenko, _Sovetskie respubliki,_ 1: 86–91.

106. Borisenko, *Sovetskie respubliki*, 1: 88.

107. GARO, f. 4071, op. 1, d. 10, l. 31.

108. Radkey, *Russia Goes to the Polls*, pp. 102–114.

109. For example, Richard Pipes, *The Russian Revolution* (New York: Vintage, 1990), pp. 555–556.

110. For example, for the countryside see Protasov, *Vserossiiskie uchreditel'noe sobranie*, pp. 224–239.

5. Forging a Social Movement

1. For the impact of the civil wars, see Donald J. Raleigh, *Experiencing Civil War: Politics, Society, and Revolutionary Culture in Saratov, 1918–1922* (Princeton: Princeton University Press, forthcoming), part 2.

2. Stephen Kotkin, "'One Hand Clapping': Russian Workers and 1917," *Labor History* 32, no. 4 (1991): 604–620; S. A. Smith, "The 'Social' and the 'Political' in the Russian Revolution," *The Historical Journal* 38, no. 3 (1995): 733–743, here at p. 734.

3. Charles Maier, *Recasting Bourgeois Europe: Stabilization in France, Germany, and Italy in the Decade after World War I* (Princeton: Princeton University Press, 1975); Gerald Feldman, "Economic and Social Problems of German Demobilization, 1918–1919," *Journal of Modern History* 47, no. 1 (March 1975): 1–47.

4. For the contemporary formulations of this narrative see *Ocherk politicheskoi istorii Vsevelikogo voiska Donskogo* (Novocherkassk: Oblastnaia tipografiia VVD, 1919), pp. 71–73, and the newspaper-journal *Donskaia volna* (Rostov, 1918–1919). This approach entered the historiography primarily through the memoirs of émigré members of the AGDH: the three-volume *DL*; Petr Krasnov, "Vsevelikoe voisko donskoe," *Arkhiv russkoi revoliutsii*, vol. 5 (1922): 191–321; [S. V.] Denisov, *Zapiski: Grazhdanskaia voina na Iuge Rossii, 1918–1920* (Constantinople: Pressa, 1921); [V.] Dobrynin, *Bor'ba bol'shevizmom na Iuge Rossii: Uchastie v bor'be donskogo kazachestva* (Prague: Slavianskoe izd-vo, 1921); I. A. Poliakov, *Donskie kazaki v bor'be s bol'shevikami* (Munich: [n.p.], 1962).

5. Pavel Kudinov, "Vosstanie verkhne-dontsov," *Vol'noe kazachestvo* 101 (1932): 12–15. Gregor Melekhov expressed identical sentiments in Mikhail Sholokhov's novel based on these events: *The Don Flows Home to the Sea* (New York: Vintage, 1940), pp. 444–446.

6. William Chamberlin, *The Russian Revolution*, 2 vols. (Princeton: Princeton University Press, 1987), 2: 134–135; Evan Mawdsley, *The Russian Civil War* (Boston: Unwin-Hyman, 1987), p. 86; Peter Kenez, *Civil War in South Russia, 1918* (Berkeley: University of California Press, 1971), pp. 122–125; Richard Pipes, *Russia under the Bolshevik Regime* (New York: Vintage, 1993), p. 19.

7. G. P. Ianov, "Don pod bol'shevikami vesnoi 1918 goda: vosstanie stanits na Donu," *DL*, 3: 21, 34, 37; *Donskie vedomosti*, March 31, 1919; A. Kozhin, "Otets khoperskogo vosstaniia," *Donskaia volna*, no. 40 (March 1919): 4–5; *Kazach'i dumy*, no. 12 (October 1923): 6–12, and no. 16 (December 1923): 2–7.

8. *Donskie vedomosti*, January 26, 1919.

9. "Cherkasskoe vosstanie," *Donskaia volna*, no. 11 (August 1918), p. 9; "Sovetskaia vlast' v Sal'skom okruge," *Donskaia volna*, no. 35 (February 1919), p. 6.

10. "Bol'sheviki v Ust'-Medveditse," *Donskaia volna*, no. 13 (September 1918),

p. 6; also "Na rodine Kaledina," *Donskaia volna*, no. 20 (October 1918), p. 7; A. V. Golubintsev, *Russkaia vandeia* (Munich: [n.p.], 1959), p. 20.

11. A. Kozhin, "V verkhov'iakh Dona," *Donskaia volna*, no. 47 (May 1918): 13–15, and no. 49 (June 1919): 10–13; A. I. Tret'iakov, "Iz bor'by donskikh kazakov," *Rodimyi krai*, no. 72 (1967): 32–38. See also *Priazovskii krai*, June 2, 1918.

12. Krasnov, "Vsevclikoe voisko donskoe," p. 206; also p. 191. See also V. Dobrynin, "Vooruzhennaia bor'ba Dona s bol'shevikami," *DL*, 1: 101; Ianov, "Don pod bol'shevikami," *DL*, 3: 26; Poliakov, *Donskie kazaki*, p. 240; Golubintsev, *Russkaia vandeia*, p. 62. Kenez provides a fine analysis of the German role (*Civil War, 1918*, pp. 126–127, 142–148).

13. See Chapter 4. Also see James Bunyan, ed., *Intervention, Civil War, and Communism in Russia, April-December 1918: Documents and Materials* (Baltimore: Johns Hopkins University Press, 1936), pp. 32–50.

14. Udo Gehrmann, "Germany and the Cossack Community in the Russian Revolution," *Revolutionary Russia* 5, no. 2 (1992): 147–171, Groener citation at p. 155; Kenez, *Civil War, 1918*, pp. 126–132.

15. Krasnov, "Vsevelikoe voisko donskoe," pp. 206–213, a defense of his pro-German policy; Anton Denikin, *Ocherki russkoi smuty*, 5 vols. (Moscow: Nauka, 1991–), 2: 338–345, provides a critique of this policy. For an overview see Kenez, *Civil War, 1918*, pp. 142–148.

16. Hannah Arendt, *The Origins of Totalitarianism*, new ed. (New York: Harcourt Brace and Company, 1979), pp. 282, 294.

17. GARO, f. 856, op. 1, d. 3, ll. 69, 72; ibid., d. 4, ll. 1, 17, 25, 35, 55; HIA, Golovin collection, box 14, "German Headquarters on Don, Correspondence, 1918," letters of May 22, 23, 24, 1918.

18. *Priazovskii krai*, May 23, 1918; ibid., June 2, 1918.

19. GARO, f. 856, op. 1, d. 3, ll. 69, 73.

20. Georges Lefebvre, *The Great Fear of 1789: Rural Panic in Revolutionary France* (Princeton: Princeton University Press, 1973).

21. The land committee guidelines can be found in *Sbornik dekretov i postanovleniia po narodnomu khoziaistvu* (Moscow: Sklad izd., 1918), pp. 465–470; excerpts of the land socialization decree, in James Bunyan and H. H. Fisher, eds., *The Bolshevik Revolution, 1917–1918* (Stanford: Stanford University Press, 1934), pp. 673–678.

22. Markov, "Epopeia generala Golubintseva," *Donskaia volna*, no. 49 (June 1919), p. 15; also Golubintsev, *Russkaia vandeia*, p. 21.

23. GARF, f. 393, op. 2, d. 30, l. 52; also "Beseda s P. Ageevym," *Priazovskii krai*, July 12, 1918.

24. Hiroaki Kuromiya, *Freedom and Terror in the Donbass: A Ukrainian-Russian Borderland, 1870s–1990s* (New York: Cambridge University Press, 1998), pp. 97–114; Theodore H. Friedgut, *Iuzovka and Revolution*, vol. 2, *Politics and Revolution in Russia's Donbass, 1869–1924* (Princeton: Princeton University Press, 1994), pp. 292, 312–314, 318–319.

25. Raleigh, *Experiencing*, chap. 2.

26. Konstantin Khmelevskii, *Krakh krasnovshchiny i nemetskoi interventsii na Donu (Aprel' 1918–Mart 1919)* (Rostov: Izdatel'stvo rostovskogo universiteta, 1965), pp. 42–45; see also the portrayal in Mikhail Sholokhov's novel *And Quiet Flows the Don* (New York: Vintage, 1940), pp. 520–554.

27. I. Borisenko, *Sovetskie respubliki na Severnom Kavkaze v 1918*, 2 vols.

(Rostov: "Severnyi Kavkaz," 1930), 1: 84; Andrei V. Venkov, *Donskoe kazachestvo v grazhdanskoi voine* (Rostov: Izdatel'stvo rostovskogo universiteta, 1992), p. 34.

28. GARO, f. 856, op. 1, d. 4, l. 25 [emphasis added]; similarly, RGVA, f. 1304, op. 1, d. 480, l. 3; "Bol'sheviki v Ust'-Medveditse," *Donskaia volna* 13 (September 2, 1918), pp. 6–7.

29. Bunyan and Fisher, eds., *The Bolshevik Revolution*, pp. 673–678; E. H. Carr, *The Bolshevik Revolution*, 3 vols. (New York: Norton, 1980), 2: 43–46.

30. A. Kozhin, "V verkhov'iakh Dona," *Donskaia volna*, no. 49 (June 1919), p. 13.

31. GARF, f. 1235, op. 82, d. 6, l. 74.

32. GARO, f. 213, op. 3, d. 1041, l. 4; GARO, f. 46, op. 1, d. 4159, ll. 4–5.

33. TsDNIRO, f. 12, op. 3, d. 1041, l. 1; see also ibid., d. 1355, ll. 1–2.

34. "Vsevelikoe voisko donskoe," p. 221.

35. V. V. Lobachevskii, *Voenno-statisticheskoe opisanie OVD* (Novocherkassk: Oblastnaia v. D. tipografiia, 1908), p. 323.

36. GARO, f. 856, op. 1, d. 4, ll. 25, 35; ibid., d. 3, l. 25; ibid., d. 15, ll. 90, 106; RGVA, f. 39456, op. 1, d. 60, ll. 42, 72, 95.

37. GARO, f. 856, op. 1, d. 76, l. 63; ibid., d. 15, ll. 127, 196.

38. RGVA, f. 39456, op. 1, d. 60, ll. 6, 86, 61, 118.

39. *Donskoi krai*, May 14, 1918; *Priazovskii krai*, May 25, 1918; June 9, 1918.

40. *Postanovleniia Bol'shogo voiskovogo kruga VVD 4-ogo sozyva, sessiia pervaia (15 avgusta–20 sentiabria 1918)* [n.p, n.d.], p. 17; GARO, f. 856, op. 1, d. 15, ll. 14, 38.

41. RGVA, f. 39456, op. 1, d. 60, l. 104. See also P. Ratner, "Kaledinskie dni," *Proletarskaia revoliutsiia na Donu*, 4 vols. ([Rostov-on-Don]: Donskaia komissiia po istorii revoliutsionnogo dvizheniia i RKP(b), 1922–1924), 4: 5; Eduard M. Dune, *Notes of a Red Guard*, trans. and ed. Diane Koenker and S. A. Smith (Urbana, Ill.: University of Illinois Press, 1993), p. 140; Belogorskii, "V dni Kaledina," *Beloe Delo* 4 (1928): 43–44.

42. Peter Kenez, "The Ideology of the Don Cossacks in the Civil War," in *Russian and East European History: Selected Papers from the Second World Congress for Soviet and East European Studies*, ed. Ralph Carter Elwood (Berkeley: University of California Press, 1984), pp. 161–183; Carsten Goehrke, "Historische Selbststilisierung des Kosakentums: ständische Tradition als Integrationsideologie," in *Osteuropa in Geschichte und Gegenwart: Festschrift für Günther Stökl zum 60 Geburtstag*, ed. Hans Lemberg (Cologne: Böhlau, 1977), pp. 359–375. Neither, however, describes how this ideology operated in prefiguring descriptions of Cossack support for the insurgency.

43. A. Kozhin, "V verkhov'iakh Dona," *Donskaia volna*, no. 49 (June 1919), p. 11; Tret'iakov, "Iz bor'by," *Rodimyi krai*, 72: 35. The same occurred in Ermakovskaia stanitsa: I. Fomin, "Nashe vosstanie," *Rodimyi krai*, no. 98 (1972), pp. 14–15.

44. GARO, f. 856, op. 1, d. 76, ll. 19, 51–52; RGVA, f. 1304, op. 1, d. 480, l. 19; ibid., d. 478, l. 10.

45. M. N., "Ust-Medveditskie partizany," *Donskaia volna*, no. 54 (July 1919), pp. 9–10; P. Vetov, "Alekseevskii partizanskii otriad," *Rodimyi krai*, no. 65 (1966), pp. 17–18.

46. GARF, f. 1235, op. 81, d. 2, l. 200.

47. Golubintsev, *Russkaia vandeia*, pp. 20–22; GARO, f. 856, op. 1, d. 76, l. 1.

48. GARO, f. 856, op. 1, d. 76, ll. 11, 18, 19, 21, 26, 28, 51–52.

49. GARO, f. 856, op. 1, d. 76, l. 25.

50. Golubintsev, *Russkaia vandeia*, pp. 40–42; TsDINRO, f. 910, op. 3, d. 606, l. 38.

51. GARO, f. 856, op. 1, d. 73, l. 3. See Chapter 7 for a discussion of such organs.

52. GARO, f. 856, op. 1, d. 73, l. 1.

53. GARO, f. 856, op. 1, d. 76, ll. 55, 61, 90; ibid., d. 15, l. 296.

54. RGVA, f. 1304, op. 1, d. 480, ll. 14, 29.

55. GARO, f. R-4071, op. 1, d. 5, l. 131.

56. GARF, f. 1235, op. 1, d. 2, l. 197b; ibid., d. 3, l. 17; ibid., d. 6, ll. 64–65.

57. RGVA, f. 1304, op. 1, d. 480, ll. 5–6, 13.

58. RGVA, f. 1304, op. 1, d. 480, ll. 18–19.

59. RGVA, f. 100, op. 3, d. 334, l. 8.

60. Kenez, *Civil War, 1918*, pp. 122–132; Ianov, "Don pod bol'shevikami," *DL*, 3: 23–25.

61. For example, Kenez, *Civil War, 1918*, p. 123, 141.

62. Poliakov, *Donskie kazaki*, p. 226.

63. L. S., "Karatel'nye ekspeditsii," in *Politicheskaia entsiklopediia*, ed. L. Z. Slonimskii, vol. 2 (St. Petersburg: P. I. Kalinkov, 1907–1908), pp. 799–800; Abraham Ascher, *The Revolution of 1905: Russia in Disarray* (Stanford: Stanford University Press, 1988), pp. 330–336; William C. Fuller, *Civil-Military Conflict in Imperial Russia, 1881–1914* (Princeton: Princeton University Press, 1985), pp. 136–141, 144–146.

64. Denisov, *Zapiski*, p. 85; also pp. 81–82.

65. GARF, f. 1257, op. 1, d. 5, l. 2.

66. *Donskoi krai*, May 14, 1918.

67. "Vsevelikoe voisko Donskoe," chap. 1. Kenez follows Krasnov's typology (*Civil War, 1918*, p. 139).

68. Khmelevskii, *Krakh krasnovshchiny*, p. 53.

69. GARF, f. 1257, op. 1, d. 2, l. 5.

70. V. V. Shapkin, unpublished manuscript (BAR, Columbia University), section two, p. 13.

71. TsDINRO, f. 910, op. 3, d. 677, l. 11.

72. RGVA, f. 40116, op. 1, d. 6, l. 16.

73. *Postanovlenie obshchego sobraniia chlenov Vremennogo voiskovogo pravitel'stva i delegatov ot stanits i voiskovykh chastei (28 aprelia 1918); Postanovleniia "Kruga spaseniia Dona," 28 aprelia po 5 maia 1918* (Novocherkassk: Oblastnaia v. D. tipografiia, 1918), p. 8.

74. *Sbornik zakonov priniatykh Bol'shim voiskovym krugom Vseveilikogo voiska Donskogo chetvertogo sozyva, v pervuiu sessiiu, 15-e avgusta po 20-e sentiabria 1918* (Novocherkassk: Donskoi pechatnik, 1918), pp. 51–52.

75. *Donskoi krai*, July 24, 1918; *Donskie vedomosti*, October 5, 10, 17, 18, 22, 1918; January 23, 24, 25, 1919; February 2, 6, 1919; RGVA, f. 39456, op. 1, d. 60, ll. 6, 86.

76. GARO, f. 46, op. 1, d. 4154, l. 36.

77. *Donskie vedomosti*, January 29, 1919.

78. GARF, f. 1257, op. 1, d. 3, l. 2; also Ivan Kalinin, *Russkaia vandeia* (Moscow-Leningrad: Gosudarstvennoe izdatel'stvo, 1926), chap. 17.

79. GARF, f. 1257, op. 1, d. 5, l. 3; *Priazovskii krai*, May 21, 1918; Krasnov, "Vsevelikoe voisko donskoe," p. 232.

80. GARO, f. 46, op. 1, d. 4156, ll. 89–90; GARO, f. 46, op. 1, d. 4154, l. 6.

81. GARO, f. 861, op. 1, d. 84, l. 32; also GARO, f. 46, op. 1, d. 4156, l. 15.

82. GARO, f. 46, op. 1, d. 4156, ll. 4–6; GARF, f. 1257, op. 1, d. 5, l. 36; *Donskoi krai*, May 14, 1918; *Postanovleniia Kruga spaseniia Dona*, p. 2.

83. GARO, f. 46, op. 1, d. 4156, l. 49; similarly, GARO, f. 46, op. 1, d. 4156, l. 50; ibid., d. 4154, ll. 15, 17; ibid., d. 4156, ll. 10, 90, 129, 167.

84. GARO, f. 856, op. 1, d. 4, l. 44.

85. Golubintsev, *Russkaia vandeia*, p. 67.

86. GARF, f. 1257, op. 1, d. 2, l. 22; ibid., d. 3, l. 2; Iu. D. Grazhdanov, *Vsevelikoe voisko donskoe v 1918 godu* (Volgograd: VAGS, 1997), p. 89.

87. GARO, f. 856, op. 1, d. 15, l. 42; GARO, f. 46, op. 1, d. 4139, ll. 2–4, 11; *Donskie vedomosti*, September 19, 1918; GARO, f. 36, op. 1, d. 4136, l. 2; GARO, f. 856, op. 1, d. 3, l. 36; Grazhdanov, *Vsevelikoe voisko*, p. 90.

88. GARO, f. 856, op. 1, d. 73, ll. 6, 8; GARO, f. 861, op. 1, d. 65, l. 1 [emphasis in original].

89. GARO, f. 856, op. 1, d. 73, ll. 27–28; GARF, f. 1260, op. 1, d. 15, l. 25; *Priazovskii krai*, July 12, 1918; also *Fillip Mironov: Tikhii Don v 1917–1921*, ed. Viktor Danilov (Moscow: ROSSPEN, 1997), pp. 55–56.

90. GARO, f. 856, op. 1, d. 15, ll. 203–204.

91. Khmelevskii, *Krakh krasnovshchiny*, p. 60; Ianov, "Don pod bol'shevikami," *DL*, 3: 30.

92. RGVA, f. 39456, op. 1, d. 60, ll. 51, 65; Vladimir Amfiteatrov-Kadashev, "Stranitsy iz dnevnika," *Minuvshee* 20 (1996): 435–637, here at p. 535.

93. GARO, f. 46, op. 1, dd. 4153, 4154, 4156, 4174.

94. Grazhdanov, *Vsevelikoe voisko*, p. 98.

95. GARO, f. 856, op. 1, d. 60, l. 3; ibid., d. 4, l. 39.

96. *RPG*, 3: 1649–1651; GARF, f. 1791, op. 2, d. 153b, l. 59; ibid., d. 19, ll. 10–11.

97. *Donskoi krai*, May 14, 1918; on the 1917 origins of this institution, see Chapter 7.

98. GARF, f. 1257, op. 1, d. 3, l. 3; GARO, f. 856, op. 1, d. 76, l. 139; ibid., d. 15, ll. 261, 264; GARO, f. 46, op. 1, d. 4153, l. 17.

99. *Osobyi zhurnal soveta ministrov*, 1914, no. 54 (July 19, 1914), point 20; *Zhurnaly zasedanii vremennogo pravitel'stva*, no. 140 (July 26, 1917), point 22 of appended instructions; *Donskoi krai*, May 14, 1918; GARO, f. 46, op. 1, d. 4153, l. 17, ibid., d. 4156, l. 8 (individuals sentenced for "spreading rumors"). For analogous Soviet instructions, see Irina Davidjan, "Voennaia tsenzura v Rossii, 1918–1920," *Cahiers du Monde russe* 38, nos. 1–2 (1997): 117–125.

100. Viktor Bortnevskii, "White Administration and White Terror," *Russian Review* 52, no. 3 (1993): 354–366; A. L. Litvin, "Krasnyi i belyi terror v Rossii, 1917–1922," *Otechestvennaia istoriia*, no. 6 (1993): 46–62; and esp. E. I. Dostovalov, "O belykh i belom terrore," *Rossiiskii arkhiv*, vol. 6 (1995): 637–697.

6. "We Will Have to Exterminate the Cossacks"

1. On the dualism of the Bolshevik party-state, see Stephen Kotkin, *Magnetic Mountain: Stalinism as Civilization* (Berkeley: University of California Press, 1994), chap. 7.

2. Karl Marx, *The Holy Family* (1845), in Karl Marx and Frederick Engels,

Collected Works, vol. 4 (New York: International Publishers, 1975), p. 123 (emphasis in original).

3. Ibid., p. 119.

4. Donald Raleigh, *Experiencing Civil War: Politics, Society, and Revolutionary Culture in Saratov, 1918–1922* (Princeton: Princeton University Press, forthcoming), chap. 4 and conclusion.

5. GARF, f. 9505, op. 2, d. 4, l. 205; HIA WMA, box 38, item 23, pp. 7–10.

6. GARO, f. R-4071, op. 1, d. 2, ll. 32–35; ibid., d. 3, l. 22.

7. GARO, f. R-4071, op. 1, d. 5, l. 160; *Bor'ba za vlast' sovetov na Donu*, ed. I. M. Borokhova (Rostov: Rostovskoe knizhnoe izdatel'stvo, 1957), pp. 353–354.

8. GARF, f. 1235, op. 82, d. 18, l. 1.

9. Lutz Häfner, "The Assassination of Count Mirbach and the 'July Uprising' of the Left SR Party," *Russian Review* 50, no. 3 (1991): 324–344; Ettore Cinnella, "The Tragedy of the Russian Revolution: Promise and Default of the Left Socialist Revolutionaries in 1918," *Cahiers du monde russe* 38, no. 1–2 (1997): 45–82; and esp. the judicious conclusions in *Partiia levykh sotsialistov-revoliutsionerov: dokumenty i materialy, iiul' 1917–mai 1918*, ed. Ia. V. Leont'ev (Moscow: ROSSPEN, 2000), pp. 27–29, 37, 39. For how this event unfolded in Saratov in ways similar to the Don Territory, see Donald Raleigh, "Cooptation amid Repression: The Revolutionary Communists in Saratov Province," *Cahiers du monde russe* 40, no. 4 (1999): 625–656.

10. Cinnella, "Tragedy," pp. 66–69.

11. Stalin, *Sochineniia*, 13 vols. (Moscow: Gosudarstvennoe izdatel'stvo politicheskoi literatury, 1946–1951), 4: 118, 420.

12. GARF, f. 1235, op. 81, d. 2, l. 252; ibid., d. 3, l. 51; RGVA, f. 40435, op. 1, d. 16, l. 76.

13. GARO, f. R-4071, op. 1, d. 2, ll. 5, 31, 40; ibid., d. 12, l. 36; ibid., op. 2, d. 15, l. 20. On centralization and localism, see Robert Service, *The Bolshevik Party in Revolution: A Study in Organizational Change, 1917–1923* (New York: Barnes and Noble, 1979), pp. 103–111; Raleigh, *Experiencing*, chap. 3.

14. GARO, f. R-4071, op. 1, d. 2, l. 13; ibid., d. 12, l. 1; ibid., d. 13, ll. 1–3.

15. *Bor'ba na Donu*, p. 364; GARF, f. 1235, op. 82, d. 5, l. 112.

16. RGVA, f. 40435, op. 1, d. 16, ll. 41–42, 78; also ibid., d. 53, l. 1.

17. *Direktivy glavnogo komandovaniia krasnoi armii, 1917–1920: Sbornik dokumentov*, eds. N. M. V'iunova, N. I. Deeva, and T. F. Kariaeva (Moscow: Voennoe izdatel'stvo, 1969), pp. 74–75.

18. GARF, f. 1235, op. 82, d. 18, l. 28; also ibid., d. 6, ll. 63–65.

19. GARF, f. 1235, op. 82, d. 3, l. 18.

20. André Mazon, *Lexique de la guerre et de la revolution en Russie, 1914–1918* (Paris: É. Champion, 1920), p. 40.

21. RGASPI, f. 17, op. 4, d. 36, ll. 29–31, 48; *Perepiska sekretariata TsK RSDRP(b) s mestnymi partiinymi organizatsiiami*, 8 vols., eds. G. D. Obichkin, A. A., Struchkov, and M. D. Stuchebnikova (Moscow: Gosudarstvennoe izdatel'stvo politicheskoi literatury, 1957–1974), 4: 240–241.

22. For discussion of the groupings [*gruppa, grupporovka*] within the Don Bureau, see GARF, f. 1235, op. 82, d. 15, l. 320; RGASPI, f. 17, op. 65, d. 34, l. 138; ibid., d. 35, l. 122; RGASPI, f. 554, op. 1, d. 4, l. 6.

23. Mark von Hagen, *Soldiers in the Proletarian Dictatorship: The Red Army and*

the Soviet Socialist State, 1917–1930 (Ithaca: Cornell University Press, 1990), pp. 36–54.

24. *Iuzhnyi front: mai 1918-mart 1919: Bor'ba sovetskogo naroda s interventami i belogvardeitsami na Iuge Rossii: Sbornik dokumentov*, eds. L. I. Bukhanova, N. M. V'iunova, N. M. Korneva, and Ia. A. Perekhov (Rostov: Rostovskoe knizhnoe izdatel'stvo, 1962), pp. 90–91, 226–241.

25. *Partiino-politicheskaia rabota v krasnoi armii, aprel' 1918–fevral' 1919: Dokumenty*, eds. L. D. Znamenskaia, V. P. Portnev, and L. M. Chizhova (Moscow: Voennoe izdatel'stvo, 1961), pp. 36–37; *Direktivy komandovaniia frontov Krasnoi Armii*, 4 vols., ed. T. F. Kariaeva (Moscow: Voenizdat, 1971–1978), 4: 252; *Iuzhnyi front*, pp. 222–223, 365–366.

26. RGVA, f. 100, op. 2, d. 235, ll. 58–59; also *Partiino-politicheskaia rabota v Krasnoi Armii, 1918–1919*, pp. 69–70, 137–138; von Hagen, *Soldiers*, pp. 80–89.

27. Nikolai Kakurin, *Kak srazhalas' revoliutsiia*, 2 vols. (Moscow: Izdatel'stvo politicheskoi literatury, 1990; original, 1925–1926), 1: 151–154, cartogram no. 5.

28. Robert McNeal, *Tsar and Cossack, 1855–1914* (New York: St. Martin's Press, 1987), pp. 220, 256; Evgenii Saval'ev, *Krest'ianskii vopros na Donu v sviazi s kazach'im: Istroichesko-statisticheskii ocherk* (Novocherkassk, 1917), p. 76.

29. *RPG*, 1: 210–211; *The Bolshevik Revolution*, eds. James Bunyan and H. H. Fisher (Stanford: Stanford University Press, 1934), pp. 279–280.

30. Mikhail Bernshtam, "Storony v russkoi grazhdanskoi voine," *Vestnik russkogo khristianskogo dvizheniia*, no. 128 (1979): 252–357; Vladimir Brovkin, *Behind the Front Lines of the Civil War: Political Parties and Social Movements in Russia, 1918–1922* (Princeton: Princeton University Press, 1994), pp. 101–106; V. L. Genis, "Razkazachivanie v Sovetskoi Rossii," *Voprosy istorii*, no. 1 (1994): 42–55.

31. GARF, f. 1235, op. 82, d. 15, l. 20; RGVA, f. 100, op. 2, d. 11, ll. 144–145; ibid., d. 78, ll. 78, 83; ibid., d. 106, l. 9.

32. Andrei V. Venkov, *Donskoe kazachestvo v grazhdanskoi voine* (Rostov: Izdatel'stvo rostovskogo universiteta, 1992), pp. 62–63; Ivan I. Dedov, *V sabel'nykh pokhodakh* (Rostov: Izdatel'stvo rostovskogo universiteta, 1989), pp. 50–52, 106; RGVA, f. 100, op. 2, d. 165, l. 42.

33. GARF, f. 1235, op. 82, d. 15, l. 123; similarly, RGVA, f. 100, op. 2, d. 106, l. 119; RGVA, f. 193, op. 2, d. 144, ll. 1–2.

34. For example, RGVA, f. 100, op. 2, d. 20, l. 1; ibid., d. 11, l. 182.

35. *Bol'shevistkoe rukovodstvo: perepiska 1912–1927*, eds. A. V. Kvashokin et al. (Moscow: ROSSPEN, 1996), p. 42; Joseph Stalin, *Works* (Moscow: Foreign Language Publishing House, 1953), pp. 124–128.

36. Peter Holquist, "To Count, to Extract, and to Exterminate: Population Statistics and Population Politics in Late Imperial and Soviet Russia," in *A State of Nations: Empire and Nation-Making in the Age of Lenin and Stalin*, ed. Terry Martin and Ron Suny (New York: Oxford University Press, 2001), pp. 111–144; Eric Lohr, "Enemy Alien Politics in the Russian Empire during World War One" (Ph. D. dissertation, Harvard University, 1999).

37. Orlando Figes, *A People's Tragedy: The Russian Revolution* (New York: Penguin, 1998), p. 570; *Sbornik zakonov priniatykh Bol'shim voiskovym krugom Vseveilikogo voiska Donskogo chetvertogo sozyva, v pervuiu sessiiu, 15-e avgusta po 20-e sentiabria 1918* (Novocherkassk: Donskoi pechatnik, 1918), pp. 51–52.

38. Don government's usage: GARO, f. 856, op. 1, d. 15, l. 127; ibid., d. 76,

l. 133; RGVA, f. 39456, op. 1, d. 60, l. 64. Red Army usage: RGVA, f. 100, op. 2, d. 162, ll. 25, 53; ibid., d. 106, l. 144; RGVA, f. 193, op. 2, d. 117, ll. 92–93.

39. V. V. Lobachevskii, *Voenno-statisticheskoe opisanie oblasti voiska Donskogo* (Novocherkassk: Oblastnaia v. D. tipografiia, 1908), pp. 309–317.

40. "Bor'ba s Donom," *Izvestiia narodnogo kommissariata po voennym i morskim delam*, February 2, 4, 6, 8, 1919. On this article, see Andrei Venkov, *Pechat' suvorogo iskhoda: K istorii sobytii 1919 g. na verkhnem Donu* (Rostov: Rostovskoe knizhnoe izdatel'stvo, 1988), pp. 67–68.

41. This schematic representation of social relations almost entirely dominates the historiography: see William Chamberlin, *The Russian Revolution, 1917–1921*, 2 vols. (Princeton: Princeton University Press, 1987), 1: 277; Peter Kenez, *Civil War in South Russia, 1918* (Berkeley: University of California Press, 1971), pp. 38–39.

42. GARF, f. 1258, op. 1, d. 81, ll. 139, 143; *Trudy mestnykh komitetov po nuzhdam sel'sko-khoziaistvennoi promyshlennosti* (St. Petersburg: Tip. V. Kirshbauma, 1903), vol. 50, p. 295; D. Iablokov, "Rezul'taty vyborochnogo ucheta zemli v 1922 godu," *Donskoi statisticheskii vestnik*, book 2 [1923], pp. 36–37; *Otchet voiskovogo nakaznogo ataman o sostoianii OVD za 1915* (Novocherkassk: Oblastnaia tipografiia, 1915), p. 43.

43. GARO, f. 46, op. 1, d. 4154, l. 6; ibid., d. 4156, l. 136; ibid., d. 4174, ll. 1–2.

44. TsDNIRO, f. 4, op. 1, d. 65, l. 436.

45. GARF, f. 393, op. 2, d. 30, l. 52 (emphasis in original); also, RGVA, f. 1304, op. 1, d. 489, l. 171.

46. GARO, f. 856, op. 1, d. 15, l. 106; A. A. Maslovskii, ed., *Boevoi put' blinovtsev: Istoriia boev i pokhodov 5 Stavropol'skoi im. tov. Blinova divizii, 1919–1929* ([Rostov-on-Don]: "Severnyi Kavkaz," 1930), pp. 203–204.

47. GARF, f. 1235, op. 81, d. 2, l. 197b.

48. Lev Trotsky, *How the Revolution Armed*, 5 vols. (New York: New Park, 1979–1981), 1: 490; earlier usage cited in Venkov, *Donskoe kazachestvo*, p. 54.

49. RGVA, f. 100, op. 2, d. 94, l. 51.

50. Ibid., d. 51, l. 250.

51. GARF, f. 1235, op. 82, d. 15, l. 320; RGASPI, f. 17, op. 65, d. 34, l. 85.

52. *Izvestiia TsK KPSS*, no. 6 (1989): 177–178.

53. RGVA, f. 100, op. 2, d. 235, l. 6; also RGASPI, f. 17, op. 65, d. 34, l. 47.

54. RGVA, f. 100, op. 2, d. 42, l. 31; RGVA, f. 193, op. 2, d. 144, l. 63. There are two variants of the Southern Front's "Instructions": see HIA, Bykadorov Collection, Folder "Prikazy," "Instruktsiia," which is more moderate; and *Filipp Mironov: 'Tikhii Don' v 1917–1921*, ed. Viktor Danilov (Moscow: "Demokratiia," 1997), pp. 145–146, which is less discriminating.

55. GARF, f. 1235, op. 82, d. 15, l. 320.

56. *Perepiska TsK*, 6: 482; formalized the following day in RMC Order no. 171 (RGVA, f. 100, op. 2, d. 42, l. 31).

57. RGVA, f. 100, op. 2, d. 106, l. 20; ibid., d. 162, ll. 24–25.

58. Venkov, *Pechat'*, pp. 78–80; Pavel N. Kudinov, "Vosstanie verkhnedontsov," *Vol'noe kazachestvo*, no. 79, pp. 8–9; no. 80, p. 8.

59. RGVA, f. 100, op. 2, d. 146, ll. 16–19; also *Donskie vedomosti*, June 3 and 15, 1919.

60. RGASPI, f. 554, op. 1, d. 1, ll. 5–6, 18; also GARF, f. 1235, op. 82, d. 15, ll. 172–173.

61. RGVA, f. 100, op. 2, d. 146, l. 30; GARF, f. 1235, op. 82, d. 15, ll. 311–312.

62. For this argument regarding the Wehrmacht's conduct in the East, see Omer Bartov, *The Eastern Front: German Troops and the Barbarization of Warfare* (New York: St. Martin's, 1986).

63. Kudinov, "Vosstanie," no. 80, p. 8; Venkov, *Pechat'*, pp. 80–81. Lists of individual victims compiled by the insurgents immediately after the uprising (GARF, f. 1258, op. 2, d. 66, ll. 2–4) provide much more modest figures (12 in Veshenskaia, 24 in Migulinskaia) than reports of hundreds mentioned in later agitational broadsheets.

64. White intelligence estimated more than 1,000 executions in Kotel'nikovo and 700 in Tsimlianskaia (GARF, f. 452, op. 1, d. 32, ll. 18–21; ibid., d. 19, l. 4).

65. These figures from both Soviet and anti-Soviet sources: RGVA, f. 192, op. 2, d. 197, l. 13; RGASPI, f. 554, op. 1, d. 1, l. 67; *Donskie vedomosti*, June 24, 1919; *Priazovskii krai*, June 25, 1919; *Sever Dona*, July 17, 1919.

66. RGVA, f. 100, op. 2, d. 43, ll. 6–7; ibid., d. 51, l. 57; *Perepiska TsK*, 6: 190–195; RGASPI, f. 17, op. 4, d. 36, ll. 52–53.

67. *Perepiska TsK*, 6: 34, 36.

68. *Perepiska TsK*, 6: 48, 77–78, 287–288, 481–482; *Izvestiia TsK KPSS*, no. 7 (1989), pp. 148, 155; RGASPI, f. 554, op. 1, d. 1, ll. 71–76.

69. *Perepiska TsK*, 6: 77–78, 287–288; RGASPI, f. 17, op. 65, d. 34, l. 66.

70. RGASPI, f. 17, op. 4, d. 36, l. 53; similarly, RGASPI, f. 17, op. 65, d. 35, l. 56.

71. RGASPI, f. 17, op. 65, d. 34, l. 164; similarly, RGVA, f. 192, op. 2, d. 197, l. 53; Danilov, ed., *Filipp Mironov*, p. 146.

72. RGASPI, f. 17, op. 65, d. 35, l. 61; also GARF, f. 1235, op. 82, d. 15, l. 320.

73. Vladimir Lenin, *Polnoe sobranie sochenenii*, 5th ed., 55 vols. (Moscow: Izdatel'stvo politicheskoi literatury, 1958–1965), 50: 387.

74. RGVA, f. 192, op. 1, d. 66, ll. 14–15; GARF, f. 1235, op. 82, d. 15, l. 260; GARF, f. 1235, op. 83, d. 6, l. 91.

75. RGASPI, f. 17, op. 4, d. 36, ll. 53–54.

76. RGASPI, f. 554, op. 1, d. 1, ll. 80, 83; portions of Syrtsov's report are found in *Perepiska TsK*, 7: 261–262.

77. RGASPI, f. 17, op. 65, d. 35, l. 15.

78. RGVA, f. 100, op. 2, d. 94, l. 51.

79. RGVA, f. 193, op. 2, d. 144, l. 63. Orders through April reiterated that Order no. 178 remained in force: RGVA, f. 100, op. 2, d. 67, l. 20; GARO, f. 3441, op. 1, d. 66a, l. 16; *Perepiska TsK*, 7: 508–509.

80. HIA, Bykadorov Collection, Folder "Prikazy," "Instruktsiia."

81. As is asserted by Bernshtam ("Storony," p. 318) and Evgenii Losev (*Mironov* [Moscow: "Molodaia gvardiia," 1991], p. 317). Losev places responsibility for the "Cossack genocide" on the Jews. For a scrupulous refutation of this canard, see Aleksandr Kozlov, "Razkazachivanie," *Rodina*, no. 6 (1990): 64–71, and no. 7 (1990): 43–47, here at 6: 65–66.

82. *Polozhenie o polevom upravlenii voisk v voennoe vremia* (St. Petersburg: Voennaia tipografiia, 1914), articles 11, 647; RGIA, f. 1276, op. 10, d. 895, ll. 76–80. For the military administration of Galicia see A. Iu. Bakhturina, *Politika rossiiskoi imperii v vostochnoi Galitsii v gody Pervoi mirovoi voiny* (Moscow: AIRO, 2000); for Armenia, see RGVIA, f. 13227, op. 2, d. 149, ll. 1–20.

83. A. V. Smolin, *Beloe dvizhenie na severo-zapade Rossii, 1918–1920* (St. Petersburg: Dmitrii Bulanin, 1999), pp. 129, 174, 177.

84. RGVA, f. 192, op. 1, d. 66, l. 13; GARO, f. 3441, op. 1, d. 66a, l. 16; RGASPI, f. 17, op. 4, d. 36, l. 53.

85. *Izvestiia TsK KPSS*, no. 8 (1989): 161, 163–164.

86. RGASPI, f. 17, op. 65, d. 35, l. 7.

87. *Perepiska TsK*, 7: 260; RGVA, f. 192, op. 2, d. 197, l. 55.

88. *Perepiska TsK*, 7: 508–509. There the order is erroneously dated April 7, its date of receipt by the CC: see RGVA, f. 192, op. 1, d. 66, l. 9.

89. Reviews of the failed policy began citing this case early on: GARF, f. 1235, op. 82, d. 15, l. 298; RGASPI, f. 17, op. 65, d. 34, l. 87. Almost every later account of de-Cossackization invokes it; see Kozlov, "Razkazachivanie," no. 6, p. 64; Genis, "Razkazachivanie," p. 46; Brovkin, *Behind*, p. 104.

90. GARF, f. 1235, op. 82, d. 15, ll. 172–173; Genis, "Razkazachivanie," p. 46.

91. RGASPI, f. 554, op. 1, d. 1, ll. 83, 87–88; Venkov, *Pechat'*, p. 135.

92. Danilov, ed., *Filipp Mironov*, pp. 221–222.

93. RGASPI, f. 17, op. 65, d. 34, ll. 163–164; Danilov, ed., *Filipp Mironov*, 145–146.

94. RGASPI, f. 17, op. 65, d. 34, l. 115.

95. RGASPI, f. 17, op. 6, d. 83, ll. 1–10; edited version found in *Perepiska TsK*, 7: 259–271. The editors of the *Perepiska TsK* erroneously ascribe the report to the Don Bureau, whereas it was actually titled "Syrtsov's report." Syrtsov simultaneously presented the Don Bureau's "Resolution": RGASPI, f. 17, op. 65, d. 34, l. 170.

96. RGASPI, f. 17, op. 65, d. 35, l. 13; RGASPI, f. 554, op. 1, d. 1, ll. 83, 85, 87.

97. Danilov, ed., *Filipp Mironov*, pp. 187–188.

98. RGVA, f. 192, op. 2, d. 197, l. 53; RGASPI, f. 17, op. 109, d. 77, l. 158ob.; ibid., op. 65, d. 35, ll. 60–61.

99. *Donskie vedomosti*, September 27, 1919; also, GARF, f. 1235, op. 82, d. 15, l. 320.

100. Aleksandr Nikolaevich Naumov, *Iz uselevshikh vospominanii, 1868–1917*, 2 vols. (New York: Russian Printing House, 1955), 2: 379–380.

101. Holquist, "To Count"; Eric Lohr, "The Russian Army and the Jews: Mass Deportations, Hostages, and Violence during World War I," *Russian Review* 60, no. 3 (2001): 404–419.

102. *Bol'shevistkoe rukovodstvo*, pp. 107–110.

103. RGASPI, f. 17, op. 109, d. 44, ll. 135–141ob., citations at 140ob.–141.

104. RGASPI, f. 17, op. 65, d. 34, ll. 115, 85–89.

105. RGVA, f. 192, op. 1, d. 66, l. 44.

106. GARF, f. 1235, op. 82, d. 4, l. 50.

107. GARF, f. 1235, op. 82, d. 15, l. 290.

108. GARF, f. 1235, op. 82, d. 15, ll. 303–304; also ll. 175–177.

109. GARF, f. 1235, op. 83, d. 6, ll. 92–93; RGASPI, f. 17, op. 65, d. 35, ll. 20, 32.

110. Reports were solicited by the Party's Central Committee (RGASPI, f. 17, op. 65, d. 34, ll. 81–82, 85–89, 97–100); by the Cossack Section (GARF, f. 1235, op. 82, d. 15, ll. 172–176, 298–300, 303–304, 309, 311–314, 320–323); and by the Republic's Military-Revolutionary Council (*Kazaki Rossii: donskoe kazachestvo v grazhdanskoi voine* [Moscow: Institut etnologii i antropologii, 1993], pp. 288–301).

111. RGASPI, f. 17, op. 65, d. 116, l. 99.

112. *Perepiska TsK*, 7: 539; also 97, 105.

113. RGASPI, f. 17, op. 65, d. 35, l. 84; ibid., d. 153, l. 74.

114. Danilov, ed., *Filipp Mironov*, pp. 255–486.

115. RGVA, f. 100, op. 1, d. 6, l. 55; *Izvestiia TsK KPSS*, no. 2 (1990), p. 156; RGASPI, f. 17, op. 65, d. 35, l. 105.

116. *Krasnoarmeets*, September 4, 1919 (emphasis in original).

117. RGASPI, f. 17, op. 109, d. 44, l. 177.

118. Kozlov, "Razkazachivanie," no. 7, p. 46; *Izvestiia TsK KPSS*, no. 2 (1990), pp. 160–162, 169–172.

119. Danilov, ed., *Filipp Mironov*, pp. 427–430, 447, 453, 456–459.

120. RGASPI, f. 17, op. 6, d. 82, l. 13; GARO, f. R-97, op. 1, d. 622, l. 4; ibid., d. 613, ll. 7–10; RGVA, f. 192, op. 2, d. 385, ll. 27–28 (quote).

121. RGASPI, f. 17, op. 6, d. 82, l. 13; GARF, f. 393, op. 13, d. 523, ll. 489–490; TsDNIRO, f. 4, op. 1, d. 5, l. 11; ibid., d. 14, l. 15.

122. Kakurin, *Kak srazhalas' revoliutsiia*, 2: 329. I. M. Kalinin, *Pod znamenem Vrangelia: zapiski byvshego voennogo prokurora* (Rostov-on-Don: Rostovskoe knizhnoe izdatel'stvo, 1991), pp. 11–12, 335; GARO, f. R-97, op. 1, d. 616, l. 1; TsDNIRO, f. 4, op. 1, d. 35, l. 2.

123. *Prikazy sovetskim voiskam 9 Armii* [n.p., n.d.], p. 340; *Rezoliutsii i postanovleniia 2-ogo Donskogo oblastnogo s"ezda sovetov* (Rostov: [n.p.], 1920), pp. 17–18; GARO, f. R-97, op. 1, d. 516, l. 36.

124. Robert Armeson, *Total Warfare and Compulsory Labor* (The Hague: Martin Nijhoff, 1964), pp. 39–40; Jean-Claude Farcy, *Les Camps Concentration Français de la Prémière Guerre Mondiale* (Paris: Anthropos, 1995); Panikos Panayi, *The Enemy in Our Midst: Germans in Britain during World War One* (Oxford: Oxford University Press, 1991).

125. TsDNIRO, f. 4, op. 1, d. 35, l. 2; RGVA, f. 25896, op. 2, d. 11, l. 6.

126. RGVA, f. 25896, op. 2, d. 11, l. 1; also GARO, f. R-97, op. 1, d. 617, l. 1; ibid., d. 710, l. 69; TsDNIRO, f. 4, op. 1, d. 5, ll. 30, 39.

127. GARO, f. 861, op. 1, d. 107, ll. 89, 93; RGVA, f. 191, op. 1, d. 70, ll. 1–2; RGVA, f. 192, op. 2, d. 385, l. 28; RGVA, f. 192, op. 1, d. 136, l. 71.

128. RGVA, f. 25896, op. 1, d. 3, l. 1.

129. Dedov, *V sabel'nykh pokhodakh*, p. 121.

130. Adrian Lyttelton, "Fascism and Violence in Post-War Italy," in *Social Protest, Violence, and Terror in Nineteenth and Twentieth Century Europe*, ed. Wolfgang Mommsen and Gerhard Hirschfeld (New York: St. Martin's, 1982), pp. 257–274, here at pp. 259, 271; Richard Bessel, *Germany after the First World War* (Oxford: Clarendon, 1993), pp. 254–284, here at p. 261.

131. Raleigh, *Experiencing*, chap. 4 and conclusion.

132. *Pace* Ernst Nolte, *Das Vergehen der Vergangenheit* (Berlin: Ullstein, 1987), and *Der europäische Burgerkrieg, 1917–1945* (Berlin: Propyläen, 1987); Richard Pipes, *Russia under the Bolshevik Regime* (New York: Vintage, 1993), pp. 240–281.

133. Maxim Gorky, *Untimely Thoughts: Essays on Revolution, Culture and the Bolsheviks, 1917–1918*, trans. Herman Ermolaev (New Haven: Yale University Press, 1995), pp. 9–12, 76–77, 128–130, 185, 195–199, and Isaac Babel's story cycle *Red Cavalry* in *Collected Stories* (New York: Penguin, 1994). See also Roger Pethybridge, *The Social Prelude to Stalinism* (New York: St. Martin's Press, 1974), chap. 3.

134. N. Voronovich, ed., *Zelenaia kniga: istoriia krest'ianskogo dvizheniia v chernomorskoi gubernii* (Prague: Chernomorskaia krest'ianskaia delegatsiia, 1921), pp. 27–28, 152–154; also, Kudinov, "Vosstanie," no. 77, p. 7, and no. 101, p. 13.

135. RGVA, f. 100, op. 2, d. 235, ll. 219, 266.

136. Hannah Arendt, "On Violence," in *Crises of the Republic* (New York: Harcourt, Brace, Jovanovich, 1972), p. 150.

137. *Pace* Arno Mayer, *The Furies: Violence and Terror in the French and Russian Revolutions* (Princeton: Princeton University Press, 2000), p. 28; later he asserts that it was "above all, force of circumstance" that drove Soviet leaders to violence (p. 10).

138. See also Raleigh, *Experiencing*, conclusion.

139. Hannah Arendt, *On Revolution* (New York: Viking Press, 1963), pp. 10, 13–14, 28.

140. Arendt, "On Violence," p. 154.

7. *"Psychological Consolidation"*

1. E. A. Sikorskii, "Sovetskaia sistema politicheskogo kontrolia nad naseleniem v 1918–1920 godakh," *Voprosy istorii*, no. 5 (1998): 91–100; A. Berelovitch, V. Danilov, Nicolas Werth, V. Vinogradov, and V. Dvoinikh, eds., *Sovetskaia derevnia glazami VChK-OGPU-GPU: Dokumenty i materialy*, vol. 1: *1918–1922* (Moscow: Rosspen, 1998); N. Werth and Gaël Moullec, eds., *Rapports secrets sovietiques: La société russe dans les documents confidentiels, 1921–1991* (Paris: Gallimard, 1995); Vladlen Izmozik, *Glaza i ushi rezhima: gosudarstvennyi politicheskii kontrol' nad naseleniem Sovetskoi Rossii v 1918–1928* (St. Petersburg: Izdatel'stvo St. Peterburgskogo universiteta ekonomiki i finansov, 1995); V. Danilov and A. Berelowitch, "Les documents de la VCK-OGPU-NKVD sur la campagne sovietique, 1918–1937," *Cahiers du monde russe* 35, no. 3 (1994): 633–682; N. Werth, "Une source inédite: les svodki de la TCHEKA-OGPU," *Revue des etudes slaves* 64, no. 1 (1994): 17–27.

2. Keith Baker, "A Foucauldian French Revolution?" in *Foucault and the Writing of History*, ed. Jan Goldstein (Cambridge, Mass.: Harvard University Press, 1994), pp. 187–205.

3. Sidney Monas, *The Third Section: Police and Society in Russia under Nicholas I* (Cambridge, Mass.: Harvard University Press, 1961), esp. pp. 22–23, 294; Jonathan Daly, *Autocracy under Siege: Security Police and Opposition in Russia, 1866–1905* (DeKalb: Northern Illinois University Press, 1998). For Germany, see Wolfram Siemann, *'Deutschlands Ruhe, Sicherheit und Ordnung': Die Anfänge der politischen Polizei, 1806–1866* (Tübingen: M. Niemeyer, 1985).

4. Dominic Lieven, "The Security Police," in *Civil Rights in Imperial Russia*, eds. Olga Crisp and Linda Edmondson (Oxford: Clarendon Press, 1989).

5. John Bossy, "The Counter-Reformation and the People of Catholic Europe," *Past and Present*, no. 47 (1970): 51–70, here at pp. 64–66.

6. Daly, *Autocracy*, pp. 5, 42.

7. Z. I. Peregudova, *Politicheskii sysk v Rossii (1880–1917 gg.)* (Moscow: ROSSPEN, 2000), pp. 275–288; S. Maiskii, "'Chernyi kabinet': iz vospominanii byvshego tsenzora," *Byloe*, no. 13, book 7 (July 1918): 185–197; R. Kantor, "K istorii 'chernykh kabinetov,'" *Katorga i ssylka*, no. 37 (1927): 90–99.

8. *Osobyi zhurnal soveta ministrov*, no. 54 (July 19, 1914); for the military guidelines on staffing these organs, see *Polozhenie o polevom upravlenii voisk v voennoe vremia* (St. Petersburg: Voennaia tipografiia, 1914), articles 118, 126, and 516.

9. Iu. P. Khranilov, "'Chto im delo do chuzhikh pisem, kogda briukho syto': voennaia tsenzura Viatskoi gubernii v bor'be za pobedu nad germantsami," *Voenno-istoricheskii zhurnal*, no. 2 (1997): 22–29.

10. For example, RGVIA, f. 13841; ibid., f. 2048, op. 1, dd. 1353–1358; ibid., f. 13216, op. 6.

11. Peregudova, *Politicheskii sysk*, pp. 278–279; *Tsarskaia armiia v period mirovoi voiny i fevral'skoi revoliutsii*, ed. A. Maksimov (Kazan': Tatizdat, 1932), p. 4; Khranilov, "Chto im delo," p. 24; also Mikhail Lemke, *250 dnei v tsarskoi stavke* (St. Petersburg: Gosudarstvennoe izdatel'stvo, 1920), pp. 405–406.

12. Lemke, *250 dnei v tsarskoi stavke*, pp. 405, 436–437, 442.

13. *Tsarskaia armiia*, , pp. 4, 96–103, 103–107; Khranilov, "Chto im delo," p. 24.

14. Irina Davidjan, "Voennaia tsenzura v Rossii, 1918–1920," *Cahiers du Monde russe* 38, no. 1–2 (1997): 117–125, here at p. 118.

15. *Revoliutsionnoe dvizhenie v armii i na flote v gody pervoi mirovoi voiny*, ed. A. L. Sidorov (Moscow: Nauka, 1966), p. 281; *Tsarskaia armiia*, p. 24; Khranilov, "Chto im delo," pp. 28–29.

16. A. Miroliubov, "Dokumenty po istorii departmenta politsii perioda pervoi mirovoi voiny," *Sovetskie arkhivy*, no. 3 (1988): 80–83.

17. "Politicheskoe polozhenie Rossii nakanune fevral'skoi revoliutsii v zhandarskom osveshchenii," *Krasnyi arkhiv* 17 (1926): 3–35; "Tsarskaia okhranka o politicheskom polozhenii v strane v kontse 1916 g.," *Istoricheskii arkhiv* 1 (1960): 203–209. For Ufa, see TsGIA RB, f. 87, op. 1, d. 551, ll. 12–13, 28, 90–91, 95, 99. I am grateful to Professor Charles Steinwedel for generously sharing this material with me.

18. John Horne, "Remobilizing for 'Total War': France and Britain, 1917–1918," in Horne, ed., *State, Society, and Mobilization in Europe during the First World War* (Cambridge, England: Cambridge University Press, 1997).

19. Siemann, *Deutschlands Ruhe*, pp. 428–430.

20. Wilhelm Deist, ed., *Militär und Innenpolitik im Weltkrieg 1914–1918*, 2 vols. (Dusseldorf: Droste, 1970), 1: 378–379; Bernd Ulrich, "Feldpostbriefe im Ersten Weltkrieg: Bedeutung und Zensur," in *Kriegsalltag: Die Rekonstruktion des Kriegsalltags als Aufgabe der historischen Forschung und der Friedenserziehung*, ed. Peter Knoch (Stuttgart: J. B. Metzler, 1989), pp. 57–58.

21. John Horne, "Mobilizing for Total War, 1914–1918," in *State, Society, and Mobilization in Europe*, pp. 2, 5; and Horne, "Remobilizing for 'Total War,'" p. 195; Michael Geyer, "The Stigma of Violence, Nationalism and War in Twentieth Century Germany," *German Studies Review*, special issue (1992): 75–110, here at p. 84.

22. Scott Seregney, "Zemstvos, Peasants, and Citizenship: The Russian Adult Education Movement and World War I," *Slavic Review* 59, no. 2 (Summer 2000): 290–315. For measures in Kostroma Province, see *Voina i kostromskaia guberniia (po dannym ankety statisticheskogo otdeleniia)* (Kostroma: Tipografiia Gelina, 1915), pp. 66–77, 141–142.

23. Jean-Jacques Becker, *The Great War and the French People* (Dover, N.H.: Berg, 1985); Eugen Weber, *Peasants into Frenchmen: The Modernization of Rural France, 1870–1914* (Stanford: Stanford University Press, 1976).

24. See especially Peter Gatrell, *A Whole Empire Walking: Refugees in Russia during World War I* (Bloomington: Indiana University Press, 1999), pp. 37–40, 201, 208–209.

25. Hubertus Jahn, *Patriotic Culture in Russia during World War I* (Ithaca: Cornell University Press, 1995), pp. 40, 42, 155–157, 164–166.

26. E. Krivtsov, "Kniga i gazeta na voine," *Voennyi sbornik*, no. 11 (1915): 85–92. See also *Voina i Kostromskaia derevnia*, pp. 73–76.

27. Vera Slavenson, "Sovremennyi plakat," *Russkaia mysl'*, no. 3–4 (1917): 81–94.

28. GARF, f. 9505, op. 1, d. 1, l. 1; ibid., d. 3, ll. 11, 13.

29. Hilde Hardeman, *Coming to Terms with the Soviet Regime: The "Changing Signposts" Movement among Russian Émigrés in the Early 1920s* (DeKalb: University of Northern Illinois Press, 1994), pp. 78–79.

30. GARF, f. 9505, op. 1, d. 1, ll. 3, 8.

31. Ibid., d. 4, ll. 9–10; op. 2, d. 5, ll. 1–16. Daily maps, arranged by subject ("support for Provisional Government"; "Agrarian unrest"; "Food-supply crisis"), can be found in op. 2, dd. 7–10, 13, 16.

32. Horne, "Remobilizing for 'Total War,'" pp. 198–200.

33. GARF, f. 9505, op. 1, d. 3, ll. 1, 3, 7–8, 9–11; ibid., op. 2, d. 1, l. 50.

34. RGVIA, opis' description to f. 2005; RGVIA, opis' description to f. 366; RGIA, f. 1276, op. 10, d. 723, ll. 121–131.

35. V. B. Stankevich, *Vospominaniia, 1914–1919* (Berlin: Ladyzhnikov, 1920), pp. 140–147, quote at p. 141; Fedor Stepun, *Byvshee i nesbyvsheesia*, 2nd ed. (St. Petersburg: Aleteiia, 2000), pp. 373–442, quotes at pp. 394, 396.

36. *Partiino-politicheskaia rabota v Krasnoi Armii, aprel' 1918–fevral' 1919: Dokumenty*, eds. L. D. Znamenskaia, V. P. Portnev, and L. M. Chizhova (Moscow: Voennoe izdatel'stvo, 1961), pp. 77, 79–84.

37. William Fuller, *Civil-Military Conflict in Imperial Russia, 1881–1914* (Princeton: Princeton University Press, 1985), pp. 192–218, 262–263; Joshua Sanborn, "Drafting the Nation: Military Conscription and the Formation of a Modern Polity in Tsarist and Soviet Russia, 1905–1925" (Ph.D. dissertation, University of Chicago, 1998), pp. 49–54.

38. RGVIA, f. 366, op. 2, d. 56, ll. 24–25 (emphasis in original).

39. RGVIA, f. 2003, op. 4, d. 3, ll. 23–24, 40–42ob.

40. *Vestnik vremennogo pravitel'stva*, September 30, 1917.

41. *Kratkii ocherk kul'turno-prosvetitel'noi raboty v krasnoi armii za 1918 god* (Moscow: [n.p.], 1919); Mark von Hagen, *Soldiers in the Proletarian Dictatorship: The Red Army and the Soviet Socialist State, 1917–1930* (Ithaca: Cornell University Press, 1990), pp. 89–114.

42. *Zhurnaly zasedanii vremennogo pravitel'stva*, no. 140 (July 26, 1917), points 11 g-d and appended instructions; also, *Tsarskaia armiia*, pp. 138–139.

43. RGVIA, f. 2003, op. 4, d. 37, ll. 38–41, 1, 11. For officers of the old army entering the Red Army, see A. G. Kavtaradze, *Voennye spetsialisty na sluzhbe respubliki sovetov, 1917–1920* (Moscow: Nauka, 1988).

44. RGVIA, f. 2003, op. 4, d. 37, ll. 54–55, 64–65.

45. RGIA, f. 1282, op. 3, d. 120, l. 2; *RPG*, 1: 244.

46. *Sbornik tsirkuliarov MVD za period Mart-Iiun' 1917* (Microfilm at Hoover Library on War, Revolution, and Peace), pp. 63–64. Reports on the "peasant movement" in GARF, f. 1791, op. 6, dd. 401, 420–421. *Krest'ianskoe dvizhenie v 1917 godu*, eds. K. G. Kotel'nikov and V. L. Meller (Moscow-Leningrad: Gosudarstvennoe izdatel'stvo, 1927), reprints many of these reports.

47. GARF, f. 1791, op. 6, d. 278, l. 4; also found in *Krest'ianskoe dvizhenie v*

1917 g., p. 413. On the Main Militia Directorate's Information Department, see GARF, f. 1791, op. 6, d. 401, l. 148.

48. GARF, f. 1791, op. 6, d. 278, ll. 18–19, also found in *Krest'ianskoe dvizhenie v 1917 g.*, pp. 417–419; RGVIA, f. 2003, op. 4, d. 31, ll. 44, 70–70ob.

49. *Militär und Innenpolitik*, 1: 328–352, 2: 816–837, 841–846, 961–967; "Outline of a Scheme for the Patriotic Education for the Troops," July 29, 1917, in General [Erich] Ludendorff, *The General Staff and Its Problems: The History of the Relations between the High Command and the German Imperial Government as Revealed by Official Documents*, 2 vols. (London: Hutchison and Co., 1920), 2: 385–400.

50. Mark Cornwall, "Morale and Patriotism in the Austro-Hungarian Army," in Horne, *State, Society, and Mobilization*, pp. 184–187; Richard Plaschka, Horst Haselsteiner, and Arnold Suppan, *Innere Front: Militärassistenz, Widerstand u. Umsturz in d. Donaumonarchie 1918* (Vienna: Verlag für Geschichte und Politik, 1974), pp. 233–250; Péter Hanák, "Die Volksmeinung während des letzten Kriegsjahres in Österreich-Ungarn," in *Die Auflösung des Habsburgerreiches*, eds. Richard Plaschka and Karlheinz Mack (Vienna: Verlag für Geschichte und Politik, 1970).

51. Nicholas Hiley, "Counter-Espionage and Security in Great Britain during the First World War," *The English Historical Review* 101, no. 400 (July 1986): 635–670; David Englander, "Military Intelligence and the Defense of the Realm," *Bulletin of the Society for the Study of Labor History* 52, no. 1 (1987): 24–32.

52. David Englander, "The French Soldier, 1914–1918," *French History* 1, no. 1 (1987): 49–67, here at p. 49; Becker, *The Great War*, pp. 217–301; P. J. Flood, *France, 1914–1918: Public Opinion and the War Effort* (New York: St. Martin's, 1990), pp. 147–157.

53. William Rosenberg, "Social Mediation and State Construction(s)," *Social History* 19, no. 2 (1994): 169–188, here at p. 188.

54. HIA WMA, box 50, folder 3, "Order no. 7"; Christopher Lazarinski, "White Propaganda Efforts in the South during the Russian Civil War, 1918–1919," *Slavonic and East European Review* 70, no. 4 (October 1992): 688–707, here p. 696, n. 36.

55. Peter Kenez, *Civil War in South Russia, 1918* and *1919–1920*, 2 vols. (Berkeley: University of California Press, 1971 and 1977); William Rosenberg, *Liberals in the Russian Revolution: The Constitutional-Democratic Party, 1917–1921* (Princeton: Princeton University Press, 1974).

56. HIA WMA, box 47, files 8–12.

57. Lazarinski, "White Propaganda Efforts," p. 696; HIA WMA, box 50, folder 3, "Order no. 7." For agitational and surveillance efforts in the anti-Soviet movement in a different region, see A. V. Smolin, *Beloe dvizhenie na severo-zapade Rossii, 1918–1920* (St. Petersburg: Dmitrii Bulanin, 1999), pp. 198–199, 225, 286–287.

58. For example, Kenez, *Civil War, 1919*; Lazarinski, "White Propaganda," reevaluates the extent and success of anti-Soviet measures.

59. HIA WMA, box 50, folder 3, "Order no. 7"; Serge Chakhotin, *The Rape of the Masses: The Psychology of Totalitarian Political Propaganda* (New York: Alliance, 1940), p. 165. "Maps of political meteorology" prepared for the Provisional Government can be found in GARF, f. 9505, op. 2, dd. 7–10, 13, 16.

60. HIA WMA, box 50, folder 3, "Order no. 315"; Lazarinski, "White Propaganda," p. 698. For samples of reports from these far-flung branches, see HIA WMA, box 50, folder 35.

61. "'Bol'shevistskii karfagen' dolzhen byt' razrushen: Pis'mo S. G. Svatikova V. L. Burtsevu," *Otechestvennaia istoriia*, no. 2 (1993): 148–152; also K. N. Sokolov, *Pravlenie generala Denikina* (Sofia: Rossiisko-Bulgarskoe knigo-izdatel'stvo, 1921), p. 95; N. M. Mel'nikov, "Pochemu belye na Iuge ne pobedili krasnykh," BAR Mel'nikov collection, box 4, p. 122.

62. HIA WMA, box 29, file 20, "Doklad" (January 17, 1919).

63. "'Bol'shevistskii karfagen'"; Vladimir Amfiteatrov-Kadashev, "Stranitsy iz dnevnika," *Minuvshee* 20 (1996): 435–637, here at pp. 565–568; Aleksandr Drozdov, "Intelligentsiia na Donu," *Arkhiv russkoi revoliutsii* 2 (1921): 45–58, esp. p. 57.

64. Kenez, *Civil War, 1919–1920*, pp. 65–78; and "K istorii osvedomitel'noi organizatsii 'Azbuka,'" *Russkoe proshloe* 4 (1993): 160–193.

65. GARO, f. 861, op. 1, d. 107, l. 80; Amfiteatrov-Kadashev, "Stranitsy iz dnevnika," pp. 597–598.

66. Amfiteatrov-Kadashev, "Stranitsy iz dnevnika," pp. 575–576; Sokolov, *Pravlenie*, p. 95.

67. Amfiteatrov-Kadashev, "Stranitsy iz dnevnika," pp. 566–567; Mel'nikov, "Pochemu belye na Iuge ne pobedili krasnykh," p. 120.

68. Amfiteatrov-Kadashev, "Stranitsy iz dnevnika," pp. 576–577; Mel'nikov, "Pochemu belye na Iuge ne pobedili krasnykh," pp. 120–122; Sokolov, *Pravlenie*, pp. 98–99; Kenez, *Civil War, 1919*, pp. 75–77.

69. HIA WMA, box 50, folder 35; ibid., box 47, folders 5–7; ibid., box 48, folders 6–10; ibid., box 55, folders 8, 13–14.

70. HIA WMA, box 38, folder 18; also GARF, f. 452, op. 1, d. 14, l. 5.

71. "Dokumenty Guverskogo arkhiva o grazhdanskoi voine v SSSR," *Otechestvennye arkhivy*, no. 1 (1992): 63–66; HIA WMA, box 38, folder 18.

72. "Iz dokumentov belogvardeiskoi kontrrazvedki," *Russkoe proshloe* 2 (1991): 340–347, here at pp. 341–342; Sokolov, *Pravlenie*, p. 113.

73. Amfiteatrov-Kadashev, "Stranitsy iz dnevnika," pp. 565–566, 587, 595–601; Mel'nikov, "Pochemu belye na Iuge ne pobedili krasnykh," p. 123.

74. Lev Anninskii, "Krov' obagrila—smert' pobedila," *Rodina*, no. 9 (1996): 10–14; François-Xavier Coquin, "Une source méconnue: les affiches contre-revolutionnaires (1918–1920)," in *Russie-URSS, 1914–1991: Changements de regards*, eds. Wladimir Berelowitch and Laurent Gervereau (Paris: BDIC, 1991).

75. *Donskoi krai*, May 14, 1918.

76. *Kazaki Rossii: donskoe kazachestvo v grazhdanskoi voine* (Moscow: Institut etnologii i antropologii, 1993), pp. 244–245.

77. *Kazaki Rossii*, pp. 183–192, 243–244.

78. Ibid., p. 184; also RGVA, f. 39456, op. 1, d. 60, ll. 1–118.

79. GARF, f. 452, op. 1, d. 32, l. 10; ibid., d. 14, l. 11; GARF, f. 113, op. 1, d. 4b, l. 1; *Donskie vedomosti*, October 22, 1919.

80. GARO, f. 861, op. 1, d. 102, ll. 52–62, 77, 80; these reports are divided between GARF, f. 452, op. 1, d. 14, and GARO, f. 861, op. 1, d. 107.

81. Drozdov, "Intelligentsiia na Donu"; Roz-v., "Belaia pechat' na Iuge Rossii," *Byloe* 34 (1925): 206–221; also GARO, f. 861, op. 1, d. 107, l. 55. The anti-Soviet Northwest Government did the same. The editor of its official newspaper was none other than Peter Krasnov, the former ataman of the AGDH (Smolin, *Beloe dvizhenie*, pp. 198–199).

82. Drozdov, "Intelligentsiia na Donu," pp. 52, 56–58.

83. GARO, f. 861, op. 1, d. 107, l. 54. For examples, cf. GARF, f. 113, op. 1, d. 4b, l. 1, and *Donskie vedomosti*, December 31, 1919; GARO, f. 861, op. 1, d. 107, l. 155, and *Donskie vedomosti*, January 3, 1920.

84. *Vechernee vremia*, August 8, 1919; *Donetskaia zhizn'*, November 15, 1919.

85. GARO, f. 861, op. 1, d. 107, l. 101a.

86. RGVA, f. 39456, op. 1, d. 60, ll. 7, 14; GARF, f. 452, op. 1, d. 32, l. 18; *Donskie vedomosti*, June 20, 1919; GARO, f. 861, op. 1, d. 107, l. 115. For a similar response among peasants in Russia's northwest, see Smolin, *Beloe dvizhenie*, p. 191.

87. For the "intellectuals in uniform" staffing the army committees in 1917, see Alan Wildman, *The End of the Russian Imperial Army*, 2 vols. (Princeton: Princeton University Press, 1980 and 1987), 2: 402–403.

88. Michael David-Fox, *Revolution of the Mind: Higher Learning among the Bolsheviks, 1918–1929* (Ithaca: Cornell University Press, 1997), pp. 1–23; Yuri Slezkine, *Arctic Mirrors: Russia and the Small Peoples of the North* (Ithaca: Cornell University Press, 1994).

89. See treatment above in text. See also Izmozik, *Glaza*, p. 37.

90. Izmozik, *Glaza*, p. 43; Daly, *Autocracy*, p. 42.

91. Vladlen Izmozik, "Pervye sovetskie instruktsii po perliustratsii," *Minuvshee* 21 (Moscow–St. Petersburg: Feniks, 1997): 155–174; Davidjan, "Voennaia tsenzura," pp. 117–125.

92. Izmozik, *Glaza*, pp. 48, 54, 57.

93. For example, RGVA, f. 25896, op. 2, d. 11, ll. 1–11, 41–43, 47–48, 94–95, 132–133, 145, 149; RGVA, f. 192, op. 2, d. 385, ll. 2, 11, 17, 27–28, 38; RGASPI, f. 17, op. 109, d. 80, ll. 2, 3, 9, 15, 20–23.

94. For example, RGVA, f. 25896, op. 2, d. 11, ll. 46, 98.

95. *Partiino-politicheskaia rabota, 1918–1919*, pp. 92–93.

96. M. A. Molotsygin, *Raboche-krest'ianskii soiuz* (Moscow: Nauka, 1987), pp. 36–37; Sikorskii, "Sovestkaia sistema," pp. 92–93; Izmozik, *Glaza*, pp. 37, 42; examples found in RGVA, f. 100, op. 2, dd. 162, 165–166.

97. *Partiino-politicheskaia rabota, 1918–1919*, pp. 63–76; Von Hagen, *Soldiers*; Izmozik, *Glaza*, pp. 38–40.

98. Izmozik, *Glaza*, p. 75.

99. The following is based upon L. Borisova, V. Vinogradov, A. Ivnitskii, and V. Kondrashin, "Informatsionnye materialy VChK-OGPU za 1918–1922 kak istoricheskii istochnik," in *Sovetskaia derevnia glazami VChK-OGPU*, pp. 23–53; also pp. 59–79.

100. Borisova et al., "Informatsionnye materialy," pp. 28–30; GARO, f. R-97, op. 1, d. 772, ll. 19–21.

101. For example, TsDNIRO, f. 12, op. 5, d. 153, ll. 25, 33–40, 55; GARO, f. R-97, op. 1, d. 759, l. 25.

102. Borisova et al., "Informatsionnye materialy," p. 54; Izmozik, *Glaza*, p. 55.

103. Izmozik, *Glaza*, p. 66.

104. Sikorskii, "Sovetskaia sistema"; Izmozik, *Glaza*, pp. 23–36; N. G. Tsyganash, "Obshchestvenno-politicheskie nastroeniia sel'skogo naseleniia Dona i severnogo Kavkaza v period perekhoda k NEPu," in *Oktiabr'skaia revoliutsiia i izmeneniia v oblike sel'skogo naseleniia Dona i severnogo Kavkaza (1917–1929)*, ed. V. E. Shchetnev (Krasnodar: Kubanskii gosudarstvennyi universitet, 1984).

105. Borisova et al., "Informatsionnye materialy," pp. 36–38. For the development of Soviet surveillance in the following years, see Izmozik, *Glaza*, pp. 79–156;

Olga Velikanova, "Berichte zur Stimmungslage: zu den Quellen politischer Beobachtung der Bevölkerung in der Sowjetunion," *Jahrbücher für Geschichte Osteuropas* 47, no. 2 (1999): 227–243; *Sovetskaia derevnia glazami OGPU*, vol. 2, *1923–1929*, eds. Borisova et al. (Moscow: ROSSPEN, 2000).

106. For example, *Derevnia glazami*, pp. 7, 8, 9, 52.

107. Sergei Chakhotin, "V Kanossu!" *Smena vekh*, 2nd ed. (Prague: Otto Elsner, 1922), pp. 160–164.

108. George Mosse, *Nationalization of the Masses: Political Symbolism and Mass Movements from the Napoleonic Wars through the Third Reich* (Ithaca: Cornell University Press, 1975), pp. 10–11; Geyer, "Stigma," p. 92.

109. Charles Maier, "Between Taylorism and Technocracy: European Ideologies and the Vision of Industrial Productivity in the 1920s," *Journal of Contemporary History* 5, no. 2 (1970): 27–61.

110. These figures from Peregudova, *Politicheskii sysk*, p. 277; Izmozik, *Glaza*, p. 50.

111. For example, A. Verkhovskii, "Propaganda kak boevoe sredstvo," *Voennyi vestnik*, 43 (1924); D. Zuev, "Gazeta vo vremia voiny," *Voennaia mysl' i revoliutsiia* (1924), book 3: 11–25; F. Blumental', *Burzhuaznaia politrabota v mirovuiu voinu 1914–1919: Obrabotka obshchestvennogo mneniia* (Moscow-Leningrad: Gosudarstvennoe izdatel'stvo, 1928); Sergei Denisov and Vul'f Rzheznikov, *Politicheskaia obrabotka soldat v burzhuznykh armiiakh: nashi zapadnye sosedi* (Moscow-Leningrad: Gosudarstvennoe izdatel'stvo. Otdel voennoi literatury, 1929); Iu. Aliaritskii and S. Semeshevskii, *Propaganda v armiiakh imperialistov* (Moscow: Gosudarstvennoe voennoe izdatel'stvo, 1931).

112. For food supply, see Nikolai Kondrat'ev, *Rynok khlebov i ego regulirovanie vo vremia voiny i revoliutsii* (Moscow: Nauka, 1991), pp. 192, 197–199.

8. The Revolution as Orthodoxy

1. TsDNIRO, f. 4, op. 1, d. 5, ll. 70–72, 58–59; for debates on this question, see ibid., ll. 21–22, 25, 30, 38–39, 88.

2. *Rezoliutsii i postanovleniia 2-ogo Donskogo oblastnogo s"ezda sovetov* (Rostov: [n.p.], 1920), pp. 5–6; also pp. 19–20.

3. GARO, f. R-97, op. 1, d. 276, ll. 3–4.

4. *Otchet 3-mu s"ezdu sovetov* (Rostov: Donpoligrafotdel, 1920), p. 4; *Otchet 4-mu s"ezdu sovetov* (Rostov: Gosudarstvennoe izdatel'stvo-Donskoe otdelenie, 1921), pp. 3–13.

5. TsDNIRO, f. 4, op. 1, d. 8, ll. 53a, 89–90; for similar statements, see ibid., d. 5, l. 102; ibid., d. 66, l. 106.

6. *Otchet 3-mu s"ezdu*, p. 29; *Sbornik statisticheskikh svedenii po soiuzu SSR, 1918–1923 (Trudy TsSU, tom XVIII)* (Moscow, 1924), pp. 107, 112.

7. M. Pokrovskii, "Na Donu," *Revoliutsionnaia Rossiia*, no. 9 (June 1921): 30–32, here at p. 31.

8. GARF, f. 1258, op. 1, d. 81, ll. 140, 143–146; M. A. Kushnyrneko-Kushnyrev, *Polozhenie sel'sko-khoziaistvennogo promysla v Oblasti voiska Donskogo* (Novocherkassk: Donskoi pechatnik, 1913), pp. 37–38; A. N. Abramov, "K voprosu o sostoianii kazach'ikh i krest'ianskikh khoziastv Donokruga," *Severo-kavkazskii*

krai, no. 6 (1925): 115–120, here at p. 119; *Litso donskoi derevni k 1925: Po materialam obsledovaniia DKK i DonoRKI* (Rostov-on-Don, 1925), pp. 5–6.

9. *Otchet 3-mu s"ezdu,* p. 1; GARO, f. R-97, op. 1, d. 611, l. 8.

10. RGVA, f. 1304, op. 1, d. 5, l. 42; RGVA, f. 192, op. 1, d. 136, ll. 70–71; GARO, f. R-97, op. 1, d. 775, l. 34.

11. RGASPI, f. 17, op. 6, d. 82, l. 11; I. V. Ustinovskii, *Leninskaia agrarnaia programma i ee osushchestvlenie na Severnom Kavkaze* (Rostov: Izdatel'stvo rostovskogo universiteta, 1989), p. 54; *Donskoi statitisticheskii ezhegodnik,* 1922: 41.

12. *Rezoliutsii 2-ogo Donskogo s"ezda,* p. 23; GARO, f. R-97, op. 1, d. 611, ll. 4, 19, 62.

13. TsDNIRO, f. 4, op. 1, d. 11, l. 34a.

14. Ibid., d. 5, l. 11; GARO, f. R-97, op. 1, d. 626, l. 39; also *Proletarii Dona,* December 5, 1921.

15. Iakov Bukshpan, *Voenno-khoziaistvennaia politika: Formy i organy regulirovaniia khoziaistva za vremia mirovoi voiny, 1914–1918* (Moscow-Leningrad: Gosizdat, 1929), p. 104; Arthur Marwick, *The Deluge: British Society and the First World War* (New York: Norton, 1970), p. 271.

16. Robert Moeller, "Winners as Losers in the German Inflation: Peasant Protest over the Controlled Economy," in *Die deutsche Inflation: Eine Zwischenbalanz,* ed. Gerald Feldman et al. (New York: Walter de Guyter, 1982), pp. 276–282; Richard Bessel, *Germany after the First World War* (Oxford: Clarendon Press, 1993), pp. 197, 213–219.

17. Yanni Kotsonis, *Making Peasants Backward: Agricultural Cooperatives and the Agrarian Question in Russia, 1861–1914* (New York: St. Martin's, 1999); for collectivization in this light, see Lynne Viola, *Peasant Rebels under Stalin: Collectivization and the Culture of Peasant Resistance* (New York: Oxford University Press, 1997).

18. RGVIA, f. 2009, op. 2, d. 105, ll. 6–8, 12, 18a, 97, 105, 112–113, 129–131, 138–139, 157, 183.

19. Ibid., ll. 158, 160, 180, 184.

20. *Polnoe sobranie sochinenii,* 5th ed., 55 vols. (Moscow: Izdatel'stvo politicheskoi literatury, 1958–1965), 36: 399, 401–402, 407, 430.

21. *Sistematicheskii sbornik dekretov i rasporiazhenii po prodovol'stvennomu voprosu,* 4 vols. (Nizhnii Novgorod–Moscow: Narkomprod, 1919–1920), 1: 33–34; translation found in Silvana Malle, *The Economic Organization of War Communism, 1918–1921* (New York: Cambridge University Press, 1985), pp. 359–361.

22. RGVIA, f. 499, op. 1, d. 1657, ll. 234–235; *Sistematicheskii sbornik,* 1: 32. For similar formulations, see *Prodovol'stvennaia politika v svete obshchego khoziaistvennogo stroitel'stva sovetskoi vlasti: posobie dlia prodovol'stvenno-agitatsionnykh kursov* (Moscow: Gosudarstvennoe izdatel'stvo, 1920), pp. 192–193; *Dekrety sovetskoi vlasti,* 15 vols. (Moscow: Gospolitizdat, 1957–), 9: 34; *Otchet 3-mu s"ezdu sovetov,* p. 6.

23. *Sbornik zakonov priniatykh bol'shim voiskovym krugom VVD, 15 aug.-20 sent. 1918* (Novocherkassk, 1918), pp. 24–27.

24. N. M. Mel'nikov, "Pochemu belye na Iuge ne pobedili krasnykh," BAR, Mel'nikov collection, box 4, pp. 66–82, citation at p. 73.

25. *Sistematicheskii sbornik,* 1: 33–34; Malle, *Economic Organization,* pp. 329–338.

26. Nikolai Kondrat'ev, *Rynok khlebov i ego regulirovanie vo vremia voiny i revoliutsii* (Moscow: Nauka, 1991), p. 186.

27. Lars Lih, *Bread and Authority in Russia, 1914–1921* (Berkeley: University of California Press, 1990), pp. 167–198.

28. RGVA, f. 25896, op. 2, d. 11, ll. 41, 47.

29. TsDNIRO, f. 4, op. 1, d. 5, l. 35; RGVA, f. 25896, op. 2, d. 11, ll. 41–42, 94, 98; *Zhurnal oblastnogo prodovol'stvennogo soveshchaniia* (Rostov: [n.p.], 1920), pp. 6–8.

30. *Donskoi statisticheskii ezhegodnik*, 1922: 107, 112. For the Civil War period, see N. M. Mel'nikov, "Kratkaia zapiska o sostoianii sel'skogo khoziaistva Donskogo voiska k 1922," BAR, Mel'nikov collection, box 5, p. 10; GARO, f. R-97, op. 1, d. 607, l. 6. On the general causes of the fall in marketed grains, see Malle, *Economic Organization*, pp. 437–439.

31. *Prodovol'stvennaia politika*, pp. 42, 61; analogous statements at pp. 12–13, 42, 64–65, 72, 78, 87, 93, 95, 102, 117, 180, and 211. For other Soviet directives distinguishing the periphery from the Soviet Republic's core, see *Dekrety*, 9: 408; 10: 73; 13: 369.

32. *Prodovol'stvennaia politika*, p. 262; P. Popov, *Proizvodstvo khleba v RSFSR* (Moscow: Gosudarstvennoe izdatel'stvo, 1921), p. 53; Kondrat'ev, *Rynok*, p. 358; RGIA, f. 456, op. 1, d. 206, l. 220.

33. *Dekrety sovetskoi vlasti*, 9: 3, 348–349, 408–409; 10: 73–76, 78, 285, 351, 353–355; 12: 210–211; 13: 369, 387–388. This is only a partial listing: for similar telegrams from Lenin to Don officials, see *Khleb i revoliutsiia: Prodovol'stvennaia politika Kommunisticheskoi partii i Sovetskogo pravitel'stva v 1917–1922*, ed. A. S. Iziumov (Moscow: "Sovetskaia Rossiia," 1972), pp. 240, 243, 246, 253, 257, 259, 274, 285, 289, 295.

34. TsDNIRO, f. 4, op. 1, d. 5, ll. 113–115; ibid., d. 14, l. 8b; *Zhurnal oblastnogo prodovol'stvennogo soveshcheniia*, p. 9.

35. TsDNIRO, f. 4, op. 1, d. 5, l. 115.

36. Ibid., d. 2, l. 9; *Dekrety sovetskoi vlasti*, 11: 385–386; published on the Don in *Biulleten' Donprodkoma*, no. 2 (December 1, 1920), p. 16; *Donskaia bednota*, November 25, 1920; *Khoperskaia pravda*, December 16, 1920.

37. TsDNIRO, f. 4, op. 1, d. 5, ll. 39, 44; RGVA, f. 25896, op. 2, d. 8, l. 39; *Sovetskoe stroitel'stvo na Donu*, no. 2 (September 1920), p. 58.

38. GARO, f. R-97, op. 1, d. 775, ll. 33–38; similarly, *Zhurnal oblastnogo prodovol'stvennogo soveshchaniia*, p. 7; GARO, f. R-1891, op. 1, d. 76, l. 91; TsDNIRO, f. 4, op. 1, d. 37, l. 3a.

39. GARO, f. R-1891, op. 1, d. 88, l. 245; d. 388, l. 11; GARO, f. R-97, op. 1, d. 616, ll. 4–5. This was a general policy: Lih, *Bread and Authority*, p. 170.

40. RGVA, f. 25896, op. 2, d. 11, ll. 6, 95, 133, 145.

41. Ibid., l. 98; similarly, l. 46.

42. TsDNIRO, f. 4, op. 1, d. 2, l. 9; ibid., d. 8, l. 97; *Donskaia bednota*, November 25, 1920; *Biulleten' Donprodkoma*, no. 2 (December 1, 1920), p. 5.

43. GARO, f. R-97, op. 1, d. 690, l. 43; also ibid., d. 650, l. 521; TsDNIRO, f. 12, op. 5, d. 153, l. 68.

44. TsDNIRO, f. 4, op. 1, d. 14, l. 48; GARO, f. R-97, op. 1, d. 644, l. 49.

45. GARO, f. R-97, op. 1, d. 276, ll. 3–4; *Proletarii Dona*, May 22, 1921.

46. Malle, *Economic Organization*, pp. 402, 406.

47. TsDNIRO, f. 4, op. 1, d. 8, ll. 52a, 81a, 89.

48. RGVA, f. 25896, op. 2, d. 11, ll. 6, 42–43, 95, 98, 132–133.

49. GARO, f. R-1891, op. 1, d. 373, l. 46; ibid., d. 88, l. 369; TsDNIRO, f. 4, op. 1, d. 35, l. 6a.

50. TsDNIRO, f. 4, op. 1, d. 37, l. 2b; also *Biulleten' Donprodkoma*, no. 4/5: 24.

51. TsDNIRO, f. 4, op. 2, d. 2, l. 9.

52. TsDINRO, f. 4, op. 1, d. 8, l. 94; Afanasii Selishchev, *Iazyk revoliutsionnoi epokhi: Iz nabliudenii nad russkim iazykom poslednikh let (1917–1926)* (Moscow: Rabotnik prosveshcheniia, 1928), p. 131.

53. TsDNIRO, f. 4, op. 1, d. 35, l. 4.

54. GARO, f. R-1891, op. 1, d. 76, l. 94; *Verkhne-Donskaia pravda*, November 7, 1920.

55. Lih, *Bread and Authority*, pp. 167–198.

56. Kondrat'ev, *Rynok*, p. 222.

57. *Dekrety sovetskoi vlasti*, 10: 78; *Donskoi prodovol'stvennik i kooperator*, no. 1 (November 15, 1920), p. 18.

58. *Dekrety sovetskoi vlasti*, 9: 385–386, printed on the Don in *Biulleten' Donprodkoma*, no. 2 (December 1920), p. 16.

59. *Biulleten' Donprodkoma*, no. 2, p. 4.

60. *Vnutrennie voiska Sovetskoi respubliki, 1917–1922: Dokumenty i materialy*, ed. Vasilii Dushen'kin (Moscow: "Iuridicheskaia literatura," 1972), p. 205; *Dekrety sovetskoi vlasti*, 10: 78; Iurii Konstantinovich Strizhkov, *Prodovol'stvennye otriady v gody grazhdanskoi voiny i inostrannoi interventsii* (Moscow: Nauka, 1973), pp. 246–247; GARO, f. R-1891, op. 1, d. 178, l. 52.

61. TsDNIRO, f. 4, op. 1, d. 43, l. 13; GARO, f. R-1891, op. 1, d. 171, l. 18; ibid., d. 211, l. 16.

62. GARO, f. R-1891, op. 1, d. 543, l. 21.

63. *Otchet 3-mu s"ezdu sovetov*, p. 150.

64. GARO, f. R-1891, op. 1, d. 171, ll. 18–20, 31–32, 81.

65. Ibid., d. 76, l. 99. For territory-wide figures, see ibid., d. 166, ll. 208–271, and *Otchet 3-mu s"ezdu sovetov*, p. 148.

66. *Biulleten' Donprodkoma*, no. 2 (December 1, 1920), pp. 4–5; *Otchet 3-mu s"ezdu sovetov*, p. 150.

67. *Otchet 3-mu s"ezdu sovetov*, pp. 148, 154–155; *Biulleten' Donprodkoma*, no. 4/5 (January 1921), p. 21.

68. GARO, f. R-1891, op. 1, d. 166, l. 20; ibid., d. 178, ll. 77a, 78.

69. TsDNIRO, f. 4, op. 1, d. 33, l. 60; GARO, f. R-1891, op. 1, d. 76, l. 148; *Biulleten' Donprodkoma*, no. 4/5 (January 1921), p. 21.

70. GARO, f. R-1891, op. 1, d. 171, ll. 32, 81–82.

71. *Biulleten' Donprodkoma*, no. 4/5, p. 21.

72. *Sistematicheskii sbornik*, 1: 33–34 (quotation), 38, 106–107, 204–217; 3: 141, 148–149; 4: 237; and *RPG*, 2: 618–622, 641–642, 644.

73. For example, *Proletarii Dona*, November 18, 1920.

74. GARO, f. R-1891, op. 1, d. 543, l. 17.

75. *Dekrety sovetskoi vlasti*, 9: 386; *Biulleten' Donprodkoma*, no. 2 (December 1, 1920), p. 16.

76. *Donskaia bednota*, December 3, 1920; *Otchet 3-mu s"ezdu sovetov*, p. 147.

77. GARO, f. R-1220, op. 1, d. 9, l. 543.

78. *Otchet 3-mu s"ezdu sovetov*, p. 148.

79. *Biulleten' Donprodkoma*, no. 4/5 (January 1921), pp. 22–23; GARO, f. R-1891, op. 1, d. 76, ll. 119, 133, 136–137, 148, 167.

80. GARO, f. R-97, op. 1, d. 532, ll. 28, 31, 33; *Donskaia bednota*, December 11, 1920; *Biulleten' Donprodkoma*, no. 6 (February 1921) [unpaginated; p. 11]; *Krasnyi listok*, October 2, 1921.

81. GARO, f. R-1220, op. 1, d. 41, ll. 6–8.

82. *Sistematicheskii sbornik*, 3: 148–149.

83. GARO, f. R-97, op. 1, d. 532, l. 21.

84. Ibid., ll. 18–19, 21–22, 26, 28–29, 31, 33; broadsheets, ll. 36, 38–47.

85. *Biulleten' Donprodkoma*, no. 4/5, p. 22; GARO, f. R-97, op. 1, d. 532, l. 48.

86. *Proletarii Dona*, January 16, 1921.

87. *Trudovoi Don*, October 6, 1921; *Krasnyi listok*, October 2, 1921.

88. For example, GARO, f. R-97, op. 1, d. 532, l. 31.

89. *Krasnyi Don*, February 2, 1921.

90. *Donskaia bednota*, December 22 and 23, 1920; *Biulleten' Donprodkoma*, no. 4/5 (January 1921), p. 23.

91. GARO, f. R-97, op. 1, d. 532, ll. 26, 28, 31, 33.

92. *Dekrety*, 13: 387–388.

93. GARO, f. R-97, op. 1, d. 644, l. 64; GARO, f. R-1891, op. 1, d. 76, ll. 136, 148, 264, 266, 268–269.

94. GARO, f. R-97, op. 1, d. 759, l. 25; ibid., d. 772, ll. 41, 57–58, 62; *Biulleten' Donprodkoma*, no. 2 (December 1920), p. 25; *Donskaia bednota*, November 25, 1920.

95. GARO, f. R-97, op. 1, d. 772, ll. 57, 66; GARO, f. R-1891, op. 1, d. 76, ll. 112, 148.

96. TsDNIRO, f. 4, op. 1, d. 37, ll. 2–4b.

97. Ibid., d. 73, l. 1; GARO, f. R-97, op. 1, d. 48, l. 5; ibid., d. 276, ll. 1–2.

98. GARO, f. R-97, op. 1, d. 48, l. 10; *Dekrety sovetskoi vlasti*, 12: 210–211.

99. *Zhurnal oblastnogo prodovol'stvennogo soveshchaniia*, p. 9.

100. TsDNIRO, f. 12, op. 5, d. 155, l. 12.

101. GARO, f. R-1891, op. 1, d. 76, ll. 206, 215–219, 223, 226–227.

102. Ibid., l. 227.

103. *Otchet 3-mu s"ezdu sovetov*, p. 148.

104. RGVA, f. 28087, op. 1, d. 81, ll. 50, 44, 71.

105. TsDNIRO, f. 12, op. 5, d. 153, l. 36; GARO, f. R-1220, op. 1, d. 31, ll. 56–59.

106. *Biulleten' Donprodkoma*, no. 6: [8]; *Otchet 3-mu s"ezdu sovetov*, pp. 154–155.

107. GARO, f. R-97, op. 1, d. 653, ll. 98–99; TsDNIRO, f. 12, op. 5, d. 155, ll. 34–35; GARO, f. R-1891, op. 1, d. 76, ll. 227, 287.

108. *Dekrety sovetskoi vlasti*, 13: 245. On the impact of NEP's introduction, see E. H. Carr, *The Bolshevik Revolution*, 3 vols. (New York: Norton, 1980), 2: 269–297; William H. Chamberlin, *The Russian Revolution, 1917–1921*, 2 vols. (Princeton: Princeton University Press, 1987), 2: 445–449; Lih, *Bread and Authority*, pp. 228–230; Orlando Figes, *Peasant Russia, Civil War: The Volga Countryside in Revolution, 1917–1921* (Oxford: Clarendon Press, 1989), pp. 321, 356.

109. Strizhkov, *Prodovol'stvennye otriady*, p. 288.

110. *Otchet 4-mu s"ezdu sovetov*, p. 49.

111. TsDNIRO, f. 12, op. 5, d. 155, ll. 34–35; *Krasnyi Don*, May 19, 1921; also

June 25, 1921. There was a similar response in Tambov: S. A. Esikov and L. G. Protasov, "Antonovshchina: novye podkhody," *Voprosy istorii*, no. 6/7 (1992): 47–57, here at p. 51.

112. Strizhkov, *Prodovol'stvennye otriady*, p. 288.

113. GARO, f. R-1220, op. 1, d. 31, l. 4; TsDNIRO, f. 4, op. 1, d. 96, l. 11.

114. TsDNIRO, f. 4, op. 1, d. 67, ll. 53–54.

115. *Khoperskaia pravda*, July 31, 1921.

116. TsDNIRO, f. 4, op. 1, d. 73, l. 20; *Sovetskaia derevnia glazami VChK-OGPU-NKVD*, vol. 1: *1918–1922*, eds. A. Berelowitch, V. Danilov, Nicolas Werth, V. Vinogradov, V. Dvoinikh (Moscow: ROSSPEN, 1998), pp. 436, 448, 496.

117. Lars Lih, *The Bolshevik Sowing Committees of 1920: Apotheosis of War Communism?* Carl Beck Papers, no. 803 (Pittsburgh: University of Pittsburgh Center for Russian and East European Studies, 1990); A. M. Terne, *V tsarstve Lenina: Ocherki sovremennoi zhizni v RSFSR* (Moscow: Skify, 1991), pp. 179–180.

118. *Donskoi statisticheskii ezhegodnik*, 1922: 107–108, 112. For the shortfall in seed grain, see *Krasnyi listok*, April 13, 1921, and May 12, 1921; GARO, f. R-97, op. 1, d. 267, l. 58; ibid., d. 691, l. 30.

119. *Otchet 4-mu s"ezdu sovetov*, p. 4; *Sovetskoe stroitel'stvo na Donu*, no. 7 (August 1921), p. 52; TsDNIRO, f. 4, op. 1, d. 66, ll. 148, 152; TsDNIRO, f. 12, op. 5, d. 153, ll. 34, 77. On Siberia, see Vladimir Shishkin, "Krasnyi banditizm v sovetskoi sibiri," in *Sovetskaia istoriia: Problemy i uroki*, ed. Vladimir Shishkin (Novosibirsk: Nauka, sibirskoe otdelenie, 1992), p. 73.

120. GARO, f. R-1891, op. 1, d. 741, l. 39.

121. *Otchet 4-mu s"ezdu sovetov*, pp. 51, 47.

122. *Krasnyi Don*, September 22, 1921; *Otchet 4-mu s"ezdu sovetov*, p. 51; GARO, f. R-97, op. 1, d. 691, l. 31; TsDNIRO, f. 4, op. 1, d. 98, l. 278.

123. *Verkhne-donskaia pravda*, October 22, 1921; TsDNIRO, f. 4, op. 1, d. 98, ll. 275–278.

124. GARO, f. R-1220, op. 1, d. 46, l. 9; ibid., d. 31, ll. 46–47; *Otchet 4-mu s"ezdu sovetov*, pp. 190–194.

125. GARO, f. R-1220, op. 1, d. 31, ll. 36, 46–47, 49; *Sovetskaia derevnia glazami VChK-OGPU-NKVD*, 1: 529; D. Rodin, "Revoliutsionnye tribunaly v 1920–1922 gg.," *Vestnik statistiki*, book 13, nos. 1–3 (January-March 1923): 155–189.

126. GARO, f. R-97, op. 1, d. 691, l. 31; TsDNIRO, f. 12, op. 5, d. 153, ll. 34, 81.

127. *Otchet 4-mu s"ezdu sovetov*, pp. 51–54.

128. TsDNIRO, f. 4, op. 1, d. 67, l. 65a; also GARO, f. R-97, op. 1, d. 691, ll. 29–31.

129. On Siberia, see Shishkin, "Krasyni banditizm," pp. 73–76; on Tambov, see Esikov and Protasov, "Antonovshchina," p. 52.

130. Representative formulations of this view can be found in Chamberlin, *Russian Revolution*, 2: 436–439; Carr, *Bolshevik Revolution*, 2: 271–273; Vladimir Brovkin, *Behind the Front Lines of the Civil War: Political Parties and Social Movements in Russia, 1918–1922* (Princeton: Princeton University Press, 1994), pp. 143–145, 404, 416; Richard Pipes, *Russia under the Bolshevik Regime* (New York: Vintage, 1993), pp. 137–138; Orlando Figes, *A People's Tragedy: The Russian Revolution, 1891–1924* (New York: Penguin, 1997), pp. 729–730; Andrea Graziosi, *The Great Soviet Peasant War: Bolsheviks and Peasants, 1917–1933* (Cambridge, Mass.: Ukrai-

nian Research Institute, 1996), pp. 16–37. "Age-old shell" is found in Moshe Lewin, *The Making of the Soviet System* (New York: Pantheon, 1985), pp. 17–18, 43, 50–51, 266, 296.

131. For Germany, see Vejas Liulevicius, *War Land on the Eastern Front: Culture, National Identity and German Occupation in World War I* (New York: Cambridge University Press, 2000), pp. 227–246; Richard Bessel, *Germany after the First World War* (New York: Clarendon Press, 1993), pp. 261–262; on Italy, Adrian Lyttelton, "Fascism and Violence in Post-War Italy: Political Strategy and Social Conflict," in *Social Protest, Violence, and Terror in Nineteenth and Twentieth Century Europe*, eds. Wolfgang Mommsen and Gerhard Hirschfeld (New York: St. Martin's, 1982), pp. 257–274.

132. *Obzor banditskogo dvizheniia v Sibiri s dekiabria 1920 po ianvar' 1922* (Novonikolaevsk: Tipografiia predstavitel'stva V.Ch.K. v Sibiri, 1922), p. 18.

133. *Trudovoi Don*, October 2, 1921; similarly, TsDNIRO, f. 4, op. 1, d. 35, l. 6a. This is also the trajectory of Gregor Melekhov in Mikhail Sholokhov, *The Don Flows Home to the Sea* (New York: Vintage, 1940), pp. 681–777.

134. GARO, f. R-1891, op. 1, d. 184, l. 38; ibid., d. 178, l. 78; TsDNIRO, f. 4, op. 1, d. 8, l. 100.

135. GARO, f. R-97, op. 1, d. 644, ll. 50–51; TsDNIRO, f. 12, op. 5, d. 155, l. 28; RGVA, f. 25896, op. 2, d. 11, ll. 43, 133.

136. GARF, f. 1235, op. 84, d. 9, ll. 351–353; GARO, f. R-97, op. 1, d. 653, ll. 98, 101, 105.

137. Pokrovskii, "Na Donu," p. 31.

138. RGVA, f. 28087, op. 1, d. 81, ll. 44, 71, 211.

139. *Otchet 3-mu s"ezdu sovetov*, p. 4; Pokrovskii, "Na Donu," p. 32; GARO, f. R-97, op. 1, d. 653, l. 106.

140. *Ocherki geografii vsevelikogo voiska Donskogo* (Novocherkassk: Izdatel'stvo otdela narodnogo prosveshcheniia, 1919), p. 493; "Spisok naselennykh mest," supplement to *Donskoi statisticheskii ezhegodnik za 1922*, p. 10; GARF, f. 452, op. 1, d. 14, l. 31.

141. GARO, f. 856, op. 1, d. 4, l. 25; RGVA, f. 39456, op. 1, d. 60, ll. 98, 107; GARF, f. 452, op. 1, d. 14, l. 37.

142. GARO, f. R-1891, op. 1, d. 389, ll. 6–7; ibid., d. 166, l. 212; RGVA, f. 28087, op. 1, d. 81, ll. 67–68; GARO, f. R-97, op. 1, d. 772, l. 203; ibid., d. 653, ll. 88, 99–101.

143. GARO, f. R-97, op. 1, d. 653, l. 100.

144. TsDNIRO, f. 12, op. 5, d. 153, l. 26; ibid., d. 155, ll. 2, 25–26, 35.

145. *Trudovoi Don*, October 6, 1921.

146. As argued in *Antonovshchina: dokumenty i materialy*, ed. Viktor Danilov (Tambov: Redaktsionno-izdatel'skii otdel, 1994); Oliver Radkey, *The Unknown Civil War in Soviet Russia: A Study of the Green Movement in the Tambov Region, 1920–1921* (Stanford: Hoover Institution Press, 1976); Graziosi, *The Great Soviet Peasant War*.

147. On Red Army men as the backbone of Soviet power in the countryside, see J. L. H. Keep, *The Russian Revolution: A Study in Mass Mobilization* (New York: Norton, 1976), pp. 451–453; Sheila Fitzpatrick, "The Legacy of the Civil War," in *Party, State, and Society in the Russian Civil War*, eds. Diane Koenker, William

Rosenberg, and Ronald Suny (Bloomington, Ind.: Indiana University Press, 1989), pp. 390–395.

148. RGVA, f. 25896, op. 2, d. 11, l. 46; TsDNIRO, f. 4, op. 1, d. 90, l. 6; GARO, f. R-97, op. 1, d. 607, ll. 1, 18; generally, Mark von Hagen, *Soldiers in the Proletarian Dictatorship: The Red Army and the Soviet Socialist State, 1917–1930* (Ithaca: Cornell University Press, 1990).

149. GARF, f. 1235, op. 84, d. 9, l. 429; RGVA, f. 25896, op. 1, d. 3, l. 15; GARO, f. R-97, op. 1, d. 267, l. 2.

150. Von Hagen, *Soldiers*, pp. 127–132; Terne, *V tsarstve Lenina*, p. 75.

151. GARO, f. R-97, op. 1, d. 759, l. 25; ibid., d. 644, l. 44; TsDNIRO, f. 12, op. 5, d. 153, l. 75; ibid., d. 155, ll. 34–35.

152. *Prikazy voiskam Donskoi oblast, 1921* (n.p., n.d.), p. 7; GARO, f. R-1891, op. 1, d. 166, l. 204; ibid., d. 543, l. 132; *Sovetskaia derevnia glazami VChK-OGPU-NKVD*, 1: 407.

153. TsDNIRO, f. 12, op. 5, d. 153, l. 35.

154. GARO, f. R-1891, op. 1, d. 741, l. 45; RGVA, f. 28087, op. 1, d. 81, l. 117a; Budennyi, "Proidennyi Put'," *Don*, no. 8 (1970), 66–107, here at p. 74.

155. Von Hagen, *Soldiers*, pp. 308–325; V. Mikhailova and N. Tarkhova, *"Medynskoe delo" v Krasnoi Armii* (Toronto: University of Toronto Press, 2000), pp. 9–10.

156. This typology holds true for Siberia and Tambov as well: S. A. Esikov and V. V. Kanishev, "Antonovskii NEP," *Otechestvennaia istoriia*, 1993, no. 4: 60–72, here at p. 65; Shishkin, "Krasnyi banditizm."

157. *Sovetskaia derevnia glazami VChK-OGPU-NKVD*, 1: 386.

158. In *Quiet Flows the Don* and *The Don Flows Home to the Sea*, Sholokhov gives a portrayal of Fomin that is generally consistent with the historical record: see S. N. Semanov, *V mire "Tikhogo Dona"* (Moscow: Sovremennik, 1987), pp. 140–145; Andrei Venkov, *Pechat' surovogo iskhoda: K istorii sobytii 1919 g. na verkhnem Donu* (Rostov: Rostovskoe knizhnoe izdatel'stvo, 1988), pp. 41, 51–53, 55, 60–61.

159. TsDNIRO, f. 12, op. 5, d. 155, ll. 12, 56; GARO, f. R-1891, op. 1, d. 76, l. 287.

160. TsDNIRO, f. 12, op. 5, d. 155, ll. 27–28, 57, 69; ibid., d. 153, l. 62; TsDNIRO, f. 4, op. 1, d. 90, ll. 48–48v; RGVA, f. 25896, op. 1, d. 8, l. 2; GARO, f. R-1891, op. 1, d. 745, l. 2; *Sovetskaia derevnia glazami VChK-OGPU-NKVD*, 1: 409–410, 517, 532, 535, 549, 557, 564, 570, 579, 588.

161. *1917 god v Saratove* ([Saratov]: Istpartotd. gubernskogo komiteta RKP(b), 1927), pp. 96–97; Danilov, ed., *Filipp Mironov*, pp. 588–590, 593–595, 602–605, 607–614, 618; Figes, *Peasant Russia*, pp. 343–345.

162. *Sovetskaia derevnia glazami VChK-OGPU-NKVD*, 1: 796; TsDNIRO, f. 12, op. 5, d. 155, ll. 25–26; RGVA, f. 28087, op. 1, d. 44, l. 110.

163. GARO, f. R-97, op. 1, d. 48, l. 43.

164. *Otchet 4-mu s"ezdu sovetov*, p. 57.

165. Ivan Trifonov, *Klassy i klassovaia bor'ba v SSSR v nachale NEPa (1921–1925)*, 2 vols. (Leningrad: Izdatel'stvo leningradskogo universiteta, 1964, 1969), 1: 210–213; *Dekrety sovetskoi vlasti*, 13: 514. On the Soviet category of "banditry," see Figes, *Peasant Russia*, pp. 340–343.

166. TsDNIRO, f. 12, op. 5, d. 155, ll. 2, 14; *Otchet 3-mu s"ezdu sovetov*, 8a–8b.

167. RGVA, f. 28087, op. 1, d. 81, ll. 77, 87; *Vnutrennie voiska Sovetskoi respubliki*, pp. 596–599.

168. Trifonov, *Klassy i klassovaia bor'ba*, 1: 213.

169. TsDNIRO, f. 12, op. 5, d. 155, ll. 2, 14; RGVA, f. 25896, op. 1, d. 8, ll. 31–32.

170. TsDNIRO, f. 12, op. 5, d. 155, ll. 51, 56, 67; TsDNIRO, f. 4, op. 1, d. 66, l. 151.

171. RGVA, f. 25896, op. 1, d. 8, ll. 9–11; DTMA Order no. 5, issued August 31, was widely publicized in the local press: *Trudovoi Don*, September 2, 1921; *Proletarii Dona*, September 11, 1921; *Krasnyi Don*, September 20, 1921.

172. TsDNIRO, f. 12, op. 5, d. 153, l. 68.

173. RGVA, f. 25896, op. 1, d. 8, ll. 7, 10–11.

174. Operational decrees, orders, and directives are found in Danilov, ed., *Antonovshchina*; see esp. documents 174–177, 179–181, 189, 200, 212, 221, 259, 272, 275.

175. RGVA, f. 25896, op. 1, d. 8, l. 15.

176. RGASPI, f. 17, op. 109, d. 148, ll. 2–3, 11; RGVA, f. 25896, op. 6, d. 65, ll. 38–44.

177. *Trudovoi Don*, May 1, 1922; see also Figes, *Peasant Russia*, pp. 352–353.

178. GARO, f. R-97, op. 1, d. 267, l. 3; also, TsDNIRO, f. 4, op. 1, d. 66, l. 106.

179. Donald Raleigh, *Experiencing Civil War: Politics, Society, and Revolutionary Culture in Saratov, 1918–22* (Princeton: Princeton University Press, forthcoming), chaps. 9, 12.

180. *Otchet Ust'-Medveditskogo okruzhnogo ispolnitel'nogo komiteta 8-mu okruzhnomu s"ezdu sovetov* (Mikhailovka: n.p., [1922]), pp. 26–27; *Sovetskaia derevnia glazami VChK-OGPU-NKVD*, 1: 614; *Otchetnyi doklad Prezidiuma khoperskogo okruzhnogo ispolkoma za vremia s 24-go noiabria po 25-e noiabria 1923* (Uriupino: [n.p.], 1923), pp. 21, 27.

181. On the enduring impact of this ideal, see Jochen Hellbeck, "Speaking Out: Languages of Affirmation and Dissent in Stalinist Russia," *Kritika*, 1, no. 1 (2000): 71–96.

182. Ustinovskii, *Leninskaia agrarnaia programma*, pp. 54, 76, 98.

183. Bessel, *Germany after the First World War*; Charles Maier, *Recasting Bourgeois Europe: Stabilization in France, Germany, and Italy in the Decade after World War I* (Princeton: Princeton University Press, 1975); Gerald Feldman, "Economic and Social Problems of German Demobilization, 1918–1919," *Journal of Modern History* 47 (1975): 1–47.

Conclusion

1. Karl Marx and Frederick Engels, *Selected Correspondence* (Moscow: Foreign Languages Publishing House, 1956), p. 460.

2. A. Gozulov, "Opyty izhucheniia vliianiia moshchnosti khoziaistva na sotsial'no-gigienicheskoe sostoianie derevni," *Vestnik statistiki*, book 23, nos. 10–12 (October-December 1923): 181–213, here at pp. 185–186, 211; *Donskii statisticheskii ezhegodnik*, 1922: 43–45.

3. Gozulov, "Opyty," p. 211; V. Dobrynin, "Vooruzhennaia bor'ba Dona s

bol'shevikami," *Donskaia letopis'*, 3 vols. (Vienna: Izd. donskoi istoricheskoi komissii, 1923–1924), 1: 93–130, here at p. 130.

4. *Donskoi statisticheskii ezhegodnik*, 1922: 107–108, 112, 116, 131–132, 140; N. L. Ianchevskii, *Kak zhivet i chem boleet derevnia: po materialam komissii obsledovaniia derevni na Iugo-vostoke* (Rostov-Moscow: Priboi, 1924), pp. 22–24; *Litso donskoi derevni k 1925 godu (po materialam obsledovaniia DKK i DonoRKI)* (Rostov, 1925), p. 21.

5. Richard Pipes, *Russia under the Old Regime* (New York: Scribner's, 1974); Orlando Figes, *A People's Tragedy: The Russian Revolution, 1891–1924* (New York: Penguin, 1997).

6. Stéphane Courtois et al., eds., *The Black Book of Communism: Crimes, Terror, Repression* (Cambridge, Mass.: Harvard University Press, 1999).

7. Alfred J. Rieber, "The Sedimentary Society," in *Between Tsar and People: Educated Society and the Quest for Public Identity in Late Imperial Russia*, ed. Edith W. Clowes, Samuel D. Kassow, and James L. West (Princeton: Princeton University Press, 1991), pp. 343–366, here at p. 362.

8. John Hutchinson, *Politics and Public Health in Revolutionary Russia, 1890–1918* (Baltimore: Johns Hopkins University Press, 1990), pp. xix–xx; Yanni Kotsonis, *Making Peasants Backward: Agricultural Cooperatives and the Agrarian Question in Russia, 1861–1914* (New York: St. Martin's Press, 1999), p. 94.

9. Alexis de Tocqueville, *The Old Régime and the French Revolution* (New York: Doubleday, 1983), p. 192.

10. Jochen Hellbeck, "Speaking Out: Languages of Affirmation and Dissent in Stalinist Russia," *Kritika* 1, no. 1 (Winter 2000), 71–96, here at p. 86–87.

11. Mark von Hagen, *Soldiers in the Proletarian Dictatorship: The Red Army and the Soviet Socialist State* (Ithaca: Cornell University Press, 1990), pp. 335–340.

12. Memoirs of the period portray this dynamic: Viktor Shklovsky, *A Sentimental Journey: Memoirs, 1917–1922* (Ithaca: Cornell University Press, 1984); Victor Serge, *Memoirs of a Revolutionary, 1901–1941* (Oxford: Oxford University Press, 1980); and Isaac Babel, *Red Cavalry*, in *Collected Stories* (New York: Penguin, 1994).

13. Donald Raleigh, *Experiencing Civil War: Politics, Society, and Revolutionary Culture in Saratov, 1918–1922* (Princeton: Princeton University Press, forthcoming), chap. 4 and conclusion.

14. Stephen Kotkin, *Magnetic Mountain: Stalinism as Civilization* (Berkeley: University of California Press, 1994); Igal Halfin, *From Darkness to Light: Class, Consciousness, and Salvation in Revolutionary Russia* (Pittsburgh: University of Pittsburgh Press, 2000); Amir Weiner, *Making Sense of War: The Second World War and the Fate of the Bolshevik Revolution* (Princeton: Princeton University Press, 2001).

Index

Ageev, Pavel, 29–30, 65, 72, 89, 114, 117, 163
Agrarian specialists, 17–19, 30, 40, 94, 96, 104–105, 246–247. *See also* Cooperatives and cooperative activists; Educated society
Aleksandrovsk-Grushevskii, 84, 116, 132
Alekseev, Mikhail, 115, 119, 123
All Great Don Host (AGDH), 144–145, 160–165, 194, 223, 228, 247; Don Department of Surveillance (DDS), 223, 226, 228–229
All-Russian Congress of Soviets: Third, 133; Fourth, 137, 148; Fifth, 168–169
Amfiteatrov-Kadashev, Vladimir, 225, 226
Anisimov, Viktor, 20, 105–106, 247, 285, 319n119
Anticommercial sentiments, 18–19, 26, 33–34, 40, 44, 94, 97–98, 102–103, 226. *See also* Ministry of Agriculture (Imperial), anticommercial disposition of; Speculation
Antonov-Ovseenko, Vladimir, 117–118, 120, 123, 126–127, 130–132
Armed Forces of South Russia (AFSR), 222, 228; Special Council of, 222–224, 229, 247. *See also* OSVAG (civilian surveillance organization); Volunteer Army
Army, Russian imperial, 67, 79, 83, 90–92, 216, 232; and role in food supply, 17, 21–

22, 102–104, 107, 109, 246. *See also* Red Army; Soldiers; War Ministry
Austria-Hungary: food supply in, 33, 35, 107, 246, 248; propaganda and surveillance in, 220–221

Banditry, 269, 274–279
Berezovskaia stanitsa, 137, 148, 184
Bilibin, Ivan, 225
Bobrinskii, Aleksei, 37, 39–41
Bogaevskaia stanitsa, 58–59
Bogaevskii, Metrofan Petrovich, 68, 117
Bogoiavlenskaia stanitsa, 259
Bolshevik Party, 83, 173, 194, 235–236; in Don Territory, 53, 57, 116–118, 122, 124, 131–132, 135–141, 150, 167–174, 321n18; ideology of, 166–167, 204–205, 239–240, 254, 262, 280–281, 287–288; Central Committee of, 172, 178, 186, 188, 191–192, 195, 197; Orgburo of, 178–182, 184, 186, 188, 197–198, 200; Eighth Congress of, 186, 196, 199; Tenth Congress of, 264; members' involvement in anti-Soviet rebellions, 271, 274. *See also* Centralism, and role of Center in policy; Don Bureau; NEP
Brest-Litovsk Treaty, 130–131, 137
Britain: food supply in, 20, 33–35, 245; propaganda and surveillance in, 214, 220, 224

353